Mysteries of Templar Treasure & the Holy Grail

THE SECRETS OF RENNES-LE-CHÂTEAU

Lionel & Patricia Fanthorpe

WEISER BOOKS

Boston, MA/York Beach, ME

To Guy N. Smith

a great writer,

a great friend,

and a kindred spirit

This edition first published in 2004 by
Red Wheel/Weiser, LLC
York Beach, ME
With offices at:
368 Congress Street
Boston, MA 02210
www.redwheelweiser.com

Text copyright © 1992 Lionel and Patricia Fanthorpe
Introduction copyright © 2004 Red Wheel/Weiser, LLC

The Library of Congress has cataloged the original paperback edition as follows: 91-43311

ISBN 1-57863-315-X

Printed in the United States of America
BJ

11 10 09 08 07 06 05 04
 8 7 6 5 4 3 2 1

The paper used in this publication meets the minimum requirements of the American National Standard for Information Sciences-Permanence of Paper for Printed Library Materials Z39.48-1992 (R1997).

CONTENTS

Page

Introduction to the Mystery 1

Chapter 1: Rennes-le-Château and its Area 9

Chapter 2: The History of Rennes-le-Château 22

Chapter 3: Theological and Religious Factors 35

Chapter 4: The Real Messianic Message 46

Chapter 5: Lines, Shrines and Signs 55

Chapter 6: Codes, Ciphers and Cryptograms..74

Chapter 7: Magicians, Alchemists and Men of Mystery 100

Chapter 8: The Habsburg Connection 130

Chapter 9: Priests and Prelates 136

Chapter 10: The Overseas Enigma 143

Chapter 11: Glimpses and Glances 153

Chapter 12: Conclusions 164

Appendices 185

Bibliography 229

Index 233

Foreword to the 2004 Edition
by
Tim Wallace-Murphy

The mystery of the Abbe Berenger Saunière, the free-spending parish priest of the small hilltop village of Rennes-le-Château has, over the last thirty years, taken on a vibrant life of its own, enlivened with tales of hidden treasure, accusations of heresy, and allegations of fraud, murder, and general mayhem in a manner that almost defies belief. This tiny and otherwise insignificant, remote village now attracts over twenty thousand visitors a year from all over the world; modern pilgrims who wend their way on foot, on horseback, by car, or by bus up the narrow, twisting, mountainous road that leads from Couiza to the village. The short sandy traverse from the first houses to the car park, which occupies a considerable portion of village, is a vivid reminder of how small this hamlet really is and that despite its superb location, its mere existence cannot explain why it has such an apparently insatiable, truly international appeal that transcends all barriers of race, culture, or creed.

The village of Rennes-le-Château was virtually unknown to the English-speaking world until 1972 when a television documentary, *The Lost Treasures of Jerusalem*, presented by the masterful storyteller, Henry Lincoln, was broadcast by the BBC. This program recounted the tale of Berenger Saunière, a parish priest who in the later years of the nineteenth century was appointed to Rennes-le-Château after some unspecified misdemeanour and who rose from abject poverty to immense wealth with bewildering speed without ever giving the slightest indication of the source of his new-found riches.

Henry Lincoln wove a fascinating tale of hidden treasure, intrigue, and medieval mystery, telling of an ancient, heretical conspiracy that spanned the ages from the time of Jesus down to the twentieth century. Two other documentaries followed the first, each separated by several years—*The Priest the Painter and the Devil* in 1974 and *The Shadow of the Templars* in 1979. Their impact was considerable, but it was nothing compared to the international furore that erupted in 1981 with the publication of the book, *The Holy Blood and the Holy Grail*, written by Henry Lincoln in collaboration with Michael Baigent and Richard Leigh.

To say that this book caused a sensation would be the understatement of the century. Depending on their personal bias, various critics described it as "a brilliant piece of detective work," a book "which will infuriate many ecclesiastical authorities," or simply "blasphemous." It soon achieved best-seller status and was translated into nearly every known language in the world. This one book, a humanly flawed masterpiece, turned a small trickle of interest in esoteric matters into a veritable tidal wave of insatiable curiosity.

The Holy Blood and the Holy Grail was followed by another book by the same authors entitled The Messianic Legacy. The publication of these two books provoked a literary cascade and as early as 1988, two English bibliographers had counted over 473 books, essays, and articles, plus more than one thousand Web pages on the Internet all devoted to the mystery of Rennes-le-Château. Since then the flood of publications has shown no sign of abating; indeed I added to it myself with Rex Deus: The True Mystery of Rennes-le-Château.

Most of the books and articles on the subject swallowed Lincoln's, Baigent's, and Leigh's research without question. It was almost as if the original authors, having castigated "Holy Mother the Church" for dogmatism had inadvertently created yet another form of "holy writ" that was held to be infallible and above criticism. Indeed for many aficionados of the genre, the medieval Priory of Sion that featured as the main narrative device of the original book was as real and as tangible as the local fire brigade or police department.

Some of the authors who rushed so precipitately into print reached conclusions that were as surreal as they were incredible. One "proved" that Jesus was buried a few short kilometers from the village, while another suggested that the "Head of Christ" was buried under Rosslyn Chapel in Scotland. Others proposed that the mystery was inextricably linked to pirate treasure in Oak Island, Nova Scotia, and a variety of authors busied themselves drawing lines on maps and using their questionable results to demonstrate their own capacity to fantasize. This illusory euphoria was not to last, however. Reality eventually began to rear its ugly head as the muddy waters of fantasy and surreal speculation were clarified by the revelation of certain bizarre facts.

A catholic theologian, the American Margaret Starbird, was so incensed at the The Holy Blood and Holy Grail's heretical idea that Jesus had married and founded a dynasty, that she was determined to refute it. It is a tribute to her intellectual and spiritual integrity that the book she eventually published after many years of careful research, The Lady with the Alabaster Jar, did not merely fail to refute this particular "heresy," it reinforced it almost beyond question.

Then came the revelation confirming what many had suspected from the beginning: that the original three authors had been duped and that the coded documents and dossiers secrets on which they had lavished so much research were, in fact, modern creations—forgeries confected by a certain Pierre Plantard and his dissolute, but intellectually brilliant associate, Antoine de

Cherisey. This came in a superbly researched BBC documentary *The History of a Mystery*, broadcast as part of the Timewatch series.

Furthermore, extensive archival research by Georges Keiss of the Centre des Études et du Recherche Templieres at Campagne-sur-Aude established that the majority of Templar attributions of ownership of property in the vicinity of Rennes-le-Château, paraded as proven fact in *The Holy Blood and the Holy Grail*, were completely bogus and without foundation. For example, the allegation that the one-time Grandmaster of the Templar Order, Bertrand de Blanchefort, who was described by Lincoln, Baigent, Leigh as being born near Rennes-le-Château, was actually born in the Guyenne several hundred kilometers from the village. He did not own any property near Rennes-le-Château and thus could not have given the Chateau Bezu to the Templars. Indeed, Chateau Bezu was never in the possession of the Knights Templar and its only real claim to fame is that it was used as a center for the falsification of the coinage some centuries later.

Thus, to tales of buried treasure, sacred bloodlines, historical conspiracy, persecution, Cathar heresy, genocide, and inquisitorial torture we now have to add forgery, fantasy, downright error, and complete fabrication.

Yet bizarre though it may seem, when the miasma of fabrication, questionable research, fantasy, and fabrication are stripped away, several very real and puzzling mysteries still remain, all surrounding that enigmatic priest, Berenger Saunière, and the events that took place at Rennes-le-Château in the years between 1886 and 1917.

What was the source of Saunière's mysterious and sudden wealth? Was it treasure in the form of good old-fashioned loot such as gold, silver, or jewels? Was it documentary evidence of some great secret that could damage the Church or one of the great royal houses of Europe? Was it the ancient secret of alchemy, the philosopher's stone perhaps? Why was Saunière sacked from his post as priest at Rennes-le-Château? Who brutally murdered one of his elderly colleagues? What secrets could possibly undermine the authority of the Vatican? What is the true interpretation of the bizarre symbolism in the church he so lovingly restored? Who were the mysterious mourners at his funeral? Despite the plethora of books, articles, essays, and websites, each plugging their preferred theories, explanations, and fantasies, these questions remain unanswered to this day.

There are as many ways to seek answers to this mystery as there are people. For the local residents fixated on material treasure, there is one method that is pursued with unflagging enthusiasm: despite the rusting notice at the entrance to the village forbidding unauthorized archaeological excavations, the quiet of siesta time in Rennes-le-Château is often disturbed by the constant clinking of hammers from the caverns that permeate the rock the village is built on. Other seekers still publish and speculate using reason, research, intuition, astrology, and every arcane art, real or imagined, that can be brought into play. Yet the mystery remains unsolved. So what need is there of yet another book on the subject and one that is a reissue at that?

The answer comes from the fact that *Mysteries of Templar Treasure and the Holy Grail: The Secrets of Rennes-le-Château* is unique among the vast majority of works on the subject. Lionel and Patricia Fanthorpe do not seek to prove any theory—either their own, or one proposed by anyone else. Instead they provide an all-embracing examination of the circumstances that seeks to discover where the possible answers may lie, without falling into the trap of finding "proof." Presented with the blessed qualities of humour, humility, and commendable scholarship, *Mysteries of Templar Treasure and the Holy Grail* is a work that puts every aspect of the Saunière mystery under the intellectual microscope and then weighs the results with independence and clarity. Nothing relevant is ignored or dismissed without in-depth examination. Every possible line of investigation, however remote, that might shed further light on the subject is followed to its logical conclusion. The authors' own bias, which they admit with transparent honesty and commendable brevity is that, as devout Christians, they do not question the New Testament accounts of the life and work of Jesus. Yet they also freely admit that, on this subject, readers are perfectly entitled to reach their own conclusions.

The location of Rennes-le-Château and the country surrounding it are described with loving detail that is obviously based upon first-hand knowledge and prolonged, personal exploration. The Fanthorpes present the history of the area in a lucid exposition of the complex web that has molded the Languedoc, its people, and its culture from Greek, Roman, Visigoth, Merovingian, Cathar, Templar, and Inquisitorial times up to the present day.

The difficult and oft-times controversial subject of sacred geometry in the magnificent landscape of the Languedoc is given due attention and the authors describe the various theories floated by Henry Lincoln, David Wood, and others, evaluating them all, accepting with reservation, aspects of some, and dismissing others with considerable humour.

The coded documents and the so-called *dossiers secret* lodged at the Bibliothèque Nationale, which are central to the original story promoted by Henry Lincoln, are examined with due diligence and proper critical analysis that leads the authors to make conditional statements such as "if the Priory of Sion actually existed." To the authors' credit, this justifiable scepticism does not prevent them from exploring all possible consequences of that secret society's putative existence, as if indeed it was a viable entity in the medieval era as described by Henry Lincoln.

The tentacles of the mystery of Saunière's millions are wide reaching, for as well as arcing back into the mists of the past they stretch, in geographical terms, across western Europe and possibly even the Atlantic. The narrative flows easily from Rennes-le-Château to Paris, Rosslyn Chapel near Edinburgh, Shugborough Hall in England, and on to Oak Island and the Money Pit in Mahone Bay, Nova Scotia. The authors' knowledge of the European esoteric tradition is profound and displayed to the reader's advantage as they examine the wide spectrum of possible contributors to the mystery in fascinating detail, including Sir Francis Bacon, the Ansons, John Napier, Nicolas Flamel and, of course, the ubiquitous and mysterious Comte de St. Germain. In addition, brief but informative studies of the Templars, the Cathars, the Rosicrucians, and the Troubadors form the setting for a critical and highly astute analysis of the Priory of Sion.

What more could any student of the mystery of Rennes-le-Château reasonably ask for? Yet there is more that is both pertinent and informative. Lionel is a priest in the Church of England and his professional view of Berenger Saunière, his eminence grise, the Abbe Boudet, and the inexplicable murder of the elderly priest, Abbe Gelis, brings the reader insights denied in other works on this mystery.

Another rare and highly treasured addition to this meticulous approach can be found in the colourful pen portraits of many of the living commentators and investigators in this field who still live in the vicinity of the village. These are all drawn with tolerance, respect, and often times affection and add a distinctly warm and highly relevant human touch to the book that again marks its difference from other works in the field.

I recommend this book on many levels. It is a superb introduction to the mystery of Rennes-le-Château that is written with open-mindedness and erudition and that is mercifully free from bias and from the desire to "prove" some pet theory, and it is an investigation that treats its subject matter and its readers with the respect that they both truly deserve.

While I would not necessarily accept all of the conclusions the authors' reach, I respect their courage and their integrity in presenting them. For far too long, this subject has spawned an incalculable number of books that have unquestioningly accepted the conclusions of their predecessors as irrefutable statements of truth. We are at the point where we are in danger of replacing the tyranny of Church dogma with the absolute dictatorship of a revisionist consensus based on fantasy and not on fact. This book will encourage debate, personal investigation, and the dissemination of rational, dissenting opinions in order to arrive at truth.

It is time for many flowers to bloom in this particularly well-hoed furrow and Lionel and Patricia Fanthorpe's book, *Mysteries of Templar Treasure and the Holy Grail* is a major contribution to the debate on Rennes-le-Château. More importantly, it is a damned good book that, whether or not you agree with all the points raised within its covers, is informative, provocative, entertaining and, above all, honest.

Tim Wallace-Murphy

FOREWORD
by Canon Stanley Mogford, MA

This book will attract many readers and will continue to do so for many years to come — unless and until Rennes-le-Château finally and convincingly yields up its many secrets. It will deserve every one of those readers, not merely for the quality and cogency of its writing, but for the transparent honesty and thoroughness with which it has been researched. Shakespeare in his Hamlet makes the following declaration: "If circumstances lead me I will find where truth is hid, though it were hid within the centre". They could well have been the inspiration behind these authors. They have looked for the truth and looked hard, sparing no pains in their long search.

No doubt the most avid among the readers, and the most to be feared, will be the many other like-minded researchers who, over the years, will have been equally tormented by the mysteries of the area, and by the leading characters in the drama, seeking, in their turn, to penetrate to the heart of the secrets they uncovered. The authors are clearly aware of them, have given due weight to their views, and have analysed fairly the several conclusions so many of them have drawn. They have given credit where it is due; they have on occasions been justifiably critical of conclusions they saw as only loosely justified by the evidence, but always in a generous, kindly way. They know only too well how certain clues seem to promise great things and then, disappointingly, lead nowhere. No doubt these like-minded researchers will, in their turn, look closely at this new study, the product of fifteen years' research, and be equally as generous and kindly in the judgments to which they come.

Research of any kind can be a lonely business. There are secrets being probed, reputations are being made or lost, and there are others in the field equally resolved to be first with their conclusions. The wise researcher will of necessity for long periods keep his workings to himself. The moment will eventually come when he presents his final work to the scrutiny of others, and then he has the equally lonely experience of hearing and, perhaps, having to endure, the unwelcome shafts of their criticism. Generations of us, for example, have now long benefited from the researches of men like Lister and Pasteur and will envy their achievements. Few, however, would have envied them the prejudice and misunderstanding that for so long impeded their work. It has always been much the same. The good researcher struggles alone, or with one devoted and totally reliable partner, but never loses his determination to reach an honest conclusion. Many like researchers, then, will read this book and, no doubt, will respect it as a genuine hard-working piece of scholarship.

Readers of mystery stories will be fascinated by Rennes-le-Château, but, sadly, they will yet have to provide their own final diagnosis and solution. The writers are not Hercule Poirot, tying up all the loose ends, and able to satisfy all their readers with a neat and defensible solution to the events they describe. Some mysteries persist and perhaps they always will. Long years ago now, in Whitechapel in Victorian London, the area was ravaged by a series of brutal murders. The murderer has gone down into history as Jack the Ripper but no one to this day is certain of his identity. There were, and there are still, theories in plenty and notable people named, but no one could ever be sure of the facts. Only the murders remain certain. So, perhaps, whatever the quality of research, the mystery of Rennes-le-Château will never be finally resolved. It covers not merely the secret of the unknown treasure. What did Bérenger Saunière find all those years ago? There are mysteries within the mystery. Why was he so fearful of his future, wary of visitors and living behind a steel door? Who killed the old priest, Antoine Gélis, in nearby Coustaussa? What did Saunière say to his confessor that seemed so shocking as to warrant neither penance nor absolution? What can even now be made of the three decayed corpses found in 1956 in Saunière's garden, all three having been shot? Were these and other happenings like them simply coincidence? Coincidence, no doubt, has a long arm but can it be long enough to cover so many such tragedies in so limited an area?

Were they all part of the one great mystery that surrounded Bérenger Saunière to the day of his death? Readers of the mystery genre will be glad of this book but, long after they have read it, it will continue to torment them to find a solution that satisfies everything they have found.

Students of the human psyche also will be equally fascinated by this study, and the character of the hero, if such he may be called, may continue to baffle them. Only the very few and wonderfully privileged ever make great and lasting discoveries. When they do it is natural and irresistible to share with others the thrill of such discoveries.

One of the many outstanding exhibits in the British Museum is the so-called Rosetta Stone. For long years much hieroglyphic writing from the long distant past was known but no one could read any of it. The writing was like a code which no one could decipher. Its secrets might have remained hidden forever had not a young Frenchman in 1799 unburied a basalt stele at the mouth of the Nile at a place called Rosetta. It bore an inscription in several languages, one known, the others in hieroglyphics. It is said that when the young man realised the value of his find he fainted. The known language slowly unlocked the secret of the other, and thus opened to the world the whole vast range of ancient Egyptian writing. No one who made such a discovery could have kept it to himself.

Tutankhamun may have been one of the lesser Pharaohs, in supreme authority for only nine years and dying young as long ago as 1352 BC, but his name has been invested with a rare glamour following the chance discovery of his tomb in the Valley of the Kings in 1922. Perhaps chance is not a fair word. Lord Carnarvon and his associate, Howard Carter, discovered the tomb following a search lasting all of sixteen years, but their reward was that of the first intact royal burial chamber ever found in Egypt with its occupants and artifacts undisturbed as they were at the time of the burial all those centuries before. No one could keep such a discovery from the rest of the world.

The treasure unearthed by Bérenger Saunière, whatever it was, was not in this league. Nonetheless, certainly it was of vital import to him and for him. Where his life had known poverty and limitation, now it began to exude considerable wealth and extravagance. It will indicate a rare man, and a strange make-up, if it can be shown that he kept to the end of his life, exclusive to himself, the secret of what he discovered and the use he made of it. It is normal human nature to hint, to confide, to gossip, to bribe through promises of gifts to come. It is said he shared his secret with his housekeeper, Marie Dénarnaud. Can we be all that certain that he did? It is equally part of human nature to claim what one would like to have happened. She had many opportunities to share the secret with others if she really knew it. Did he reveal everything finally to his confessor? The confessional will never tell. Perhaps what he longed to share with his priestly neighbour was something alarming but totally unrelated. It may be a fact that Bérenger Saunière was that rarest of men, self-contained, self-enclosed, capable of learning a secret and taking it with him to the grave. Those who enjoy the unusual, the supernatural, the fantasy world, will find much to attract them in these researches. Co-author Lionel Fanthorpe was once a writer of much science fiction and libraries everywhere contain stories from his wide-ranging imagination. In this present work he has had no need to invent anything. Everything fanciful and unusual is already there in Rennes-le-Château. All he had to do, where once he invented, is now to record. There are descriptions of esoteric triangles, pentagons, hidden cryptic clues found in paintings, on tombstones, in the very landscape itself. There are allusions to strange religious cults, heresies, secret societies and the like. Cryptograms, ciphers, codes abound, and he invented none of them. How could so limited an area produce not only the treasure, whatever it was, but so many enigmas, labyrinthine caves, subterranean burial sites, all of which long to be disco-vered then solved, but, if and when they are, seem merely to lead to new problems and other enigmas? Those who love solving problems, cryptog-rams, etc., will have a field day in these chapters, but no doubt, in their turn, they will in the end admit defeat. Rennes-le-Château will not have covered its secrets in vain.

Treasure seekers, those who look for crocks of gold at the foot of a rainbow, will have some encouragement from this book. Perhaps it is possible even yet for some of the great elusive treasures to be found.

Solomon of old was once offered by God any one wish he desired, and chose well. His choice was wisdom, the ability to choose discreetly between good and evil. Midas of old, given a similar choice, chose badly, insisting that everything he touched should turn to gold. A golden plate would be acceptable but golden food would not. A golden child would be an image not a son.

Most of us more ordinary mortals, loving life and enjoying its comforts, given such a choice, might well elect to ask for the so-called Elixir of Life, the formula that would halt the ageing process, and extend life as long as we needed it. Was this long-sought formula the treasure Saunière disco-vered? Or was it the so-called Philosopher's Stone, believed to exist some-where by almost every generation, the process by which base metals could be turned into gold? Ordinary mortals might find such a treasure attractive, and greater ones would pay a great price for it. Was this the treasure he claimed to find? Did he find somewhere the Holy Grail, the sacred chalice Jesus once used at the last Supper with his disciples? It would be priceless, but if Saunière discovered it who has it now? Did he find the lance once buried in the side of Jesus at the moment of his death and later maybe smuggled away by the soldier who was ordered to use it? Any such Christian relic would be worth a king's ransom within the Christian world. But who could credit that Christendom would ever buy it, or anything like it, from one of its own Christian priests? Such will-o'-the-wisp treasures are still attractive and men will always hope to find them.

Anything of quality will always have its detractors. Nothing satisfies everyone all of the time. The Christian religion has drawn more than its just share of criticism, for all the good it has achieved throughout the world and the quality of lives it has helped to create. Sadly, no doubt, some of these strictures have been deserved, but not all. One co-author of this book is a priest of the twentieth century, and his subject a priest of the nineteenth century. The one brother in Christ is seeking to understand the other. The authors patently are incapable of believing certain things. Initially, they will never be able to accept from anyone that the death of Jesus and his resurrection can ever have involved a piece of deception, that Christ, in fact, survived the cross, was allowed to escape and later joined his life with that of Mary Magdalen and settled down well away from the troubled area of Palestine. Equally, one co-author, the priest of the twentieth century, cannot be persuaded that the priest of the nineteenth found evidence of this survival and flight and marriage, and that he used it to blackmail the Catholic hierarchy, and was well paid for suppressing what he found. Christendom may have had many faults, for which it will be judged, but not one so wholly remote from the facts. The Christian religion was born on the Gospel of the Resurrection; its power has come from it; Christ died and was buried and rose again from the dead. The priest of the twentieth and the priest of the nineteenth century, the one British and the other French, along with people all over the world, will surrender nothing of that truth. The Christian religion stands or falls by it.

So what was it Bérenger Saunière found all those years ago? It was treasure of a kind and it made him wealthy far beyond his earliest hopes and dreams. Those who read the book, and, perhaps, be drawn one day to visit the area, will form opinions of their own. There may be much of his treasure still to find. It would be sad to think he was just a grave robber. Whatever it was it made him rich and through his money it made him powerful. But is it unfair to see him as a man certainly not loved by everyone, and in large measure not at peace within himself? Towards the end he seemed to lose interest in it or ceased to exploit it. The mystery has not yet been laid to rest. Bérenger Saunière, Priest of the Parish, 1885 – 1917, now lies at rest in the churchyard side by side with Marie Dénarnaud. May he have found in the eternal world the peace and forgiveness he failed to find in his lifetime.

Canon Stanley Mogford, MA

Cardiff, 1991

INTRODUCTION TO THE MYSTERY

Praemonitus praemunitus.

In the evening twilight Rennes-le-Château is a silhouette on a small hill: the contoured edge of a Yale key — a curious watchtower, an ancient church, a crumbling château. What mysteries can that key unlock?

Fly as far as Toulouse; drive down the motorway; go on through Limoux; turn up the narrow mountain road at Couiza — and there it is: Rennes-le-Château. Ordinary, everyday reality has just given way to Lewis Carroll's Wonderland. This is the sort of place that the Pevensey children found when they hid in the Professor's wardrobe. This resembles the realm in which George MacDonald's narrator-hero in *Lilith* found himself after stumbling through the weird mirror in the ancient library. This is the country where memories of Tectosages, Celts, Romans and Visigoths are still strong; where Cathars, Templars and Troubadours once explored the limestone crags and caves; where Bérenger Saunière, the priest, became immensely and unaccountably rich.

And that's where the mystery begins — with Bérenger Saunière. Born on April 11th, 1852, he was appointed Parish Priest of Rennes on June 1st, 1885. Not long afterwards he began spending money on a massive scale. Whether he found an ancient treasure, or whether he gained access to some means of creating or obtaining wealth, cannot be proved absolutely from the evidence now available. Nevertheless, the tower, the orangeries, the villa, the statues, paintings and decorations in his refurbished church of St Mary Magdalen all demonstrate beyond a shadow of doubt that a great deal of money flowed through his hands during the thirty-two years he spent at Rennes before his death on January 22nd, 1917.

Exploring and researching the Rennes mystery can be compared to peeling a gigantic onion — except that the explorer seems to be working from the inside, always working from a smaller layer to a larger one. Each tantalising new discovery serves only to highlight the need for more and more research.

From the one sure fact that Bérenger Saunière spent a great deal of money arises the question: where did he get it? There are many possibilities: some are wildly far-fetched and improbable; others jostle nose to nose for the role of first favourite.

Without pre-empting the chapter which deals in detail with the coded manuscripts, which Saunière may or may not have discovered in or beside the Visigothic altar pillar, a strong contender for the source of his wealth must be an ancient buried treasure of some kind.

According to one popular explanation, which although plausible is not without its serious critics, coded messages led Saunière to a cache of Visigothic gold, silver and jewels hidden with the body of King Dagobert II in a crypt below the ancient church. An elaboration of this theory traces the treasure — or a major part of it — back to Solomon and the Treasure of Zion in the Holy Land. Some historians have suggested that the Jewish treasure was taken to Rome by Titus (part of it at least is shown on his triumphal arch) and looted from the Roman treasury by Alaric the Visigoth in A.D. 410. There is strong historical support for the idea that what is now the tiny village of Rennes-le-Château was once a major Visigothic centre, and substantially fortified.

Another variant suggests that Saunière actually discovered the whereabouts of several ancient tombs in which it was customary for the nobility to be buried in all their finery, complete with jewels and golden ornaments. Supporters of this idea reinforce their case by referring to the long, secretive walks the priest allegedly took, and which he "explained" as expeditions to gather interesting stones for his collection.

There were Cathar strongholds at Montségur, at Puivert, at Usson, at Peyrepertuse, Quéribus and Puilaurens. Before Montségur fell to the Catholic crusaders in 1244, it seems that a handful of Cathars escaped with "the treasures of their faith". It is not possible to say with certainty what form these treasures took, but there are strange echoes from the torture chambers of the Inquisition about their being *pecuniam infinitam* — literally "unlimited money". Was it this mysterious Cathar treasure which Saunière discovered?

After the fall of the Cathars, the Templars took centre stage: bankers to the Crusaders, enigmatic warrior-priests who lead the treasure hunter inexorably back in the direction of Zion and Solomon's Temple again. There are ancient Samaritan legends of a hidden treasure on Mount Gerizim in the Holy Land, and there was certainly a Templar settlement on that mountain. Did they find the treasure? Did they bring it to a suitable Templar stronghold such as the Château Blanchefort near Rennes-le-Château was thought to be? Was that what Saunière eventually uncovered?

Some of the stranger, more esoteric theories tell of alchemists (one tower of the crumbling Château Hautpoul in Rennes is called "The Tower of Alchemy") and of Rosicrucians. Modern nuclear science can transmute one element into another, but the process is so expensive and time-consuming that it is far more economical to mine for gold than to manufacture it! But what if the ten million to one long shot was right? What if some medieval genius had actually found the legendary Philosopher's Stone? And what if he had left his secret for Saunière to rediscover in the late nineteenth century?

The alchemists and Rosicrucians were alleged to guard two priceless secrets: the Philosopher's Stone, which had the power of transmuting base metals into gold; and the Elixir of Life, which conveyed great longevity and prolonged youthfulness, even if it did not give absolute immortality. In view of his own stress-induced, premature ageing, and death at the comparatively early age of sixty five, it seems highly unlikely that this was the alchemical secret which Saunière was selling. Yet there is a curious link between Rennes and the secret of longevity, and that link is forged by the Man in the Iron Mask.

A later chapter will deal fully with the curious affair of Nicolas Fouquet, French Superintendent of Finance in the days of Louis XIV, but the outline can be given here. Fouquet and his younger brother were involved in some mystery connected with Poussin the painter and, through him, with Rennes-le-Château. Fouquet fell from power, and, according to some historians, may have become the Man in the Iron Mask. When the nameless masked prisoner eventually died, it was allegedly reported by some witnesses that the face beneath the mask had not aged perceptibly during the long years of incarceration. If Poussin had pointed Fouquet in the direction of the secret of the Elixir of Life, and if Fouquet had stubbornly refused to pass it on to Louis XIV, might not that explain the very curious circumstances under which the masked prisoner was held incommunicado for so many years? Fouquet knew that once Louis had the secret, nothing would prevent the King from disposing of his prisoner: Louis knew that keeping Fouquet alive and totally isolated was his one hope of acquiring the longevity and renewed youth and vigour that he craved. It was, therefore, a classic stalemate.

Another team of investigators has suggested that Saunière stumbled into the inner sanctum of a politico-religious secret society, perhaps "The Priory of Sion", and that they then paid him handsomely to be their "representative" in Rennes.

There was some talk of a closely guarded secret "bloodline" and innuendoes about a "genealogy" that linked the local Counts of Razès (and their contemporary descendants) to the Merovingian Kings and beyond them to Jesus himself, who, according to this theory, was secretly married to Mary Magdalen. The implication was that the "evidence" which Saunière was supposed to have found was so profoundly shocking that the Church authorities paid him to keep it quiet.

There is evidence linking Rennes with ancient Egypt – millennia before the Christian era. The enigmatic Hermes Trismegistus, or Thoth, is prominent in this theory, one suggestion being that it was his legendary (and priceless) Emerald Tablets which found their way to Rennes, and ultimately into Saunière's hands. There is also a connection with Isis, mother-goddess of the holy family in Egyptian mythology, sister-wife of Osiris and mother of the infant Horus – who grew up to overthrow the evil god Set and avenge his father, Osiris, who was then triumphantly resurrected. The mother-goddess theme is persistent in Rennes.

One advanced student of magic, to whom the authors talked at great length, felt certain that Saunière was secretly performing a ritual known as "The Convocation of Venus". According to this informant, that ritual is a very effective and accurate way of forecasting the future. In her opinion, Saunière – with the aid of Marie Dénarnaud – was charging vast sums for the accurate predictions he was able to give to the wealthy clients who came regularly to consult him, or whom he visited during his travels. This particular spell was believed to have been facilitated by the presence of a "natural" pentagon on the ground at Rennes, and by its correspondence to the celestial pentagon which the planet Venus appears to trace out every eight years. It was also hinted that there were strong sexual overtones in the convocation ritual, as Venus-Aphrodite was traditionally the goddess of physical love. Is it remotely possible that Saunière's deathbed confession in 1917 contained sordid secrets of this kind – perhaps involving Marie Dénarnaud – and that it was for this reason that, like Tannhäuser in the legend, he was refused absolution?

Other investigators have suggested that he betrayed someone wealthy and important, blackmailing him, or her, following the revelation of a dark secret in the confessional.

Another thoughtful researcher has suggested that the real savant of Rennes was not Saunière but Henri Boudet, the old priest at Rennes-les-Bains: "Saunière was the voice and the legs — Boudet was the brain. Saunière was the colourful marionette on a well lit stage: Boudet was the puppet master in the shadows behind it." In 1886 the brilliantly academic Boudet wrote a very curious book entitled *La Vraie Langue Celtique et le Cromleck de Rennes-les-Bains* (The True Celtic Language and the Cromlech at Rennes-les-Bains). It seems to be liberally sprinkled with paronomasia and cryptic double meanings. One short sample is probably enough to indicate something of its enigmatic flavour: on pages 298 and 299 Boudet writes about the hunt (*la chasse*) of the wild boar (*le sanglier*) and the bear (*l'ours*).

The addition of a circumflex accent changes the meaning of *chasse* to "shrine" or "reliquary" and *sanglier* divides very easily into "ties" or "bonds" of "blood" or "lineage". *L'ours* not only conjures up all sorts of connections with King Arthur as *The Bear of Britain* (Edward Frankland, published by MacDonald, London, 1944) but is also very close to the French word for gold (*l'or*). This kind of symbolism and word-play can be dismissed as coincidence fermented by the work of an effervescent imagination, but when it occurs in sufficient quantity it gives grounds for more serious reflection. If *la chasse sanglier* is a cipher for the Holy Grail (the sacred reliquary, or container, of the "Blood which Unites") then the connection with Arthur, the Bear of Britain, becomes more significant because of the Grail Quest by his Knights of the Round Table.

There are hints that Saunière may have had a connection with the Habsburgs, and that he may have approached the old Imperial House of Austria-Hungary to try to dispose of some priceless religious relic which he had uncovered in a royal tomb at Rennes. Although Francis II had effectively done away with the title of Holy Roman Emperor in August of 1806 to prevent Napoleon from seizing it, the Habsburgs still had the clearest and most legitimate claim to it. A priest could hardly hope to sell an illicitly acquired relic to the Vatican; but the "rightful" Holy Roman Emperor would have been a logical customer. This raises very profound questions: did Saunière offer something to the Habsburgs? Did his contact with them have any connection at all with the tragedy of Rudolf's death in the hunting lodge at Mayerling in 1889, or the subsequent flight and alleged disappearance at sea of the young Habsburg Archduke Johann Salvator, who, at the time of his reported death, had renounced his former titles and was known simply as Johann Ort — which also means the bear?

A completely different theory suggests that considerable quantities of gold may still lie hidden in the ancient mines on the southern slopes of the hill on which Rennes-le-Château stands. Certainly there are accounts of German miners being brought in to do some secret work there a few centuries ago: from their employer's point of view, their inability to communicate in Languedoc French with the local people could have been a great advantage. There are also reports of unidentified skeletons found later in the area, which could well have been those of the German miners.

There, in briefest outline, are a few of the ways in which Bérenger Saunière might have become wealthy; but although Saunière's unaccountable wealth is the first clear fact in the Rennes mystery, the mystery itself is far broader, deeper and older than a nineteenth century village priest's mysterious acquisition of money. The adventures of Marie Dénarnaud and Bérenger Saunière are only a peep-hole through which something much bigger and stranger can be glimpsed.

Rennes and the area around it have an intriguing geography, geology and topography. Its ancient landmarks line up in unaccountably strange patterns. If the old Abbé Boudet was right, the cromlechs, dolmens and menhirs around Rennes are particularly intriguing. From the Celts to the Cathars, from the Templars to today's geometricians and surveyors, many of those who have explored — or who are currently exploring — the landmarks in and around Rennes are convinced that the solution to a great and ancient mystery is to be found among these enigmatic shapes and the curious lines and angles that connect them.

The mystery surrounding Rennes-le-Château has some of its deepest roots in religion and theology. Once the tired old red-herring about Jesus and Mary Magdalen (which is only a pale, hollow and echoing recrudescence of an ineffectual attack made on the early church long ago) has been disposed of, there are some important and serious ancient Chaldean, Hebrew, Egyptian and Celtic religious explorations to be made.

At least part of the mystery of Rennes is hidden in codes, ciphers and cryptograms of the most complex type: and they turn up everywhere. There is a mysterious tombstone at Axat, beneath which Henri Boudet was buried in 1915: it bears a coded message of some sort on what looks like a stone replica of his very unusual book *La Vraie Langue Celtique*, which was itself a mass of coded messages. There is also a de-consecrated church at Axat with a curious star and roses design on the wall below its bells and above its clock.

The tombstone of Marie de Nègre was carefully erased by Saunière, but not before its fascinating cipher had been copied by an antiquarian and published in a small monograph. The inscription on that stone is a perfect anagram of the message which is eventually distilled from the parchments which were allegedly found inside the Visigothic altar pillar in the church at Rennes. What is the meaning of the three strange "griffouls" on the ancient fountain outside the house in Montazels where Saunière was born? Saunière's bellringer, whose great grandchildren still live in Rennes, found a curious little glass vial hidden in a secret compartment of an old wooden baluster. He showed it to the priest, who consequently found the knight's gravestone which is currently on display in the museum at Rennes. What was written on the parchment concealed inside that tiny glass vial? Saunière not only found clues, he left them as well: in the statues and pictures with which he filled his church . . . and probably in his tower, his orangeries and the Villa Bethania.

The mystery of Rennes spreads its tentacles like the limbs of some gigantic octopus. They are not confined to the Razès, the Midi, or even to France. In the grounds of Shugborough Hall, Staffordshire, England there is a stone reproduction, in reversed form, of Nicolas Poussin's enigmatic painting "The Shepherds of Arcadia". This eighteenth century structure is known as The Shepherd Monument, and it bears a curious inscription:

O.U.O.S.V.A.V.V
D.   M.

One possible decoding for this mysterious inscription was proposed in our earlier book on Rennes, and the subject is examined again in greater detail in a later chapter.

Michael Bradley's unusual and controversial ideas in *The Holy Grail Across the Atlantic* (published by Anthony Hawke, Canada, in 1988), take the trail several thousand miles farther and connect the Rennes mystery with the equally puzzling affair of the notorious Money Pit on Oak Island, Nova Scotia, which, coincidentally, was also the subject of our investigations in 1988. There are two divergent theories about the Money Pit: one suggests that it contains, or contained, an enormous treasure; the other suggests that it is the carefully guarded burial chamber of an ancient holy man who led a party of religious refugees to the New World centuries ago.

Following the old Paris Meridian line also leads to some very strange places including Arques (where there was once a tomb resembling the one in the Poussin shepherd painting), and Conques (where there is one of the strangest bejewelled, golden "reliquaries" ever seen). Pursuing that Paris–Arques line further north and south also takes the traveller to some surprisingly interesting ancient sites. The position of the old Paris Meridian is almost certainly more − much more − than coincidental.

Henri Boudet's whimsical predilection for verbal, phonic and etymological clues alerts the contemporary researcher to look for similar things while sifting through the data dune which buries the secret of Rennes-le-Château. It is not a long step from the "Arcadia" of Poussin's painting to Acadie, or Acadia, and the Acadians of early Nova Scotia. Under the Treaty of Utrecht (1713), the old French settlement of Acadia became British, and in 1755, when war between Britain and France seemed to be looming ominously, several thousand Acadians were forcibly deported. One major group found their way to Bayou Teche in Louisiana, where their subsequent adventures and life-style were vividly and sympathetically described in the books of George Washington Cable. The folk history, the legends and especially the songs of the Cajuns (a dialect derivative of Acadians) provide intriguing study material. The tendrils of the Rennes mystery can be discerned twining as far as the folk music of New Orleans. What is hidden in the medieval ballads of the troubadours, the twenty-two curious verses of the Good King Dagobert song and traditional Cajun folk music?

Over the centuries the Rennes mystery has accumulated its share of writers and artists, as well as musicians. As far back as 1618, Giovanni Francesco Barbieri (1591-1666) who was known as Guercino because of his unfortunate squint, painted a pioneering version of the *Et in Arcadia Ego* theme (strongly associated with the Rennes mystery) in which two young men (possibly shepherds, but not necessarily so) are looking at a skull on a plinth in a small forest. After Guercino came Poussin and the

Teniers (father and son), Delacroix and the avant-garde writer-painter, Jean Cocteau. The major nineteenth century novelist and poet Victor Hugo included an amazing section *La Confiance du Marquis Fabrice* in his epic poem *La Légende des Siècles*. One sub-section of this is entitled *Un seul homme sait où est caché le trésor*, which may be translated as "only one man knows where the treasure is hidden", and parts of this story come very close to the Rennes mystery. It seems logical, therefore, that the works of these artists, writers and poets need to be examined thoroughly for any hidden clues which they may contain.

In addition to the famous artists and writers who seem to have known more than most about the Rennes mystery, there are others who may, perhaps, be better categorised as Men of Mystery. One document (against which it is only fair to say that some serious objections have been voiced) purports to give a list of Grand Masters of the Priory of Sion, an alleged secret society which was believed by some researchers to have controlled, directed, or at least influenced the Templars prior to a reported episode at Gisors in 1188, an episode which was said to have involved the symbolic felling of an ancient elm tree.

According to this list, which may be spurious, past Grand Masters included: Nicolas Flamel, a scholarly physician who was said to have been given a definitive treatise on alchemy in Paris in 1357, Leonardo da Vinci, Robert Boyle, Isaac Newton, Victor Hugo and Claude Debussy. The same authority on magic who provided the theory about Saunière's performing "The Convocation of Venus" also said that Barnes Wallis, the inventor, had been Grand Master until his death, and that there was currently a vacancy.

Other Men of Mystery whose names have been associated in one way or another with the Rennes mystery over the centuries have included Francis Bacon (who seems to have used a secret code involving very odd watermarks when making contact with his inner circle) and the Count of St Germain, who, like the Man in the Iron Mask, may have had access to the secret of extreme longevity.

And what of the current personalities involved in the Rennes mystery? A historical demographer once pointed out that of all the scientists who have ever lived, half are living now. Substituting "Rennes researchers" for "scientists" would probably not detract from the statistical accuracy of that statement.

Way back in 1975, when we made our first visit, the enigmatic old village was very quiet and very rural. We actually slept in Saunière's Villa Bethania, which was then being run as a hotel by our friend M. Henri Buthion. There was no bookshop, no museum, no souvenir shop . . . just an atmosphere of peace, tranquillity and ancient, brooding mystery.

Today, there seem to be almost as many investigators as there are bizarre facets of the Rennes affair: our old friend, Henri Buthion, is still there in the Villa Bethania, skilfully explaining and interpreting life-like facsimiles of the coded manuscripts which Saunière is believed to have found in the ancient Visigothic altar pillar. Marcel and Antoine Captier, descendants of Saunière's bellringer, the one who found the tiny parchment rolled up in the glass vial in the baluster, are on hand with immense first-hand knowledge and experience of the village and its people. Celia Brooke is there, fluently bilingual, enthusiastic, knowledgeable and tirelessly helpful, along with Claire Corbu, daughter of Noël Corbu, the previous owner of the Villa Bethania.

Elizabeth van Buren, a descendant of the eighth President of the United States, is a prolific, widely read and deeply sensitive writer on arcane, esoteric and mystical cosmic themes. She runs the Arcadia Centre, at the foot of Rennes-le-Château, where her range of books, tapes and video films dealing with her perspective on the mystery is on sale to visitors.

On the opposite side of the spectrum are investigators like the doggedly persistent, thorough and pragmatic young Englishman, Paul Smith, who approaches the Rennes mystery in much the same way as Peter Falk's Lieutenant Columbo in the popular television series. The authors and publisher are very grateful to Paul for permission to reproduce some of his findings as one of the Appendices.

Arlette Règne and Pierre Bren have concentrated their studies on Boudet's *La Vraie Langue Celtique* and M. Bren very kindly discussed his ideas with us during a taped interview at Rennes in 1990.

After their initial success with *The Holy Blood and the Holy Grail*, which offered one speculative solution to the Rennes mystery, Baigent, Leigh and Lincoln produced a sequel entitled *The Messianic Legacy*. Baigent and Leigh then went on to write *The Temple and the Lodge* in which they endeavoured to trace the flight of the European Templars to Scotland after the tragedies of the early fourteenth century. While acknowledging their enthusiasm and energy, and the relevance of some areas of their extensive research, the present authors are diametrically and implacably opposed to those of their conclusions which relate to Jesus Christ.

Colin Wilson, rightly recognized as a leading authority on inexplicable phenomena and the paranormal in general, has also interested himself in the Rennes mystery recently, and his views are well worth reading.

Pierre Jarnac has produced a monumental and scholarly archive on the subject.

Jean Robin has put forward several interesting ideas; and Stanley James's personalised and meticulously detailed study, *The Treasure Maps of Rennes*, is also well worth perusing. James's theory is based principally on some very complex decodings which led him to what he believed to be the actual "treasure cave" just past the Berque Grande in the Bézis Valley.

Perhaps one of the most useful and authoritative studies on the priest himself is that written by Émile Saunière, a close relative of the intriguing Bérenger. For authentic details of his life at Rennes-le-Château, *L'Heritage de l'Abbé Saunière* by Claire Corbu and Antoine Captier is of immense value.

The combined ideas of these modern researchers and students of the Rennes mystery effervesce together to produce a potent liquor − a heady sort of "Hypothesis Absinthe" for the discerning reader to sip slowly, thoughtfully and with a certain prudent circumspection.

Finally, to all of this, the authors have added their own ideas − and, of course, their own solution.

CHAPTER ONE

RENNES-LE-CHÂTEAU AND ITS AREA

Non est ad astra mollis e terris via.

Not far from the Naurouze Gap which separates the eastern Pyrenees from France's central massif lies the village of Rennes-le-Château. Mediterranean chestnut, Hermes oak and cork oak all flourish here in the eastern Pyrenees. Broom grows prolifically and ubiquitously on the hillsides, and there are countless hectares of tough, drought-resistant bushes of the species which are native to Provence.

The eastern Pyrenees are cut by the valleys of the Agly, the Tech and the Tet; and the Agly has sculpted an interesting line of cretaceous marls. The neighbouring Corbières with their hard palaeozoic core seem to be fighting a stubborn rearguard action on behalf of the central massif.

Rennes and its immediate surroundings rest on cretaceous limestone: the area is rich in sharp, jagged crests with stark, singular profiles, labyrinthine caves and subterranean rivers and streams. Despite the heavy undergrowth and afforestation on most of the nearby slopes, the hill on which Rennes itself stands is comparatively bleak. Only the scant, tough, mountain grasses and an occasional shrub cover its ponderous limestone base.

This absence of cover would have appealed to its original neolithic settlers (some of whose stone axe-heads and other artefacts have been discovered in the area by M. Henri Fatin, the owner of the ancient Château Hautpoul) as well as to the Celt-related Tectosages (an interesting ethnic title probably meaning "wise builders or makers, skilled craftsmen") who were probably living in Rennes at about the same time that Pericles was guiding the Athenians. The bare slopes of the hill on which Rennes-le-Château stands give its defenders a clear view of any potential enemies while they are still several kilometres away. Military strategists among the Romans, Visigoths, Septimanians, Merovingians, Carolingians and their successors would also have found Rennes an eminently defensible site.

Couiza lies on the main D118 road between the towns of Limoux in the north and Quillan in the south, while Rennes-le-Château itself is less than five kilometres south of Couiza. Montazels, which adjoins the western outskirts of Couiza, is a fascinating old hilltop village — "Mount Hazel" in its anglicised form, and some folklorists traditionally associate the hazel with wisdom. It was here in Montazels on April 11th, 1852, that Bérenger Saunière was born in a narrow, three-storeyed house with iron verandas overlooking the curious "Fountain of the Tritons". The Tritons depicted on this fountain are reminiscent of dolphins in many respects, but their heads are grotesque. The foreheads are much too high for an aquatic mammal, or for a fish, and the rows of regular teeth look distinctly human. Some early artists portrayed Triton, the son of Neptune and Amphitrite, as a man down to the waist, the rest of him being a fish's tail. The statue in the Vatican museum which shows Triton abducting a nymph portrays him with a horse's forelegs, as well as a human torso from the waist up — rather like a centaur.

Ancient tradition places Triton's home just off the coast of Libya, where he is said to live with his parents in a beautiful golden palace below the sea.

This "Fountain of the Tritons" may well be a significant clue in the Rennes mystery. Firstly, Saunière built his watchtower looking out directly towards his old home beside that fountain in Montazels, and with the fountain just behind us, we photographed Saunière's tower during a re-search visit to Montazels in 1990. Secondly, we believe, the Rennes mystery has links with the Money Pit on Oak Island, Nova Scotia, which we studied in 1988, and interviewed Dan Blankenship, the site manager. The Money Pit is currently being explored by a syndicate called Triton Alliance with whom Dan is closely associated. Thirdly, there is a very curious legend concerning the birth of Mérovée, alias Merovech, alias Merovaeus, the founder of the Merovingian Dynasty. According to this legend, Mérovée's mother, the wife of King Clodion le Chevelu (Clodion the long-haired), was impregnated twice before Mérovée was born: first by Clodion, then by some sort of merman, sea-monster or aquatic demi-god while she was swimming. Was this the mysterious Triton (whoever or whatever Triton really was)?

The traveller who follows the banks of the River Aude from north to south, as it flows to the west of Rennes-le-Château, comes first to Alet-les-Bains, then Castel Nègre (the Black Castle) followed by the turning to the east which leads to Luc (meaning light). Once south of Couiza, the Aude trail leads through the village of Campagne, the town of Quillan and on to Belvianes. Immediately south of Belvianes, the river passes between two dramatic and curiously named natural features: to the west le Trou du Curé (the Priest's Hole, or the Priest's Canyon); to the east Les Murailles du Diable (the Devil's Ramparts). The Black Castle beside the Village of Light? The Priest's Canyon opposite the Devil's Ramparts? No more than fanciful and romantic local place names perhaps, but in view of the strange rumours and legends saturating Rennes and the surrounding area they may be a clue to something more.

It is equally interesting to follow the course of the River Sals, which means "salt", and there is yet another strange coincidence here concerning names. Saunière can mean "salt-maker" and salt is a powerful religious symbol: it is a purifying agent used in rituals of exorcism; it represents the power of goodness and light; it heals and it cleanses; both literally and metaphorically it gives flavour and meaning to an otherwise dull and tasteless existence. Jesus himself told the first disciples that they were the salt of the earth. The Rennes mystery has connections with Shugborough Hall in Staffordshire, England, home of the extremely wealthy Admiral Anson. In the grounds of Shugborough Hall stands The Shepherd Monu-ment: a mirror image in stone of Poussin's "Shepherds of Arcadia". Staf-fordshire is a salt county. Natural brine wells up to the surface in many places there. So much salt is produced that cattle standing in what the locals call the "plashes" of natural brine soon become white with crystalline salt.

A small tributary of the Sals called the Rialsesse, which flows into it from the east, passes close to the site of the Tomb of Arques, flowing at the very foot of the limestone promontory on which the tomb stood until it was unaccountably razed by the new owner of the site in 1988. The demolished tomb had been erected by an American named Lawrence in 1903, and was an exact replica of the one with the *Et in Arcadia Ego* inscription featured in Poussin's canvas.

It was Visigothic practice in the fifth century, and probably for some years afterwards, to bury their kings surrounded by their royal treasures in secret chambers concealed below river beds. The technique was to dam the river and divert its course temporarily while the bed was excavated and the burial chamber prepared. Once the dead king and his treasures were safely interred, and the waterproof subterranean chamber properly sealed, camouflaging sand and gravel would be raked over the site and the dam demolished. The all-concealing river then resumed its original course. Within a few weeks it would be almost impossible to locate the site, and, even if it was located, without sufficient manpower to divert the river again, it would be almost impossible to profane the king's tomb. Unless, of course, a secret passage was constructed . . . perhaps from the base of a tomb on the bank?

Pierre Jarnac's *Archives du Trésor de Rennes-le-Château* reproduce our 1975 photographs of the Tomb of Arques and the two coffins it then contained. Jarnac records on the same page that a M. Adams says that the tomb also contains — or once contained — a very large iron wheel, fixed in the wall, and carrying an endless chain. It did not show up on our 1975 photographs, but that does not mean it wasn't there. It might simply have been out of camera range.

The Sals rises several kilometres southeast of Sougraine, and flows on northwest through Rennes-les-Bains. Shortly before entering this ancient village, the Sals is reinforced by the River Blanque, and immediately to the west of their confluence are three very curious and significant landmarks: the Dead Man; the Devil's Armchair and the Trembling Rock. Beside the road which follows the curve of the River Blanque, and immediately south of these three strange landmarks, lie the ruins of a very ancient mine; a few hundred metres south of that mine is a hermitage.

As we follow the Sals through Rennes-les-Bains itself, we pass the ancient church where Boudet — at least as enigmatic a figure as Saunière — worked for so many years prior to the First World War, and the presbytery where he laboriously assembled his cryptic volume about the old Celtic language. This timeless settlement with its thermal springs — well-known since Roman times — has the same deep, secretive atmosphere that envelopes Rennes-le-Château.

From Rennes-les-Bains the Sals flows almost due north between the Pech Cardou to the west and the high slopes which hide the ruined Château Blanchefort to the east. Below Blanchefort juts the sinister Black Rock, and halfway up the mighty side of Cardou stands the White Rock: again that balance; again that challenge — it is as though the two cosmic forces of Good and Evil, Darkness and Light, Order and Chaos (central to the

Gnostic beliefs of the Cathars who once thronged the Languedoc) are dramatically and repeatedly symbolised in so many of the rivers, mountains and landmarks of this mysterious region.

At the tiny hamlet of Pachevan, the Sals turns due east towards the little hillside village of Cassaignes. There is a mystery here, too. In the cemetery of Cassaignes, incongruous among the nineteenth and twentieth century tombs and memorial carvings which surround it, stands an ancient, weathered stone cross, unmistakably of octagonal Visigothic cross-section. It has probably stood there for fifteen hundred years. What mystery does it cover? To what secret hiding place does it point?

Coustaussa is the next hillside village. There is a ruined château here, with gaunt stone fingers that point upwards starkly like the hand of a traveller who has died of thirst in the desert and still points accusingly at the merciless sun. In the cemetery of Coustaussa lies the body of the murdered priest, Antoine Gélis, savagely struck down by some unknown hand in his own presbytery, here in the village in 1893. A solitary and secretive old man, Gélis normally answered the door only to his niece, when she called with food or clean laundry for him. On the tragic evening when he neglected his own prudent rule, whoever − or whatever − got into his presbytery, attacked him with heavy iron fire-tongs, and finished him with an axe while he was apparently trying to struggle towards the window overlooking the street in a vain attempt to summon help. What seems even more sinister and macabre is that the murderer then coolly and calmly laid out the body − as solemnly and respectfully as a priest or an undertaker might have done.

There were three great pools of blood on the presbytery floor but there was not one telltale foot or fingerprint to be seen. Gélis had considerable sums of church money lying about the presbytery: none of these had been touched. A locked deed box, however, had been forced and the contents rifled. Very probably some interesting documents had been removed − but what were they? And what made them more important than the old priest's life? What strange, paradoxical, psychopathic type of killer could strike down a defenceless old man with an axe, and then spend vital getaway time in laying out the body?[1]

There is another mystery centred on Coustaussa, which would not have come to our attention without the invaluable help of M. Henri Fatin, the proprietor of Château Hautpoul in Rennes-le-Château. M. Fatin showed us around his fascinating and historic home, and very generously gave us several hours of his time. Among the many interesting theories he discussed with us was the possibility that the actual street layout of Rennes-le-Château had been deliberately designed to approximate to the form of an ancient "boat of the dead" − including the gigantic outline of a dead warrior, complete with helmet. He lies with his back to the north, his head to the east − towards Jerusalem, the Holy City. His feet are towards the west − the Isles of the Dead, the Twilight Lands of the Setting Sun. The casque, or helmet, of this dead warrior is very plainly outlined, and

[1]The authors are deeply indebted to their friend, M. Rousset, the doyen of Coustaussa, who most kindly and helpfully assisted them to find their way around the village, and to locate the tomb of Father Gélis. M. Rousset's courtesy is most warmly appreciated.

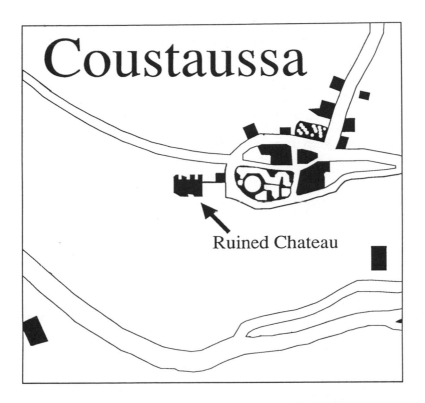

Coustaussa

Ruined Chateau

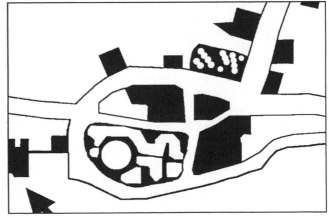

Outline Plan of the village of Coustaussa with possible "helmeted head". (Note also that Coustaussa may well be linked etymologically with *custodien*.)

Château Hautpoul occupies the midpoint of his back, approximately where the keel of the boat would join the underside of the hull. Having once been made aware of such a possibility through our discussions with M. Fatin, we noticed that the outline plan of the village of Coustaussa also bears an uncanny resemblance to the helmeted head of a dead warrior. Were these original street plans laid out as gargantuan memorials to ancient lords and heroes? Pyramids decay; the deepest lines carved on stone become indecipherable as aeons pass: but streets, tracks and roadways last as long as men walk them. *(Illustration page 13)*.

There is another possibility: deliberate designs of this size and scale are readily visible from above, and their outlines become clearer as the observer's distance from them increases. Compare this with the various giants and white horses cut into the chalk of several English hillsides, and the inexplicable lines of Nazca, which Erich von Däniken once maintained were intended for the use of ancient astronauts or aviators. In a mountainous district like that in which Rennes-le-Château is located there are numerous ridges, peaks and other viewpoints from which the layout of an entire village is clearly visible.

Almost due north of Rennes-le-Château, the Sals joins up with the Aude at Couiza, and, having briefly traced the courses of these rivers, we can centre our attention on Rennes itself and its relationship to the significant sites and landmarks nearby.

A bearing of zero degrees leads to the Black Castle. At 7 degrees we find Luc, the Village of Light; 39 degrees (significantly 13 x 3!) is the bearing for Coustaussa with its mysterious ruined château and the grave of Antoine Gélis, its brutally murdered nineteenth century priest. A bearing of 55 degrees leads to Cassaignes, where the cemetery contains the ancient Visigothic cross − incongruous among the more modern memorials. The ruined Château Blanchefort is on a bearing of 72 degrees: exactly one fifth of the 360 degrees of a full circle, and exactly the size of each external angle in a regular pentagon. In Poussin's famous picture of the "Shepherds of Arcadia", the geometry of the painting is believed by at least one expert to be based on a regular pentagon, which extends outside the frame. The centre of this pentagon is said to coincide with the head of the shepherdess. Some other investigators are convinced that pentagons feature prominently in the landscape and topography of the Rennes area, and, of course, the pentagon has been regarded for centuries as a potent magical symbol.

A bearing of 87 degrees from Rennes-le-Château points towards the mysterious cave in the Bézis Valley, near what the maps usually label the Berco Petito, but which Stanley James refers to as Berque Petite in his *Treasure Maps of Rennes-le-Château*. Taking a bearing of 105 degrees leads to Rennes-les-Bains; 114 degrees locates the village of Sougraine; 115 degrees takes us over to the Devil's Armchair; 117 degrees is the direct line to the Trembling Rock; the 121 degree line arrives first at the Dead Man and beyond that at the ancient mine close to the bank of the River Blanque where it runs parallel to the narrow, winding D14 road connecting Rennes-les-Bains with Bugarach. The 147 degree bearing leads to the ruined Château of the Templars, which lies less than two kilometres to the west of Le Bézu.

Travelling due south from Rennes-le-Château on a bearing of 180 degrees brings the traveller to several more ancient mines. Exactly two kilometres due south of Rennes lies the Aven. The fascinating black dot which marks its location on the official map produced by the Institut Géographique National for the area is shown on the key as representing *Entrée de mine, d'excavation souterraine* — entrance to a mine or subterranean excavation. Aven is close to the French word *avenir* with its sense of futurity, hopes, expectations and prospects. Merely a coincidence? Or is it another of those very curious verbal connections which appealed so strongly to the brilliant but devious mind of the author of *La Vraie Langue Celtique*, Abbé Henri Boudet?

A bearing of 202 degrees from Rennes leads to the village of Granès, while 205 degrees leads straight to the Roc de la Dent — the Rock of the Tooth — rising well over 1500 feet above sea level. At 220 degrees the track leads to the village of St Ferriol; and at 255 degrees to the village of Campagne, clustered around each bank of the Aude. The 261 degree line leads to the fascinating old hamlet of Campagne-les-Bains, with its ancient thermal source. A bearing of 285 degrees from Rennes takes the traveller to Espéraza — which is something between a large village and a small town. The hamlet of Garnaud is on a bearing of 300 degrees from Rennes-le-Château, while Saunière's birthplace of Montazels is on a bearing of 325. The interesting little town of Couiza, with its imposing château, stands just across the river from Montazels, and is on a bearing of 340 degrees from Rennes. This is the last of the landmarks on our circular tour of the immediate vicinity.

Here in Couiza, inside the church itself, there is a very interesting memorial to the dead of the First World War. It seems to be generally accepted that the man responsible for its unusual design was a priest named Duvilla, who had been a teacher at the Grand Seminary and was widely acknowledged to be a man of great scholarship. Nominated to the living of Couiza in 1917, he had previously been the priest at Axat. Gérard de Sède states clearly and categorically that Boudet and Duvilla knew each other well and that Boudet was a frequent visitor to Axat. Certainly Boudet's tomb is there, and it carries a very strange inscription. Even more significantly, de Sède says that when Archduke Jean (John or Johann) of Habsburg visited Axat he lodged with Boudet's step-sister.

The rather unusual War Memorial which Duvilla designed contains some very subtle symbolism which de Sède is convinced relates to Freemasonry, and particularly to a Scottish Masonic Degree: Knight of the Red Cross, or Rosicrucian Knight. He also argues, quite persuasively, that the rest of the symbolism relates to the Holy Roman Empire and the Imperial Habsburg family.

The Rennes mystery seems to be like a complicated piece of embroidery: the threads repeatedly cross over one another and join up again in unexpected places. It is also curiously like a spider's web. *Toile d'araignée* is the French phrase for "spider's web", and, if we pursue Boudet's concern with paronomasia, it is not too difficult to see *étoiles de Rennes* — the stars of Rennes — hidden in the spider idea. At least one of the ancient coded gravestones relating to the enigma bore a primitive design which looked very much like a spider. And are the "stars" of Rennes its glittering hidden jewels?

The unusual War Memorial at Couiza appears to link up with Freemasonry, Rosicrucianism and the Habsburgs; and to link the learned Duvilla, the scholarly Boudet and the strange code on the latter's tomb at Axat.

But there is far more than this in the geographical location of Rennes-le-Château. It is only a few kilometres from the nearest fortification forming part of the famous circuit of Cathar castles of the Languedoc with their ethos of tragic gallantry and their atmosphere of brooding mystery.

There is Carcassonne — the most amazing medieval citadel still in existence. There is the Château of Foix with its three great towers like something out of a particularly dramatic Gothic romance. There are the four great ruins at Lastours, each on its own mountain peak: Cabaret, Tour Régine, Fleur Espine and Quertinheux. Below them the rushing torrents of the Orbiel and the Grésillon have cut deep gorges as they thunder down from Montagne Noire. There is the fortified village of Minerve, where de Montfort was responsible for the deaths of 140 Cathar martyrs in 1210. There is Montségur, standing high on its almost inaccessible rocky pillar (The Pog), where four intrepid Cathars once stole away from the beleaguered fortress by night to keep "the treasures of their faith" out of the hands of the Catholic Crusaders. (Was this the mysterious *pecuniam infinitam* of the Inquisition records?) And there is Usson, where tradition says the Cathars took it.

There are the elongated defences of Peyrepertuse; the squat, square towers of Puivert; the inaccessible fortress on its crag at Puilaurens, documented in the tenth century, and probably much older. (Is there a possible connection here, too, with the Lawrence family of the Tomb of Arques . . . laurens . . . Lawrence?)

Finally, there is Quéribus, standing out like a solitary surviving tooth in an ancient jawbone; it overlooks the Grau de Maury Pass. The Celts were probably its first defenders, then the Visigoths. Here in 1256, the Cathars made their last stand. As well as being a fortress, Quéribus was a signalling tower in contact with Peyrepertuse.

Enough energy has been expended on studying the geometry of Rennes to put a dozen communication satellites into orbit; and enough detailed maps and drawings have been made to supply a university geography faculty with ample material for a full three year course. Not all the geographical geometricians agree on which patterns are the most important, but even a cursory look at the landmarks is enough to show its potential for experimental work in this field.

For example, one interesting and reasonably convincing pentacle (a five pointed star based on a central regular pentagon) can be located with its points at Rennes-le-Château, the ruins of Château Blanchefort, the menhir south-east of Rennes-les-Bains and due east of the Source of the Madeleine, the ancient château of the Templars east of le Bézu and south of la Pique, and the ruin marked just north of the narrow D46 road connecting Granès and le Bézu. This same ruin lies at the south of the Serre de Lauzet.

An even more interesting pentacle has its most northerly point on Le Berger (which means the Shepherd, and may have links with the Poussin painting) and its other points on the château at Arques, the Bézis Valley where Stanley James found the heavily silted and partly collapsed cave, the peak of Cardou, and the ancient village of Peyrolles. The centre of this pentacle is the spot where stood the enigmatic Tomb of Arques — the image of the one in the Poussin painting — until it was demolished in 1988.

It is not only the pentacle which is believed to be significant in the Rennes geometry: a triangle — especially an equilateral triangle — is also worth noting. Take the Fountain of the Tritons in Montazels (just in front of the house where Bérenger Saunière was born) as the first point; draw a line from there to the cemetery at Cassaignes where the old Visigothic marker cross has stood for centuries. The second line connects Cassaignes to the Aven which lies due south of Rennes and due south of the ancient, ruined mines. The third line connects the Aven with the Fountain of the Tritons. But this particular triangle has a triple significance: it is, in fact, three equilateral triangles inside one another: all sharing a common apex at the Fountain of the Tritons in Montazels. A line drawn from the château at Rennes to the château at Coustaussa intersects the frame of the original triangle at Les Bals in the south-west and Camp Grand in the north-east. This new line creates the second equilateral triangle enclosed in — and partly common with — the first. A new line drawn parallel to the line connecting the two ancient châteaux and passing directly through Roque Fumade creates the third equilateral triangle. This Roque Fumade could be much more interesting and important than has generally been recognized by previous investigators.

If, as some serious researchers have suggested, there was considerable gold-smelting activity going on in subterranean passages and chambers during the long and chequered history of Rennes-le-Château, the fumes from that smelting had to emerge somewhere. Even the most ancient mines had their primitive ventilation systems, which were essential to enable the miners to work at all. Some of these "systems" were simply natural and fortuitous draughts and currents of air in the shafts and tunnels; others were augmented by air holes dug deliberately, and by crude wooden air-gates and flaps operated by the workmen or slaves. It is more than possible that smoke from an underground smelting operation could carry for hundreds of metres along one of these ventilation systems and emerge through a fissure a long way from its source — giving rise to the name Roque Fumade at the point where the fissure actually allowed the smoke to escape.

As well as the mysterious pentacles and equilateral triangles which fit remarkably well on to the significant landmarks of Rennes-le-Château, there is the question of the Zodiac.

It is a fundamental tenet of Hermetic philosophy — the belief that certain Great Masters of Wisdom have possessed vital secrets since very ancient times — that certain deep cosmic truths lie hidden behind symbols in art, music, literature, configurations in the landscape and in the sky. A message intended for generations yet unborn might be preserved, as we suggested earlier, in the layout of streets and roads: how much longer it could be preserved in the constellations. Hermeticists and alchemists set great store by the aphorism "as above, so below". Hieroglyphics carved in the hardest rock will eventually be eroded and erased: hieroglyphics set in the stars will last a great deal longer.

Astronomers and astrologers would agree in defining the Zodiac as that zone of the observable sky within which the paths of the sun, moon and planets of the solar system appear to lie. Since the planetary orbits deviate only slightly from a shared plane, an observer on our earth sees the sun, moon and planets moving in a comparatively narrow band — a tiny fraction of the vast celestial sphere: they move, in fact, rather like the figures of saints around a medieval church clock when the hours strike.

At least as long ago as 3,000 B.C. in Mesopotamia, the fixed stars against which the planets moved were allocated to various arbitrary groups, and were usually given names corresponding to living things: the goat, the raven or the serpent. The Greeks called these constellations which were passed by the planets on their travels the *zodiakos kyklos* – the circle of the animals.

Undoubtedly aware of the "as above, so below" aphorism, Mrs. Katherine Maltwood, the well-known writer and sculptor, made a detailed study of the journeys of King Arthur's Knights from Camelot (which she interpreted as South Cadbury Castle) to the Isle of Avalon. Using large scale maps and aerial photographs, she put forward a careful and well balanced argument for the existence of a set of zodiacal figures in and around Glastonbury which more or less coincide with the celestial zodiac. Mrs. Maltwood demonstrated that when a stellar map of the right scale is laid over the map of Glastonbury, the stars making up the heavenly zodiac constellations fall within the figures she claimed to have discovered on the ground. At the top of the circle, near the town itself and encompassing the Tor, is Aquarius, originally an air sign in the old earth-air-fire-water theory. The Glastonbury Zodiac shows him as a phoenix, a resurrection symbol. The Tor lies inside the head of this phoenix, which is turned to face Chalice Hill, where the ancient Chalice Well was once reputed to have been the hiding place of the Holy Grail in the Christian traditions centred on the adventures of St. Joseph of Arimathea. Outside the circle, Mrs. Maltwood located the figure of The Great Dog, presumably set there to guard this Temple of the Stars. Upon the dog's head are Head Drove and Head Rhyne, which are man-made drainage ditches; in an appropriate spot above his head is Earlake Moor, while his tail contains the tiny hamlet of Wagg! Glastonbury is not alone in being strongly suspected of having an earthly zodiac corresponding to the celestial one: researchers believe that they have found similar outlines at Kingston-upon-Thames, Nuthampstead, Banbury, Wirral, Durham, Edinburgh and Glasgow.

And so back to the Rennes-le-Château area where aspects of Henri Fatin's lengthy researches tend to confirm some of Elizabeth van Buren's ideas about a zodiac on the ground in the area. Aquarius, for example, can be located over the ancient Visigothic cross in the cemetery at Cassaignes. Scorpio, also seen as a dragon, is in the immediate vicinity of Rennes-le-Château itself, and — very curiously — the dragon's mouth is close to Roque Fumade, the Smoking Rock. Rennes-les-Bains is part of Gemini, the Twins.

We move next to smaller scale studies in greater detail; from the wide geography of the ground with its possibilities of equilateral triangles, pentacles and zodiac figures, it is interesting to look at the designs of Château Hautpoul, the Church of St. Mary Magdalen, and the work which Bérenger Saunière carried out in and around the church prior to his death in 1917.

The Château Hautpoul is impressively ancient. It is impossible to say with any degree of certainty whether the Celtic Tectosages were responsible for the first fortification on its present site, but they could well have been. Certainly, aspects of its architecture show Roman influence of the type which is still to be seen at Rennes-les-Bains, and these Roman characteristics were most probably expanded and developed by the Visigothic successors to Roman Gaul. There may have been an Arabian influence later, then a Frankish one. Spanish nobles came and went. Demolitions, repairs, additions, renovations and expansions were apparently made from time to time. Today the château belongs to Henri Fatin, whose father, Marius, acquired it at the end of the Second World War. Marius had made a lengthy and detailed study of their fascinating home prior to his death, and Henri has continued and expanded this work. Between them the Fatins have produced considerable evidence suggesting that there is much strange symbolism contained within the design and structure of their crumbling château. One of their most remarkable ideas is that the twelve threshold stones of the château represent the Twelve Apostles. They might also, of course, represent the twelve signs of the Rennes Zodiac.

What we ourselves found particularly impressive during our recent studies of Château Hautpoul under M. Fatin's guidance were the egg-shaped oubliette, the very old barrel-ceilinged vaults, and the remarkable similarity between two ancient Roman-style arches in Château Hautpoul and the scenes carved between the two arches on the *dalle du chevalier* (the knight's gravestone). This stone dates from the sixth, seventh or eighth century, and is the one which Saunière discovered when it was lying face down in the floor of his church. It is now on prominent display in the museum. M. Fatin also showed us a finely drawn plan of one of the ancient château doors. Once he had pointed it out, we could clearly see that these particular doors had been deliberately constructed to resemble exactly a knight's helmet from an early period, probably the eleventh or twelfth century. When this symbol is combined with M. Fatin's other theories concerning the overall layout of Rennes as a "boat of the dead" conveying the body of a giant warrior, it is possible that this enigmatic château holds keys to more than one of Rennes-le-Château's mysteries, even if it is not directly linked to the secret of Bérenger Saunière's inexplicable wealth.

The site of what was once Bérenger Saunière's domain is also very interesting. The layout of his little "park" behind the tower and the terraces is unusual. It has a central circle from which radiate three triangles or pointers, only two of which are complete. If we complete this third one and follow the direction which it indicates, it leads directly to the first Station of the Cross inside the church. Part of Stanley James's theory, which he has worked out in minute detail in *The Treasure Maps of Rennes-le-Château*, is that each Station of the Cross indicates part of the route a treasure hunter must follow.

The lad who holds the water in which Pilate is washing his hands is black. Is this Saunière's way of hinting that the treasure hunter must pay attention to the tomb of Marie de Nègre? Yet by the time he had erected these Stations of the Cross, Saunière had already obliterated the inscription on her gravestone. Another example of his strange and tantalising sense of humour, perhaps? The figure on Pilate's right (which may be meant to represent a Jewish priest) is holding a golden coin, or perhaps a nugget. The hand that holds this piece of gold could also be pointing to its source. If it is, in fact, a nugget rather than a coin, is it meant to indicate one of the missing nuggets from the drawstring bag with a hole in it that lies at the foot of the Hill of Flowers on the mural behind the confessional? Curiously, the line from the incomplete pointer in the "park" passes through the centre of this mural. It either touches − or passes very close to − the holed money bag on its way to the First Station. There is much more to be said about clues of this kind in the pictures and statuary that Saunière left in his church, but it will be dealt with more fully in Chapter Six: Codes, Ciphers and Cryptograms.

The Magdalen Tower, which once housed part of Saunière's library, has become almost synonymous with the mystery of Rennes. It is featured prominently on the covers of many of the books about the enigma and among their inside illustrations. It is also one of the most popular of the Rennes postcards. It looks out directly towards Montazels and the weird Fountain of the Tritons. It commands wide views of the surrounding countryside. It is eminently defensible, especially for a strong, athletic man like Saunière. Strangest of all: it has a steel door. If an intruder comes over the parapet, the steel door can be slammed to prevent his getting into the main room below. If he bursts into the ground floor room, escape is possible up the stairs and the steel door can then be slammed against his ascent.

It may not be unduly melodramatic to suggest that certain dangers still lurk in Rennes-le-Château, and that those sinister forces were much more real, and much more imminent, for Saunière a century ago than they are for today's investigators. Maurice Guinguand reports the accident which killed a local notary who had asked Saunière to help him with Latin translations concerning titles to land that had belonged to the Fleury family. This man was said to have been out shooting with Saunière when it happened. Gérard de Sède tells of the grisly − and still unsolved − murder of the elderly Antoine Gélis. He also recounts the mysterious deaths of Rescanière and Boudet − both priests of Rennes-les-Bains − after they had been visited by two strangers. He also tells how three unidentified corpses were found in Saunière's garden in 1956. All of which makes a steel door a sensible precaution.

The Grotto, on which Saunière laboured for so many hours with the stones he brought back from his long, mysterious walks, and the Garden Calvary, both stand inside an equilateral triangle the northern edge of which runs parallel to the southern wall of the church and very close to it.

The church is very small and extremely old. The present building apparently stands on Visigothic or Merovingian Christian foundations, and, in all probability, there was some sort of pagan temple on the site well before the Christian era. The Stations of the Cross, the murals, the statues and the stained glass windows were placed there at Saunière's instigation, or, as some researchers would have it, at Boudet's instigation with Saunière as Boudet's agent and "front man". Either way they must rank among the strangest church ornaments in the world. A detailed attempt at their decipherment must wait for the appropriate later chapter, but in broad outline the stained glass depicts five scenes: Mary Magdalen with Jesus; Mary and

Martha of Bethany; the resurrection of their brother, Lazarus; the mission of the Apostles; and Jesus on the cross. There are nine statues: St. Joseph the Carpenter; the Virgin Mary; St. Anthony of Padua (the Hammer of the Heretics) who lectured in theology at Toulouse; St. Antony the Hermit with his traditional bell and pig; St. Mary Magdalen with a cross, and her flask of precious nard; St. Germaine, the shepardess, with her apron full of roses; St. Roch, defender against the plague; St. John the Baptist in the act of baptising Christ — strangely enough by influxion with a silver shell rather than by the total immersion method which John himself would actually have practised in the River Jordan; and, lastly, the four angels making the sign of the cross above the dish of holy water held above the shoulders of a furious and vicious looking demon. He is probably meant to represent Asmodeus, the legendary guardian of Solomon's treasure in Jerusalem. The demon's empty right hand is said to have held a trident in years gone by.

So far we have given a very short summary of the mystery and an equally brief survey of the area in which it is set: the land and the landmarks; the enigmatic old towns and villages; the challenging rivers and mountains; the uncanny symbolism of the decaying Château Hautpoul and the bizarre decorations in the church of St. Mary Magdalen The setting is undeniably strange — as strange as the semi-visible land zodiac which seems to impinge on Rennes-le-Château and the persistent triangles and pentacles connecting several significant local sites. But if the setting seems strange, the history is stranger, and we move next to an outline of the events that this tiny hilltop village has witnessed over many centuries.

CHAPTER TWO

THE HISTORY OF RENNES-LE-CHÂTEAU

Nam historia debet egredi veritatem. (Pliny the Younger)

In the shadowy interior of Château Hautpoul, Henri Fatin showed us his fascinating collection of axe-heads, scrapers and other Stone Age artefacts which he and his father had found in and around Rennes-le-Château over many years. Stone Age men lived here, hunted here, raised their families here, fought and died here before pyramids rose in the Valley of the Kings. The first inhabitants of the Rennes area were here before Abraham left Ur of the Chaldees. When the architects and engineers of Stonehenge were raising their impressive trilithons near Salisbury, men were raising dolmens, cromlechs and menhirs near what would one day be Rennes-les-Bains.

Among what archaeologists describe as the protohistorical peoples of Europe, the Celts featured prominently. Their name derives from the plural Greek form *Keltoi* which was in use from the sixth century B.C. to denote the race inhabiting transalpine Europe and the Iberian peninsula. Latin writers referred to them as Celtae. Some Celtic groups were referred to as Galatai from which the familiar New Testament word Galatians is derived. From the second century B.C. they were also known as Galli which gave rise to the more familiar term Gauls.

Greek and Roman writers regarded the Celts as unusual because of their height, their muscular strength and their fair colouring, but these features seem to have been typical of their warriors rather than of the Celts as a whole. Skeletal remains show marked differences in bodily size and skull type.

They seem to have been divided into three simple social classes: the king, the warrior aristocracy and the freemen farmers. Celtic druids, who were concerned with religious and magical practices, were drawn from the warrior aristocracy, and enjoyed a rather higher status than the straightforward warriors.

The great ancient "authority" on the Druids was the Stoic philosopher and writer Poseidonius (c. 135-50 B.C.). He was a renowned scholar and teacher, and a man who travelled widely in Spain and France. A suspected weakness, however, in his writings on the Druids was his apparent tendency to project on to them his own Stoic philosophy. If, on the other hand, what he said about them was true and based on honest, objective observation, then it might be possible to trace aspects of Gnosticism back to the Druids. That would be very significant indeed for the religious aspects of the Rennes mystery — as we shall discuss in detail in the next chapter. It is sufficient to say here that if Poseidonius was right in thinking that the Druids, whose name derives from Old Irish meaning "those who know", were a group who enjoyed genuine esoteric knowledge of a spiritual nature — some special form of "enlightenment" — then the roots of Gnosticism in the Rennes area predate Christianity by several centuries.

There is evidence that Celts, or people of Celtic origin such as the Tectosages, were in the Rennes area five or six centuries before the birth of Christ. If Celts were there, Druids and Druidic teachings would almost certainly have been there too.

It was the Romans who took this Celtish territory, and southern France soon became a popular part of the Roman Empire. From approximately 50 B.C. to the collapse of the Western Empire in the fifth century a posting to Arles was comparatively welcome: especially in those later Roman years when options could have included the Rhine Frontier or Hadrian's Wall. The end of the officially united Roman Empire came in 395 when the sons of Theodosius I, Honorius and Arcadius, took their respective controls of the western and eastern halves. In connection with the Rennes codes, and especially the Poussin painting of the Shepherds, Arcadius is rather an interesting name, as will be seen in the later chapter dealing with codes, ciphers and cryptograms. The most interesting aspect of Roman history from the point of view of the Rennes treasure mystery is a consideration of what the Romans might have acquired during their years of conquest and expansion, and what might subsequently have made its way from their treasury to a secret Visigothic hiding place at Rennes.

It is possible that some of the treasures of Solomon's Temple were taken in 591 B.C.; it is highly probable that most of the remainder of the treasure was looted by the Babylonians under Nebuchadnezzar in 586 B.C. Detailed accounts of the destruction can be found in 2 Kings 25 and Jeremiah 25. In 169 B.C. Antiochus Epiphanes, a descendant of Alexander the Great's Seleucid successors, stole not only the readily visible treasure, such as the gold on the pillars and the vessels from the altars, but he also took "the hidden treasures" as well. The episode is recorded in I Maccabees, chapter 1 : 21 – 23 In A.D. 70, Titus – then a general, later the Emperor of Rome, destroyed much of Jerusalem. His triumphal arch shows his men sacking the city and carrying away the menorah, the famous, seven-branched, golden candlestick. Where was it, and where was the rest of the Jewish treasure taken by the Romans in 410 when Alaric the Visigoth entered Rome?

Alaric died shortly afterwards at Consenza (known then as Consentia) and was buried in the Visigothic manner: the River Busento (known then as the Busentus) was dammed and diverted; a suitable burial chamber was prepared for Alaric, his armour and his treasure. The chamber was sealed; the gravel and stones raked over it. The dam was broken: the waters of the Busentus flowed over the concealed tomb — and they still flow over it to this day. Alaric lies silent, still . . . undisturbed.

It is rather misleading to write of Alaric "taking" Rome. He had made two previous unsuccessful attempts to capture the city, and it was only because the gates were treacherously opened for him on August 24th that he succeeded on this third attempt. He did not enjoy a particularly success-ful military career: he lost more battles than he won. In the years leading up to 410 there was so much confusion and semi-anarchy stirring the dying embers of the Roman Empire that it could fairly be described as a continual conflict between the unauthorised barbarians outside and the authorised barbarians inside. Alaric's main rival, Stilicho, was a Pannonian Vandal; the legions in Gaul were under the command of a Frank; and the Emperor Theodosius I was himself a Spaniard who depended upon the support of Visigothic legionaries. It was an ideal period for an ambitious adventurer with sufficient armed men at his command to help himself to whatever treasure was available. It is probable that the treasures of Sion — including the "hidden treasures" — left Rome in 410, and it is even more probable that they left in Visigothic hands.

What of the Visigoths of Rennes during this period? There are various etymological possibilities for the derivation of Rennes, and one of the more likely is that it comes from the Visigothic word meaning "travelling chariots". Louis Fédié, among others, has envisaged a vast encampment of Visigothic living wagons — like a huge warrior-gypsy site, or a massive wagon train drawn up for the night as it crossed the early nineteenth century American prairies — surrounded by a defensive dyke, perhaps reinforced by a wooden stockade. Certainly in the twilight years of the Roman Empire and during the Visigothic ascendancy which came after, Rennes was a strategic site of some importance. It commanded the crossroads of two significant Roman routes which intersected at Couiza: one from the Paradise Pass leading to Narbonne; the other from the Saint Louis Pass leading first to Bugarach and then on towards Perpignan.

Many strange things — both military and political — happened during the dying years of the Western Roman Empire, things which affected the area around Rennes-le-Château. From 462 until 486 Gaul was more or less notionally under the control of the autonomous Roman Governor, Syagrius, but the first Frankish Dynasty — the House of Mérovée — was already established there as well. The Merovingians can be traced back to Clodion le Chevelu (Clodion the Long-haired) who was a King of the Salian Franks from 428 to 448.

Mérovée, who gave his name to the dynasty, was Clodion's son — or rather, according to the legends, partly his son and partly the son of something else. In their anxiety to substantiate their very questionable hypothesis about Jesus and Mary Magdalen in *The Holy Blood and the Holy Grail*, Baigent, Leigh and Lincoln suggest that the legends concerning the miraculous circumstances surrounding Mérovée's conception are allegorical or symbolic representations of an intermarriage between Clodion's line and a very important and mysterious family from overseas: the descendants of Jesus via Mary Magdalen. The derivation of the name Mérovée is interesting, and may even be significant as far as the legends are concerned. *Mer* gives the idea of both "mother" and "sea", while *ovée* has the same root as "egg". There are also etymological connections with *ovis* meaning "sheep" and thus a possible link with Poussin's "Shepherds of Arcadia". *Ovo* carries the sense of triumphing, exulting, or celebrating a victory by loud shouts and cheers.

Stated in their clearest and simplest form, the legends relate how Clodion's wife went swimming in the sea while already pregnant with Mérovée. She encountered a mysterious sea-being, perhaps a Triton, which either raped or seduced her, somehow blending its genetic material with that of the developing human foetus she was already carrying. According to the legends, this made Mérovée grow up with supernatural powers; he became a sorcerer-king, a monarch-magician. One ancient Latin source describes the sea creature as "resembling a Quinotaur", which raises the question of what a Quinotaur might be. The *quin* part would seem to be derived from the root word meaning "five", which is not particularly informative. However, the Pythagoreans used *quin* in a special way when working out their theories of the elemental forms which constitute matter. In addition to the accepted four elements of earth, air, fire and water, they believed in a fifth element, the quintessence, something purer and subtler than fire, something that always seeks to leap upwards, the substance of which the stars are made. Does the etymology of Quinotaur suggest a being who came from the stars?

There is a fascinating parallel to be found in the legend of the Assyrian Princess Semiramis, who lived circa 800 B.C. The sources are the writings of Diodorus Siculus, Justin and Ctesias of Cnidus, together with the archaeological researches of Professor Lehmann-Haupt of Berlin. Semiramis was the daughter of the fish-goddess, Atargatis. She was fed by doves until she was rescued by Simmas, the royal shepherd. After two marriages she took over the kingdom and proceeded to work miracles of civil engineering for over forty years, building vast cities and driving roads through mountains.

Yet another fish-divinity parallel can be found in the strange being called Odakon, featured in Babylonian mythology. He is a curious blend of two other gods — Dagon and Ea. Dagon was widely (but incorrectly) thought of as a fish-god, although the first book of Samuel 5:4, makes it clear that Dagon's image was in ordinary human form. Ea was the fish-god, and was accordingly depicted on ancient Babylonian seals with the hands and face of a man but the body of a fish. One such seal (currently in the British Museum) carries an inscription describing Ea as "the god of pure life", which is not very distant from the Pythagorean idea of *quin*, the fifth element, purer than fire and more dynamic . . . the element of the stars.

Are these siren speculations luring us dangerously close to the treacherous rocks and shoals characteristic of the shores of "Von-Däniken Land"? Or, in this infinite and mysterious universe — in which other intelligent life is almost certain to exist — dare we suggest that the legends of Ea, Semiramis, Atargatis, Triton, the Quinotaur and Mérovée are possibly mythologised half-memories of encounters with aquatic extra-terrestrials?

Mérovée ruled from 448 until 457, and seems to have become something of a legend in his own lifetime. At the great Battle of Mauriac, where Aetius brought the Hun invasion to a juddering halt in the blood-stained Catalonian fields, the Roman army was powerfully reinforced by Frankish foederati commanded by Mérovée. The history of his son, Childeric I, benefits from being told in reverse order — we learn of his life from the discovery of his grave. This was found in 1653 in the Belgian town of Tournai, which lies a little way north of the River Scheldt. Jacques Chifflet published *Anastasis Childerici Primi* (The Resurrection of Childeric I) in 1655. By a curious coincidence after the etymological analysis of "quinotaur" and Pythagorean quintessence, the grave was actually discovered by a stonemason named Quinquin who was a deaf mute!

The treasures which Chifflet recorded as having been buried with the king included: a gold and garnet belt; gold buckles; a gold bracelet; a Roman official's brooch of office (which Chifflet understandably mistook for a writing instrument); a francisca or throwing axe; accessories for a scramasax (a sword with only one edge); and a number of gold bees.

It is possible that there is a curious and very significant ritualistic connection between these gold bees in Childeric's grave, and the strange ceremony which took place when Bérenger Saunière died on January 22nd, 1917: the sorrowing villagers of Rennes-le-Château filed past their hero's body and each plucked a small red pompom from the cloth in which he was wrapped.

At the end of the sixth century Gregory of Tours wrote of Childeric's battle at Orléans, the assumption being that Childeric and his Franks were either allied to Aegidius or fighting at Orléans on behalf of their Roman allies. There is further important early evidence about Childeric in the letter which Bishop Remigius of Rheims wrote to Clovis I, Childeric's son:

"A powerful message has reached us that you have become the administrator of the Second Province of the Belgians. This is nothing new: you have now started to be what your ancestors always were."

Dr. Gaston Sirjean was responsible for a very scholarly and reliable genealogy of the Merovingians, which may safely be regarded as definitive and which is available for consultation in the Bibliothèque Généalogique, 3 rue Turbigo, 75001, Paris, along with several similar records. According to Dr. Sirjean's researches, Childeric was the father of Clovis I, who was in turn followed by his son Clotaire. He lived from 497 until 561 — a remarkable achievement in an epoch whose continual warfare gave most warrior-kings a life expectancy of less than thirty years — and in so doing earned himself the soubriquet of *le Vieux* (the Old).

Clotaire I was followed by his son Chilperic I, who lived from 523 — 584 and sired eleven children by his three wives: Audevere, Galsonte and Fredegonde, the last of whom outlived her husband and was the mother of his successor, Clotaire II. This Clotaire reigned from 584 to 613 as King of Soissons, and from 613 to 629 as King of France. He was distinguished from his grandfather by being nicknamed *le Jeune* (the Young).

Clotaire the Young's second wife, Beretrude, died in 620. She was the mother of his successor, Dagobert I, who was born in 606 and reigned from 629 until his death in 639. Dagobert had two sons: the first was Clovis II known as *le Fainéant* (the Weak), who, despite his unpromising cognomen, ranked in the main line of Merovingian Kings of France; the second was Sigebert III, who was king only of Austrasia, an area which lay roughly to the north-east of Paris. But it is Sigebert III and his descendants who are said to be involved in the mystery of Rennes. Following his death in 656 (as the commentator remarked in the Charlton Heston film "El Cid"!) we step out of history and into legend.

The traditionally accepted, definitive records of the Merovingians in the Bibliothèque Généalogique show quite unequivocally that Sigebert's son, Dagobert II — the one who is mentioned in the Rennes codes — lived from 652 until 679. He had only one wife, Mechtilde, who bore him four daughters and a son. This lad predeceased his father by a year. These

SIMPLIFIED MEROVINGIAN GENEALOGY
SHOWING THE END OF SIGEBERT III's LINE

CLODION the Long-haired
Reigned: | 428 - 448
↓

MEROVEE
Reigned: | 448 - 457
↓

CHILDERIC I
Born 436 | Died 481
↓

CLOVIS I
Born 466 | Died 511
↓

CLOTAIRE I (LE VIEUX)
Born 497 | Died 561
↓

CHILPERIC I
Born 523 | Died 584
↓

CLOTAIRE II (LE JEUNE)
Born 584 | Died 629
↓

DAGOBERT I
Born 606 | Died 639
↓

SIGEBERT III
Born 631 | Died 656
↓

DAGOBERT II (EXILE IN IRELAND)
Born 652 | Died 679
↓

SIGEBERT
Born 676   Died 678

historically reliable, academic records, however, are widely at variance with another version of Merovingian history and genealogy which is found in a quaint document called *Dossiers Secrets*, apparently deposited in the Bibliothèque Nationale in rather unusual circumstances. It is registered there under the name Henri Lobineau, which was originally thought to be the pen-name of Leo Schidlof, an Austrian expert on miniatures, who died in 1966. Henri Lobineau was subsequently believed to be the nom-de-plume of a distinguished French aristocrat, Comte Henri de Lenoncourt. It is, of course, at least equally possible that the *Dossiers Secrets* were deliberately concocted and then planted in the Bibliothèque Nationale by those interested in reinforcing the theory about Jesus, Mary Magdalen and their supposed contribution to the Merovingian bloodline.

Before outlining "Lobineau's" ideas, it may be helpful to look further into some additional elements in the life of Dagobert II, which may have a stronger basis in fact. Lanigan's *Ecclesiastical History* (Volume 3, page 101) refers to his being brought up at a monastery in Ireland. On the other hand, Mézeray, in his *Histoire de France* published in 1685, complains bitterly that the chronicles of the seventh century are both scanty and confused, and provide little if any worthwhile evidence for later historians to work on. According to Mézeray, such clues as there are suggest that Dagobert II's father, King Sigebert III of Austrasia, had only this one son, who was not quite two years old when Sigebert died. Immediately, Grimoald, the Mayor of the Palace, put the word about that Sigebert had legally adopted his (Grimoald's) son, Childebert, as his heir. In order to further his plot, Grimoald had the rightful prince tonsured by Didon, Bishop of Poitiers, and arranged for him to be taken secretly to Ireland. One writer (Archdall) says that there is an oral tradition to the effect that it was the monastery of Slane to which the boy was taken. As soon as this journey to Ireland had been safely undertaken, Grimoald made every effort to establish his own son, Childebert, on the throne. Not surprisingly, the Lords of Austrasia turned on Grimoald, and sent him as a prisoner to King Clovis, who promptly executed him. Austrasia was unsettled for some years, until Dagobert II was recalled from Ireland and installed as King in 674. He reigned for only four years before his murder in 678.

"Lobineau's" version relates that Dagobert's wife, Mechtilde, (who was actually a sturdy young Anglo-Saxon lady, not a Celt as indicated in some accounts) died giving birth to their third daughter, and that — very conveniently for the Jesus and Mary Magdalen-Merovingian bloodline theory — Dagobert then married Giselle de Razès, daughter of the Count of Razès. There is no mention whatsoever of Dagobert's second marriage in any reputable or historically reliable genealogy, as far as our extensive research has been able to reveal. The second marriage and surviving progeny supposition depends entirely upon the "Lobineau" documents, which are about as historically reliable as a confession of broomstick flying extracted from a senile geriatric on the rack.

Dagobert II, on his return from Ireland with the support of St. Wilfrid, turned out to be as vigorous and effective as some of his illustrious ancestors: a man like Clovis whose action during the famous "vase of

Soissons"[1] episode showed that he was not to be trifled with. Dagobert II was anything but a *roi fainéant*.

The bitter rivalry between the various political, religious and dynastic factions led to Dagobert II's death in December of 679. One account suggests that as he lay resting under a tree Dagobert was pierced through the eye by one of Pépin's supporters. Another version refers to an ambush of some sort near Stenay. The inscrutable *dalle du chevalier* may provide some slight clue here, contradictory to our earlier argument. Allowing just for a moment, for the sake of speculation, that the infant Sigebert had not predeceased his father in 678, could the *dalle* show a mortally wounded Dagobert II gallantly defending some narrow place while his most trusted lieutenant gallops away to safety carrying not only the child but the secret of the royal treasure of Rennes? What does a dying hero do in such circumstances?

There is a further, much more powerful argument for the non-survival of the Merovingian line: the ambition, pragmatism and efficiency of the usurping Carolingians. In the days when monarchs really ruled, dynasties, bloodlines and politics were inextricably intertwined. It was basically a raw question of survival: if you did not succeed in extirpating all possible rival claimants, one of them would inevitably turn up unexpectedly and extirpate you!

Whether we are analysing a contemporary board room power struggle, a Mafia-style duel between rival aspirants for the post of Godfather, or the intrigues of a Dark Age Frankish Court, the basic elements remain constant. The abstract theory of power still applies: it is seen as desirable by the overwhelming majority of participants; it tends to increase or decrease exponentially; it abhors a vacuum.

Merovingian kings were normally held in special reverence and regard; not a few of them — deservedly or undeservedly — enjoyed reputations as magicians or thaumaturgists. There was an increasing tendency for them to withdraw from the boring and uncongenial work of legal and financial administration and to delegate such matters to a senior official known as the Mayor of the Palace, while they got on with what interested them more. In all administrative pyramids, however, there are a series of sub-apexes from which ostensibly delegated decisions are made, but which in practice tend to become miniature power sources in their own right, and to enjoy a degree of autonomous power. The policy of the man at the top can be seriously hindered — if not completely negated — by lack of co-operation at these sub-apexes. Much then depends upon the conflicting desires and the orders of priority in the mind of the top decision maker. If the king's main interests are womanising, hunting, feasting, drinking and practising a little thaumaturgy from time to time, he may well allow more and more decisions to be made in his name by a conscientious and efficient Mayor of the Palace. A trade-off takes place between the occupants of the relative rungs of power — either implicitly or explicitly, consciously

---

[1]Following his victory at Soissons, Clovis was visited by the Bishop who begged for the return of as vase which one of Clovis' soldiers had looted from a church. Clovis magnanimously granted the Bishop's request, but the soldier concerned smashed the vase in deliberate defiance of Clovis' order. With his own hand, the King executed the disobedient soldier.

— the industrious administrator "sells" the King more and more leisure. The king "sells" the Mayor of the Palace more and more power. Interpersonal relationships then begin to play a significant part in the gradual shift of the balance of power between the two players. If it is from the Mayor of the Palace that other senior servants normally receive their orders, they will sooner or later come to view him at a subconscious level as the "real" source of authority. If, in addition, the king has a dislike of confrontation and controversy, he may well take the path of least resistance and follow the "advice" urged upon him by the Mayor of the Palace. A critical point is reached at which the balance of power shifts irrevocably in favour of the administrator and the king becomes a mere figurehead, a *roi fainéant*.

The next stage is more sinister: power begins to want to wear the trappings of power. The shadow behind the throne wants to be the man who sits on it. The enfeebled king is seen as a nuisance, something expensive and superfluous. The question is posed: who is the real king, the man with the title and the blood — or the man with the power? It is time for a withered dynasty to end and a new and vigorous one to start. Ruthlessly the deadwood is cut away. The field is cleared for the Carolingians. The survival of the Merovingian line is — to say the least — highly unlikely. If Sigebert, son of Dagobert II, had survived his father, he would not have survived him for long as a small Merovingian snowflake in a Carolingian blast furnace.

There is reasonable evidence — although it is far from conclusive — that during the centuries while the Merovingian Kings were slowly giving way before their Mayors of the Palace, massive physical changes were taking place at what had originally been a Stone Age campsite at Rennes-le-Château. Roman legionaries had expelled the Celtic Tectosages, and probably built substantial fortifications on their strategic hill top. Visigoths had subsequently replaced the Romans. According to some historians and archaeologists, the little site continued to grow. Higher and wider grew its walls. At its zenith it almost rivalled Carcassonne.

Later, the Franks drove out the Visigoths, who retreated to an area that was then known as Gothie, or Septimania, an area that is roughly equivalent to the present French departments of Aude, Garde, Hérault and Pyrénées-Orientales, but Visigothic troubles did not end there: over the blue waters of the Mediterranean, via Gibraltar and Spain, the Saracen storm blew into Septimania. There is evidence that a substantial remnant of the defeated Visigothic population withdrew into the fortifications of Rennes-le-Château, which was known to them in those days as Rhedae.

The advancing Saracens, however, met their match in Charles Martel (the Hammer) at the great battle of Poitiers in 732, a period during which Martel (a proto-Carolingian, and Mayor of the Palace) still continued to maintain the delicate fiction of Merovingian rule.

In order to understand the ultimate Carolingian supremacy over the Merovingians, it is necessary to delve quite deeply into their family origins. The Merovingian King Clotaire II (le Jeune) 584-629, had a counsellor named Arnulf. He was popularly believed to be of Gallo-Roman and Aquitanian ancestry, but was more likely to have been a Ripuarian Frank. His wife, Doda, bore him two sons, before Arnulf went into the Church as Bishop of Metz in 614. (Doda went into a nunnery at the same time.)

Arnulf later resigned his see to become a hermit-monk and was eventually honoured as Saint Arnulf, whose feast day is July 18th. One of his and Doda's sons, Ansegesil, married Begga, the daughter of Pépin the Old.

SIMPLIFIED GENEALOGY OF THE CAROLINGIANS

ARNULF

Died 641

↓

ANSEGESIL

Died 685

↓

PEPIN of HERISTAL

Died 714

↓

CHARLES MARTEL
(Pepin's illegitimate son by Alpais)

Born 689 | Died 741

↓

PEPIN the SHORT

Born 714 | Died 768

↓

CHARLEMAGNE

Born 742   Died 814

Crowned as "Augustus and Emperor"
by Pope Leo III on December 25th, 800.

Pépin the Old was also known as Pépin of Landen, which is near Trier, where he held large and prosperous estates. His son, Begga's brother Grimoald, was that same Mayor of the Palace who arranged for the rightful King Dagobert II to go into exile in Ireland while Grimoald's own son usurped the Austrasian throne. When the nobility reacted violently against this, not only were Grimoald and his son executed — Ansegesil was killed as well. Begga and her son by Ansegesil — whom they had named Pépin after his illustrious grandfather — escaped and kept a low profile for the next twenty-odd years.

This Pépin, the son of Begga and Ansegesil, was usually referred to as Pépin of Herstal (occasionally spelled Heristal). He worked long and hard to re-establish his family's political power and finally realised his ambition to become Mayor of the Palace in Austrasia. He had a dangerous rival in the person of Ebruin, Mayor of the Palace of Neustria, but defeated him resoundingly at the battle of Tertry, near Péronne, in 687, and put his own nominees into the senior positions in Neustria and Burgundy.

When Pépin of Herstal died in 714, there was a problem over the succession. His only legitimate son was dead, and the choice lay between two young grandsons and Pépin's illegitimate son, Charles, nicknamed Martel

— the Hammer. There was a ten year struggle between Charles and the forces mustered by Plectrude, Pépin's widow, but his massive victory over the Saracens established him securely from 732 until his death in 741.

Charles Martel's younger son, Pépin the Short, soon held the title of Mayor of the Palace in all three Frankish Kingdoms: he it was who finally succeeded where Grimoald had failed in the days of Dagobert II. Pépin the Short deposed the Merovingian Childeric III, and the Carolingian Dynasty was at last on the throne of France — not merely controlling it. His son, Charlemagne, was given the Imperial Title and became Holy Roman Emperor with the blessing of Pope Leo III in the year 800. There is evidence that in Charlemagne's time the County of Carcassonne was created and ruled by one of his lieutenants with the almost equally important stronghold of Rhedae as a dependency.

After Charlemagne had achieved such distinction, it is scarcely surprising that curious ancestral legends about the origins of the Franks became very popular. There is one fascinating version in an eighth century writing known as *Liber Historiae Francorum*. According to this eighth century account, some Trojans escaped from the siege of Troy and went to Pannonia where they built the city of Sicambria. From there they helped the Emperor Valentinian to beat the Alans, and he was so impressed by their courage and daring that he re-named them "Franks", meaning "the Fierce Ones". Unfortunately, underestimating his highly aggressive new allies, Valentinian unwisely sent Roman tax collectors into their territory. The tax collectors were killed and the Romans retaliated by attacking their former friends, the Franks. The latter withdrew strategically to their strongholds along the remotest regions of the Rhine, and elected as King Faramund, who was said to be a direct descendant of Priam of Troy. This account, of course, bears little resemblance to the way that Virgil recounted the history of Troy. According to the author of *Liber Historiae Francorum*, this same Faramund was the father of Clodion the Long Haired, whom other sources regard as the "half-father" of Mérovée (whose other "half-father" — as we have already seen — was thought by some to be an unearthly aquatic being, possibly what the Greeks called a Triton).

The history of Rennes-le-Château becomes something of an indeterminable maelstrom after its heyday during the relatively tranquil and civilised Carolingian supremacy. Some historians have put forward the idea that under the name of Rhedae it grew to be a very important fortified site, containing two urban centres, and shaped rather like a weight-lifter's barbell, or an amoeba about to divide into two new cells. In the eleventh century, Rennes seems to have become the property of the House of Barcelona; then, some two centuries later, it fell under the overlordship of the Trencavels — the Lords of Béziers. There was trouble with Alphonse of Barcelona towards the end of the twelfth century. He already commanded the impressive fortresses of Quéribus and Peyrepertuse, and was now setting his sights on Rhedae. Some authorities believe that Alphonse's attack was largely responsible for the destruction of many of the impressive old fortifications which were once thought to have surrounded the site.

The rise and widespread popularity of Catharism throughout the Languedoc — including Rennes-le-Château — during the twelfth and early thirteenth centuries, led to a Crusade being organised against them under the leadership of Simon de Montfort, a battle-hardened and bloodthirsty warrior, who remained in the prime of life well into his fifties.

The terror and massacres of this Crusade were followed by a period of steady rebuilding and refurbishment under the Voisin lords, who looked after Rennes until well into the fourteenth century. It is probable that it was during their time that both the Rennes churches — St. Peter and St. Mary Magdalen's — were restored to their earlier glories.

It must also be borne in mind that during the period between 1118 and 1307, the Knights Templar were a prodigious force to be reckoned with. At the height of their power, their wealth, their territories and their military prowess made them more formidable than many contemporary kings. They were secretive, cohesive and fiercely independent. A vital connection between Rennes-le-Château and the Templars is that Bertrand de Blanchefort was Grand Master of the Templars from 1156 until 1169, and there were other Templar castles in the area.

Plague and pestilence, robber bands and itinerant soldiers of fortune did much to undo the good that the Voisins had done. In particular, a Spanish bandit-lord, the dreaded Count of Trastamarre, was credited with having wrought terrible havoc in Rennes, and totally devastating the recently restored church of St. Peter.

It seems that towards the start of the fifteenth century, the Voisins married into the noble Hautpoul family, and they, in turn, eventually re-established their claim to the ancient title of Blanchefort. The last of their line was the celebrated Marie de Nègre, whose coded tombstone Bérenger Saunière went to great lengths to obliterate. Several knowledgeable researchers believe that Marie was the last guardian of some great secret that had been handed down for generations, and that when she knew herself to be dying she had passed that secret on to her chaplain, Abbé Bigou.

Abbé Antoine Bigou was one of Bérenger Saunière's precursors as Parish Priest at Rennes-le-Château, in addition to his duties as chaplain to the Hautpoul/Blanchefort family. It seems reasonable to assume that if Marie de Nègre had possessed some major secret — the whereabouts of the Blanchefort treasure, perhaps — then she would have been likely to pass that secret on to her faithful priest as her earthly life drew to a close.

Marie de Nègre died on January 17th, 1781. France was stirring with incipient rebellion and revolution. Priests were almost as unpopular as aristocrats. If it was Antoine Bigou who carved the very curious memorial stone which once marked Marie de Nègre's grave, it was one of the few tasks he undertook before going into exile rather than take the revolutionary oath. It is believed by several Rennes experts that it was also Bigou who compiled at least two of the curious manuscripts which Saunière was said to have found in a hollow Visigothic pillar supporting the altar in his church. Bigou may also have been responsible for moving and re-concealing a substantial part of Marie de Nègre's ancient Blanchefort treasure — if indeed that was what her secret was — in such a way that another priest might find it reasonably easily but the "rationalist" supporters of the revolution would not. After going sadly into exile, Antoine Bigou died in Spain.

Our brief survey of the history of Rennes-le-Château now brings us up to the 11th of April, 1852: Bérenger Saunière is born in Montazels. In 1879 he is ordained as a priest. In 1882 he is appointed curé at the tiny village of Clat. On June 1st, 1885, Monseigneur Billard, the Bishop of Carcassonne, posts him to the living of Rennes-le-Château. From the date of his mysterious "discoveries" — whatever they were — until his death on January 22nd, 1917, he spent an amount which is often estimated in millions of pounds sterling reckoned in terms of modern currency. Yet when his will was read he had almost nothing to leave: all his lands and buildings were already in the name of his housekeeper and life-long confidante, Marie Dénarnaud. She survived until 1953, having promised that when she knew herself to be dying she would reveal the secret which she and Bérenger had shared for so long: a stroke which left her speechless and paralysed her hands prevented her from keeping that promise.

CHAPTER THREE

THEOLOGICAL AND RELIGIOUS FACTORS

Domino optimo maximo. (Motto of the Benedictine Order)

If it needs a thief to catch a thief, perhaps a priest has some sort of psychological advantage when it comes to trying to get inside the heart and mind of another priest — even if their worlds are 1500 kilometres and 100 years apart.

The first, poignant and sensitive question is whether Saunière ever felt a genuine and undeniable call to the Priesthood in the first place, a real sense of vocation. Ask a dozen average priests at random what they mean by "a sense of vocation" and you will get a dozen different answers. Yet each man will be telling you the simple truth as he sees it, and each man will know at the deepest level of his being that there was nothing else he could do and nothing else he could be. One may be an industrial chaplain, another may teach, one may lecture in a theological college. The next man may be a diocesan administrator. Another may write devotional books while his nearest colleague works in a hospital, a hospice, or a prison. One may be in the army, another in the police force, one may even be a traditional rural Parish Priest. Each in his own way is doing what he believes God wants him to do.

The tragedy is that if you stop a thirteenth man as part of your random survey he may well be wearing a sacerdotal black suit, complete with a white collar back to front, but he may also be grimly disillusioned and sadly disappointed, wondering why he ever set out upon the arduous road to ordination in the first place. Is it possible that Bérenger Saunière was a thirteenth man? "Judge not, that ye be not judged," is one of the most fundamental of all Christian ethics. Far be it from any of us to dare to suggest that any other priest's sense of vocation is suspect. The only qualified and knowledgeable judges of vocation are the God who calls and the man who answers: questions from any other source are impertinent and intrusive. Yet, in view of what subsequently happened at Rennes-le-Château, we have to ask the forbidden question. Was Saunière a sincere and dedicated priest who just happened to find himself posted there, or was he a sincere and dedicated treasure hunter who went through the rigorous disciplines and deprivations of seminary training solely in order to get the living of Rennes — the most advantageous situation possible for a man who wants to search for its lost treasure. If Saunière was prepared to train for ordination simply to be in the running for the post of Parish Priest at Rennes, his faith in the existence of the legendary treasure, and his confidence in his ability to locate it once he got there, must have been of the first magnitude. It was said by those who knew him as a child growing up in Montazels, that whereas most other children played the games that children usually play, the young Bérenger Saunière would say to his contemporaries: "Let's go and look for the lost treasure of Rennes-le-Château!"

There is another relevant question mark over Saunière's head: his ancestry, or, of equal importance, what he had been told about his ancestry, or what he had come to believe about his ancestry. It is the old paradox about the image and the reality. Human beings behave in accordance with what they perceive to be the facts, not with the facts themselves. The whole point of the comedy in *The Inspector General* is that the corrupt and incompetent local civil servants behave to the penniless young stranger as if he was the dreaded Inspector General who is rumoured to be about to arrive in their town incognito to check up on them.

The villagers of Rennes-le-Château generally behaved towards Saunière as if he was their rightful and beneficent seigneur. There is certainly no record of which we are aware, that anyone complained because he had seemingly discovered some ancient treasure indigenous to the area, and was now spending it lavishly and without reference to any village authorities. In general, during his incumbency at Rennes, his people behaved rather as if their rightful ruler was simply doing what rightful rulers have tended to do for millennia: they accepted his paternal generosity gratefully and acquiesced quietly in his minor delinquencies, extravagances and eccentricities. Republican anti-clericalism and anti-royalism were not happy with the situation. Their complaints, however, were not directed against Bérenger Saunière the man, but rather against any representative of the revival of autocratic, aristocratic power. There was never any question in their minds about Saunière's right to whatever source of wealth he was tapping so prodigally — their objection was to the inegalitarianism which permitted any form of wealth, rank or privilege to flourish.

The other objections to Saunière's wealth and behaviour came from the querulous and obsessively bureaucratic Bishop Paul-Félix Beuvain de Beauséjour, who had, unfortunately for Saunière, replaced the amiable and complacent Bishop Billard in the See of Carcassonne in 1902. In his dealings with the singularly persistent and irritating Paul-Félix, Saunière usually displayed the cavalier style of a boldly autonomous local seigneur rather than the timid obsequiousness of some poor village priest plagued by the delusion that his bishop in some way spoke for God. The question must be asked: did Saunière behave as a dashing local seigneur because he believed himself to be one? Had he been told — whether it was true or false — that he carried the royal and ancient Merovingian blood? Did he believe himself to be the rightful Count of Razès, and, as such, vastly superior to any mere local bishop or demagogic republican politician? It is vitally important to solve this problem about Saunière's character, his personal beliefs and attitudes, before we can begin to try to understand any of the things he may — or may not — have done in connection with the Rennes mystery between 1885 and 1917.

If he was a sincere, dedicated, devoted and spiritually orientated Christian priest who held a completely orthodox Catholic faith, certain theories about his source of wealth are non-starters. If, on the other hand, he was an ambitious soldier of fortune, an adventurous treasure hunter whose courage and determination occasionally outweighed his moral scruples, then no theory is beyond the bounds of possibility. With that proviso in mind, we can begin objectively and dispassionately to assess the religious and theological aspects of the Rennes mystery, and our first quasi-religious investigation takes us upwards to have a look at the apparent movements of the planet Venus – "as above, so below."

There are, as we noted in the chapter concerning Rennes and its geographical location and topography, various natural landmarks and ancient man-made ones – such as mines and menhirs – which form remarkable pentagons and equilateral triangles in the vicinity of the village. In the ancient world, astrologers believed the earth to be the centre of the universe. From their point of view, every other heavenly body moved around the earth. The planets – or wanderers – created a calculation problem for early astronomers and astrologers. They did not move in a great circular sweep as the fixed stars appeared to do: planets turned up in all sorts of celestial locations, more or less regularly, and more or less predictably. For the ancients who believed that the apparent geo-centred universe was the real state of astronomical affairs, each planet seemed to have an idiosyncratic movement pattern around the sun. Mercury makes an irregular triangle, for example – but Venus makes a pentagon every eight years. For the ancient astrologers and magicians, for whom symbolism was everything, this was of vital significance, especially when combined with a pentagon on the ground in a mysterious site like Rennes-le-Château.

Scientifically, Venus is the second planet out from the sun. Its dense, cloudy atmosphere readily reflects sunlight and makes it appear extremely bright. Its mean distance from the sun is 112 million kilometres, and its nearest approach to the earth brings it within 41 million kilometres. The diameter of Venus is 13,000 kilometres, and its mass is 0.826 that of the earth. Venus performs regular transits of the solar disc: during these it appears as a black dot against the sun. These transits occur four times every 243 years at intervals of 8, 105½, 8 and 121½ years. Recorded transits took place in 1518, 1526, 1631, 1639, 1761, 1769, 1874 and 1882. The next two are due in 2004 and 2012. It would not be particularly difficult to find significant events in history to coincide with the dates of the transits, of course, but it is mildly ironic to note that in 1874 Saunière entered the seminary to begin his five years of priestly training, and in 1882 he was given his first post as priest of the tiny village of Clat. Born under the sign of Aries, the Ram, Saunière made two important "transits" which coincided with those of Venus.

Venus the goddess, after whom the planet is named, goes back a long way. Her ancient Italian origins are obscure, but she was connected in the beginning with vegetable and herb gardens. A fragment of comedy by Gnaeus Naevius, who wrote in the third century B.C., refers to cooked herbs as *Venerem expertam Volcanum*, literally "Venus having experienced the embrace of Vulcan". (Possibly the herbs were burnt!) Gnaeus is also apparently alluding to Venus under her alternative title, Aphrodite, the wife of Hephaestus, or Vulcan, the limping blacksmith of the gods. Volcanoes were once thought of as his forges. The idea of her as a goddess of gardens revives a faint echo of Eve in Eden with Adam before the Fall.

Aphrodite, the Greek goddess of sexuality and beauty, was also a goddess of fertility, and especially at Eryx, she was seen as presiding over plant growth, vegetables and successful harvests. These concepts are not far removed from the far older idea of the earth-mother goddess, reputed to be the parent of the gods, of humanity and of all nature. She was believed to be responsible for supplying food to be gathered and game to be hunted in Stone Age times. The earliest settlers at Rennes — the men who made and used the flint tools and weapons which M. Fatin has discovered in and around the village — would most likely have been among her devotees.

She was known by many names in many lands: she was Cybele in Greek and Roman writings from the time of Pindar (500 B.C.); she was also Dindymene from one of her prominent shrines on Mount Dindymon. Her sacred symbol was a small meteoric stone, which her ancient worshippers believed had fallen from the heavens.

As late as A.D. 394 under the Emperor Eugenius she was still being worshipped in Rome. Whatever her local name, her characteristics were consistent: her shrines were on mountain tops, or in caves; she was the ruler of wild nature; her traditional companions were lions; her attendants, the Corybantes, were wild, semi-demonic beings. Her priests, known as the Galli, were transvestite eunuchs, who covered themselves in perfume and wore their hair long. Is there any remote connection here with Clodion the Long Haired, the first Merovingian? Is the legend of the Triton-parent of Mérovée a veiled reference to Clodion's impotence, or emasculation as part of the worship of Cybele? Was the rather shadowy and mysterious Clodion a eunuch? If so, who was Mérovée's real father?

There is another interesting point to make about the earth-mother. The temple on the Palatine which was dedicated to her was meant to be a symbol of the mother's cave, and it was to this "cave" that the sacred pine — the symbol of the resurrected god Atys — was carried in procession on March 22nd every year. Does this provide us with a clue, a hint, perhaps, that later secret devotees of the ancient mother goddess cult might naturally tend to carry their sacred treasures to a literal cave to conceal and protect them in times of war, danger or persecution? Does this lend credibility to Stanley James's theory about the Rennes treasure being concealed in a cave? What, too, of Saunière's painting of Mary Magdalen in a cave? What does lie buried in those mysterious *avens* in the Rennes area?

There is a strong theological link connecting Cybele the earth-mother and Venus-Aphrodite with Isis, the most powerful of the Egyptian goddesses. She was also identified with Demeter (or Ceres) by Herodotus. In the Egyptian mythology, Isis is the daughter of Keb and Nut (the earth and the sky). Her worship spread to Greece; and Sulla opened a college of Isis in Rome as far back as 80 B.C. although it was frequently suppressed and persecuted. The so-called mysteries of Isis, or Isiac mysteries, portrayed the murder of her husband-brother, Osiris; the triumph of their son, Horus, over the evil god Seth; and the subsequent resurrection of Osiris. Although the prevailing view of the ceremonies is that initiates simply went through a series of purification rites, there were persistent, darker rumours of uninhibited orgiastic celebrations as well.

Images of Isis nursing the infant Horus were very widespread, and bore an undeniable resemblance to images of the infant Christ in the arms of the Virgin Mary. Opponents of the Church have often seized on this apparent similarity and attempted to argue that Christianity can be "explained" as an imitation of the Isiac Mysteries, or of the related Eleusinian Mysteries where Demeter, not Isis, was the central figure. Similar arguments have been put forward suggesting that the detailed and accurate Gospel accounts of Christ's resurrection were not historical but only symbols of the cyclic life-and-death theme of the old arable fertility religions, where a dying god returning to life was the symbol of the apparently lifeless seed buried in the ground but springing to life again as the seasons changed. A far more powerful argument is the idea that the old pagan fertility cults were like dull, translucent windows through which the first glimmerings of divine truth were able to percolate slowly. Because the wisest and most perceptive pre-Christian believers were able to see a few uncertain glimpses of some greater truth about a dying and resurrected God, the Truth when it happened was in no way diminished. The dazzling beauty of the risen sun is in no way lessened or proved to be unreal because a few early risers saw the pale shafts of dawn that heralded the morning.

Inseparable from the creative, beneficently generous element in the ancient mythologies of the mother-goddess is her sexual attraction. In her Venus-Aphrodite aspect she presents almost irresistible temptation: her ancient worship was frequently augmented by the services of prostitute-priestesses. Just as that aspect of Isis which encapsulates the concept of the protective, all-providing and loving mother — especially when she is depicted with the infant Horus in her arms — has led to her later comparisons to the Virgin Mary, so the overtly sexual aspects of Venus-Aphrodite have led to her being compared to Mary Magdalen, "the woman who was a sinner." Strangely, in the ancient, pagan goddess cults, three powerful but paradoxical and seemingly contradictory elements were frequently concurrent to a greater or lesser degree: the strength and generosity of the protecting mother; the purity of the virgin; and the blatant sexual attraction of the harlot.

No less an authority than Baring-Gould has preserved the stange legend of the Mountain of Venus, the Horselberg, which rises like a strange stone sarcophagus between Eisenach and Gotha. High on the north-west flank of that mountain, a cavern called the Horselloch opens; in its dark depths a subterranean torrent thunders. Ancient legends maintain that this is the entrance to the court of Venus-Aphrodite herself. Ethereal forms of beautiful women are said to have appeared there from time to time and lured men inside: none ever returned — except Tannhäuser — and even he went back to the cave again and disappeared into it forever.

Well known because of Wagner's opera and Swinburne's *Laus Veneris*, the basic legend of Tannhäuser tells how the hero, a romantic knight and renowned *Minnesinger* (the German equivalent of a French *troubadour*) was riding through Thuringia close by the Horselberg when he saw an exquisitely beautiful woman whom he recognized as the goddess Venus. She beckoned him into the Horselloch Cavern where he spent seven years enjoying the luxurious sensuality of her court. At last his conscience drove him from the bed of his pagan goddess and he went from priest to priest repenting and begging for absolution. All refused. At last he approached the Pope himself, who also refused. The papal comment was grimly pessimistic: "You have less hope of absolution than this dry wooden staff in my hand has of sprouting fresh green leaves!" The despairing Tannhäuser set off back to the Horselloch and his pagan goddess. Three days later the papal staff miraculously sprouted fresh green shoots: aghast at what he had done to the penitent, the Pope sent swift messengers after Tannhäuser. The messengers were too late: Tannhäuser had returned to Venus and her pagan festivities in the Horselloch until the world's end.

The curious threads and strands of the Rennes mystery keep going back on themselves in an elusive and intricate pattern: Tannhäuser was denied absolution — and so, according to some accounts, was Saunière. A few rather unlikely and unreliable traditions of the later life of Joseph of Arimathea suggest that he visited the Rennes area as a missionary after Christ's resurrection, possibly as a companion of Mary Magdalen: the entirely different account of his work in Glastonbury is much more likely to be historically accurate. The significant connection with the Tannhäuser legend, however, is the dry wooden staff which miraculously blossomed. It is also interesting to notice that in the Glastonbury version the staff is in the hands of Joseph of Arimathea — a man of authority in Israel before his conversion to Christianity, a man of considerable wealth and power. In the Tannhäuser tradition the staff is in the hands of the Pope — also an authority figure, and one who could command the wealth and power of the medieval church.

The Celtic Tectosages who once inhabited the Rennes area were also steeped in the mother-goddess tradition. Frank Delaney's brilliant and scholarly study of the Celts expresses this information about their religious thinking superbly: " . . . heroes and kings are mated with the earth-goddess, the earth-mother, from whom we spring and to whom we return . . . sometimes the peaks of mountains represented the breasts of a great mother-goddess . . . "[1]

In addition to the three paradoxical aspects of an earth-goddess, which we have already discussed, the Rennes area was subjected for many centuries to the equally strong traditions of Gnosticism and Hermeticism. The most significant aspects of these beliefs were firstly dualism — the idea that cosmic forces of Light and Darkness, Order and Chaos, were eternally ranged against each other; and secondly the existence of secret and mysterious powers, which could be made available to initiates who were shown how to acquire them by those who had already found the keys to their secret doors. Spirit and matter were incompatible and irreconcilable — but somehow artificially emulsified here on earth, like oil and water, and always seeking ways to escape from each other. Light was conceived of as being trapped in darkness: spirit was imprisoned in matter. The Gnostic and the Hermeticist sought in their different ways to find the secret of releasing them — only then, so they believed, would true freedom, happiness and everlasting life be attainable.

The Gnosticism and Hermeticism prevalent in the Rennes area were themselves significantly influenced by the teachings of Mani, or Manes, who lived circa 216 to 276. His doctrine, which became known as Manichaeanism, was partly Zoroastrian dualism (the belief that Good and

---

[1]Delaney, Frank: *The Celts,* Grafton Books, London, 1989, p. 79.

Evil are equal personal forces locked in eternal combat) and partly soteriology – the branch of theology which is concerned with the salvation accomplished by Jesus Christ. According to Mani, the human soul originated in the Kingdom of Light and is continually trying to escape from its unwelcome imprisonment in the human body. Mani regarded mankind's physical nature as a microcosm of the Kingdom of Darkness.

The philosophers and theologians of the Graeco-Roman world found it difficult to assimilate Christianity. There is a sense, therefore, in which Gnosticism may be regarded as an attempt to weld the classical thought patterns of Greece and Rome on to what was for that era "the new teaching from Galilee". Another way to look at Gnosticism is to regard it as a mixture of theology and philosophy, which exists in both Christian and non-Christian versions. One of the main planks of Gnosticism is that spirit is good and matter is evil. If a person can acquire the necessary, secret, spiritual knowledge (Greek *gnosis*), he or she can escape from the prison of matter.

It is also important to realise that Gnosticism and Manichaeanism had a powerful reciprocal influence on each other, and Manichaean teaching in turn influenced Christian thought in some areas of the world. The nominal Manichaeans spread across Europe and Asia, even reaching as far as China, until they were extinguished by persecution. The Paulicians, however, who were in one sense a Manichaean–Christian group (although they anathematized Mani himself!) survived in Asia Minor, Bulgaria and Armenia. They were more or less in evidence until the twelfth century; vanished until the eighteenth; and reappeared again in 1828 when a group of them turned up in Russian Armenia complete with a mysterious book of unknown origin which they called *The Key to the Truth*.

Information about the Paulicians is mainly derived from the *Chronicon* of Georgios Monachus, and from the ninth century *Historia Manicheorum*, one of the many scholarly and reliable works written by Photius, the brilliantly academic Patriarch of Constantinople, who lived from 820 until 891. It seems that the Paulicians regarded their founder as Paul of Samosata, the Patriarch of Antioch from 260 until 272, who taught (like the Adoptionists and Ebionites) that Jesus became the Son of God by divine adoption, rather than being the pre-existent Divine Logos of St. John's Gospel, co-existent with the Father since the Beginning. The Adoptionist heresy was naturally compatible with Gnostic doctrine as it implied that if Jesus had moved by divine intervention from the rank of ordinary man to Son of God then, by acquiring the same secret, spiritual knowledge that he had possessed, others could make the same transition.

Other Paulician teachings denied the historical existence of the Virgin Mary as a real woman of flesh and blood, regarding her instead as a symbol for the Church nourishing and protecting the Word of God, or as a symbol for what they called the Upper Jerusalem – a mysterious non-physical realm where Christ came and went. The Paulicians regarded the Eucharist as a mere allegory. They despised the cross rather than venerating it, and actually destroyed crosses when they could – a significant point in view of later reports about the Cathars and the Templars doing similar things. They repudiated Peter's role as the Rock upon which Christ founded the Church, and, rather quaintly, they regarded traditional monks' habits as an invention of the devil. Prudently — and this perhaps accounted for their stubborn survival during several of the centuries when less offensive heretics were totally obliterated by fire and sword — they permitted external conformity to the rules and regulations of the dominant Church, and taught that Christ would forgive this practice.

When the Greeks drove many of the Paulicians into the Balkan Peninsula in 872, they seem to have fallen under the influence of a new leader known as Bogomil (the name means "Beloved of God"), and, under the name of Bogomils, they took root in Bosnia and Serbia. In due course their ideas reached Italy and the area around Toulouse and Rennes-le-Château. From the Paulicians and the Bogomils grew the Cathars — otherwise known as Albigensians.

In 1167 they were so strong and numerous that the Bulgarian Bishop Nicetas (otherwise known as Nikita) convened a Council of Cathar Bishops and Priests at Saint-Félix de Caraman, near Toulouse. They had ceased to be merely a heretical sect: they had now acquired the status of a powerful rival church.

What did these twelfth century Cathars believe?

On the whole their faith was very similar to its Manichaean, Paulician and Bogomilian roots: its chief ingredients were Gnosticism and Hermeticism. The Cathar God was not the omnipotent God of Islam, Judaism or Christianity. To a Cathar the physical universe — and everything in it including his own body — was a manifestation of evil. It was the devil's creation, but as Satan could not create life, he had had to ask God's help to animate the human forms which he had made. According to the Cathars, therefore, it was the good God who had breathed life, a divine essence or spirit, into the clay forms which the devil had fashioned. Satan was then said to have lured angels down from heaven in order to utilise their souls in the bodies of the descendants of his two original human beings.

As Dr. Arthur Guirdham's deservedly famous study, *The Cathars and Reincarnation,*[2] very lucidly indicates, many Cathars actually believed in reincarnation: if the evidence of Dr. Guirdham's principal informant is to be taken seriously, and there is much in her evidence that deserves careful and sober reflection, some Cathars actually succeeded in practising it. If the original number of "kidnapped" angelic souls was thought by the Cathars to be finite, then they probably argued that those "stolen" souls migrated from one human body to another as the centuries rolled on.

It was a further aspect of Cathar faith that the good God had sent his second son, Jesus, in the form of a divine projection or image to rescue these lost angelic souls from their prisons of flesh. They believed that Satan, although now opposed to the good God, had been his first son. To the Cathars, Jesus was nonphysical, and, as he was nonphysical, they argued that he could not be born, suffer, die or experience resurrection. Not only was the cross seen as an instrument of evil instead of being the holy symbol of the Christian faith, the Cathars also hated and despised saints' relics — because they were physical. The Cathars said that those who bowed to scraps of rag, bone or hair in reliquaries were foolishly

---

[2]Published by Neville Spearman, Saffron Walden, 1990.

bowing to matter, and matter was the creation of Satan. Cathars also deplored sex and family life as being worldly and material: they disliked procreation because they believed it dragged down more and more damned souls to endure the misery of earthly incarnation. They forbade all killing of human beings, for whatever reason, and the prohibition was extended to animals as well. No food of animal origin was permitted either. This regulation even extended to eggs and milk.

It was against Cathar principles to lie, to swear oaths, or to own property, but even all of these moral, sexual and dietary prohibitions were insufficient to ensure salvation according to Cathar criteria. Salvation demanded full and proper membership of the Cathar Church, which was brought about by the laying on of hands by a Cathar Minister.

The Cathar eschatologies — their teachings about the end of the world — were dramatic and colourful; but in one place at least they seem irresolvably contradictory. The majority of Cathars believed that the reincarnative processes would continue until all souls — except a few which had been created by Satan and were, therefore, impossible to save — were safely reunited with the good God. The physical world would then be destroyed completely in a holocaust of fire and water in which fire would consume all water and water would quench all fire.

Once this holocaust was over and the elements of fire and water had proved not only mutually annihilatory but had disposed of the whole of the material creation in the process, the saved Cathar souls would enjoy a blissful eternity with the good God. The irresolvably contradictory element here is the problem of the damned souls who were said to have been "created by Satan". The main thrust of the dilemma is that in another, equally clear, piece of Cathar teaching it is made explicit that Satan cannot create anything living.

The central point of Cathar ritual was the "consolamentum". During this service it was believed that the convert received the Holy Spirit through the laying on of the Minister's hands. These Cathar Ministers were known as *perfecti* and they normally worked and travelled in pairs. A male companion was called a *socius*, and a female companion was called a *socia*. These pairs of Ministers shared all of life's hardships and dangers as they travelled through the Languedoc. The colloquial name for the *perfecti* was *bonshommes* (the good men), which tells us a great deal about the admiration and affection in which they were held by the local people, many of whom they helped.

Ordinary members of the movement were known as *credentes*, and they were not bound to follow such strict codes of behaviour as were the *perfecti*.

Each Cathar province was administered by a bishop and two assistants. These assistants were known as the *Filius Major* and the *Filius Minor* — the "greater son" and the "lesser son". When a bishop sensed that his death was not far away, he would appoint the *Filius Major* as his legitimate successor, and promote the *Filius Minor* to be the new *Filius Major*. A new *Filius Minor* would then be elected by the *perfecti* in that locality.

Although as individuals Cathars possessed nothing, the *perfecti* as a group controlled very substantial wealth. Much of it they gave directly to the poor. Some was used to support their charitable institutions — most of which were hybrids of hospitals, seminaries and monasteries. Some, it is strongly rumoured, they stored carefully either in or near some local landmark, or in one of their eminently defensible strongholds. Alas for the independent Counts of Razès, and their Cathar protégés! Montségur fell to the Catholic crusaders in 1244 and over 200 Cathars were burned alive; but there is evidence that four Cathar mountaineers climbed down the precipitous rock on which the castle stands and took with them the secret of the Cathar treasure. Was it a purely "spiritual treasure" — secret knowledge, perhaps, or some rare and precious book resembling *The Key to the Truth* which at least one group of Paulicians was known to be using as recently 1824? The most intriguing question of all is the reference to "pecuniam infinitam" or unlimited wealth, which was made by a Cathar prisoner being interrogated by the Inquisitors. What strange secret could the Cathars have had that might have led those who understood it to enjoy the control of unlimited wealth?

The mysterious religious influences saturating Rennes-le-Château by no means ended when the Cathars were suppressed. Although they are best remembered for their romantic chivalry and matchless courage, the Knights Templar were priests as well as warriors, and there are strong suspicions that their version of the Christian faith was a far cry from traditional orthodoxy. Founded in 1119, and ostensibly extinguished by their final overthrow at Castellat on November 1st, 1308, the Templars began as a redemptive and evangelical order; their rule seems to have included the principle of seeking out former knights who had been excommunicated, obtaining absolution for them and then initiating them into the new Order of the Templars.

There has always been controversy over whether the Templars followed a secret, or hidden, rule as well as their open order. Travelling adventurers, especially those coming into contact with ancient Eastern civilisations, were far more likely to encounter esoteric knowledge than those who stayed quietly at home tending their rose gardens. Byzantium — the Eastern Roman Empire — was still a rich and flourishing culture at the time of the Templars. Many an ancient Roman secret and many an ancient Roman treasure could have been preserved there. The tides of war flow over ancient cities and wash away the coverings of once-safe hiding places. A hidden chamber, once deep within an ancient tower wall, will yield its secrets to the first soldier who scrambles over the ruins as soon as the siege engines have done their work.

As we have already noted, many of the Templars were redeemed soldiers of fortune. Some of them had undoubtedly acquired considerable treasure during their former careers as plundering mercenaries. These treasures would now become the common property of their Order. What if, among these treasures, were strange and mysterious things whose origin, nature and function were only dimly guessed at?

Adventurers and travellers share the stories of their adventures with one another. What if part of a tale from Damascus linked up with half-remembered legends from Luxor or a myth from Cyprus? Did an exotic adventure in Syria make sense of a strange piece of folklore heard in distant Eschcol? The Templars also had contact with Egypt and its mysteries, and Egypt was the original home of Hermes Trismegistus, or Thoth, and of the mysterious Emerald Tablets. It is well within the bounds of possibility that the Templars of the Rennes area had brought the secrets of Hermeticism to such strongholds as Le Bézu and Blanchefort.

The religious ethos of Rennes was already sufficiently bizarre with its ancient mother-goddess background, its Gnosticism and Hermeticism, when Cathars and Templars added their mysterious contributions. But there were yet more curious strains to come: a soupçon of alchemy and Rosicrucianism filtered in as well.

The theological and religious background of the Rennes area is complex and enigmatic. Historical philosophers like Collingwood ("History is the history of thought") almost give us grounds for believing that ideas seem to have a life of their own. If ideas can be said to "live" anywhere, then, surely, strong, ancient and persistent religious ideas still live in Rennes.

We shall return to the importance of the mother-goddess theme, the secrets of the Hermeticists and the relevance of Gnostic dualism in a later chapter, but one additional point needs to be made here.

James E. Lovelock began his work as a scientific study of the possibility of life on Mars: he then began questioning the nature of life on earth. What finally emerged was the amazing – and highly controversial – Gaia Hypothesis: the proposition that all life should be regarded as a single living being, which is capable of altering the planetary environment as and when it needs to in order to sustain life. If we take the Gaia Hypothesis a few steps further and allow this one great life-form to have self-awareness, purpose and intelligence, for the sake of pursuing the argument, then we may not be a hundred kilometres away from something which our ancestors understandably described as their great mother-goddess.

CHAPTER FOUR

THE REAL MESSIANIC MESSAGE

Deo duce, ferro comitante.

In addition to their dubious suggestions in *The Holy Blood and the Holy Grail* that Jesus had not really died on the cross, that a substitute had died in his place, or that in some other curious way the historical accuracy of the Gospel accounts of his death and resurrection were to be called into question, Baigent, Leigh and Lincoln produced a sequel called *The Messianic Legacy*.

By invoking an argument as tortuous as any Orwellian *Nineteen Eighty-Four* "doublethink", *The Messianic Legacy* attempts to discredit any arguments based on subjective feelings and inner experiences. The reader is asked to imagine, for the sake of creating a parallel situation, that a modern Mexican Indian with a claim to ancient Aztec blood, might assert that he believed in the divinity of Hernán Cortés. The authors ask us to suppose that our imaginary believer might also assert that he could "feel" Cortés alive inside him, that he spoke to Cortés and that Cortés appeared to him in visions.

They admit that what an individual experiences in the private, inward secrecy of the mind must be his, or her, experience alone, and cannot be violated from outside. They go on to protest, however, that when the feelings and beliefs that belong to this inner sanctum begin to "distort, alter or transform historical fact" or when they "derange dramatically the laws of probability" the believer cannot expect other people to "condone the process".[1]

This line of thought seems to presuppose that something called a "simple historical fact" can ever be ascertained with the certainty which Baigent, Leigh and Lincoln ascribe to it. The simplicity is knocked out of most so-called simple historical − or any other kind of − facts by the theory of relativity and its comments on the position of the observer. Let's have a hypothetical situation to match our imaginary Mexican Indian who believes in the divinity of Hernán Cortés. Imagine a straightforward, down-to-earth materialist who believes that what his senses tell him is fact. We will now confront this character with a glass-sided train. Inside one transparent carriage two small boys are alleviating their boredom by throwing a tennis ball backwards and forwards to each other.

We have an athletic tramp hitching a ride by hanging underneath the train and looking up through the glass floor at the two boys who are

---

[1] Baigent, M., Leigh, R., and Lincoln, H. *The Messianic Legacy,* Corgi Books; 1989 reprint, p. 27.

throwing the tennis ball. There is also an observer on the platform watching the train with interest as it passes through this particular station at 100 kilometres an hour.

From the point of view of the observer hanging under the floor, the tennis ball is moving from a point just beyond his forehead to a point near his hips, and then back again, at a speed of about ten kilometres an hour. From his point of view it moves in a flat trajectory in a series of straight lines. Seen by the boys playing the game, however, it moves in a series of arcs: its path curves in the vertical plane. Seen by the man on the platform it moves past him at 110 kilometres an hour while being thrown towards the front of the train, and at only ninety kilometres an hour when thrown towards the rear of the train. All three observers are reporting accurately what they see: each is in a different frame of reference. If we add other observers in space craft outside the earth's gravitational field, the ball will also be following the earth's rapid axial rotation and its journey around the sun, as well as the whole solar system's trip through space. There is no single, simple, factual description of the ball's flight.

Although light travels faster than anything else we've yet discovered, its enormous velocity is nevertheless finite: the old definition of approximately 186,000 miles (just under 300,000 kilometres) a second is close enough for our present purposes. If an observer is stationed at a distance of 18,000,000 kilometres (one light minute) away from the train, his observations will differ from those of the boys, the tramp and the man on the platform. His "now" will be one minute behind their "now". An observer with an unimaginably powerful telescope on a planet 5,000 light years from earth would at this moment be watching the pyramids being built. His description of human civilisation would encompass what he could see of China, Mesopotamia and Egypt. An infinite number of observers placed at different distances from the scene of an activity would describe "now" in an infinite number of ways.

Imagine two space ships in an infinite empty void. There are no reference points from which they can get any information about their speed or position. They can see only each other, and each ship is a perfect sphere: there is no "front" or "back" on either. One ship "passes" the other. Is it overtaking, or are they moving in opposite directions? With no reference points other than themselves it is a question which cannot be resolved. It is just not possible to say that A overtook B, or that A and B were going in opposite directions and met, as a simple historical fact. There can be no absolute external certainty in this situation: what does each astronaut believe?

The comforting old world concept of "simple historical facts" received another devastating body blow from the work of Werner Heisenberg, Erwin Schrödinger and Paul Dirac, over sixty years ago. Most widely known as Heisenberg's Uncertainty Principle, the heart of what they postulated was that if you want to forecast where a particle is going, you need to know where it is now and its current velocity. The snag is that to do that you have to shine a light on it. For scientific purposes, where highly accurate measurements are desirable, you need to use light of the shortest possible wavelength, because your accuracy of measurement is governed by the distances between the wave crests of the light you're using to observe the particle: the shorter the wavelength, the more accurate the measurements. Twenty years before Heisenberg and his contemporaries worked out the Uncertainty Principle and its ramifications, Max Planck had put forward the Quantum Theory, which had dire consequences for the physics of particle observation. Planck said that light, X-rays and similar waves were emitted in minute "packets" which he called quanta. It was not possible to deliver less than one quantum: one "packet" was absolute minimum. Each finite quantum contained a certain amount of energy. The higher the frequency of the wavelength, the more energy each quantum had. Hitting a particle with a photon (a quantum of light) at very high frequency would obviously disturb the particle and change its velocity in a totally unpredictable way, so in the act of observing a particle the observer influenced its future behaviour. Heisenberg was able to demonstrate that the more accurately the observer seeks to measure the location of a particle, the less accurately can he measure its velocity; and, conversely, the more accurately he tries to measure the velocity, the less certain can he be of the particle's location! Heisenberg went on to demonstrate this mathematically: the uncertainty of the position multiplied by the uncertainty of the velocity multiplied by the mass of the particle being studied is always greater than a certain constant, which mathematicians and physicists call h, or Planck's Constant. Its actual value is 6.626×10^{-34} (joule second). It makes no difference how you measure the position, or how you measure the velocity; it doesn't even matter what type of particle you're observing: Planck's constant is always constant! Heisenberg's uncertainty principle is ubiquitous and inevitable: it's just part of the way God made our world. Its implications are massive and highly controversial. In effect, they spell the end of the kind of philosophical determinism associated with Pierre Simon, Marquis de Laplace, the great Napoleonic astronomer and mathematician, whose pioneering genius has probably been equalled only by Albert Einstein and Professor Stephen Hawking.

Laplace, whose solutions to the intricate and convoluted problems concerning the orbits of Saturn and Jupiter put him well on the way to his rightful niche in the Hall of Fame, dreamt of creating a thoroughly deterministic model of the universe in which everything could be predicted accurately — as accurately as the orbits of the planets. Heisenberg's Uncertainty Principle and the later developments of quantum mechanics make it abundantly clear that if we're not able to measure the here and now accurately (which we're not!) we haven't any chance at all of predicting the then and the there. All we can hope to do is to calculate the various probabilities. An event may be defined as the interaction of matter and energy in space and time. Some events are massively more probable than others but no event is so improbable that it is absolutely impossible.[2]

---

[2] For those readers who want to delve more deeply into this area, there is no better book than professor Stephen Hawking's *A Brief History of Time,* published by Bantam Press, Transworld Publishers Ltd., London in 1988.

Further interesting highlights on the mysterious nature of the universe appear among the case histories of incredible "coincidences" which Alan Vaughan has recorded in his books on synchronicity.[3] One of the episodes he records concerns an unpleasant nineteenth century character whose casual seduction of a girl led to her pregnancy and subsequent suicide. Her brother shot the man responsible, assumed he was dead and then shot himself. The seducer, however, got up. The bullet which had struck him without doing any serious damage had ricocheted into a tree and lodged there. Many years afterwards — now a prosperous businessman — he bought the field in which the tree stood and dynamited it as part of his land clearance scheme. The bullet flew out and killed him. Vaughan goes on from his case histories to expound a theory of synchronicity based on the thoughts of Carl Jung, the pioneer psychologist. Jung's theory was that synchronicity was an acausal connecting principle which revealed itself as what he termed meaningful coincidences in his famous archetypal situations. Vaughan's theory of synchronicity is even bolder than Jung's. Vaughan suggests that there is a sense in which consciousness is capable of creating — not merely observing — space, time and matter. It is a controversial hypothesis, but a well-reasoned one, which is well worth reading. It, too, casts doubt on the apparent simplicity of "simple historical facts".

Another nail in the coffin of "simple historical facts" is what John Michell and Robert Rickard describe as phenomenalism: the idea that there are three spheres of observation — the "hard" phenomena which can be weighed and measured (within the limits set by Heisenberg); the phenomenal, which are a kind of half-way house between "hard" phenomena and purely mental ones; and what the authors describe as psychological phenomena, the world of mental experiences. They believe that there is an overlap between these zones. Their theory is controversial, but well argued and worth serious consideration.[4]

If we have succeeded in presenting a reasonable case for the historicity of the New Testament miracles — and especially the supreme miracle of Christ's resurrection — we may proceed first to examine and then to counter the arguments put forward in *The Messianic Legacy* suggesting that Jesus was merely a mortal Messiah, a political aspirant for the throne of Judah in the tradition of David, Solomon or any other Hebrew monarch.

The writers of *The Messianic Legacy* blithely assert that although they can accept that the oldest and purest versions of Buddhism and Islam may be close to the teachings of their original founders, the same cannot be said of Christianity.

It is true that long intervening centuries and the natural weakness of fallible human conductors of divine truth have created differences among groups of the faithful. It is also true that when all those minor denominational disagreements are thrown away as the trivia they are, and when certain prominent liberal humanists are extracted from their bishops' camouflage, there still remains a massive common core of solid, bedrock

---

[3]Vaughan, Alan: *Incredible Coincidence*, Corgi Books, London, 1981.

[4]Michel, John and Rickard, R.J.M., *Phenomena: a Book of Wonders*, Thames and Hudson Ltd., London, 1977.

Christianity that can be traced directly to Jesus Christ as surely as Islam can be traced to the Prophet Mohammed.

Baigent, Leigh and Lincoln have insinuated that there was some absolutely fundamental difference between the teachings of St. Paul — whose missionary work was so deservedly successful — and the Jerusalem Church leaders like St. James, the brother of Jesus, and St. Peter. Yet Paul himself says clearly in his First Epistle to the Corinthians (written early in A.D. 56) that the Gospel which he had preached to them was the one that he himself had received. It was neither a misunderstanding nor a creation on his part: it was the basic and fundamental truth at the heart of the Christian faith. Of course, there were differences of style, doctrinal emphasis and personality between the first century apostles — just as there are among Church leaders today — but there is no evidence at all of the sort of sinister and unbridgeable gulf between a supposed group of politically motivated messianic insurgents in Jerusalem and the spiritually motivated fathers of the Church elsewhere.

The Messianic Legacy seeks to persuade the reader that Jesus was neither more nor less than one of a substantial series of messianic priest-king aspirants to the Davidic throne, and that his attempt failed. We are also asked to believe that a small inner clique of his family, friends and close supporters were "in the know" as far as this political intrigue was concerned, that the rest of his disciples and adherents were not, and that there was a subsequent misunderstanding of his person and work which led to its becoming spiritualised and mysticised into early Christianity.

For the sake of illustration, let us make a parallel hypothesis of equal, or greater, probability than the Baigent, Leigh and Lincoln ideas about Jesus. Imagine that Sir Isaac Newton was a political agitator who had planned to begin a popular revolution by providing free apples all round on a prototype of the National Health Service. He then intended to set himself up as a scientific philosopher-king of the kind envisaged in Plato's *Republic*. His scheme failed when the government got wind of it, and sent a brigade of hussars to arrest him in the orchard. He was subsequently assassinated by government agents, but it was made to look like death from natural causes. We are also required to believe that he had been secretly married to his orchard keeper's second cousin (who had had a certain reputation in the village!) The evidence for such a marriage being that he had once provided free cider at a village wedding. This clandestine marriage had produced offspring who had escaped to the Isle of Wight after Sir Isaac's death and subsequently married into the ruling family. It is also darkly rumoured that their descendants may still be around and plotting to take over the United States of Europe. Any carvings or paintings depicting apples or orchards are really sinister, secret emblems of the underground movement dedicated to putting the Newtonians into power.

Now we add the complication that one of his more naive followers (who hadn't understood the great man's real political motives in the first place) wrongly assumed — when he observed Newton hurling an apple down in frustration and disgust one day — that that gesture was really making a statement about an invisible force called gravity. This well-meaning ignoramus of a disciple was abnormally energetic and persuasive: over the course of centuries several people came to believe in his non-existent force of gravity. All properly educated people, of course, know it to be an entirely subjective experience, despite the sensation of imaginary pain that they think they feel when falling from a height on to a hard surface!

The Messianic Legacy, and its predecessor, *The Holy Blood and the Holy Grail,* both assert that the canon of scripture was deliberately edited, re-dacted and modified to remove references to the supposed political ambitions of Jesus and his inner clique.

Biblical scholars of the highest reputation certainly claim to see evidence of deliberate arrangement and reorganisation in scripture – but it is neither more nor less than the kind of planning any authors undertake when putting a serious, factual work together.

Unless you are engaged on a "stream of consciousness" novel, or some form of diary, or journal, whose contents are dictated strictly by the chronological order of events, you naturally tend to group and categorise your memories of the man of whom you are writing.

If I were writing a biography of my late father, my most vivid memories of him from over fifty years ago would be of the toy car and wheelbarrow he made for me on the carpenter's bench in his old greenhouse-cum-work-shop. That was a completely separate dimension from his work as a Special Constable during World War II; as was his Provincial Grand Rank in East Anglian Freemasonry in the 1920s. When I wrote of him as landlord of "The Crown" in Church Street, Dereham; as a soldier in World War I; as a scrap-metal dealer, and later as a small town high street shopkeeper, those memories, although clear and accurate, would be automatically or-ganised and categorised into the various areas and aspects of his life. A literary critic with time to spare and access to the Norwich archives might correct me in one or two odd places by discovering that my father had re-married in 1933 and not, as I had thought, in 1932. But no emendation or reorganisation of my categories would materially alter the central facts about my father's life and character. There is no way that he could have been a Rosicrucian, a Hermeticist, or a Grand Master of the Priory of Sion without my strongly suspecting that something of that nature was going on. I may not have known every fact about his business ventures, but I did know enough to say quite categorically that he was not a fishmonger, a bookseller, nor an antique dealer.

So it is with the accounts we have of the life and work of Jesus of Nazareth in the Gospels. The best scholarly evidence suggests that Mark's Gospel is directly based on the memories of Peter, who knew Jesus very well indeed, and that Mark himself, the son of Mary of Jerusalem, was very probably the young man in the linen garment who escaped from the garden on the night Jesus was arrested.

Was Mary Magdalen the same woman as Mary of Bethany, and was either (or were both) the same person as the woman with the precious alabaster box of ointment of spikenard? Did Jesus actually work in Joseph's carpentry shop in Nazareth in the years before his public ministry began? Did he provide and care for Mary and his younger step-brothers and sisters after Joseph, her husband, had presumably died? Was Joseph of Arimathea his uncle, and did they once visit England together on a tin trading voyage, as Blake seems to hint at in *Jerusalem*?

These are interesting questions: but they are totally peripheral. Even the remote possibility that Jesus was married to Mary Magdalen, and that they had children is totally peripheral. Christ's unique work as the Son of God and Saviour of the World is not affected one iota by whether he married or not, nor by the precise order of events in his earthly life, nor by the exact locations in which those events occurred. The great central truth of the Gospel remains absolutely unimpaired by minor disagreements about times, places and precise sequences. Christ was born to the Virgin Mary by the miraculous intervention of the Holy Spirit. He taught us the truth about God his Father, and what was necessary for our salvation. He went nobly and willingly to a death for all our sakes which he could so easily have avoided.

By the power of God he rose from the dead; not as a beautiful thought; nor as some sort of fragrant, sacred memory; nor as a pale, ethereal ghost; but in his new, immortal, post-resurrection body with powers vastly exceeding those of any terrestrial being: a body with everything gained and nothing lost. On that first Easter Morning Christ was — and is — eternally, abundantly, objectively alive. Of course it is true that he lives in the hearts and minds of his people, but it is even more true that he lives his own supra-personal life in its own external and objective right as well. Because a few drops of the great Pacific Ocean sustain the life of a tiny fish by passing through its gills, it does not mean that the ocean has no existence outside the gills of the fish!

We live in a world which is, tragically, becoming daily more obsessed by detail and bureaucratic proliferation. Some social historians spend more time working out the precise number of unemployed charcoal burners in the New Forest in 1812 than on considering who won the Battle of Waterloo and why. Some pharmacists have to spend more time filling in government claim forms neatly and correctly than in dispensing drugs to relieve pain and cure illness. Some social workers are busier writing reports, compiling statistics and attending case conferences than getting on with the vital job of feeding the hungry and housing the homeless. Some teachers have to spend more time filling in mark-books and evaluation sheets than in actually teaching their pupils to read, write and count. Whatever the trade or profession, it is becoming increasingly handicapped by this modern obsession with minutiae, analysis, records, statistics and bureaucratic regulations. We are in grave danger of losing sight of our true aims and objectives because we are preoccupied with the details of how to get there.

The obvious purpose of a road and a car is to convey human beings to and from desirable destinations quickly, comfortably, safely and conveniently: but we have to negotiate a score of hurdles of our own preposterous making before we can fulfil the fundamental aims and objectives of simply using the car. We encumber ourselves with driving lessons, tests and licences, insurances, road fund tax discs, MOT tests, log books, speed limits, tachometers, drivers' hours, one way systems, contra-flows, parking restrictions, compulsory seat belts, old uncle Tom Cobleigh and the kitchen sink! Did that same dashing warrior, Jehu (who dealt so effectively with the evil and arrogant Queen Jezebel) worry about traffic regulations when he drove his chariot so that you could tell he was coming from miles away, simply by his style with the reins? (2 Kings 9:20: "His driving is like the driving of Jehu, for he driveth furiously".)

The obvious purpose of Holy Scripture is to lead us to God, to Christ and to everlasting life, but we have encumbered that spiritual road as effectively as we have cluttered our tarmac. There are now more textual theories per verse than a diligent Bible scholar can hope to read in a year! We know the roots of every Hebrew, Aramaic, Arabic, Coptic, Greek and Latin word in the most minute detail. We know their derivations and parallel usages. What we have lost somewhere along the way is what they actually mean for us today. We are like pools winners holding a cheque for £1,000,000 in our hands and minutely studying the details of the printer's art on the cheque form – instead of getting down to the bank to pay it in and start enjoying our good fortune. The thing to do with Holy Scripture is not to spend hours quibbling over its tiny details, but to get down to its main message, the real messianic message.

That message is plain, simple, clear and straightforward. Jesus never saw himself at any time during his incarnation as any sort of earthly king: Saint Paul, the Apostles and the Church Fathers didn't misunderstand Christ, didn't wrongly spiritualise some political message about his being an earthly successor to the throne of David. They hadn't always understood at the beginning. There were several occasions when Jesus had to make it plain to the disciples that he was not the sort of messiah who was going to overthrow the Romans and the forces of Herod and the priests by force of arms. His mission was not the mission of the Maccabees: the dreaded Hammerers. His mission was to show both by words and deeds, especially by the Ultimate Deed – his death and resurrection – that God had intervened, had broken into history, for the benefit of all mankind. The real messianic message was that God the Son, incarnate in Jesus Christ, had come to save every individual human soul who would accept and believe in him, and to redeem human society and his creation as a totality. The real messianic message still is: repentance, forgiveness and abundant, eternal life in Christ. It is as far removed from the concept of an earthly, Davidic, political kingdom as the east is from the west. It is greater folly to mistake Jesus for a revolutionary politician who failed, than to mistake the first gleam of sunrise for the dying flicker of a guttering candle.

To return to the question of the hypothetical divisions and organisational arrangements of the Gospels, the Acts of the Apostles and Revelation: such divisions and taxonomised subsections of textual material as may be discerned are definitely not the product of some cunning, anti-political editor – some literary member of the "spiritual" faction – trying to bowdlerise the original text and expurgate all possible references to a "political" Jesus, a Jewish warrior-prince seeking the throne of his ancestors.

One of the best and most original of the recent, reputable, scholarly works in this field is David G. Palmer's *Sliced Bread*, published by Ceridwen Press of 17 Chargot Road, Victoria Park, Cardiff, in 1988. It is very well worth reading. David Palmer, who enjoyed a career as a successful professional architect before being ordained as a Methodist Minister in 1983, has brought his original talents to bear alongside his very considerable theological skills in analysing the Gospels, the Acts of the Apostles and the Book of Revelation in a completely new way. His theory is based on the idea of *chiasmus*, a Greek term meaning "placing crosswise". As a technical term in literature it signifies a balanced structure, like a reflection, or a step-ladder with two sets of rungs meeting at a small platform at the apex. If passages with similar themes or underlying ideas are designated by various letters of the alphabet, a chiasmus might look like a,b,c,d,c,b,a, with the letter d representing its centre, or reflective surface. Strangely enough, there is an original form of sonnet, the authors' own Fanthorpean Sonnet (devised many years before we had the pleasure of reading David's book) which has the rhyme scheme a,a,b,b,c,c,d,d,c,c,b,b,a,a. The central rhyming couplet (d,d) "reflects" or "symmetrically projects" the other rhyme schemes in both directions. Part of this sonnet form's effect depends upon linking the ideas in the first (a,a) rhyming couplet with those in lines 13 and 14, the final couplet, which must also be (a,a). The poet using this chiasmic sonnet form also endeavours to encapsulate his major thought, or theme, inside the (d,d) central couplet. With these points in mind, let us consider this verse:

Saunière was Curé of Rennes-le-Château	(a)
And laboured there a century ago.	(a)
What did he find in Visigothic stone?	(b)
What secret shared with Dénarnaud alone?	(b)
Strange, cryptic clues from Hautpoul's tomb erased:	(c)
Bigou's inscription, curiously phrased.	(c)
And what of Boudet, up at Rennes-les-Bains?	(d)
A scholarly and enigmatic man.	(d)
His Celtic language riddles questions raised –	(c)
Which Monsieur Bren both analysed and praised.	(c)
Gélis struck down: slain by a hand unknown.	(b)
Dark rumours round that savagery have grown.	(b)
The timeless quest goes on until we know	(a)
The hidden secrets of Rennes-le-Château.	(a)

The great value of chiasmic arrangements in a society where books in the form of codices and scrolls were rare and expensive was that chiasms were easy to memorise, and they had an added liturgical beauty and rhythm when read aloud to groups. Truth is in no way impaired by being arranged in a form that makes it easier to listen to and easier to recall.

In *Sliced Bread*, David Palmer puts forward a scrupulously researched, logical and convincing argument for the Gospels, Acts and Book of Revelation having been assembled in this way. It is vastly more probable that the evidence of editing and redacting which biblical scholars claim to have found is the result of chiasmic design for entirely honest and laudable purposes than that it indicates the surreptitious suppression of "embarrassing" political messianic references. The New Testament does not read like a book that has been censored: it reads like a book that has been organised to enhance the clarity and memorability of the truth it contains.

CHAPTER FIVE

LINES, SHRINES AND SIGNS

Abyssus abyssum invocat.

If you could drop a naked human brain armed with at least one sensory input organ and miraculous powers of survival into a chaotic maelstrom, devoid of form or meaning, the gallant, God-given mind inside that brain would slowly struggle to make some sort of order out of its unknown environment.

Sit in a train rattling over the irregularities in a railway line and before long the repeated, meaningless noises are beginning to sound like speech. There was even a famous old 78 which was popular on "Housewives Choice" a few decades ago in which the artist impersonated a chattering train. Mystics and seers "see" things in crystals, teacups, glowing coals on the fire and the patterns of moving clouds. Roman soothsayers and augurs read the future from the entrails of animal sacrifices. The mind compares and contrasts; it creates shapes and patterns, then refers back to them.

This is not to say, of course, that there are no genuine external patterns — it is merely to suggest the need for a little caution and circumspection. To see the true signs, to read the genuine portents, to decipher the real clues — these are all immensely helpful and informative things to do. To be deluded by quaint and curious but perfectly natural formations, to follow the scent of a noxiously decaying red herring, or to be hopelessly misled by something which a clever hoaxer has devised — these are all singularly unhelpful and misleading things. They waste a great deal of the researcher's precious time. Sadly, the mystery of Rennes-le-Château is not without its share of these blind alleys and wills-o'-the-wisp.

The balanced and most positive position would seem to be a rational mixture of due caution and confident optimism. It is far more likely that there is some deep and genuine mystery at Rennes-le-Château than that there is not. On the other hand, in the course of the search for that mystery, investigators need to be shrewd and selective in their choice of leads and clues. Nowhere is this caution more necessary than in the pursuit of the real or imagined lines, shapes, patterns and Gestalts which may, or may not, have any bearing on the Rennes mystery.

Barry Bayley, a gifted SF and fantasy writer, with a keen and enquiring mind and an instinct for locating unusual phenomena, drew our attention to some significant statements that J. C. Campbell had made a few years earlier in *Astounding Science Fiction*. Campbell had pointed out that there was something more than a little curious about the number five.

Atoms have atomic weights and atomic numbers ranging from one to more than 240. Although boron, a group IIIa element in the periodic table, has five as its atomic number, its actual atomic weight is 10.811. The atomic number of a chemical element is simply its number in the periodic table. (The basis of this system is that it arranges the elements in an order which depends broadly upon the number of protons in the nucleus, or the number of electrons outside the nucleus.) The atomic weight of an element gives the relative "weight", or preferably mass, of that element. It is reckoned in multiplies of a basic unit of 1.66033×10^{-27}kg, or 1/12 of the mass of an atom of carbon-12. Although boron has the atomic number five, Campbell maintained that no element had five particles in its atomic nucleus. The actual atomic mass of boron is twice as big at 10.811 and the only two elements having an atomic mass anywhere near five are helium at 4.002 602 and lithium at 6.941. So the Campbell-Bayley idea begins to look interesting. Where does it take us next?

Campbell also pointed out in his original article that expert crystallographers maintain that no crystal can have pentagonal symmetry, that topologists can produce any plane or spherical map using only four colours − a fifth is never necessary − and that five soap bubbles cannot meet at a point, whereas four can!

Bayley and Campbell then give us an intriguing pointer to Bode's Law of Planetary Distances. Johann Elert Bode lived from 1747 until 1826, and became Director of the Berlin Observatory in 1786. Although Johann Daniel Titius of Wittenberg actually announced this Law of Planetary Distances in 1766, it was Bode who popularised it. According to Bode's Law, there ought to be a planet between Mars (the fourth out from the sun) and Jupiter (the fifth). There isn't! The space is filled by the asteroid belt, which looks very convincingly like the shattered debris of a planet.

Another point which aroused Campbell's curiosity was that it looked to him as if living matter (active biochemical matter) only seemed able to remain living as long as it was chemically unstable. Like all broad generalisations, it's open to questions and arguments − but it's easy enough to see what Campbell was suggesting: there is, perhaps, a biochemical tendency for unstable fives to become flat fours and stable sixes. He then went on to look at pentagonal symmetry in nature: the starfish, for example. That very basic little creature has amazing powers of recuperation: if it loses a limb, not only does it grow a new one − the severed limb grows a new starfish. Campbell also argued that having four limbs and a head made human beings (and a fair number of other creatures) pentagonal. Certainly a great many of the higher forms of life on land have five-digited limbs. (See Appendix I for a discussion of the "Bearskin Rug" pattern).

Since time immemorial "magicians" have regarded the pentagon and the pentacle as having supernatural powers, but the origin of this belief was possibly mathematical rather than esoteric.

The Pythagoreans were interested in the pentagram because it was a way of expressing the Golden Mean − a ratio between two parts which makes the relationship of the smaller to the larger the same as the relationship between the larger and the whole. The ancient Greeks were fascinated by this ratio and regarded it as the perfect proportion. They found it in the human body and they used it in their art and architecture − including the design of the Parthenon.

The Golden Mean can also be expressed algebraically as:

$$\frac{a}{b} = \frac{b}{a+b} \qquad \text{or} \qquad b^2 = a\,(a+b)$$

This formula uses "a" to represent the smaller part and "b" to represent the larger part of the original line. It is also possible to express the Golden Mean by using a series of arithmetical approximations:-

$$
\begin{aligned}
5/8 &= 0.625\\
8/13 &= 0.615\\
13/21 &= 0.619\\
21/34 &= 0.618\\
34/55 &= 0.618\\
55/89 &= 0.618\\
89/144 &= 0.618
\end{aligned}
$$

Each successive denominator is obtained by adding together the numerator and denominator of the previous fraction. Each denominator in turn becomes the numerator of the next fraction in the series. (The series of denominators thus generated is known as the Fibonacci series after its appearance in a mathematical problem posed by Leonardo Fibonacci in his *Liber Abaci* — a manual of arithmetic and algebra — published in 1202 and revised in 1228.[1]) If the length of the original line is 1, the lengths of the two parts are 0.382 and 0.618.

The conjunctions of Earth and Venus as seen from the sun (i.e. when the two planets are lined up together on the same side of the sun)[2] would

---

[1]For more information on the Fibonacci series and the golden section, see Chapter 13 of *Mathematical Circus* by Martin Gardner (Pelican Books, 1979).

[2]The interval between such conjunctions is approximately 583.9 Earth days (8/5 Earth years, 13/5 Venusian years). Now the axial spin of Venus is not only from east to west (the opposite direction to that of all the other planets), but is extremely slow. An observer on Venus (assuming he could see through the clouds) would find Venusian solar days very long, each lasting some 116.8 Earth days. The Sun would rise in the west and set in the east. Most strange, however, is the fact that the conjunctions referred to above — which our hypothetical observer would see as oppositions between the Earth and the Sun — would occur *exactly* every five Venusian days.
Interactions between a planet or satellite's rotation and its orbit around its parent body are fairly common, and are reminiscent of the "spin-orbit coupling" of the electrons within an atom, invoked by spectroscopists to explain the finer details of atomic spectra. Thus, the rotational period of Mercury is 58.65 Earth days, while its orbital period around the Sun is 87.97 Earth days — the spin period is exactly 2/3 of the orbital period. Closer to home, we find that the spin of our Moon is coupled in 1:1 ratio with its orbit around the Earth, with the effect that the Moon always presents the same face to us.
However, the Venus spin/Earth orbit coupling in the ratio 5:1 discussed above is different — it is the only known example of a coupling between the spin of one planet and the orbit of a *different* planet.
[Footnote by Paul Townsend, M. Sc., based on data from *The Realm of the Terrestrial Planets* by Zdenek Kopal (Institue of Physics Bristol and London, 1979), pages 179-180.]

more or less create a pentagram around the sun if you could join up the points on some imaginary interplanetary draughtsman's board. The complete figure takes eight earthly years (which is equivalent to thirteen Venusian years) to complete. The Golden Mean ratio of 8/13 between the average orbital motions of Earth and Venus is striking and curious, and brings the argument back to the Titius-Bode Law of Planetary Distances.

In its simplest form this Law says that if you write down the number four against each planetary position, add three for Venus, then go on doubling that three for each planet you come to as you travel outwards from the sun, you get a fair approximation of the relative distances from the sun of the planets in our solar system — all except Neptune.

Planet	Predicted Distance (units of 15,000,000 km)		Actual Distance
Mercury	4	= 4	3.86
Venus	4 + 3	= 7	7.21
Earth	4 + 6	= 10	9.97
Mars	4 + 12	= 16	15.19
(Asteroids)	4 + 24	= 28	22 − 35
Jupiter	4 + 48	= 52	51.89
Saturn	4 + 96	= 100	95.13
Uranus	4 + 192	= 196	191.27
Neptune			(299.87)
Pluto	4 + 384	= 388	393.33

Barry Bayley goes on to make a very perceptive and convincing argument for the existence of a pentagram — or at least an essential aspect of a pentagram — in a law governing the relative distances of all the planets, including Neptune which escaped from the original Titius-Bode net! Bayley points out that when any line in a pentagram cuts another, it divides it in the Golden Mean ratio. He also notes that if you join any point of the five-pointed star to its two opposite points it forms an incomplete isosceles triangle. When drawn in to complete the triangle, the third side (the short side, or base) is in the Golden Mean ratio to either of the two longer and equal sides. Bayley points out that the Earth and Venus mark out the corners of just such a triangle with every three successive passes they make of each other. He then makes a breathtaking quantum leap and suggests that the Golden Mean was actually the harmonic rule which governed the formation of the original conglomerations out of a pre-planetary disc of dust, rubble and gas.

Painters — as well as the early astronomers and astrologers — were fascinated by the relationship between the Golden Mean and the pentagram. Their actual technique of construction was quite elegant. First draw a line PQ which is to be the length of one side of the pentagon. From the point Q draw at right angles to PQ a line QR and make it exactly half the length of PQ. Join the point P to the point R. Place the point of the compasses on R and draw an arc with radius RQ so that it intersects the line PR at a point S. Place the point of the compasses on P and draw an arc with radius PS to intersect the line PQ at a point T. This construction has created the Golden Mean along the line PQ: the ratio of TQ (the shorter part) to PT (the longer part) is the same as the ratio of PT to PQ (the original line). The length of PT divided by the length of PQ equals the length of TQ divided by the length of PT, and both calculations produce the answer 0.618.

$$\frac{PT}{PQ} \quad = \quad \frac{TQ}{PT} \quad = \quad 0.618$$

Once this Golden Mean has been obtained it is possible to construct the pentagon PXUVW. Extend the line PQ to the point U so that QU is equal in length to PT. The line PU is now one of the diagonals of the pentagon. Place the point of the compasses on P and draw an arc radius PQ. Repeat with the point on U. The intersection of these arcs is the point X of the pentagon. Join PX and UX and proceed in a similar manner to locate points V and W.

These early painter-geometricians were also intrigued by the infinite reproducibility of the Golden Mean. Marking off the length of the shorter line against the longer line resulted in a new Golden Mean. Adding the length of the longer line to the original whole line also gave a new Golden Mean. To the mysterious Rosicrucian Brotherhood this was clear mathematical confirmation of their esoteric belief that the microcosm and the macrocosm were related: as above, so below – the same rules were valid for specks of dust, human beings, planets, stars and nebulae.

Certainly the idea appealed to Nicolas Poussin, the seventeenth century painter who is deeply and inextricably involved in the Rennes mystery. The closest and most intriguing point of contact between Poussin and Rennes-le-Château is his canvas "The Shepherds of Arcadia". This famous painting shows three shepherds and a shepherdess standing beside a table-tomb situated in a wild and mountainous landscape, very similar to that between Rennes and Arques. The men are examining the inscrutable inscription *Et in Arcadia Ego*; the girl, serene and beautiful, looks down towards it. The whole geometry of the painting is governed by the geometry of the pentagon which extends for a considerable distance out-side the frame and is centred on the head of the shepherdess. In the coded message which allegedly derives from the broken and defaced tombstone of Marie de Nègre and the parchments said to have been found in the Visigothic altar pillar, the first word is "Shepherdess". These parchments and the inscriptions on the gravestones are dealt with in detail in the chapter on codes and ciphers.

Poussin's pentagon and Marie de Nègre's grave-marker both give the same clue, but how does the mysterious shepherdess help the treasure hunter? Is it the direction of her gaze? The way her hands are held? She is depicted midway between the two background mountains: is the treasure buried at some point between them, but on yet another curious line?

Who exactly was Nicolas Poussin and which of his life experiences may have connected him with the Rennes-le-Château mystery?

He lived from 1594 until 1665 and is generally venerated by art critics as the greatest and most characteristic French painter of the seventeenth century. He is acknowledged to be one of the leading exponents of pictorial classicism: not only of his own century, but arguably of all time. He was born near Les Andelys in Normandy, moving to Paris in 1610 and working there until 1624. He was taught by several different Mannerist artists, and spent a great deal of time studying the royal collections of sculpture, engraving and paintings. He met his first significant patron, the Italian poet Marino, at the court of the queen mother, and Marino commissioned Poussin to make a series of drawings for him to illustrate Ovid's *Metamorphoses*.

Poussin went to Rome in 1624 where he met Marcello Sacchetti and Cardinal Barberini. During this period Poussin's style was almost indefinable because he seems to have been experimenting in several different directions at the same time. However, the influence of the Bolognese classical artist, Domenichino, seems to have been decisive. As early as 1629 Poussin painted "The Martyrdom of St. Erasmus" as the altar piece for St. Peter's. In the same year he did at least one version of "The Shepherds of Arcadia" – the one in Chatsworth House in Derbyshire. From then until about 1633 he seems to have selected his ideas from classical mythology. He turned next to Raphael and themes from ancient times, including such Biblical scenes as "The Worship of the Golden Calf", which was probably completed in about 1636. In 1640 he was invited (ordered?) to go to Paris by King Louis XIII and Cardinal Richelieu, but stayed only until 1642. During his time in Paris, however, he formed a valuable friendship with Fréart de Chantelou.

It is interesting that during the 1640s and 1650s both Poussin's religious and secular paintings were very often concerned with difficult emotional and moral decisions, or moments of crisis. He seems to have deliberately selected as his heroes rather austere characters who rejected vice and sensual pleasures in favour of rational and ethical behaviour. His style itself seems to have been intended to emphasise the austerity of these characters. His trees and shrubs are geometrical; and the normal disorder of nature is dragooned into patterns. There is tension and stress in his work, as if he never quite managed to resolve the conflict between austerity and liberality, puritanism and freedom. The human figures from his final period are cold and formal like classical statues, but there is also an undeniable hidden life trying to burst out of their sombre immobility. They may be as motionless as the steel casings of massive dynamos – but the living energy inside them will not and cannot be suppressed forever. To what extent do those curious living-dead figures reveal the conflict inside Poussin himself? What did he know of Rennes-le-Château, its mysteries and secrets, which made the hidden depths of his innermost being try both to freeze and to explode with life simultaneously?

Was it during his formative years in Les Andelys that he acquired a deep knowledge of the two things that recur so regularly in his many canvases: dancing and forests?

Poussin's father was a soldier and peasant farmer: not, perhaps, a man ideally suited to raise a sensitive, artistic and highly intellectual son. Poussin's move to Paris may well have been in the nature of an escape from his father, at least in part.

To return to the detail of "The Shepherds of Arcadia", Poussin had an incredible eye for detail. He watched everyone and everything. He studied the most minute objects to see how they contributed to the patterns and forms of larger ones. He did not look simply at the surface of objects; he examined them and tried to analyse them. Does this attitude of his perhaps account in some measure for the contradiction in those paradoxical later-period figures where the evidence of so much vibrant inner life is in stark contrast to the evidence of so much formal, external, classical stillness?

Poussin had married a Roman girl, and he died in Rome on November 19th, 1665. His mausoleum in the church of St. Lorenze in Lucina, Rome, shows the artist's head and shoulders carved above a bas-relief copy of "The Shepherds of Arcadia". This mausoleum carries the inscription: "François-René de Châteaubriand to Nicolas Poussin for the glory of the arts and to the honour of France."

There is an odd problem concerning the precise current whereabouts of "The Shepherds of Arcadia". Firstly, there might be more than one version extant. In *La Race Fabuleuse,* Gérard de Sède intimates that the vital painting is not on public display. During the 1970s Henri Buthion, who still lives in Saunière's old house, showed us a copy of what he then believed to be this second version which is not on display. On one of our early research visits to the Louvre in 1975 one version was certainly on public display, and we bought some transparencies and postcard–sized colour reproductions of it. We have also taken numerous photographs of it on subsequent occasions. However, as the facsimiles of our letter of inquiry to the Louvre and M. Foucart's reply (included as an appendix) seem to indicate, there may well be some sort of mystery about this alleged second version. It is perfectly possible that those letters can be explained as a simple misunderstanding; it is equally possible, however, that another Poussin canvas of "The Shepherds of Arcadia" is being carefully concealed and protected. If so, by whom? And why?

There are other curious and interesting facts about "The Shepherds of Arcadia". In 1685, twenty years after Poussin's death, the picture was acquired by Louis XIV, who had it placed in his private apartments at Versailles. In Edward Lucie-Smith's *A Concise History of French Painting* (Thames and Hudson, London, 1971), there is a reproduction of a totally different version of Poussin's "The Shepherds of Arcadia". Lucie-Smith says it is the first version and that it was probably painted at the end of the 1620s. In this canvas the shepherdess and two shepherds stand on the left. A third "shepherd" sits at the right. His gaze is directed towards the ground and he is pouring liquid from a container.

It is possible to see hidden Christian symbolism in this version. The woman and two men examining the tomb may be meant to represent Mary Magdalen, St. John and St. Peter at the empty tomb on the first Easter Morning. The seated figure with his back to us at the right of the canvas may symbolise the risen Christ. He wears a crown of leaves; perhaps a hint at the crown of thorns? He is pouring water (or might it even be mystical wine?) over his feet: perhaps a coded reminder that Christ washed the disciples' feet, or even a link with the incident during which Mary Magdalen (or some other penitent sinner) washed his feet with her tears and dried them with her hair. Jesus also told the Samaritan woman at the well that he had "the living water" which gave eternal life. Again there is the symbolic use of water in baptism, and the frequent use of holy water in religious services. Does the vital liquid being poured here represent the work of Christ, the Creator and Sustainer of the world, pouring the Water of Life into the parched, necessitous earth?

In this 1620s version, the standing shepherd nearest to the tomb traces the inscription with his hand. A dark cliff rises behind: does it symbolise the dark and towering mystery of death? The tomb bows out like the side of a violin, or like the profile of the sailing ships and galleons of Poussin's time. With his love of symbolism and his close involvement with detail, Poussin may have had the Ship of Death in mind when he gave the tomb a galleon-like cross section. Does that link up, however tenuously, with the theory M. Fatin raised with us about the whole village ground plan at Rennes possibly representing a funeral ship carrying away the body of some great dead warrior?

A thick tree trunk rises from behind the tomb and reaches the top of the canvas near its centre. A thinner one rises beside it, parallel to it, but closer to the cliff face. The top of the tomb is festooned with shrubs, clinging determinedly to the stone. The shepherd nearest the shepherdess carries a staff held at much the same angle as the one in the better known version. The shepherd who is touching the inscription carries a crook in his left hand.

The original is now part of the Devonshire Collection in Chatsworth House. There are certain important similarities between the two versions as well as significant changes. In both paintings it is the heavily bearded shepherd who carries a crook and touches the inscription. There are three shepherds and a shepherdess in each version. All are barefoot in the Chatsworth version; three wear sandals in the Louvre version, and the shepherdess is far more formal and less attractive in the later design. The most significant differences are the shapes and positions of the tombs in the two pictures. It would be interesting to know whether the tomb in the Chatsworth Poussin resembled the actual tomb of Arques before the work which was reportedly done on it in 1903.

According to the very detailed information in Pierre Jarnac's *Archives du Trésor de Rennes-le-Château*, an American named Louis Bertram Lawrence went to France as a soldier in 1916. He stayed on after the end of World War I, and so might − just conceivably − have known Saunière during the last year or so of the priest's life. Lawrence's widowed mother and grandmother (who was originally Spanish) joined him in France soon afterwards. He ran a small electrical and chemical business at Ille-sur-Tet in the Pyrénées-Orientales, for which − rather curiously in view of Childeric's association with bees − he adopted a bee as a logo.

Another possible connection between Lawrence and the Rennes mystery is his interest in music and his talent as a singer. At 8 p.m. on Saturday, March 15th, 1919, he was a member of the organising committee and one of the soloists at a concert given aboard the S. S. Rotterdam. Is there any possibility that his musical interests also brought him into contact with Emma Calvé, the internationally known opera star and friend of Saunière? Known to Saunière and Calvé or not, Lawrence was certainly in the area, and was linked with the mysterious tomb near Arques − a replica of the one which featured in Poussin's second version of "The Shepherds of

Arcadia".

Lawrence had a business associate, a M. Jean Galibert, who owned a mill at Pontils. In 1903, M. Galibert's grandson arranged with a stonemason named Bourriel from Rennes-les-Bains to work on the tomb of Arques. Some years later the Galibert family left Pontils for Limoux and the tomb of Arques with its small parcel of land passed into Lawrence's hands. He himself died on July 25th, 1954, only one year after the death of Marie Dénarnaud, Saunière's housekeeper and confidante. There is some evidence, however, that the tomb of Arques is centuries older than the work of Bourriel in 1903. It is said that after Fouquet, Louis XIV's Minister of Finance, fell from royal favour and was replaced by Colbert, the latter went to Rennes and dug over many of the most important archaeological sites – including the tomb of Arques.

If a tomb of the same dimensions as the one in the Louvre's public display version existed long before Colbert's supposed treasure hunting expedition, it may reasonably be assumed that it was the model for either of the versions (Chatsworth and Louvre) which Poussin painted. If an ancient tomb did not exist on the site prior to Bourriel's work in 1903 the argument goes the other way: the twentieth century monument was a copy of the tomb in the painting and not vice versa.

Of two things, however, we can be absolutely certain – or at least as absolutely certain as is possible in a world where so-called "absolute certainties" need to be treated with caution in accordance with Heisenberg, Einstein and Schrödinger's ideas!

When we visited the tomb for the first time in the 1970s some previous investigator had broken away a large section of the top and then replaced it. I lifted this piece and held it up while Peter Rice, the expedition's professional photographer, took flash pictures of the tomb's interior. The base was much wider than the top and two decaying coffins lay side by side at the bottom, about four metres down. Those pictures were featured in our first book on the Rennes mystery in 1981 and were reproduced in Pierre Jarnac's *Archives du Trésor de Rennes-le-Château* in 1988.

Poussin was by no means the only painter to be interested in the *Et in Arcadia Ego* theme. There is, for example, a painting by Giovanni Francesco Barbieri (who was nick-named Guercino because of his unfortunate squint) in the National Gallery in Rome. Barbieri's picture shows two shepherds looking at a skull with a hole above the left eye. Guercino lived from 1591 to 1666, which makes him a contemporary of Poussin. Robert Gavelle, the art critic, writing in *Bulletin of Studies of the 17th Century* in 1953 compared Barbieri's work to a late 16th century German engraving carrying the same inscription. This old German engraving shows the King of the New Sion dethroned after having started the Golden Age. This could be a reference to the shadowy and mysterious Priory of Sion. The King of the New Sion could well have been the title of the then master of the Priory. The "Golden Age" may refer obliquely to the artist's secret geometry, what they believed to be the magical Golden Mean.

Poussin by himself is puzzling enough, but the Rennes code adds the name of Teniers, and this is still more difficult to unravel. Two Flemish artists, father and son, bore the name David Teniers; both were contemporaries of Poussin, and both were born at Antwerp. The older was a specialist in religious themes and homely subjects. The younger was very ambitious, and his art was highly commercialized; he specialized in cheerful, vivacious outdoor scenes. The elder's dates were 1582-1649, the younger's 1610-90. Poussin was fifty-seven when the elder Teniers died; the younger Teniers was fifty-six when Poussin died; both Teniers were alive and active as artists while Poussin was painting his various versions of "The Shepherds of Arcadia".

The younger Teniers was made a Master of the Artists' Guild in 1632. In 1637 he married Anne Breughel, ward of the great Paul Rubens and daughter of Jan Breughel the Elder. This marriage boosted Teniers' prestige considerably. In 1651 he became court painter in Brussels and curator to Archduke Leopold-William, moving later to the service of Don Julin of Austria — another member of the Habsburg family. When Anne died, Teniers married the daughter of the Secretary to the Council of Brabant, and, if anything, he became even more ambitious than before. Paintings came off his easel like cars off an assembly line. Students and assistants were used as production resources. Inevitably quality suffered, but there was an insatiable demand for canvases bearing Teniers' signature.

As we discuss in detail in the next chapter entitled Codes, Ciphers and Cryptograms, the parchments which were allegedly found inside the Visigothic altar pillar in Saunière's church say that Poussin and Teniers "guard the key", but which Teniers holds the key referred to in the Rennes code? Was it passed from father to son? If David Teniers the Younger had a link with the Habsburgs, his father certainly had a link with some of the other code words: "St. Anthony no temptation". The elder Teniers was a specialist in religious art and St. Anthony was one of his favourite subjects. Like many robustly masculine but celibate saints, Anthony was frequently alleged to have been troubled by thoughts of attractive young women. In the picturesque language of the time, he was "assailed by demons in the guise of lewd wenches". No doubt this theme gave the painter ample opportunity for nude compositions (which he probably enjoyed!) and it is said that only once did he paint St. Anthony without showing the saint being tempted. This particular Teniers painting was reported to have been at Shugborough Hall, along with some of Poussin's canvases and various copies, but they were not on public display when we made our research visits to Shugborough.

One thing is certain about the younger Teniers: his ambition was not an idle one. He rose to fame and fortune via his connection with the Habsburgs, but there was also in him something of Bérenger Saunière's drive, energy and relentless purpose. Both men achieved what they did by stamina, persistence and application. Both had enough courage and dynamism to turn ambition into fact. Both could also have been members of the enigmatic Priory of Sion — if it really exists — and their ruthless and unflagging determination to succeed may well be characteristic of members of the Priory in general.

From lines and shapes on canvas, and the esoteric geometrical skills of painters such as Poussin and the Teniers, we turn to lines on the surface of the earth itself, and to one great line in particular — the Paris Meridian. In 1666, Louis XIV ordered an observatory to be designed and built at Paris at the edge of the St. Jacques suburb. On June 21st of that same year the meridian line was established by such expert astronomers and topographers as Cassini, Picard, Huygens and Boemer. The architect Claude Perrault, who was also a Doctor of Medicine, was responsible for the observatory. This Claude Perrault was the elder brother by some eight years of the more widely known Charles Perrault, the writer. Charles was a protégé of the redoubtable Jean Baptiste Colbert, the Minister of Finance for Louis XIV; that same Colbert who had engineered the downfall of his predecessor, Nicolas Fouquet (who had also been one of Charles Perrault's friends); that same Colbert who was reported to have hurried to Rennes to dig over many of the significant sites and ruins there after Fouquet's fall from royal favour.

It was the indefatigable Colbert once again who acquired the services of the brilliant Dutch scientist Christiaan Huygens for the king's Paris Meridian Project. This mathematician, astronomer and physicist who lived from 1629 to 1695 made one vital discovery after another: the wave theory of light; improvements to the telescope; new methods of grinding and polishing lenses; improvements to clock mechanisms — especially pendulums; and theorems on centrifugal force in circular motion which were of great assistance to Sir Isaac Newton.

What a line these savants drew for their king! It took in the belfry of the ancient church at Dunkirk dedicated to a Merovingian Bishop, a patron saint of goldsmiths; an area of Pas de Calais known as Arques, and reminiscent of that other Arques in Aude where the tomb replicating the one on the Poussin canvas once stood; and on to Somme with its multitudinous subterranean labyrinths. It sped southwards to Amiens, sprinkled with prehistoric graves: Amiens where Mérovée was crowned; where Jules Verne wrote most of his fantastic stories, and where he lies buried near the Church of St. Mary Magdalen. The meridian goes on to the important church of St. Jacques, once a beacon on the medieval pilgrim's road. Near the Boulevard of St. Sulpice stands the church of St. Roch, the limping saint. Roch's statue stands prominently in Saunière's church at Rennes, first on your right as you enter. It is flanked by the tenth and eleventh Stations of the Cross and faces St. Germaine across the nave.

The Cathedral at Amiens was built by Robert de Luzarches, whose very unusual name is thought by some researchers to provide a clue linking Luz (or ancient Bethel, the site of Jacob's view of the sacred ladder by which angels ascended and descended between Earth and Heaven) with the village of Arques near Rennes, or even with Arcadia. The meridian goes on to Boves, to the south of Amiens where there is a weird nexus with some words carved in the Chapel of the Angels in St. Sulpice in Paris: Psalm 69 verse 15 (in the French Sainte Bible, Louis Segond version of 1910): *Retire-moi de la boue, et que je n'enfonce plus.* The King James, or Authorized, Version, has the English equivalent at verse 14 of the same Psalm: "Deliver me out of the mire and let me not sink". The French word *boue* which is usually translated into English as "mire" or "mud" is very similar indeed to the name Boves, especially when it is remembered that the Latin alphabet did not always distinguish U and V. *Bove*, like *aven*, can indicate either natural or artificial subterranean galleries. There is even a remote, but faintly possible, link with La Fontaine's fable of the frogs who lived in the mud and wanted a king.

Jean de La Fontaine was born in 1621 and died in 1695. He was a great friend and admirer of Fouquet; he knew Colbert and Louis XIV, who both distrusted him; and he also knew Perrault, who had once compared La Fontaine's *Fables* very favourably with Aesop's. La Fontaine's most informed literary critic, Silvestre de Sacy, said of his stories that they appealed in three ways: their vigour and narrative freshness attracted children; their literary perfection and style caught the attention of serious students of literature; and their deep, perceptive meanings made mature and sophisticated readers reflect on their social and philosophical penetration and accuracy.

The meridian moves south from Boves. It passes through Campremy, connected with St. Remy, and the ancient kings of France, who travelled that way to their coronation ceremonies. It moves on to Saint-Denis, where many kings of France lie buried in the basilica: their forebears having been laid to rest in the ancient cemetery of St. Germain des Prés, where St. Sulpice now stands. It was Dagobert I who had the basilica built circa 630. Constantine's famous Labarum — the sacred flag of the Christian Emperors bearing the words *In hoc signo vinces* — was also placed there.

The meridian reaches Paris itself where it passes through the Great Synagogue with its seven branched chandelier; the National Library with its seven million volumes — the greatest collection in the world — and its priceless souvenirs of Dagobert, Childeric and Clovis. The meridian passes through the royal palace, and skirts the church of St. Roch very closely. Next the line passes through the Louvre with its recently constructed, strange pyramid, said to contain exactly 666 panes of glass — a darkly symbolic number in eschatology. The meridian sweeps us on to St. Sulpice, where we can pause to admire Delacroix's famous frescos. Sulpice himself, known originally by his Romanised name, Sulpicius, died at Bourges in the year 647 on January 17th, and this duly became his feast day. Although many of the relics vanished during the French Revolution, the church at Villefranche de Conflent in the Pyrénées-Orientales (and on the meridian!) treasures what it claims to be — and what in all probability is — the skull of Saint Sulpice.

South of Paris the meridian continues to run through many more fascinating old towns and villages: Fleury-Merogis, Vert-le-Petit, Saint-Benoit-sur-Loire, Cerdon, Bourges and Lussat. Here, with Lussat as its centre, it is possible to draw a huge circle whose circumference passes through: Reims, Varennes, Toul and Sion in the northeast; another Sion just north of Mont Blanc almost due east of Lussat; Rennes-le-Château and Montségur in the south; St Nazaire, Sion les Mines, Redon and Rennes in the northwest; and Rouen on a bearing of 345 degrees just before the circle is completed in the north.

As the meridian moves farther south it passes through Conques, a stopping place on the route to Santiago de la Compostela. The Benedictine Abbey here in Conques was founded in the eighth century and shelters the relics of St. Foy. There is another very peculiar relic here, sometimes referred to as the "A of Charlemagne". It seems to be a symbol with fourteen points marked on its circle, and is believed by some researchers to be connected with the Gregorian calendar, the pyramid and the control of what some researchers refer to as cosmo-telluric forces. The intersecting A and V of this unusual object are reminiscent of the masonic square and compasses, and might also be intended to represent "As above, so below" — the central concept of Hermeticism.

David Wood's ideas in *GenIsis* are, to say the least, distasteful, sensational, highly controversial and totally opposed to what we ourselves would seek to defend as the simple, rational, central and inviolable facts at the heart of traditional Christian faith, but — as Henry Lincoln says in his introduction to Wood's book — the Rennes geometry which Wood claims to have discovered is truly amazing. With commendable frankness, honesty and common sense, Lincoln makes the further point that Wood's geometry can be checked: it is there, or it isn't. A map, a pair of compasses, a ruler and a protractor are easy enough for any interested investigator to use. But let us always beware of falling into the trap which engulfed an obsessively enthusiastic pyramidologist a few years ago. Having spent half a lifetime working on his theories he finally reached the Great Pyramid and began taking measurements "on the ground". He was caught by a custodian in the act of removing a piece of ancient stone because it didn't fit in with his theories!

Wood's geometry suggests that there may be some huge "structure" — possibly a "temple" — laid out over some forty square miles of territory incorporating Rennes-le-Château, Rennes-les-Bains, Cassaignes and Coustaussa. But as we said at the start of this chapter, the human mind has a remarkable, God-given capacity for making order out of chaos, and for devising form and meaning from haphazard and random shapelessness: perhaps this is one aspect of humanity being "made in God's image". Needless to say, Louis XIV's intriguing Paris meridian features prominently in Wood's vast geometric design. It is certainly possible that Wood (and other researchers including Lincoln himself) have actually traced some real and objective "design" or "structure" over the terrain around Rennes-le-Château, and that what they may have found is interesting and of great age. There is, however, little or no justification for the agglomeration of bizarre Freudian nightmares, grotesque pagan sexual myths and darker Jungian archetypes which Wood has superimposed on whatever geometrical patterns may (or may not!) subsist in the Languedoc landscape.

There are other strange places on the Paris meridian which also merit closer attention: there is Mazamet, for example, originally the ancient domain of the noble House of Hautpoul, founded by Ataulphe, a Visigothic King who was an ally of Alaric's at the sack of Rome in 410, and was known to his contemporaries as "The King of the Black Mountain". His descendants, along with the de Fleury family and the de Voisin family were the dominant people in and around Rennes for many centuries. In 1644 (during the period of Louis XIV, Poussin, Teniers, Fouquet, Colbert, et al.!) François Pierre d'Hautpoul deposited his will and some important old papers about the family's origins with a lawyer in Espéraza. As far as can be ascertained these papers all disappeared mysteriously until 1780 when they reappeared in the keeping of another lawyer who stubbornly refused to reveal their contents. Tough, autocratic and resourceful Marie de Nègre finally retrieved them and entrusted them to the safe custody of her chaplain, Abbé Antoine Bigou, Priest of Rennes-le-Château. Marie died there in her castle on the highly significant 17th January, 1781 (St.

Sulpice's Day and the day of St.Roseline — Roux sillon, etc). Abbé Bigou — as we shall discuss in detail in the next chapter — carved her enigmatic tombstone very carefully indeed — and a century or so later Bérenger Saunière took equal care to obliterate it! So much for Mazamet: the Paris meridian rolls on.

It cuts through Salsigne with its important gold mines and runs on to Arques where a "Mont St. Michel" (usually a clear indication that an old pagan shrine has been Christianised) rises to 666 metres above sea-level and is said to be exactly 666 kilometres from Paris. Arques also embraces the site of the notorious Poussin-Lawrence tomb. From Arques the meridian speeds on to Rennes-les-Bains, where Boudet wrote his Lewis Carroll style *La Vraie Langue Celtique*: they were contemporaries as well and a whole new volume could probably be written comparing Carroll's riddles with Boudet's. It is purely speculative to ask whether those two ever met or corresponded. Carroll too was a clergyman, though only a deacon, not a fully ordained priest.

At Rennes-les-Bains there stands a mysterious Black Stone: some researchers have even compared it to the Black Stone of Mecca, Al Khema, from which the word "alchemy" is derived. There are also said to be possible links between Rennes-les-Bains and St. Roch.

The meridian leads us next to Bugarach, where the Pic de Bugarach may well have been an ancient volcano, and was the legendary crossroads of the four cardinal winds. Some witnesses claim to have seen strange lights on its summit, and another legend maintains that the Pic de Bugarach marches steadily northwards at the rate of a score or so centimetres each year. Latitude 42 degrees 53 minutes north intersects the Paris meridian at Bugarach and then leads away into Asia where — by an astounding coincidence — it also cuts right through the Bagrach Kol in Sinkiang, on the eastern shore of the lake near the towns of Yenki and Kurla. Etymologically the name may derive from Hebrew meaning a "sad", "devastated" or even "accursed" place. The Valley of Baca is the valley of weeping, and Bakbuk has the sense of being emptied or devastated. An alternative derivation would be from the Bulgars or Bogomils, closely associated with the Cathar heresy.

Villefranche-de-Conflent also lies on the Paris meridian. As we mentioned earlier, it is reputed to house the skull of St. Sulpice in its eleventh century church. As you leave Villefranche heading south along the Paris meridian towards Vernet-les-Bains you encounter the Grottoes of the Canalettes and the domain of the Fuilla family, who also own the castle of Valhala. Etymologically this connects with Norse mythology and the home of the Viking gods. Not far away is the village of Thorrent (Thor?) and another — right on the meridian — called Sahorre. Could this possibly connect with Saohrimir, the wild boar associated with the Valkyries in Norse legends? The last village before the Paris meridian crosses the Spanish frontier is Py (π) — and the imagination takes off again in the direction of Greek mathematicians and the relationship between the circumference of a circle and its diameter!

In *The Sign of the Dove* by the highly sensitive and mystically orientated Elizabeth van Buren (Neville Spearman, Suffolk, UK, 1983) chapter twelve goes into great depth about the pentacle in general and the pentacle over

Coumesourde near Rennes-le-Château in particular. In *Refuge of the Apocalypse* (C.W.Daniel, Saffron Walden, UK, 1986) Elizabeth van Buren demonstrates how she has identified an entire zodiac on the ground in the Rennes area, stretching from between Antugnac and Luc-sur-Aude in the northwest down to Sougraigne in the southeast.

The village of Rennes itself, of course, contains its share of mysterious lines, shrines and signs. One local researcher showed us the site of the ancient church of St.Peter, not far from Saunière's church of St.Mary Magdalen. This itself is the holy of holies as far as lines, signs, codes and ciphers are concerned. Stanley James's *The Treasure Maps of Rennes-le-Château* (Seven Lights Publishing, Bow, London, UK, 1984) is by far the most ingenious and complex study of Saunière's church and its contents which has yet been assembled. In every stained glass window, every mural, every statue and every station of the cross which Saunière erected after finding whatever the source of his wealth was, James has seen clue after clue, and one paronomasian verbal association after another. It is a case of A leads to B which sounds like C which reminds us of D which points to E . . . and so on, until the church which Saunière refurbished begins to sound like The House that Jack Built!

The inscriptions over the door include *Terribilis est locus iste* ("This place is terrible"). Is it merely an appropriate part of the dedicatory anthem, or is there some deeper reason behind Saunière's choice of wording here? At the apex of the triangle above the door is carved *in hoc signo vinces* ("In this sign [i.e. the cross] you shall conquer"). Absolutely true, of course, but did Saunière have some other reason for choosing to inscribe it there? Are we being told to seek for hidden signs and secret symbols as we look around this church?

First on your left as you enter the building is the curious group — arranged rather like a North American Indian totem pole — comprising: a demon (arguably Asmodeus, a traditional treasure guardian in mythology); a bowl of water; fire-lizards or salamanders; and — right at the top — four angels. Each of the angels is in the process of making one part of the sign of the cross and the inscription may be taken to mean "By this sign you shall conquer him." The pronoun at the end presumably refers to the vanquished demon above whom the triumphant angels stand.

The stations of the cross begin beside the pulpit at the eastern end of the nave and run anti-clockwise along the north wall, so that station fourteen is on the south wall opposite the pulpit, close to the statue of St. Anthony of Padua and the stained glass window depicting the mission of the apostles. This arrangement means that as we enter the church and turn left past the group of statuary surmounted by the victorious angels, we next encounter stations nine and eight respectively.

In the centre of the west wall stands the confessional with the painting called "Terrain Fleury" above it. This is a large and striking mural, ostensibly showing our Lord preaching on a flower covered hill. But "Fleury" is a name to reckon with in the vicinity of Rennes-le-Château.

On the far left of the painting stands a man holding a staff. His thumb divides it: is that division intended to be the Golden Mean yet again? Is he the shepherd from the Poussin painting? He bears some resemblance to the shepherd on the far left of the Louvre version, and he does not look unlike the leftmost of the three male figures in the Chatsworth version, but in that version it is the lovely young shepherdess who is on the extreme left of the composition. In the mural above Saunière's confessional the man with the staff holds up his left arm towards Christ, and Christ's right hand is directed towards him.

There are roses (Rosicrucian symbols?) among the flowers below the Lord's feet, and the lowest of these — an exquisitely painted pink one — almost touches the top of the enigmatic bag with a hole in it that lies at the foot of the hill. Some researchers have described this as a money bag: its draw-string and general shape give it the overall appearance of the kind of purse popularly associated with rich merchants in the Middle Ages. It is the kind of money bag that Errol Flynn used to take from wealthy travellers in the Hollywood Robin Hood films. It is reminiscent of the pantomime moneybags which the tax collectors inevitably use in the scenes where they exploit the unhappy peasants in Act I. But it may not be one. Examine it closely. That is not money which peeps through the hole. Gold nuggets perhaps? Uncut precious stones? Even fragments of the bones of a saint? Just some of the mysterious "rocks" which Saunière ostensibly collected for his grotto when he went with Marie on those long walks in the Rennes countryside? The bag with the hole undoubtedly has a deep significance, but regarding it merely as a moneybag may be too simplistic.

As we move north along this west wall of the church we pass stations seven and six; we turn right so that we are walking along the north wall and we find ourselves studying the statue of our Lord with St. John the Baptist. It is possible to suggest from the angle of Christ's head that he is studying the chequered floor of the church: is that floor meant to represent a cosmic chessboard over whose squares the battle between Good and Evil is being constantly waged? Does the ugly and sinister figure of Asmodeus represent Christ's opponent in this great game where the stakes are nothing less than the eternal future of the human race? Other strong, clear eyes are also studying the squares — the eyes of John the Baptist: the powerful new Elijah, the challenger of a lecherous puppet king, the fearless herald of the Messiah. The banner he holds aloft says simply: *Ecce agnus dei* — Behold the Lamb of God. Is the treasure hunter being advised to look closely at the statue of Christ, or is John's text to be read at face value in its normal scriptural sense?

Between stations five and four stands the statue of St. Germaine. Her apron is filled with flowers — many of which are roses (Rosicrucianism again?) — and there are more flowers and two lambs at her feet.

We proceed eastwards to the third and second station with the statue of St. Anthony the Hermit between them. This famous Egyptian hermit saint lived from 251 to 356. From 286 until 306 he lived entirely alone in an abandoned fortress in Pispir, where according to tradition he underwent that series of temptations with which many hermit-saints are traditionally associated, and which Teniers frequently recaptured on his canvases. Does St. Anthony's Egyptian background provide a vital clue linking Saunière's church at Rennes-le-Château with Hermes Trismegistus and the mysteries of ancient Egypt? St. Anthony's Feast Day — and the day of his death — is the highly significant January 17th; and it is said by some researchers that a ray of sunlight enters the church through the stained glass window in the opposite wall and falls directly on the saint's statue on that day each year.

Immediately beside the pulpit is the first station of the cross and the pulpit itself is profusely decorated with statues of the four evangelists: Matthew, Mark, Luke and John, complete with their appropriate sacred emblems.

In the village today there still lives at least one direct descendant of the man concerned, who relates a fascinating story of a carved supporting pillar — part of the pulpit in Saunière's time. This decorated wooden structure contained a secret compartment, and Saunière's old bellringer apparently found it by accident one day when he discovered that the pillar had tumbled over. As he righted it he found a small glass bottle, or vial, inside the hiding place. Dutifully, the old man took his discovery to show the priest. Expressing little apparent interest in the mysterious vial, or the slip of parchment rolled up inside it, Saunière dismissed it in the bellringer's presence as merely a holy relic of some sort; but he told the bellringer not to mention it. We shall see in a later chapter that, according to one version of Saunière's life history, this scrap of parchment was the vital clue which enabled the priest to find the entrance to a Merovingian mausoleum below the church of St. Mary Magdalen.

As we approach the eastern end of the church and enter the sanctuary area around the altar itself, we see the first of the stained glass windows: Mary and Martha at Bethany. The central window behind the altar shows Mary Magdalen's meeting with the risen Christ on the first Easter Morning; and the southern window depicts the resurrection of Lazarus.

Some researchers have observed a curious optical phenomenon connected with these windows. In winter, at midday, when the sun shines through the stained glass, there is said to be an optical effect which has been described as "blue apples". As the sunlight moves on, the "apples" appear to ripen although some remain blue.

As we shall explore in more depth in the next chapter, which deals with codes and ciphers, one suggested decipherment of the mysterious parchments which Saunière was said to have found in a hollow, Visigothic altar pillar ended with the words "blue apples". The words could conceivably relate to these alleged effects of low winter sunlight on stained glass, but there are other alternatives which are well worth exploring.

To the north of the altar is a statue of St. Joseph, the carpenter of Nazareth and husband of the Virgin Mary. He is holding the infant Christ in his arms.

To the south of the altar the Virgin Mary also holds her divine son. These statues are perfectly understandable separately: both Mary and Joseph are simply showing their devotion to the infant Christ. Unfortunately, various weird and ridiculous legends about Christ having a twin brother have been fuelled by the statuary where Mary and Joseph are each depicted holding the infant Christ.

The stained glass window in the sacristy shows our Lord on the cross.

Moving westwards along the south side of the church takes us past stations fourteen and thirteen and on to the very striking statue of St. Mary Magdalen. She holds a staff with a cross head in her right hand and the alabaster jar of precious ointment in her left. This re-opens the vexed question as to whether Mary Magdalen, Mary of Bethany and the penitent woman with the expensive vase of perfume were all one and the same person — and even whether she might also have been the same woman who was on the brink of being stoned for adultery when Christ saved her: "Let him who is without sin among you, cast the first stone at her."

There is one further very obscure possibility connected with this statue and the manuscript and tombstone codes. It is almost certain that the Poussin referred to in the codes is Nicolas Poussin, the painter. However, *poule, pousse,* or *poussin* can be slang, dialect or argot for prostitute. If that is so then it might just conceivably be a reference to St. Mary Magdalen's traditional former life style before her conversion. So when the coded message says "Poussin holds the key . . . " are we meant to look literally at what the statue of St. Mary Magdalen (the former *poussin?*) is holding in her hands? Is it something to do with an alabaster vase of precious ointment, or is it the cross-headed staff . . . like the one St. John the Baptist holds . . . or like the one in the cave in the painting of St. Mary Magdalen below the altar . . . which Saunière is said to have painted himself? Or could it be a verbal clue indicating an anagram of "Poussin" and "Teniers"?

Between stations eleven and ten is the statue of the lame St. Roch, who was said in some legends to have had a red birthmark on his chest in the shape of a cross — reminiscent, perhaps, of the birthmarks traditionally associated with the mysterious kings of the Merovingian dynasty.

Several of the stations of the cross have their subtle and curious details. The slave boy who holds the bowl in which Pilate washes his hands in station one is black; and what is the tower we can see in the distance through the archway beyond the Roman soldier?

Why is a trumpet being sounded in station three? What is the precise meaning of the three great silver discs on what appears to be a Roman standard behind the cross in station four?

The towers and walls appear again in stations seven and eight, and in the latter a child in its mother's arms is clutching what some researchers have said is a Scottish highland tartan — but it does not pertain to any clan that we can trace.

The unusual feature in station ten is that the faces on the dice are actually visible: and they show the numbers three, four and five. Now a three-four-five triangle is a right-angled triangle — is that significant in the light of Poussin's geometry in the "Shepherds of Arcadia?"

In station twelve the sorrowing woman who kneels at the foot of the cross is almost certainly intended to represent St. Mary Magdalen. Her face is very similar indeed to the face of St. Mary Magdalen in the cave with the skull and cross-headed staff which Saunière is said to have painted on the panel below the altar.

These are only a few of the intriguing lines, signs and shrines leading to Rennes-le-Château, or to be found in or near the village itself. Some are undoubtedly very meaningful; others have only peripheral significance; a few may be no more than coincidence – but all are worth pondering, just in case.

We turn next to a detailed examination of the codes and ciphers on the ancient tombstones and parchments.

CHAPTER SIX

CODES, CIPHERS AND CRYPTOGRAMS

Ars est celare artem.

Marie de Nègre's Tombstone and the Rennes Coded Manuscripts

In the churchyard at Rennes-le-Château lies a broken defaced tombstone: the stone is rectangular with a pointed top. Local tradition says that Saunière himself went to the trouble of erasing the inscription because it held a vital coded message — the key, or one of the keys, to the treasure. Unfortunately for Saunière, the stone had been copied by an antiquarian before the priest found and defaced it. Here, with its odd imperfections, is the inscription:

CT GIT NOBLe M	(a)
ARIE DE NEGRe	(b)
DARLES DAME	(c)
DHAUPOUL De	(d)
BLANCHEFORT	(e)
AGEE DE SOIX	(f)
ANTE SEpT ANS	(g)
DECEDEE LE	(h)
XVII JANVIER	(i)
MDCOLXXXI	(j)
REQUIESCAT IN	(k)
PACE	(l)
(P.S.) PRAE-CUM	(m)

There are 128 letters in the inscription, and this, together with their abnormal arrangement, may be a clue to the decipherment. There are eight odd or misplaced letters. The I of "CI" in line (a) has been carved as a T. The final e of "NOBLe" in the same line is lower case. The M of "MARIE" has been left stranded on the end of the line. In line (b), the final e of "NEGRe" is the wrong size and the wrong fount. The first word in line three should, perhaps, be "DABLES" with a B not an R. The final e in line (d) is the wrong size and fount. The p of "SEpT" in line (g) is too small and has been carved low. The second C (Roman for 100) in the date in line (j) has been carved as an O. The incorrect capitals are, therefore, T M R and O; the misplaced small letters are e e e and p. These eight letters can be rearranged into *MORT épée* or "DEATH sword". They can also be subjected to two minor changes and used to produce the word *emprunté*, which means "false", "assumed" or "borrowed".

Is the inscription, therefore, false? Has the gravestone been "borrowed" for the purpose of transmitting a coded message? To arrive at *emprunté*, we turn one of the lower case e's on its side and use it as an n. The wrong fount e's as they appeared on the stone were similar to n's if turned sideways. The misplaced O in the date has to become a U, but if we go back to the original Roman C and turn it sideways like the lower-case wrong fount e which became an n, the problem of finding the U is not insoluble. The danger here is of running into the "enthusiasm trap" as did the dedicated pyramidologist whom we mentioned in the previous chapter! There is substantial evidence that Saunière, and perhaps Bigou, too, had an irreverent sense of humour. The letters can also be arranged to form *emportée* meaning "she has been carted away"! Perhaps Bigou bore a grudge against Marie de Nègre.

It seems more likely that *MORT épée* is the clue we want. There are eight letters, four of each kind. There are eight squares per line in a chess board, and a chess board – or rather two chess boards – will feature in the later stages of the decipherment. It now becomes necessary to have some preliminary involvement with the longer of the two strange coded manuscripts which were said to have been found in, or near, the Visigothic altar pillar in Saunière's time. They will be dealt with in greater detail later in this chapter. At this juncture it is sufficient to say that this manuscript contained 140 unnecessary extra letters. Much time and effort have been expended on trying to make sense of the stone's inscription, and there is still considerable controversy over the clear text which finally seems to emerge.

In essence, students of the Rennes-le-Château mystery are broadly agreed that the vital decoding processes include the key *MORT épée* to decipher the message, followed by a knight's tour of two chess boards. A final step which readers can easily carry out for themselves is an anagrammatic check on the 128 letters on the stone and the 128 letters of the clear message.

One important point must be borne in mind through the following discussion: the message which has been encoded in the tombstone inscription is in French, and the encryption procedure has used the French alphabet. This contains twenty-five letters: the letter W is not used in French and is omitted from the alphabet. With the exception of W, the French alphabet is the same as our own.

The decipherment procedure makes use of the position values of the letters in the French alphabet, counting A as 1, B as 2, and so on to Z which becomes 25:

A	1	F	6	K	11	P	16	U	21
B	2	G	7	L	12	Q	17	V	22
C	3	H	8	M	13	R	18	X	23
D	4	I	9	N	14	S	19	Y	24
E	5	J	10	O	15	T	20	Z	25

For example, suppose that the key word is SAUNIERE and that the cipher reads:

AQIEFMLNAZVPEILN

Copy the key word as often as necessary until every letter of the cipher is covered by a letter of the repeated key word.

Cipher: A Q I E F M L N A Z V P E I L N . . .
Key Word: S A U N I E R E S A U N I E R E . . .

To begin deciphering the message, find the position values of the letters A (the letter from the encoded message) and S (the first letter from the keyword). These are 1 and 19 respectively. Their sum, 20, is the position value of the letter T, which becomes the first letter of the plaintext. The second enciphered letter is Q (17), the key letter is A (1), giving 18 (R) as the second plaintext letter.

In the third case, the position values are 9 (I) and 21 (U) which sum to 30. Since this runs off the end of the alphabet at 25, we begin again at A (26) and count round to E (30). Alternatively, 25 may be subtracted from the sum to give 5 (E).

Proceeding thus to the end gives the decoded message *Trésor est à Rennes* . . .

Cipher: A Q I E F M L N A Z V P E I L N ·. . .
Key Word: S A U N I E R E S A U N I E R E . . .
Clear: T R E S O R E S T A R E N N E S . . .

The longer of the two coded manuscripts said to have been found in the Visigothic altar pillar in Saunière's time contains 140 superfluous letters. The twelve central letters are raised: so the cryptographer rejects them. This leaves 128 to work on: exactly the same number as were carved on to the tombstone of Marie de Nègre: presumably by Abbé Bigou circa 1781. One school of thought approaches the problem by taking these letters and using them in conjunction with the inscription from the tombstone. Another approach concentrates on the inscription alone. In either case, it is considered important to lay out the letters on two chess boards and make a knight's tour of both.

The 128 letters in question run as follows:

VCPSJQROVYMYYDLTPEFRBOXTODJLBKNJFQUEP
AJYNPPBFEIELRGHIIRYBTTCVTGDLUCCVMTEJHP
NPGSVQJHGMLFTSVJLZQMTOXANPEMUPHKORPK
HVJCMCATLVQXGGNDT

The complication here is that two key words are used. The first is *MORT épée*, which has to be written sixteen times below the letters. The second keyword is the whole of the inscription from the gravestone of Marie de Nègre including the "(P. S.)" and "prae cum". To complicate matters still further, this keyword has to be used backwards. We start in the bottom right-hand corner and work from right to left and from the lowest line upwards. The full set up is:

Cipher:	V C P S J Q R O V Y M Y Y D L T . . . T L V Q X G G N D T
Keyword 1:	M O R T E P E E M O R T E P E E . . . E E M O R T E P E E
Keyword 2:	M U C E A R P S P E C A P N I T . . . E L B O N T I G T C
Stage 1:	X N L S P A N N A S I T T I A T . . . E D L V E V U L D C

To decode the message, each letter of the cipher must have the position values of the corresponding letters in both keywords added to its own position value. Thus the first letter is V (22) + M (13) + M (13) = 48 (X second time round), the second letter is C (3) + O (15) + U (21) = 39 (N second time round). Note that it is now possible to complete *two* passes through the alphabet: this happens on the sixth letter, which is Q (17) + P (16) + R (18) = 51 (A *third* time round).

Proceeding right through the message gives the following:

X N L S P A N N A S I T T I A T E X R R P B T E U C A E E N I R X T G E E N
D E L O R S I A A O E L E F S D Q R P E D C U P G X A I E M U I D O C E J
D N M E G M C O C E E P D S H R X A I A D H A T M O A E S E B I C E L E
R N E E A I E E D L V E V U L D C

This text is in fact a perfect anagram of the letters on the tombstone, but it is unreadable because the letters are not in the correct sequence. We now introduce the knight's tour.

In chess, the knight moves one square laterally followed by one square diagonally. An alternative way of considering his move is to say that he moves two squares laterally followed by one square at right angles to his original direction. During the game a knight can pass over any other piece in his path, provided that his landing square is either empty or occupied by an opposing piece which he then takes.

There are many ways of working out the knight's tour — a kind of chess problem in which the object is to cover every square on the board using the legal moves of a knight and visiting each square once only.

Modern chess notation is algebraic. The co-ordinates for each square are built up from the lower case letters a — h and the Arabic numerals 1 — 8. Each player should have a white square at the right-hand corner of his back rank. A line of squares running directly from player to player is known as a file, and these files are given the letters a — h, starting with a on the left of the player with the white pieces. The ranks are numbered from the white player's back row (1) to the black player's back row (8).

The solution shown on the next page begins on the white king's knight's starting square, g1. The rest of the moves are:

        2 – e2;   3 – c1;   4 – a2;   5 – b4;   6 – d3;   7 – c5;   8 – a6;
 9 – b8; 10 – d7; 11 – f8; 12 – h7; 13 – g5; 14 – e6; 15 – g7; 16 – h5;
17 – f6; 18 – e8; 19 – c7; 20 – a8; 21 – b6; 22 – d5; 23 – c3; 24 – a4;
25 – b2; 26 – d1; 27 – f2; 28 – h1; 29 – g3; 30 – e4; 31 – d6; 32 – b5;
33 – a7; 34 – c8; 35 – e7; 36 – g8; 37 – h6; 38 – f5; 39 – e3; 40 – g4;
41 – h2; 42 – f1; 43 – d2; 44 – b1; 45 – a3; 46 – c4; 47 – e5; 48 – g6;
49 – h8; 50 – f7; 51 – d8; 52 – b7; 53 – a5; 54 – c6; 55 – d4; 56 – b3;
57 – a1; 58 – c2; 59 – e1; 60 – f3; 61 – h4; 62 – g2; 63 – f4; 64 – h3;

In the grid below, the starting square (g1) is numbered "1", the square reached by the first move (e2) is numbered "2", and so on until square 64 (h3). Note that a single valid knight's move links square 64 back to square 1 - this tour is described as "circular" or "re-entrant".

8	20	9	34	51	18	11	36	49
7	33	52	19	10	35	50	15	12
6	8	21	54	31	14	17	48	37
5	53	32	7	22	47	38	13	16
4	24	5	46	55	30	63	40	61
3	45	56	23	6	39	60	29	64
2	4	25	58	43	2	27	62	41
1	57	44	3	26	59	42	1	28
	a	b	c	d	e	f	g	h

The above is one example of a knight's tour. There are many millions of other possible solutions to this problem, some of which form magic squares when written out as shown above. To complete the decipherment of the message we begin by writing out the decoded text on two chessboards, filling up the left board then the right:

8	X	N	L	S	P	A	N	N
7	A	S	I	T	T	I	A	T
6	E	X	R	R	P	B	T	E
5	U	C	A	E	E	N	I	R
4	X	T	G	E	E	N	D	E
3	L	O	R	S	I	A	A	O
2	E	L	E	F	S	D	Q	R
1	P	E	D	C	U	P	G	X
	a	b	c	d	e	f	g	h

8	A	I	E	M	U	I	D	O
7	C	E	J	D	N	M	E	G
6	M	C	O	C	E	E	P	D
5	S	H	R	X	A	I	A	D
4	H	A	T	M	O	A	E	S
3	E	B	I	C	E	L	E	R
2	N	E	E	A	I	E	E	D
1	L	V	E	V	U	L	D	C
	a	b	c	d	e	f	g	h

On two further chessboards we fill in the knight's tour solutions. The solutions shown below are mirror images of each other. The decipherment is obtained by laying out the letters in the order in which the knights' tours proceed.

8	60	15	46	29	62	17	44	31
7	47	28	61	16	45	30	63	18
6	16	59	6	3	8	1	32	43
5	27	48	9	36	5	34	19	64
4	58	13	4	7	2	21	42	33
3	49	26	37	10	35	40	53	20
2	12	57	24	51	38	55	22	41
1	25	50	11	56	23	52	39	54
	a	b	c	d	e	f	g	h

8	25	50	11	56	23	52	39	54
7	12	57	24	51	38	55	22	41
6	49	26	37	10	35	40	53	20
5	58	13	4	7	2	21	42	33
4	27	48	9	36	5	34	19	64
3	16	59	6	3	8	1	32	43
2	47	28	61	16	45	30	63	18
1	60	15	46	29	62	17	44	31
	a	b	c	d	e	f	g	h

We begin with the left-hand board, and find the first move of the knight's tour - square f6. In square f6 of the letter grid we find the letter B, which becomes the first letter of the decode. Knight's move 2 is square e4; letter grid square e4 contains E. We continue through all 64 squares of the left-hand board, taking the letters in the order determined by the knight's moves. Having exhausted the left-hand board, we proceed to the right-hand board and continue in the same way.

The final message reads:

BERGERE PAS DE TENTATION QUE POUSSIN TENIERS GARDENT LA CLEF PAX DCLXXXI PAR LA CROIX ET CE CHEVAL DE DIEU J'ACHEVE CE DAEMON DE GARDIEN A MIDI POMMES BLEUES

The literal translation is:

SHEPHERDESS NO TEMPTATION TO WHICH POUSSIN AND TENIERS KEEP THE KEY PEACE 681 WITH THE CROSS AND THIS HORSE OF GOD I REACH THIS DEMON GUARDIAN AT MIDDAY BLUE APPLES

Bremna Agostini, whose knowledge of idiomatic early languages is considerable, has suggested some quite startling alternatives. Instead of SHEPHERDESS WITHOUT TEMPTATION Bremna has suggested THE DOG WITHOUT FORM OR SUBSTANCE . . . and thinks that it might mean Cerberus guarding the passage of the Styx. *MIDI*, she says, can mean mid-day or The Midi, the region of France around Rennes-le-Château. *ACHEVE* could also mean DESTROY or KILL. *BERGERE* can mean an easychair, perhaps even a throne? Even more curious is her suggestion that in archaic French, *CLEF* or *CLE* could mean crown.

CHEVAL can at a push mean SUPPORT, in the sense that a clothes "horse" supports clothes. The French verb *chevaler* means to "prop", or "shore up". *GARDIEN* can also mean keeper, door-keeper, trustee, warden, or even the Superior of a Franciscan Religious House! *Gardien(ne)*, used adjectivally, can mean tutelary as well as guardian, with perhaps an edge of tuition along with the implied guarding, or protecting. Rennes-le-Château has an official *gardien*, as have similar French villages of comparable size. Is there anything in the code relating to the work of such an official? *POMMES* has a far wider range of meaning than simply "apples". It can be a knob or ball, the head of a walking cane, etc. It is possible that *POMMES BLEUES* refers to the huge grapes in another of Poussin's paintings, with a mountain background very similar to that near Rennes-le-Château.

The mists begin to clear when the shepherdess of the coded message is linked with Nicolas Poussin, the painter. When Eugenio d'Ors wrote about this enigmatic artist he said, "There always have been and always will be certain truths, aristocratic truths, which it is a privilege to know." This theme — that Poussin was one who knew strange secrets — is amplified in a mysterious letter written to Nicolas Fouquet, France's very wealthy and powerful Minister of Finance during the reign of Louis XIV. Fouquet's younger brother had been entrusted with a secret mission to Rome in the spring of 1656. Here he delivered a message to Poussin, and on April 17th wrote the following report to his elder brother:

> "I have given to Monsieur Poussin the letter that you were kind enough to write to him; he displayed overwhelming joy on receiving it. You wouldn't believe, sir, the trouble that he takes to be of service to you, or the affection with which he goes about this, or the talent and integrity that he displays at all times.
>
> He and I have planned certain things of which in a little while I shall be able to inform you fully; things which will give you, through M. Poussin, advantages which kings would have great difficulty in obtaining from him and which, according to what he says, no one in the world will ever retrieve in the centuries to come; and, furthermore, it would be achieved without much expense and could even turn to profit, and they are matters so difficult to inquire into that nothing on earth at the present time could bring a greater fortune nor perhaps ever its equal."

What did young Fouquet mean by that letter? What strange secrets had Poussin revealed to him — if, in fact, he had actually got that far and was not merely holding out the promise of some great revelations to come. The decipherment of the parchment is certainly "very difficult to enquire into" if that's what Poussin was getting at, but, having been deciphered what does it tell us? Poussin may well have known the deep meanings behind its enigmatic phrases — if there really are any. One of the disconcerting questions that comes to the researcher's mind in this area of the investigation is that the enormous complexity and difficulty of the code seems to hide almost nothing. It is as though a massive pyramid primed with intricate booby traps, falling stones, spring-loaded spears and trapdoors over chasms hid only the mummified remains of Tutankhamun's cat wrapped in his mother's shopping list.

The investigator is tempted to read the BERGERE PAS DE TENTATION . . . message and come away thinking "So what?" But is this the double (or even triple) bluff in this whole anfractuous affair? Are we supposed to do something further with the BERGERE PAS DE TENTATION letters to reveal a clear and vital clue to the real mystery? Simple and unambiguous directions, perhaps, for finding a chest full of Merovingian treasure? The Elixir of Life? The Philosopher's Stone? The Emerald Tablets of Hermes Trismegistus? Some alien artefact from Atlantis or a distant galaxy? Even the Holy Grail itself?

ET FACTVM EST EVM IN
SAbbATO SECVNdO PRIMO A
biRE PER SCCE TES dISCIPVLIAVTEM ILLITRISCOE
PERVNT VELLERE SPICAS ET FRICANTES MANIbVS + MANdV
CAbANT QVIdAM AVTEM dE FARISAEIS dI
CEbANT E ECCE QVIA FACIVN TdTS CIPVLITVISAb
bATIS + QVOdNON LICET RESPONdENS AVTEM INS
SET X ITAdEOS INVM QVAMbOC
LECISTIS QVOd FECIT dAVTd QVANdO
ESVRVT IPSE ET QVI CVM EO ERAI + INTROIbIT IN dOMVM
dEI ET PANES PROPOSITIONIS   REdIS
MANdVCAVIT ET dEdIT ET QVI   bUS
CVM ERANT IVXVO QVIbVS Nd
NLICEbAT MANdVCARE SINON   SOLIS SACERdOTIbVS

The shorter of the texts appears to be an inaccurately copied version of an episode recorded in Luke 6: 1-4, Matthew 12: 1-4 and Mark 2: 23-26. Jesus and his disciples are walking through the fields on the sabbath day, rubbing the ears of corn in their hands and eating the grains. The Pharisees criticize them for "working" (that is, threshing corn!) on the sabbath. Jesus replies that King David once took the sacred shewbread from the altar and gave it to his hungry followers. He adds that the Son of Man (a title he frequently uses to describe himself) is lord of the sabbath.

By reading the raised letters we read:

A DAGOBERT II ROI ET A SION
EST CE TRESOR ET IL EST LA MORT

"To Dagobert II, King, and to Sion, is this treasure, and he is there dead [or: and it is death]".

At the start of the parchment there is a curious triangle, resembling the legs of the Hanged Man in the Tarot. It could have a number of symbolic meanings: the three sides may represent the Trinity; the mark in the centre could mean "one in three"; there is a character outside the triangle which might either be a Greek omega (the last letter in the Greek alphabet) or the Arabic 3, or M for Mary — depending upon the angle from which it is viewed. The triangle may be a stylized linear form of the Greek alpha (the first letter in the Greek alphabet). The combined religious symbolism might then represent God as the Trinity (Three in One and One in Three) and as Alpha and Omega (the Beginning and the End).

This triangle could also be one of the keys to the decipherment of the curious text which follows. By drawing a triangle as shown in the illustration and taking the raised letters:

1	5	7	9	8	6	2	4	3	10
a	d	a	g	e	i	r	a	c	o

which occur inside that triangle, it is possible to form:

arcadia ego

The top line of the message inside the triangle begins with *et* and ends with *in*. Adding these words to the anagram produces our by now familiar phrase:

Et in Arcadia Ego

Leaving the triangle message and passing to the four bottom lines, we find that their last letters, read vertically, produce the word SION in block capitals. The P S at the end of the message may refer once more to the mysterious Priory. *Redis*, in a strangely isolated position in the centre of the lower right-hand quarter of the document, probably refers to the ancient name of Rennes-le-Château.

As we have already noted it is possible to translate *et il est la mort* either as "and he is there dead" (taking *la* as *là* there) or as "and it is death" (where *la* is the ordinary definite article the). If the latter is correct, what is the nature of the mortal danger which lurks near the treasure?

The tortuous and confused annals of alchemy have always stressed the dangers inherent in alchemical processes. The only method of performing transmutation known to modern science is by radiation bombardment. The high-energy particles required would be lethal for an unshielded operator. Only by the wildest stretch of the imagination dare it be suggested that some ancient alchemist found a sufficiently powerful natural radioactive energy source by accident, that he used it for transmutation and that he finally passed the hazardous secret to the Cathars (great healers who might have attended the dying alchemist in his last hours). Did the Cathars in turn pass it on to secret disciples after the fall of Montségur? Did it go from those secret disciples in Aude or Razès (parts of the Midi) to the noble and ancient Blanchefort family with their castle near Rennes-le-Château? Was it passed from the Blancheforts to the Templars and from them to the Priory of Sion? However unlikely, it is a possibility that we have to consider along with more probable answers.

✦

JESV. MEDELA. VULNÉRVM ✦ SPES. VNA. POENITENTIVM.
PER. MAGDALÁNÆ. LACRYMAS ✦ PECCATA. NOSTRA. DILVAS.

The second and longer manuscript is an equally inaccurate Latin rendering of John 12: 1-11. Here we take the decoding technique referred to in detail previously, pinpoint the 140 letters which do not appear to fit this passage, remove the twelve central ones and use the remaining 128 in conjunction with the position value cipher and the knights' tours of the two chess boards.

In addition, there are eight very small letters occurring randomly in the second, third, fourth, sixteenth, seventeenth, nineteenth and twentieth lines. These eight letters spell *Rex Mundi*, "king of the world". The Cathars believed that the earth was in the hands of an evil deity whom they called *Rex Mundi*. The peculiar subscription to the document may be meant to represent Adonis as well as Sion in reverse. In Greek mythology, Adonis was a handsome youth with whom the goddess Aphrodite (Venus), fell in love. He was the son of Cinyras, King of Cyprus, and Myrrha. Adonis was fatally wounded by a wild boar: curiously, Abbé Boudet mentions the *sanglier* — "the wild boar" — on pages 298 and 299 of his mysterious book. The anemone flower was said to have sprung up where his blood soaked into the earth. He was restored to life by the magic of Proserpine and thereafter spent six months of the year with her in the Underworld and the remaining six months with Aphrodite. This is evidently an aetiological myth to explain the seasons; it is similar to the myth of Proserpine, or Persephone, herself, and the six pomegranate seeds which confined her to the Underworld with Pluto, or Hades, for six months of the year. The cult of Adonis, as a seasonal nature spirit, was widespread in Syria and the Middle East, where he was known as Thamuz. Did the Templars encounter his worship there and amalgamate it with the Cathar ideas of *Rex Mundi?* The strange horned statue in the church at Rennes-le-Château could represent the demon Asmodeus, or a nature-spirit like Pan. Could Adonis, god of the seasons, be identified as one and the same being as *Rex Mundi,* god of the earth? Adonis died, and was resurrected by the agency of Persephone, who subsequently enjoyed a relationship with him in addition to her relationship with Hades. Adonis in turn spent half his time with Proserpine and half with Aphrodite, his sex goddess. The symbolism of Adonis has two main themes: sexual relationships and resurrection. These two themes lead back to the selected passage from John's Gospel, and from there to Rennes-le-Château. John 12: 1-11 contains the story of how Jesus stayed at the villa of Mary and Martha in Bethany, where Lazarus, whom Jesus had resurrected, was among the guests. Mary anointed Christ's feet with the very expensive ointment of spikenard and wiped them with her hair. Judas Iscariot complained that the ointment could have been sold and the proceeds given to the poor, but Jesus praised Mary's generous action and related it to his own impending death.

There are certain early Christian traditions — though they are by no means conclusive — that Mary of Bethany, Mary Magdalen and "the woman who was a sinner" were one and the same person, and that she might also have been the woman whom Jesus saved from the Pharisees who were intending to stone her for adultery. (Related in John 8: 1-11, and mentioned earlier with reference to the statue in the church.)

Did the middle-aged Bérenger Saunière have a sexual relationship with his attractive eighteen year old housekeeper, Marie Dénarnaud? She certainly shared the secrets of his mysterious wealth: how close were they in other ways? His church was dedicated to Mary Magdalen; the house he built with the wealth he discovered was called the Villa Bethania. Above the ancient Visigothic pillar which allegedly guided him to his fortune in 1891, he placed the statue of the Virgin Mary with the carved inscription *Pénitence! Pénitence!* The large mural along the church's west wall entitled The Mountain of the Beatitudes is also called *Terrain Fleuri*, "The Land of Flowers". The hill on which Jesus stands in this painting is certainly covered with flowers as we have already noted: some of those flowers could well be anemones – the blood of Adonis? Saunière may be saying that there is a connection between Adonis, the resurrected flower-god and the strange source of wealth waiting to be tapped at Rennes.

The Tarot, or Putting Two and Two Together to make Twenty-Two

If the codes in stone and parchment are obscure and mysterious, they are no more inscrutable than the Tarot – and the Tarot may also hold clues to the treasure of Rennes-le-Château. The Tarot, sometimes called the Tarocchi, is a pack of seventy-eight cards. There are four suits of fourteen cards each; the cards of each suit are the same as those of standard playing cards with the Cavalier as an additional court card in each suit. These fifty-six cards comprise what is called the Minor Arcana, or "lesser mystery". There are also twenty-two curious picture cards bearing symbolic designs and known as the Major Arcana, or "greater mystery". Twenty-two is a very strange number indeed.

Apart from the twenty-two cards of the Major Arcana in the Tarot it was in 598 B.C. that Solomon's Temple was destroyed: $5 + 9 + 8 = 22$. July 22nd is the Feast of St. Mary Magdalen. Dagobert II was assassinated in 679: $6 + 7 + 9 = 22$. The unfortunate Jacques de Molay who was burnt at the stake was the twenty-second Grand Master of the Templars. The French transliteration of Christ's cry from the cross – *Elie, elie, lamah sabactani* – contains twenty-two letters and is also the opening verse of Psalm 22. On January 22nd, 1917 ($2 + 2 + 1 + 9 + 1 + 7 = 22$), Bérenger Saunière died . . .

Just a string of curious coincidences . . . ?

Back to the Tarot! The first Tarot suit is shown as sticks or batons. It is equivalent to diamonds in ordinary playing cards. Some authorities interpret the symbol as a magic wand; others regard it as a sceptre. The second suit is known as cups, goblets or chalices, and corresponds to hearts in the normal pack. The third suit consists of swords, and is equivalent to spades; the fourth suit has a circular emblem, and is variously described as coins, circles or pentacles.

The twenty-two cards of the Major Arcana are very complex, and several thousand words could be devoted to a description of each of them, together with an explanation of their elaborate symbolism. One or two brief examples will serve to illustrate the point. Card number one is called the Juggler or the Magician. He stands in front of a table full of magical devices. In some versions of the Tarot he looks almost like a priest presiding over a sacred celebration at the altar. One hand holds a wand in the air, the other points to the earth below his table. He wears a wide-brimmed hat, known to the medieval world as a "cap of maintenance". The posture of his body and limbs represents the Hebrew letter *aleph*. Most occultists regard him as the symbol of willpower, desire and ambition. Card number ten is called the Wheel of Fortune. It has seven spokes and rotates between two vertical supports, shown as mystical rose-trees in some versions. A blindfolded figure of Fate turns the wheel, while human beings ascend and fall. The card symbolizes chance or fortune, good or bad luck.

The origins of the cards are mysterious and uncertain. At one extreme a claim is made for their origin in China over 6,000 years ago. There are also Egyptian and Babylonian claims, and Jacques Gringonneur, the astrologer, is credited with having invented the Tarot in 1392 to amuse Charles VI, known as "Charles the Foolish" (born 1368, reigned 1380-1422) but it is more likely that Gringonneur merely added to, or embellished, a much older pack.

The most probable connection between the mystery of Rennes-le-Château and the Tarot would seem to lie in Saunière's reported visits to various experts in Hermeticism when he was looking for help with decoding the manuscripts and tombstones. Most students of the occult have encountered the Tarot cards, and the parallel symbolism would be fairly obvious. Once Saunière had been shown a pack and had that symbolism explained to him, he could have begun devising ways of incorporating Tarot clues into the subsequent decorations of his church.

The Tarot, like Rennes-le-Château, is associated with alchemy. Card number twenty-one, the highest card, the World, shows a man, a bull, a lion and an eagle. These symbolize the four elements of alchemical theory: water, earth, fire and air respectively. It can be argued that the group of mysterious carvings immediately inside the church at Rennes-le-Château also represents the four elements: the demon-like *Rex Mundi* is King of the Earth; there is water in the dish he holds above his head; salamanders (fire creatures) writhe above the water; and angels (air dwellers) are poised above the salamanders. The earth symbol, *Rex Mundi,* is far larger than the rest of the figures. This may be a clue to Tarot card twenty-one — the World. The statue could be Saunière's way of drawing attention to the Tarot as one of the keys to the mystery of Rennes-le-Château.

Let us take the four suits of the Tarot: coins, swords, cups and staffs. Coins may represent the treasure; swords could symbolize the Templars and fit in with the key words *MORT épée* (DEATH sword) on the tombstone code; the cups, drawn in the shape of chalices, might indicate the Holy Grail, the religious element in Templarism, the Albigensian heretics, or the church at Rennes-le-Château; the staffs tie in with Poussin's painting of the "Shepherds of Arcadia".

The tenth Station of the Cross in the church at Rennes-le-Château shows three dice arranged in an L formation. The face of the dice show a three above a four on the left and a solitary five on the right. Can these dice be manipulated to give number combinations?

First, add the digits as in numerology:

$$3 + 4 + 5 = 12$$

followed by:

$$1 + 2 = 3$$

Card number three of the Major Arcana is the Empress. She symbolizes fertility and represents Gaea, Ceres Demeter, the earth mother, and that connection with Rennes is already strong. In some Tarot sets there are trees and a running river behind her: earth and water again — two of the four alchemical symbols. (There is also a small river below the tree-lined slopes leading up towards the ruins of Château Blanchefort.) Her sceptre suggests control over nature. There is a jewelled crown on her head, and in some Tarot packs her left hand points to it significantly, like the pointing fingers of the shepherds in Poussin's picture, or the pointing hand of the statue of John the Baptist in the church at Rennes.

The dice showing three and four are shown together, away from the five. Adding the three and four to produce the "mystic" number seven leads to the seventh Tarot card: the Chariot. This chariot also has alchemical significance: four columns support its canopy — each column represents one of the four alchemical elements.

The fourth card is the Emperor. Tarot writers are in general agreement in regarding him as the symbol of earthly authority or temporal power. He would be Dagobert II, or some crusading king connected with the Templars; perhaps their Grand Master.

The fifth card is the Pope (or, in some packs, Jupiter). Is this an indication that the Church guards the treasure? He holds a staff, or sceptre, in his left hand, and his right is raised with two fingers giving a benediction. He has creatures on each side of him — the traditional "sheep" and "goats" of "divine judgement". These sheep might also be a clue to the church at Rennes, to the shepherd's staff and the shepherd's fingers pointing to the inscription on the tomb in Poussin's painting.

The twelfth card is the Hanged Man. Some authorities on the Tarot regard him as the symbol of Atys, a Syrio-Hellenic god, who stands for the sun and the seasons. Atys free is the summer solstice; bound and hanging upside down he is the winter solstice. The Hanged Man's legs form a peculiar triangle like the triangle on the shorter coded manuscript.

Should the treasure hunter follow a shadow cast by one of the Rennes district landmarks at dawn or midday on the shortest day and work out his triangle from it? Or does a shaft of light enter the church at a particular angle at midday on a special day? "Blue apples" formed from cleverly situated stained glass and sunlight? One decoding of the manuscripts suggests that the "daemon guardian" was "achieved at midday". Could the mid-winter sun reveal something when it falls on the statue of the demon guardian, *Rex Mundi,* just inside the church door?

Multiplying the three and four together and adding the five gives seventeen. The seventeenth card of the Major Arcana is the Star. In fact it shows seven stars above the head of a girl who pours water into the river on the left of the card. These seven small stars are the daughters of Atlas, transformed into the Pleiades, visible at night near the back of the Bull in the zodiac. The seven celestial bodies may also refer to the seven bodies of the alchemical tradition: Sun — gold, Moon — silver, Mars — iron, Mercury — quicksilver, Saturn — lead, Jupiter — tin, and Venus — copper. The young woman on the card is identified by some authorities as Hebe, Goddess of Youth, cup-bearer to the gods and the one who supplied them with nectar. The fluid in her vases is also regarded by some traditions as the Elixir of Life, another alchemical goal. Saunière may be hinting that something infinitely more precious than worldly wealth is hidden at Rennes-le-Château.

The statuary and painting at Rennes seem to suggest that Saunière had a bizarre sense of humour; there is a mischievous, teasing element in some of the tantalizing clues he has left there. The Star is the symbol of hope — prime requisite of all treasure hunters! Could this be what he is getting at, or one of the things he is getting at, in his 3, 4, 5 dice code?[1]

In some ways the Rennes mystery resembles a conjuror's top hat from which one code after another springs like a rabbit — only to hop away into its labyrinthine warren before it can be caught and fully deciphered.

The Atbash Cipher and Baphomet

In the late sixties the authors were at Gamlingay Village College in Cambridgeshire, where Lionel Fanthorpe was the Further Education Tutor. Dr. Hugh Schonfield — author of *Those Incredible Christians* and several other scholarly works — was one of our guest lecturers during that period. After he had given his talk we drove him home to London where we enjoyed both his amiable company and his delicious coffee, although we would now differ strongly, albeit respectfully and affectionately, from his theological conclusions! Among Dr. Schonfield's discoveries is the Hebrew Atbash Cipher, which has to be seen in the context of the Hebrew alphabet (twenty-two letters!) in order to be properly appreciated. Its very name, Atbash, comes from the juxtaposition of those Hebrew letters from which it is formed.

Hebrew Letter	Name of Letter	Sound	Object from which the letter was originally derived
א	Aleph	An interrupted breath as in "re-enter" or "cooperation."	Ox
ב	Beth	b, bh (v)	House or dwelling
ג	Gimel	g, gh	Camel

---

[1] Our friend Paul Townsend has suggested another interpretation of the 3,4,5 dice. Observing that dice are cubes, he has pointed out that just as:

$$3^2 + 4^2 = 5^2$$

(the simplest case of Pythagoras' Theorem in integers), so:

$$3^3 + 4^3 + 5^3 = 6^3$$

In contrast to the infinity of integral solutions to Pythagoras' Theorem using squares, this is the only case of consecutive cubes adding to give another cube. Interpreting 6^3 as 6x6x6, we seem to have the (in)famous Number of the Beast.

Hebrew Letter	Name of Letter	Sound	Object from which the letter was originally derived
ד	Daleth	d, dh	Door or doorway
ה	He	h	A ventilation hole, a lattice
ו	Waw	w	hook or barb
ז	Zayin	z	Spear, sword or weapon of war
ח	Heth	a slightly different form of h	Hedge or fence
ט	Teth	a slightly different form of t	Snake, serpent or scorpion
י	Yodh	y	Hand
ך כ	Kaph	k, kh	Curved hand
ל	Lamedh	l	Goad
ם מ ס	Mem	m	Water
ן נ	Nun	n	Fish
ס	Samekh	one form of s	Support, trestle or prop
ע	Ayin	A stronger breathing than aleph, almost an h	Eye

Hebrew Letter	Name of Letter	Sound	Object from which the letter was originally derived
ף פ	Pe	p, ph	Mouth
ץ צ	Cadhe	A sibilant c, or an s	Fisherman's hook
ק	Qoph	q	Back of skull or, perhaps, needle's eye or narrow gate.
ר	Resh	r	Head
ש שׂ	Sin, shin	s, sh	Tooth
ת	Taw	t, th	Cross, sign, marker or indicator.

The Atbash cipher is formed by folding the Hebrew alphabet in the middle so that Aleph comes opposite Taw; Beth comes opposite Shin, and so on. This produces the sounds of "a – t – b – sh", hence Atbash.

א	Aleph	Taw	ת
ב	Beth	Sin, Shin	ש שׂ
ג	Gimel	Resh	ר
ד	Daleth	Qoph	ק
ה	He	Cadhe	ץ צ
ו	Waw	Pe	ף פ
ז	Zayin	Ayin	ע
ח	Heth	Samekh	ס
ט	Teth	Nun	ן

'	Yodh	Mem	מ ם
כ ך	Kaph	Lamedh	ל

Now the Hebrew word for Wisdom is *hokhmah*, the Greek word is *sophia*. Dr. Schonfield's Atbash cipher reportedly indicates that the word Baphomet – the name of the curious idol which the Templars were accused of worshipping – can be deciphered as Wisdom. There is wide conjecture about the physical appearance of this object and about the meaning of its name. One suggestion is that it is a Latin abbreviation spelt backwards just as the inscription on Marie de Nègre's tombstone is reversed in order to provide a position value keyword. *Templi omnium hominum pacis abhas* ("The father of the Temple of universal peace among men") is abbreviated to *Tem o h p ab* and then read – like Hebrew – from right to left to produce the word *Baphomet*. Another possible derivation is *baphe metios* or "baptism of wisdom".

It may safely be assumed that ninety-nine percent of the accusations laid against the Templars concerning their alleged heresy, blasphemy, idolatry, immorality and black magic were nothing more than the product of Philip IV's vicious propaganda augmented by spectacular Templar "confessions" extracted under the most extreme torture. It is infinitely more probable that the Templars revered Sophia, the Divine Wisdom, than that they dabbled in black magic and idolatry.

The Reverend Doctor Benjamin Wisner Bacon, a former Professor of New Testament Criticism and Exegesis at Yale, wrote with great authority and expertise on the theological and philosophical concept of Wisdom. He points out that in the *Hokhmah*, or Wisdom literature, Wisdom is seen as the Divine Spirit manifesting the redeeming love of God and going out to seek and save the lost. One vitally important aspect of Templarism was to locate and redeem knights who had fallen from their original high calling. Wisdom is personified in the Book of Job (Chapter 28), says Bacon. By the time of Philo Judaeus (30 B.C.–A.D. 40) hypostatisation has taken place and Wisdom and the Logos are synonymous, cosmological and soteriological. The mysterious Book of Enoch shows Wisdom, rejected by humanity, re-ascending to her seat in Heaven to return during the Messianic Age to bless and inspire the elect.

This personification and hypostatisation of Wisdom was rigorously resisted by the scribes of the Akiba period, during the rivalry between Church and Synagogue in Palestine (A.D. 70-135). In some Jewish texts *hokhmah* (wisdom) was even altered to *torah* (law).

The sum of the evidence here seems to suggest quite strongly that far from embracing vestigial traces of weird eastern paganism, demonology and black magic, the Templars did nothing worse than compound the idea of the Divine Logos (as in St. John's Gospel) with Sophia, the Divine Wisdom: hardly a blasphemy; scarcely a heresy; more fairly described as an emphasis of reverence – akin to the high churchman's special esteem for the Virgin Mary and the Saints or the low churchman's due regard for scriptural authority and vigorous evangelical preaching.

Curious Watermarks

As we shall endeavour to show in Chapter 7, "Magicians, Alchemists and Men of Mystery", Sir Francis Bacon and his brother could well have been among the elect group who knew more than most about the Rennes-le-Château mystery. There is also some evidence that the Bacon brothers were among those initiated into the use of an enigmatic watermark code, a small sample of which is examined below.

EXAMPLES OF THE SECRET WATERMARK CODES

FIGURE A

FIGURE B

FIGURE C

FIGURE D

FIGURE E

FIGURE F

FIGURE G

FIGURE H

FIGURE I

FIGURE J

FIGURE K

FIGURE L

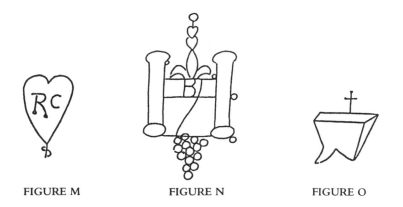

FIGURE M   FIGURE N   FIGURE O

The Poussin and Teniers period was a time of vigorous interaction between Britain and the Continent. Ideas were crossing the Channel in both directions – some openly and some secretly. One of the most intellectual and most secretive Englishmen of the time was Sir Francis Bacon, and his interest in codes and ciphers is well known. It seems likely that Bacon and his brother Anthony were deeply involved in at least one secret society which had European connections. It is also possible that their society was linked with the Rosicrucians and the Priory of Sion. It seems possible, even probable, that the Bacons used watermarks not only as symbols but as codes in which messages were communicated to members of whatever secret society they had created, revived, or adapted to their own purpose. The watermark symbols themselves go back much further than Elizabethan times. Figure A, the ellipse with a cross above it, goes back to the beginnings of the fourteenth century at least. The ellipse may be meant to represent an egg, the sealed mystery, the emblem of eternity, immortality and resurrection. If it is, it ties up with the Latin acrostic *ova* ("eggs") from the Shepherd Monument in the grounds of Shugborough Hall, to be dealt with later in this chapter. The cross could well be the sign of the Templars, surmounting a circle representing the world. Figure B is almost equally old and traceable at least as far back as the middle of the fourteenth century. Here the circle and cross idea is repeated, but the cross has been rotated into a diagonal position. It is now perhaps the emblem of St. Andrew, or it may be read with the upright of the original cross as a six-pointed star. Perhaps it is Davidic, the star of Sion? The lines could be the points of the compass, or it may even be part of some unknown, secret alphabet. Figure C is similar to A and B, but this time the symbol surmounting the circle is the two–armed cross of Lorraine, symbol of the Free French in the Second World War. The first three watermarks read together are reminiscent of questions in IQ tests where the testee is asked to complete the series or to distinguish one incompatible figure from the others in the group. They are equally reminiscent of electronic circuitry or computer diagrams. There is a possibility that, as is suspected of the strange *rongo-rongo* script of Easter Island, these water-mark codes are mnemonic triggers – not decipherable in the accepted sense unless the memorized material is known to the reader.

Figure D dates from 1315; and it is thought that the ellipses here may represent the sacred scarabs of ancient Egypt. As we have already noted, the Hermetic philosophy of Trismegistus had Egyptian roots, was linked with Manichaeanism and Catharism and seems to lead in the general direction of the Templars, the Priory of Sion and Rennes-le-Château. Figure D also contains diagonal crosses on the St. Andrew pattern, unless they are six-pointed stars again.

Figure F could have considerable significance. It can, of course, be dismissed fairly superficially as the triple crown of England, Scotland and Wales (although this raises some historical problems), surmounted by the universal symbol of Christendom. Another suggestion is that it represents biblical mountains with mystic significance: Moriah, Sinai and Golgotha (or Calvary). It was at Moriah that Abraham was on the verge of sacrificing his son, Isaac, until he was told not to, and sacrificed the ram instead. The original name Moriah meant the "bitterness, fear or doctrine of the Lord". (Genesis 22: 2 and 14). Tolkien comes close to this idea in Chapter IV of Book Two of The Fellowship of the Ring when he gives the name "Moria" to the system of underground caverns where Gandalf plunges into an unfathomed abyss while locked in mortal combat with a balrog. For the hobbits and their companions, the loss of Gandalf is exceedingly bitter; Moria is a bitter place for them — a place of sacrifice. The parallel ideas continue, however, for great things came of Abraham's willingness to sacrifice Isaac, and great things came of Gandalf's willingness to sacrifice himself. The doors of Tolkien's Moria were sealed with a magic password. Gandalf, expert in such matters, explained that some doors opened only at certain times, others opened only for selected people, some had hidden locks and keys which were still required when all other conditions had been fulfilled. It is remotely possible that Tolkien's doors of Moria are a clue to the mysteries of Rennes-le-Château. Tolkien must have had good reason for describing them in such elaborate detail. The designs on the doors in his illustrations closely resemble the weird watermarks in Bacon's books. Tolkien's Moria once contained, among other things, a dead king and his treasure. Tolkien was also a member of the group known as The Inklings which included C. S. Lewis and Charles Williams whom we shall refer to again more fully in the next chapter.

There are other remarkable similarities between Tolkien's picture of the door of Moria and the old watermarks. Figure N, for example shows a circle above two hearts with a fleur-de-lis below them and a letter B below that. The vertical columns could be meant to represent candlesticks or pillars. The door in Tolkien's picture has a pillar at each side; a tree twines around each pillar; a star is set between the trees; and an arch links the pillars at the top. Below this top arch is another arch of seven stars, the uppermost one decorating the high point of a crown. There is a hammer and anvil device below the crown. Three ancient runes, or similar linguistic symbols, also appear: one at the base (between the trees) and one in each upper corner.

Figure O shows an anvil watermark found in a Dutch account book between 1416 and 1421. A German manuscript of the fifteenth century carries a similar, but not identical, anvil watermark, which is surmounted by an incomplete Maltese cross and a letter which could be either a Roman block capital H or a greek *eta*, the long "ee" sound.

Double pillars, double candlesticks or gatepost watermarks can be found in Arthur Hilderson's *Lectures on St. John* (1628). One Latin passage in the Rennes manuscript codes is an extract from St. John's Gospel. The 1633 edition of Marlowe's *Jew of Malta* also carries a strange watermark; it resembles two pillars joined by an arch at the top — above the arch is a diamond-shaped cluster of grapes. Is the word Jew in the title a clue to Sion yet again? And is Malta a reference to the old crusading routes and the strongholds of the Templars and Hospitallers?

There are several curious crown watermarks in the 1623 edition of Shakespeare in the British Museum. More than one of these has a broad similarity to Tolkien's crown drawn on the gates of Moria, but there are essential differences in the details.

Moving on from the possible connections between Tolkien's Moria and the Old Testament Moriah where Abraham almost sacrificed Isaac, it is worth noticing in passing that Moriah was also the site of Solomon's Temple (2 Chronicles 3: 1).

The second mystical mountain, Sinai, was the scene of Moses' communion with Yahweh and the giving of the sacred law to the Israelites. The third, Golgotha, was the site of the crucifixion.

Figure G appears to be a five-pointed star within a circle, but the lower left-hand point is unjoined. This could be a magician's pentagon, or a Jewish star pointing the way back to Sion, the Holy Land and the Crusades. The opened point in the bottom left corner is significant. It might be nothing more than an error of draughtsmanship, or a flaw in the production process, but the figure might be a leaf with an open stem rather than a star. It could be a torn hoop of paper through which someone or something has jumped like an acrobat at a fair. In some old formulas, the star with five points stood for the soul of the world. In others, a star was thought to be a heavenly messenger, a guide, a teacher, even an angel. The circle which surrounds the star is usually the symbol of the world or the earth. Could this be connected with *Rex Mundi* again?

As was noted in our comments on the Tarot, the seventeenth card (possibly significant in the dice code in the church at Rennes) is the Star. There are seven small stars on this card, and one larger one, which coincides exactly with the stars drawn on Tolkien's gate to Moria. The young woman on the Tarot Star is Hebe, Goddess of Youth, and in the picture on the card she is shown pouring out the Elixir of Life. This strange symbolic, allegorical trail seems to curve its tortuous way back once more in the direction of Alchemy and Rennes-le-Château.

Figure H shows a pair of scales with the tilted right-hand pan badly out of balance. This watermark, from about 1590, is visible on records in the British Museum dating back as far as 1400. Figures I, J and K have nautical connections. Each shows an anchor. J is particularly interesting in that it may also suggest the Moorish or Saracen crescent. The hull of the ship (or base of the anchor) could also be an eastern scimitar. What became of the "lost" Templar fleet? Is the ground plan of Rennes an Egyptian "Boat of the Dead"? And, as we shall ask in a later chapter, who sailed to Oak

Island, Nova Scotia and what did they carry with them? The emblem is curious and ambiguous. Figure K could be the Greek *Chi*, the initial of Christ in Greek. It is odd to notice that the top and top-right arms are open-ended, whereas the rest are closed except for the base and the top of the anchor. About a dozen varieties of these anchor watermarks have been found, mainly in old Dutch account books, dating from the mid-fifteenth century.

Sir Nicholas Bacon spent a considerable time in Holland — what did he learn there? What old Dutch secrets might he have passed on to his sons?

Some of Anthony Bacon's correspondence is preserved in the Tennison Manuscripts in Lambeth Palace, and this is where figure L was found. It appears to be a dog-headed snake, or a dog-headed horn. Is it a cornucopia, signifying plenty, or is it a symbol of something that twists and struggles through the underground labyrinth of secret service work? Is Anthony saying here that his mind, his head, is that of a hunting dog on the scent, even though his body is twisted and handicapped by disease?

Figure M shows the heart-shaped background signifying love and brotherhood, with the letters R.C. Is this Rosicrucian imagery again? At the base of the heart is what looks like a letter S. By reversing the figure and reading the curve of the S against the line around which it is entwined it is possible to find a letter P as well. P and S as well as R and C could suggest a link between the Rosicrucians and the Priory of Sion.

However the watermarks are read, and whatever the strange career of the Bacon brothers may have had to do with secret societies or the treasures of Rennes-le-Château, there can be little doubt that Ben Jonson summed up Francis in the ode he wrote to celebrate Bacon's sixtieth birthday:

> Hail! happy genius of this ancient Pile!
> How comes it all things so about thee smile?
> The fire! the wine! the men! and in the midst
> Thou standst as if some mystery thou didst . . .

> January 22nd 1621

The question remains: what was the mystery?

The Shepherd Monument at Shugborough

Shugborough Hall in Staffordshire, ancestral home of the Ansons, is another spot to which the Rennes codes may have extended. In the grounds is a curious structure called "The Shepherd Monument". It is a *bas-relief* of Poussin's "Shepherds of Arcadia" but strangely re-arranged. The actual tomb resembles the ornately elaborate one in the Chatsworth version: but the figures are all from the Louvre picture and they stand in a mirror image relationship to their positions in that canvas, with the line of reflectional symmetry below their feet. The Atbash cipher, the two chess boards for the knights' tours, and Shugborough's The Shepherd Monument taken in conjunction with the Louvre version of "The Shepherds of Arcadia" all employ this "folding" technique. The two latter examples produce reflectional symmetry as a result.

There is a clue below the carved shepherds of Shugborough. Cut into the stone are the letters:

O.U.O.S.V.A.V.V

D.   M.

There are eight letters in a line, with a D and an M below them. All the letters, with the exception of the final V of the upper line, are followed by dots. The exact positioning of the dots, not on the line but at half the height of the letters, may also be significant.

The eight letter arrangement is an immediate reminder of the *MORT* *épée* code on the tombstone at Rennes. It is also significant in terms of a chessboard with its eight rows of eight squares. One widely held view is that these letters are simply an abbreviated memorial inscription, commemorating some important event connected with the Ansons. On the face of it, this is highly likely, and if each letter is simply the start of a word in Latin or English, the possibilities for creating a family reminder of this sort are almost endless.

But if, as some researchers believe, a link between Rennes and Shugborough can be established, then the letters on the Shepherd Monument may have something important to say. Here is one suggested solution which uses all ten letters and involves the kind of geometrical arrangement which appealed to the code makers of the mid-eighteenth century. It is also the shape of the ancient "thorn" letter (þ) found in the English alphabet until a few centuries ago, and still in use in Icelandic:

D
O   V   O
M   V
U   V   A
S

The literal meanings of the words so created are *DOMUS*, "house"; *OVO*, "I rejoice"; *OVA*, "eggs" (the symbols of eternal life, e.g. the old custom of celebrating resurrection with easter eggs); *UVA*, "grapes". Suppose that the house refers to Shugborough or to one of the curious buildings in the grounds such as the Chinese House. The idea of rejoicing may be to celebrate the sailor's safe return, the discovery of his treasure or something even more valuable. Anson's wife or brother may have felt that their Admiral's series of miraculous escapes from storms, enemies and tropical diseases warranted a permanent memorial. The Poussin-style tomb may have suggested to them an incredible escape from the mouth of the grave.

The eggs, symbols of resurrection and eternal life, follow immediately after the rejoicing; they are in fact connected to it in the diagram of letters. Because an egg is enclosed, it is also an ancient symbol of mystery, of hidden things, of the unseen. The rejoicing which links the house to this strange old nature symbol could be a rejoicing over something which is unseen but known to exist. Did the Admiral hide some of his Spanish gold as an insurance against future eventualities, and does the monument tell where? Perhaps *DOMUS* is not Shugborough but Moor Park in

Hertfordshire, which is now a golf course, for Moor Park was once the Admiral's home.

The fourth and last word UVA is the most significant one. Nicolas Poussin painted a picture entitled "L'Automne, ou la grappe de la terre promise" as part of his series on the four seasons which he completed between 1660 and 1664. This canvas shows two men in the central foreground with a staff across their shoulders. From the staff hangs an enormous bunch of grapes; each grape is the size of an apple (or, perhaps, an egg?) and the grapes are dark blue. (The tombstone code at Rennes referred to "blue apples".) Above the grapes in the painting rises a background mountain peak. It could be the peak of Cardou near Rennes, or even the small mountain on which Rennes stands. There are other ancient buildings and fortifications to the left and right of the central figures, and a river runs behind them. Scenery like this could very easily be fitted into the Aude district of southern France or the northeastern slopes of the Pyrenees.

The grapes may have yet another bearing on the mystery. Mrs. Henry Pott suggests in *Francis Bacon and his Secret Society* that the various grape watermarks used in Sir Philip Sidney's book *Arcadia* are codes, known only to members of that society. The Latin UVA ("grapes") on the Shepherd Monument at Shugborough may be confirmation of the connections joining Bacon, Sidney, the first William Anson and the society if, indeed, it exists.

The alternative title of Poussin's picture, "or the grapes of the promised land", leads to an interesting Old Testament reference from Numbers 13. In this story Moses is commanded by God to send spies into Canaan, to bring back reports about the land and its inhabitants. Moses selects a representative prince from each of the twelve traditional tribes of Israel, and they undertake the reconnaissance. They reach Eschol (the name actually means "a bunch" or a "cluster"), and cut down one branch laden with grapes, so large and heavy that it needs two men to carry it. The spies return with this and other samples to Moses and make their report. Only Caleb, Prince of Judah, is in favour of attacking. The other eleven princes counsel caution because of the great number and vast size of the indigenous population, some of whom they called Nephilim, or giants.

During the Crusades there was a Templar stronghold at Eschol. Some of the treasure from that stronghold could have found its way back to Rennes. The original giant grapes of Eschol could be the mysterious "blue apples" of the tombstone code. Those grapes of Eschol may have been the same secret, symbolic grapes as the grapes on the watermarks of Sir Philip Sidney's *Arcadia* and another curious seventeenth century publication called *Twenty-Seven Songs of Sion*. The 1652 edition of George Herbert's *A Priest of the Temple* also contains the grape watermarks. The titles of these works certainly suggest a connection: Arcadia, Sion, the Temple.

Boudet's Book(s)

One last mystery before we leave the subject of codes and ciphers: Henri Boudet's grave at Axat. If Boudet left any clues to the Rennes treasures they are cunningly concealed in his strange book *La Vraie Langue Celtique*.

What could well be intended to be a representation of this book is carved on his gravestone. On its "front cover" is the inscription:—

ΙΧΟΙΣ

Boudet tomb inscription

Turning the letters over and around — or taking a mirror image of them — gives:-

ƸΙΟΧΙ

Mirror-image of the Boudet tomb inscription

Does that mean pages 310 and 311 of the original 1886 edition of his book? Or is the stone "book" meant to represent a Priest's Bible or New Testament? In which case the apparently curious inscription would simply be the early Christian

ΙΧΘΥΣ

ICHTHUS

a fish, from which is derived, in Greek, the acrostic: "Jesus Christ, Son of God and Saviour".

CHAPTER SEVEN

MAGICIANS, ALCHEMISTS AND MEN OF MYSTERY

Eo magis praefulgebat, quod non videbatur. (Tacitus)

To add to the intriguing mysteries posed by the Rennes codes and ciphers are the even deeper mysteries of the enigmatic personalities who created them.

Sir Francis Bacon

In order to get anywhere near an answer to the watermark codes, it is important to penetrate the historical mists obscuring the enigmatic and controversial figure of Sir Francis Bacon. He was born on January 22nd, 1561, and he died on April 9th, 1626 which makes him a contemporary of Poussin and both the Teniers. He was twenty-nine when the elder Teniers was born, and the younger Teniers was in his teens when Bacon died. His other contemporaries included the mysterious Dr. John Dee (1527-1608) famous for mathematics, astrology, crystallomancy and magic in general. One of Dee's many books was entitled *Treatise on the Rosie Crucian [sic] Secrets*, and there is little doubt that he also included alchemy among his occult interests. Dee is a likely candidate for membership, or even mastership, of the Priory of Sion.

The general outline of Bacon's career is straightforward enough on the surface. His father was Sir Nicholas Bacon, Lord Keeper during Queen Elizabeth's reign. Sir Nicholas, who was born c. 1510, had worked his way up via a place at Cambridge which had been awarded to him because of his ability. He was in Paris for a short while after completing his university course and then studied law at Grays Inn. His chance came when Archbishop Heath, the Lord Chancellor, refused to carry out Elizabeth's orders. Bacon took over much of Heath's work without actually taking the title of Lord Chancellor.

Sir Nicholas had six children by his first wife, Jane Ferneley, and then married Anne Cooke. Her father had been tutor to Edward VI and her sister was married to William Cecil, the Lord Treasurer. Anne was intelligent and well educated but decidedly odd, and in old age her sanity deserted her altogether. Ostensibly, Sir Nicholas had two children by her: Anthony and Francis.

There is a curious paradox about Sir Nicholas. He was grossly overweight, and his portrait tends to make him look earthy, brutal and cunning. Yet every historical record tells of his shrewdness, kindness, intelligence, generosity and good humour. Did Sir Nicholas play more than one role? Did Francis inherit a streak of abnormality from his mother, but learn from Sir Nicholas how to feel one emotion while simulating another?

In 1564, Sir Nicholas unwisely wrote a booklet entitled *A Declaration of the Crown Imperial of England* in which he advocated the claims of the House of Suffolk. Not surprisingly, this did not please Elizabeth. Although Bacon had used the name John Hales as a pen-name, Robert Dudley, Earl of Leicester, told Elizabeth who the author was, and Sir Nicholas fell from royal favour for some time. He was eventually restored, but he often impressed upon his sons the importance of concealment, camouflage and Machiavellian methods in affairs of state. He warned them particularly about the dangers of traceable authorship.

Anthony, three years older than Francis, had a profound influence over his younger brother. There is strong and consistent evidence that the brothers were devoted to each other, and remained so until Anthony's untimely death at the age of forty-three in 1601.

The most remarkable suggestion made about Francis is that he was not the Bacon's child at all, but Queen Elizabeth's. The story is based on the Biliteral Cipher found by Mrs. Gallup among Francis Bacon's works, but the evidence is not conclusive and the affair needs to be studied cautiously. According to the encoded story, Lord Robert Dudley, Earl of Leicester, who was responsible for the murder of his wife, Amy Robsart, in 1560, had been secretly married to Queen Elizabeth in Lord Pembroke's house. Those present at this exclusive private ceremony included Sir William Cecil and the Bacons. The Queen, who, according to the story, had been Dudley's mistress for some time, was already pregnant when the wedding took place, and the child (Francis) was born in the following January. Lady Bacon was Elizabeth's Chief Lady-in-Waiting and offered to take the boy and bring him up as her own son.

Before dismissing the story as total fantasy, it should be remembered that the Bacons were staunch Protestants and that Sir Nicholas in particular had an almost obsessional hatred of Elizabeth's rival, Mary Queen of Scots. Supposing for a moment that the story were true, if Elizabeth's mar 'age to Dudley and their subsequent production of a son had become known, the throne would have rocked. To Protestants as fanatical as the Bacons, the consequences would have been unthinkable in an era of bloody religious controversy. In their scale of moral comparisons, concealing Francis's true parentage was as nothing when weighed against the dangers of a Catholic monarch's replacing Elizabeth.

As Francis grew up he became interested in psychic phenomena as well as in more orthodox philosophy and science. Macaulay's *Essay on Bacon* (1837) records how the young Francis went to a vault in St. James's Park to study an unusual echo which sounded there. He also studied the performances of travelling jugglers and conjurors to see whether they produced their startling results by trickery or by using genuinely supernormal powers.

Francis and his brother Anthony went to Cambridge together in April 1573, when Francis was twelve, and they studied at Trinity as pupils of that Dr. Whitgift, who later became Archbishop of Canterbury. Perhaps partly because of the bitter religious controversy between Whitgift and Cartright's Calvinists, Francis became an astute and penetrating critic of the university system. In *The Advancement of Learning,* he refers to the "excellent Liquor" (of knowledge), and complains that instead of getting on with the job of researching and teaching, the so-called scholars are trapped in a narrow Aristotelian framework and their energies are dissipated in shallow controversies. This idea of knowledge, or wisdom, as some kind of precious liquid, a wine or an elixir, ties in with Bacon's watermark codes, many of which take the form of grapes and wine jugs. Neither is this attitude to wisdom a million miles away from Philo's ideas as expounded by Professor Bacon of Yale. (The coincidence of names is interesting, too!)

Shortly after leaving Cambridge, Francis became a member of Grays Inn, which was then as much of a training ground for aspiring courtiers and statesmen as it was a law school, but his studies here were interrupted by his trip to France in the party led by Sir Amyas Paulet, the newly appointed ambassador. Several historians have suggested that it was while he was on this journey that the "truth" about Francis Bacon's birth was revealed to him.

This French adventure lasted from 1576 to 1579, and Francis made a return visit to France in 1582. Anthony's French activities were even stranger and more significant than his brother's. There can be little doubt that Anthony was involved in the primitive but complex secret service activities of the time – no James Bond, but a suspicious, sensitive man tormented by gout and weakened by chronic lung disease. Anthony returned to England in 1591, but prior to that his life abroad had been a tangle of secrecy and intrigue. Both Francis and Anthony had encountered powerful Huguenot leaders, and it is possible that there was a link between the Huguenots and the Cathars. With the help of their influential and well-informed contacts in Europe, some of whom might possibly have been members of the Priory of Sion – if it really existed – the Bacon brothers could well have built up their own secret society, or expanded and developed one that already existed in an attenuated or vestigial form.

Francis Bacon seems to have had exactly the right kind of temperament and attitude – and the necessary power and influence – for resurrecting the dormant underground remains of the Templars or the Priory: he was discreet, secretive and cautious; he also felt an insatiable longing for the power, prestige and authority which he believed to be his birthright but which so often eluded his grasp.

He was fascinated by codes and ciphers – as were many Elizabethans – but in his case the interest seems to have been more than academic or something employed for simple political security.

The Ansons: William, William, William and George

In the later chapter dealing with the overseas links of Rennes-le-Château we shall take a closer look at Shugborough in Staffordshire, where the curious Shepherd Monument still displays its enigmatic inscription. But it is interesting to note briefly here that Shugborough was bought in 1624 by William Anson, a successful lawyer who must have known Sir Francis Bacon, who had risen to become Solicitor General in 1607, Attorney General in 1613 and Lord Chancellor in 1618. Bacon fell from power in 1621, but it was during the period of his greatest legal ascendancy that William Anson of Staffordshire was also a highly successful lawyer.

William died in 1644, and his son, also named William, took over the estate, to be followed by yet another William Anson, grandson of the first. This third William was born in 1656 and began building a new hall in 1693. His structure forms the heart of the present building. William married Isabella Carrier, a wealthy girl from Derbyshire, and they had three children: Thomas, George and Janette. Thomas (1695-1773) was a great lover of Greek architecture and statues. At a date between 1755 and 1758, he erected the Shepherd Monument in the grounds of his home. George Anson, destined to become Lord Admiral Anson, was a strong, able, determined and adventurous man. Born in 1697, George went to sea when he was only fourteen and became a naval lieutenant in 1716. He commanded his own small warship, The Weazle, in 1722. From his winnings at cards he bought land in Carolina and owned 17,000 acres there in 1735. He had, apparently, the characteristic eighteenth century Englishman's appreciation of wine, women and song. A friend in Carolina wrote of him: " . . . he greatly admires a fine woman . . . is passionately fond of music . . . and loves his bottle . . ." Praise indeed!

In 1744, after enduring desperate hardships, surviving fierce storms, resisting virulent diseases and winning numerous hard fought sea and land battles, George Anson sailed home in triumph with the best part of £2,000,000 in Spanish treasure.

Although he lived mainly at Moor Park in Hertfordshire, George was a frequent visitor to his brother's estate at Shugborough until his death in 1762. The Shepherd Monument was therefore built during the last years of the life of this very wealthy admiral, who had circumnavigated the globe, fought the French and confiscated huge quantities of Spanish gold. Did he have a secret message to conceal in that stone?

During his many voyages Anson could well have visited sites on coasts that once belonged to Visigoths and Merovingians. In his encounters by sea and land, he could have taken important French prisoners who were willing to exchange secrets of ancient treasures for their lives.

Victor Hugo

The French poet and novelist Victor Hugo has been named as one of the supposed Masters of the Priory of Sion, and, just as Poussin and Teniers may have left clues in their pictures, so it has been suggested that Hugo left clues in his epic poem *La Légende des Siècles*.

Hugo was born at Besançon on February 26th, 1802, and the first thirteen years of his life were destined to affect his psychological development dramatically. His father rose high in Napoleon's favour and was — at least in theory — a very wealthy and important man. Victor's mother, however, disliked Napoleon almost as much as she disliked her husband. During their period in Spain, young Victor was treated with suspicion by his Jesuit teachers and with the disdain given to "foreign upstarts" by his aristocratic Spanish schoolmates.

In 1812 the French position in Spain was sufficiently precarious for Victor's father to send his family back to Paris. Here his mother hid an elderly political conspirator, General Lahorie, from the police, and Victor must have been affected by the tense atmosphere of adventure, suspense, discontent and intrigue.

In analysing Victor Hugo's work and character, the following factors must be taken into consideration: his education was frequently interrupted; his mother and father were not compatible; his early prospect of wealth and splendour faded into the subsequent disappointing reality of comparative poverty; the ostentation, glamour, drama and violence of the Napoleonic era were his first encounter with a social environment.

As a schoolboy and student from 1815 to 1822, he was a prodigy. He attended lectures at Louis-le-Grand and studied for three years at the Pension Cordier. During these years he wrote many acrostics and riddles, and they were literary forms which appealed to him.

His mother died in 1821 and Victor starved for a year in a garret rather than accept money from his hated father. He had a success in 1822 with some poems which appealed to the Court of Louis XVIII, and was rewarded with a pension.

In 1822, he married Adèle Foucher in St. Sulpice (the same St. Sulpice to which Bérenger Saunière took his manuscripts to be deciphered). Victor's brother, Eugène, went mad, as he was also in love with Adèle. Eugène died in an asylum in 1837.

From 1827 to 1830, Victor was involved in the wave of literary romanticism which flooded France. In 1829, one of his most important creative years, he produced most of *Notre Dame de Paris, Hernani, Les Orientales* and *Marion de Lorme*. In 1833, an attractive little courtesan named Juliette Drouet played the role of Princess Negroni in Hugo's *Lucrezie Borgia*. She became his mistress, the heroine of some of his best poems, and his most faithful supporter and companion until her death in 1883.

Victor was involved in politics. He was an academician. He was an exile in Guernsey from 1852 until 1870. His life was a dramatic kaleidoscope of eventful experiences. His output was enormous. His critics have frequently referred to his egoism as if it were some sort of intellectual or moral fault, but Hugo was simply in love with life, with his own ability to receive its countless impressions and understand them, and with the self that made such reception possible.

His links with the treasure of Rennes-le-Château are to be found in his reputed Mastership of the Priory of Sion and in the eighteenth section of *La Légende des Siècles*, which deals with a vicious, petty, Italian tyrant who bears the ideally villainous name of Ratbert, King of Arles, c. 1310. This Ratbert, according to Hugo, was the son of Rodolphe and grandson of Charles. (There was a Holy Roman Emperor named Rudolf of Habsburg from 1273 to 1291, and between 961 and 1277 Italy was subject to the Empire.) Ratbert is said to be the son of Agnes, Countess of Elsinor, and he also claimed Messalina as an ancestor!

In the poem, Ratbert calls a council of Italian nobles and priests, at which he thinks up various schemes to bring down his enemies. He places an axe on the table to encourage democratic discussion! The various speakers compliment Ratbert on his brilliant plans and each sycophant is rewarded with a grant of land. Ratbert then goes to Carpi, where Onfroy, the town's leader, politely refuses Ratbert's demands. Unwisely, Onfroy accepts an invitation to supper with Bishop Afranus, one of Ratbert's hatchet men, and succumbs predictably to the ingredients.

The next section of the poem is entitled *La Confiance du Marquis Fabrice*. Bearing in mind Hugo's fascination with codes, riddles and acrostics, it is just possible that Final in this poem is a symbol for Rennes. It is also quite likely that he knew the story of the treasure in the tomb and the general description of the scenery, but not the exact location. There is also a chance that the treasure originally stored at Final was subsequently moved to a new hiding place in or near Rennes.

Fabrice d'Albenga, Marquis of Final, is eighty years old when Hugo takes up the story. The Marquis has a five year old granddaughter, Isora, whom he adores. The child's parents are dead, and she is heiress to the rich Marquisate of Final. Old Fabrice himself is the illegitimate son of Otton, and was, like Macduff in Shakespeare's Macbeth, "from his mother's womb untimely ripped". He is known as Fabrice the Unborn, and was for fifty years one of the greatest knights and most valiant fighters in Europe. The date of his birth is given as 1230, which puts Ratbert's reign at about the same date as that of Philip IV of France. Again, keeping Hugo's love of symbolism in mind, it is possible that brave old Fabrice is a personification of the Templars, or, with the name d'Albenga, even a symbol for the Albigensians, or Cathars. Does Final represent any Templar castle? Is Ratbert a cipher for Philip IV or one of his despised agents? The evil Bishop Afranus then becomes a symbol for William, Philip's Grand Inquisitor. The application of torture to Fabrice later in the poem draws the parallel with the Inquisition even more distinctly.

Fabrice, like Shakespeare's King Lear, lives in the past and suffers from what Hugo calls "holy credulity". In the section headed *Aieul Maternel* Hugo describes Fabrice's deep affection for young Isora. Each night he takes her to the chapel. Sometimes, in the first light of morning, she runs as free as Rousseau's child of nature around the estate, chasing butterflies among the tombs.

The next section is entitled *Un seul homme sait où est caché le trésor* — "Only one man knows where the treasure is hidden" — and it is here that Hugo comes closest to the mystery of Rennes. He describes the value of the income of the estate as sufficient to weigh down twenty mules with massive purses. He describes the location in poetic detail: a tall watchtower in the middle of a blue sky, with clear views to north, south, east and west, having the four evangelists, Matthew, Mark, Luke and John, carved and gilded upon it. Two châteaux guard the mountain where the tower stands, like stone soldiers with iron beneath their cloaks. The treasure is secured in bolted chests, which, when their lids are raised, reveal glimpses of jewels. The treasure is walled up in a hidden cave and only the reigning marquis knows the secret. One of the rarest and most dazzling pieces is a priceless helmet decorated with a diamond Phoenix rising from a fire of rubies.

The remainder of the poem is as sad as the history of the downfall of the Templars. Ratbert sends toys for Isora and visits Final, where Fabrice welcomes him loyally. A crow, the bird of ill-omen, appears. There is a description of the tomb of Isora's parents, deep in a cavern, illuminated by an oil lamp. (The painting of Mary Magdalen, which can be seen in the church at Rennes, shows a young woman in a cave kneeling before a cross. There is an open book by her left knee and a skull by her right. Admittedly, the connection between the poem and the picture is tenuous, but it may still be worth further investigation.)

Ratbert arrives with his entourage. The castle has been spring cleaned in his honour. Special mention is made of a tapestry embroidered by Blanche d'Est, which is hung over the doorway. Is there any connection between this Blanche and the Blancheforts of Rennes?

Little Isora is dressed in regalia suitable for the king's visit. Fabrice mourns for Isora's mother. Eagles and birds of prey are seen near the castle — harbingers of the coming tragedy. Festivities are held in Ratbert's honour, but there is an atmosphere of decadence, death and lurking evil. Some of Fabrice's men are killed and birds of prey swoop on the bodies.

Suddenly Fabrice is accused of opposing the Church at some period in his earlier military career. He is arrested as a traitor, and Ratbert announces his intention of confiscating the estate of Final. Ratbert demands the secret of the treasure, but despite threats and torture Fabrice remains silent. The body of Isora is brought in. The child has been murdered. Fabrice blames himself for her death — he calls himself a fool for admitting Ratbert to his castle. In a powerful rage the old warrior curses the tyrant.

Afranus arrives and tells Ratbert that the treasure has been found. The king orders his executioner to decapitate Fabrice, but, at the same instant when the old warrior's head falls, Ratbert's head falls too, and disappears into a crevice in the earth, presumably en route for hell. Old Fabrice's head, by contrast, flies heavenwards. The vision of an angel is seen wiping a bloody sword on a cloud.

There are a number of interesting similarities between the Fabrice story and the Rennes story. The *dalle du chevalier* in the church at Rennes shows a crowned head on horseback and a child. It has been interpreted in various ways, usually as the infant Sigebert escaping with a loyal retainer from the ambush which proved fatal to Dagobert II. It might equally well represent Fabrice and the infant Isora attempting unsuccessfully to escape the attention of Ratbert. Fabrice's treasure, the treasure of Final was said to be buried in a cave or tomb, the exact location of which was a closely guarded secret. The treasure of Rennes was said to be buried in or near a tomb, or in a cavern beneath a tomb. The Fabrice story is set in Italy. Poussin went to Italy and it was from Italy that he sent his mysterious message concerning a valuable secret to Fouquet, via Fouquet's younger brother. The tombstone code contains the word *darles*, apparently as a misprint for *dables*, but could it not be *d'Arles*? Ratbert's kingdom of Arles was in Albigensian crusade territory during the thirteenth century. Can yet another link be forged between the treasure, the Albigensians and the Templars?

The symbolism is worth a second look when it comes to the beheading at the end of the poem. The evil king (Ratbert/Philip IV) strikes off the head of noble old Fabrice as Philip strikes down Jacques de Molay, Head of the Templars, but is immediately struck down as well. (Philip IV died in the same year that Jacques was burnt.)

The last enigma which Hugo leaves behind is in the preface to *La Légende des Siècles*: "All these poems . . . are condensed historical reality or guesses at historical reality."

John Napier

Another man of mystery who was contemporary with Sir Francis Bacon was the remarkable Scots mathematician, John Napier, sometimes rendered as Neper, the deviser of logarithms. He was born at Merchiston Castle, near Edinburgh in 1550 and was a redoubtable inventor, innovative mathematician and formidable religious controversialist until his death there on April 4th, 1617: the same year in which he published *Rabdologiae, seu Numerationis per Virgulas Libri duo*. This was his account of some ingenious new methods of performing multiplication and division using "rods" or "bones".

He went to the University of St. Andrews in 1563 when he was only thirteen years old, but seems to have left without taking a degree. From 1563 until 1571 little is known of his whereabouts, but he is said to have travelled abroad extensively: certainly this was the custom for young Scots nobles in the sixteenth century. Did he visit Holland and France during those years? Did he meet any of the people whom the Bacon brothers knew on the Continent? Did he meet any Priorists, alchemists or Rosicrucians? Did he get as far south as Rennes-le-Château?

In any event, he was back in Scotland again in 1571, and he married Elizabeth Stirling in 1572. She had a son and a daughter before her tragically early death in 1579, and a few years later John married Agnes Chisholm, daughter of Sir James Chisholm. She had five sons and five daughters and then went on to outlive John.

In 1594 Napier wrote a commentary on the Revelation of St. John and sent a copy to James VI of Scotland, whom he feared might be nursing secret Catholic sympathies: Napier was an unswerving and uncompromising Protestant. Is it just remotely possible that his depth of anti-Catholic sentiment might be a residual trace of Cathar sympathy after the tragedies of the Albigensian Crusade?

As though afraid that during the bitter religious dissension and acrimony of the times a Catholic-Protestant war was inevitable, Napier next turned his brilliantly inventive mind to the subject of weaponry, and this is where the mystery intensifies. Napier maintained that he had invented a piece of artillery — or some similar means of projecting or directing a missile, which was then capable of passing "not lineally through the enemy . . . " but was rather a projectile which " . . . rangeth abroad within the whole appointed place, not departing forth till it hath executed his whole strength . . . " What Napier seems to be describing is a missile which can change direction as it roams the battlefield and home in on more than one target: something scarcely within the capability of the most highly sophisticated contemporary electronic devices. He claimed that his invention would be just as devastating at sea and would "cut down by one shott the whole mastes and tackling of so many ships as be within the appointed bounds . . . "

He also claimed to have invented a fast and highly manoeuvrable light tank or armoured car capable of discharging volleys of arquebus (light musket) shots as it moved.

There is further reference in Napier's writings to a boat which can sail underwater and to a system of mirrors capable of directing intense heat towards an enemy position — rather like a modern laser weapon.

These are not the fantastic imaginings of a sixteenth century Scots precursor of Baron Munchausen, nor those of a North British Jules Verne: these are the sane and sober claims of a brilliantly inventive mathematician.

Sir Thomas Urquhart of Cromarty (1611 − 1660) wrote that Napier had invented "an almost incomprehensible device" which could clear a field with a circumference of four miles of all living things which stood over a foot high. Urquhart also maintained that in response to a bet Napier had once actually demonstrated this incredibly potent weapon very successfully, killing sheep and cattle up to a mile away in the process. Again, according to Urquhart, when Napier was on his deathbed an old friend asked him to disclose the secret of this amazing weapon. Napier is alleged to have said: "I will not allow humankind to be diminished by any new device of mine."

The insistent question remains: if the treasure of Rennes includes some strange esoteric power or knowledge did Napier incorporate some of it into his secret weapon? Like Marie Dénarnaud some three centuries later, Napier took his secret to the grave with him.

Le Comte de St. Germain

Of all the enigmatic characters to weave their puzzling strands across the courts of eighteenth century Europe few were stranger than the man who called himself the Comte de Saint Germain. Almost nothing definite is known of his real origin: there is some evidence that he came from a Jewish family in Portugal; that he was of royal blood (a Habsburg perhaps?); or that he was Polish, Italian or Spanish. What can be said with reasonable certainty is that he resided at several European Courts; that he was a very accomplished linguist; and that Louis XV of France entrusted him with several important diplomatic missions.

Friedrich Melchior, Baron de Grimm (1723-1807), the literary critic and diplomat, whose famous confidential fortnightly newsletters reached most European monarchs after 1753, described St. Germain as the most able man he had ever met. The Comte was certainly a very efficient and know-ledgeable chemist by eighteenth century standards: he claimed to know a secret method for removing the flaws from diamonds, to be able to transmute metals and to possess the elixir of life.

Horace Walpole wrote of him in 1743 that he had been arrested as a Jacobite spy, but was released shortly afterwards. Walpole added that St. Germain was alleged to have married a very wealthy Mexican lady: then deserted her, taking her jewels with him to Constantinople. (St. Germain was also said to be an ordained priest.) In due course he turned up in St. Petersburg where he was said to have had a hand in the conspiracy which brought Catherine II to power.

The almost equally strange Cagliostro wrote about St. Germain in his memoirs. The Comte was last heard of with any degree of certainty in Schleswig in the 1780's. Some accounts say that he died there, but little or nothing appears to be known of either the date or the precise circum-stances of his death. According to St. Germain himself he was many centuries old, and had been at King Solomon's Court when the Queen of Sheba paid her famous state visit there.

His valet claimed to have been given the elixir of life as well, and was once asked whether it was true that his master had been a guest at the wedding at Cana of Galilee where Jesus turned water into wine. "I can't say, sir," replied the valet with due gravity, "I myself have been in the Comte's service for only a century."

One old lady claimed that she had known him fifty years before in Venice, and that he had looked then more or less as he looked at the time when she was describing that encounter of half a century earlier.

His wealth was alleged to be as remarkable as his longevity: those who knew something about the technicalities of such matters said that his collection of precious gems was priceless — others alleged that the stones were fakes and cheap imitations. Whatever the rest of his collection may or may not have been worth, he presented King Louis XV with a diamond worth many thousands of pounds.

Did the Comte de St. Germain ever visit Rennes-le-Château? Surely his interest in alchemy, Rosicrucianism and occultism in general must have brought him into contact with the continental members of any mysterious groups who were involved.

Dr. Edward de Bono's stimulating books on lateral thinking and problem solving techniques advocate the use of supposing that something wildly improbable is true just for the sake of solving the problem. This supposition — however unreal — can then be used as a vital stepping stone to reach some other mental vantage point from which the problem can, hopefully, be studied from a fresh and more productive angle. Applying that technique to the Comte de St. Germain and the Rennes mystery, we might dare to suppose — purely for the sake of discovering some new argument — that the Comte was who he said he was; that he could do what he claimed to do; and that he had been where he claimed to have been centuries ago.

The feeling is much less substantial than what the older thriller and detective writers would have described as "a hunch", but there are times when the very curious atmosphere in and around Rennes-le-Château seems to give even the most objective, detached and pragmatic researchers the feeling that the oddness in this ancient place is being controlled, directed and manipulated by someone or something. You feel almost as if you have opened a door marked "Private" and stumbled inadvertently into an exclusive inner sanctum where venerable patriarchs, priests and archimandrites perform secret rituals and chant unknown liturgies in a language you cannot speak; or where expert players move grotesquely carved pieces in a game whose rules you do not understand. Yet there is also the disturbing feeling that they may be trying to involve you in whatever it is that is going on there . . . and that your opening of their forbidden door was not quite as inadvertent as you had originally assumed . . .

What if that wildly improbable supposition is true, and he who called himself the Comte de St. Germain in the eighteenth century still lives and seeks to exert some strange influence over events in Rennes?

Nicolas Flamel

Feet back on the ground! Our mysterious Comte de St. Germain was not the only alleged time transcender: there were also Nicolas and Perrenelle (or Petronella) Flamel, the alchemists. General accounts record that Nicolas Flamel was born in Pontoise in the early years of the fourteenth century and began his working life as a scrivener, a poet and a painter. Then he became an astrologer. He obtained a copy of a book on transmutation written by "Abraham the Jew" — a strange volume comprising twenty-one leaves made of tree bark and inscribed with some sharp metal instrument. The calligraphy was beautiful: the Latin text and the illustrations were cryptic in the extreme. After many years of unsuccessfully attempting to decipher this strange book, Flamel went to Spain to obtain help from expert rabbis there. It is recorded that this brought him success. On February 13th, 1382 it is reported that he produced silver, and, on April 25th of the same year, gold. There is no doubt that he and Perrenelle became immensely wealthy and, if the records are reliable, they both lived to be well over 100 years old. Like Saunière five hundred years later they spent lavishly: endowing churches, hospitals and charitable institutions.

In the course of his seventeenth century travels, Paul Lucas met a distinguished Turkish philosopher who claimed that far from being dead, Nicolas and Perrenelle were among his closest friends. In 1761 they were alleged to have been seen at the Paris Opera. Nimian Bres, the nineteenth century author of *Le Corbeau Menteur* claims that he saw both the Flamels in the Boulevard du Temple and recognised Nicolas instantly because of the many hours he had spent poring over *The Book of Abraham the Jew* in the Bibliothèque Nationale. Bres claimed that a drawing on the fifth leaf clearly showed Flamel's face among those depicted searching for gold.

Flamel is also listed among the supposed grand-masters of the Priory of Sion — if, of course, it ever existed at all.

Before examining the very curious case history of James Price, another alchemist, it might be worth recalling a quotation from *Suducismus Triumphatus* by Joseph Glanvill, D.D., F.R.S., who flourished in the second half of the seventeenth century.

"Facts ought not to be denied because we cannot see how they could have happened. It is unreasonable to presume a thing is impossible and then to conclude that it cannot be proved. Every action should be judged by evidence, not evidence by our prejudices about the action."

James Price and Dr. Irish

The quest for a stone or powder having the power to transform base metals into gold possibly began with the Spagyric Philosophers whose history is long, and whose beginnings are vague. Their beliefs included the idea that all metals were fundamentally the same. Throughout the Middle Ages many a court and many a castle employed — or was quietly exploited by — its resident mystic who combined magic and primitive chemistry in his search for the vital catalyst that would turn base metals into gold. Very few of them seemed to get very far — apart from Flamel, the Comte de St. Germain and whatever may, or may not, have happened at Rennes-le-Château — until the notorious James Price controversy in England in 1782. In that year Price bought an estate at Stoke near Guildford which had previously belonged to an old recluse named Dr. Irish. Neighbours hinted that Irish had died in his laboratory in mysterious circumstances. Young Price took his fiancée to inspect their future home, and, in the course of looking round the house, they discovered a manuscript attached to a sample of reddish-brown powder. In brief, the manuscript recorded that old Dr. Irish had admitted a wandering stranger in 1753 and that he had been very favourably impressed with the wanderer's scholarship and conversation. The stranger, according to Irish, had produced a curious looking oriental casket and shown him the four lumps of reddish-coloured, translucent substance that it contained. The wanderer had claimed that these were samples of the Philosopher's Stone, and had then conducted an experiment which had convinced Irish that it was possible to carry out transmutation. After the stranger left, Irish repeated the experiment, using a tiny fragment of the Stone which the mysterious visitor had given him. Again it worked, but he had used up the last of the Stone. He devoted his life to making more and to describing his experiments. He wrote persistently and constantly of the dangerous nature of the work and described how the tincture was placed in wax, how six drachms of mercury were added, how there was a hissing sound and the appearance of nitrous gases and how in fifteen minutes the mercury turned to purest gold. Irish's manuscript ended with the reiteration that his life was in danger and that he was now too old and ill to carry on. Price insisted on repeating the experiment and claimed that it succeeded. His fiancée left him in horror, convinced that it was black magic and against the laws of nature. Price became a recluse as Irish had been. He worked long and hard to discover the secret of the reddish powder, claimed to have done so, and then began giving demonstrations. The Royal Society invited him to disclose the process: he did not do so. Eventually, Sir Philip Clarke and Dr. Spence went to Guildford with an ultimatum: Price must prove his claim or face the consequences. He used up the last of his powder in one final unsuccessful experiment, snatched up and drained a flask of prussic acid . . . and died leaving his enigma behind him.

Of more direct relevance to the Rennes mystery than Price's tragedy is the question of old Dr. Irish and the identity of the mysterious wandering stranger who brought the four samples of the Philosopher's Stone to him in the first place: could that wanderer have been Nicolas Flamel or the Comte de St. Germain?

The Rosicrucian Order

From the mysteries of alchemy to the enigma of Rosicrucianism is a comparatively short step. The name was apparently unknown prior to 1598, but became famous in 1614 in Cassel in Germany after a pamphlet appeared there. It was entitled *The Fama of the Fraternity of the Meritorious Order of the Rosy Cross Addressed to the Learned in General and the Governors of Europe*. It claimed to be a message from some anonymous wise men who were concerned to improve the future of the world. The leaflet proposed that all intellectuals should join forces and thus synthesize science and the arts. The leaflet also advocated that science needed a drastic cleansing reformation — such as the one that the Church had just undergone — and so did the world's political and administrative structures. The leaders of the Rosicrucian Brotherhood were, of course, ideally suited to this work and would be more than happy to accept the responsibility of leading humanity to perfection!

The leaflet also gave a brief history of the Rosicrucian Order. Their leader was known as "C.R.C." who had been educated in a convent before going on to the Holy Land with "P.A.L." who died on the way.[1] Despite being only fifteen years old "C.R.C." went on alone and reached Damascus where he learnt of some theosophists of great erudition who lived in a mysterious unknown city called Damcar. He found his way there and was told by the illuminati that he was expected. After three years' training in Damcar he went to Egypt, as they had instructed him, where he learnt a great deal more and then travelled to Spain. He then spent five years in a hermitage in Germany before beginning to collect the nucleus of his future Rosicrucian Brotherhood around him.

In contrast to the remarkable information offered in the *Fama* about C.R.C. (Christian Rosencreutz?), the Rosicrucian ideas seem more likely to have emanated from a mystic and alchemist named Simon Studion who lived in Nuremberg at the time.

After a lapse of nearly a century, Rosicrucianism emerged again in Germany in 1710 when Sigmund Richter published a treatise on how to prepare the Philosopher's Stone, attached to which were the Rosicrucian rules for initiating new members. Another publication dealing with their sacred symbols was produced in Altona in 1785.

Taken together these documents give a broad picture of the Rosicrucian ideals. They seem to have included the doctrine of the Microcosmos which regards man as a miniature of the universe containing all its potentialities – this is in line with what Paracelsus taught. The Rosicrucians believed in elemental spirits, which is again a Paracelsan idea. They claimed to know how to operate the alchemical transmutation process and how to prepare and use the Elixir of Life.

One of their most famous English exponents was Robert Fludd (also named as a grandmaster of the elusive Priory of Sion). Fludd (or Flud) was born at Milgate House, Bearsted, in Kent. His father, Sir Thomas Fludd, served Queen Elizabeth as "Treasurer of War in the Low Countries". Robert went to Oxford at seventeen and graduated after five years, later studying medicine. Ultimately, he became a Fellow of the College of Physicians and built up an extensive practice in the Fenchurch Street area, a practice which flourished partly because of his genuine skills, and partly because of his dynamic personality. Dr. Fludd travelled a great deal: Italy, Spain, Germany – he may even have visited Rennes-le-Château. Settled in England again, he founded a Rosicrucian School, and wrote widely on magnetic medicine and alchemy. He moved later to a house in Coleman Street where he died in 1637.

The Knights Templar

No serious investigation of the Rennes mystery is possible without some close reference to the Templars. They were rashly adventurous, mysterious

---

[1]Both sets of initials, C.R.C. and P.A.L., are familiar in connection with modern technology. C.R.C. stands for "Cyclic Redundancy Check", used by computers to check the integrity of data received via some form of interface (from the outside world or from their own discs). The procedure involves performing a mathematical calculation on the data received, and comparing the answer with that received along with the data itself. If the two agree, the data is assumed to be correct. If there is a discrepancy, the computer assumes that the data has been garbled in transmission and asks for a repeat.

P.A.L. stands for "Phase Alternating Line", the television signal transmission system currently used in the U.K. PVST and reputedly the wealthiest order in medieval Christendom.

The dawn of Catharism mingled with the Merovingian sunset; the Templars and Cathars were contemporaries for all but the last fifty years of Templarism.

The Blancheforts, whose château was so close to Rennes, were said to have had Templar connections. The great stronghold of Bézu was near Rennes. The mysterious codes which we have examined in detail appear to have been put together in Templar style.

The Templars were known as the "Knights Templar" and the "Poor Knights of Christ and of the Temple of Solomon". Their Latin title was *pauperes commilitones Christi templique Salomonici*, and they were a true military order from their foundation in 1119 to their final overthrow at Castellat on November 2nd, 1308. Their founders were Godfroi de St. Omer from the north of France, and Hugues de Payns of Burgundy. These two took it upon themselves to protect the pilgrims who headed for Jerusalem and other shrines in Israel after the First Crusade. They were joined by six other knights who shared their ideals, and these eight adventurers swore an oath to the Patriarch of Jerusalem. They vowed "to give up worldly chivalry, to guard the public roads, to live in chastity, poverty and obedience and to fight with purity of mind for the true and supreme King".

Baldwin II, king of Jerusalem during 1118-1131, gave the Templars part of his palace for their headquarters. This section was adjacent to the al-Aksa mosque, which was popularly called Solomon's Temple, and it was from here that the Order took its title.

In their earliest period, the Templars were poor and had no special dress or habit. They were also a redemptive and evangelical order: their rule seems to have included the duty to seek out former knights who had been excommunicated, to obtain absolution for them from the bishop and to take them into the Order.

Israel was at that time infested with what Bernard of Clairvaux described as "rogues, impious men, robbers, committers of sacrilege, murderers, perjurers and adulterers". The Templars undoubtedly performed an important social function in reclaiming these outcasts and outlaws and welding them into a trained, disciplined fighting force. This may well have produced a number of famous Templar characteristics, not unlike those later associated with the French Foreign Legion and romanticized, though not unrecognizably, in P. C. Wren's novel *Beau Geste*. There was a rugged, independent, pioneering, warrior spirit about these early Templars. A fighting man's honour was more important to him than his life in the twelfth century.

The Order later enjoyed many important privileges, one of which was a link with its earliest days — members were immune from excommunication by parish priests and bishops. At a time when excommunication was taken seriously, this gave the Templars an enormous advantage. A powerful leader's excesses could often be curtailed by the threat of excommunication. Freedom from this made a Templar free indeed: like the knight on a chess board, which was often used as a Templar symbol, he could jump with impunity over pieces that blocked the moves of others.

Hugues de Payns knew that he needed official sanction at the highest level if he was to avoid the backlash of those whose powers he was short-circuiting. He went to Europe in 1127, where he obtained the backing of the very powerful Bernard of Clairvaux, contained in *De laude novae militiae*. In 1128, the Order was given official recognition at the Council of Troyes.

There has always been controversy over whether there was a secret or hidden rule of the Templars as well as the open rule, given in French as *Règle du Temple*. No manuscripts of the earliest open rule have been found, but historians are mainly agreed that the later copies which have survived are probably close to the Templars' original practice. This open rule contains the constitution, the regulations about dress and worship, the jobs and privileges of different ranks, methods of conducting meetings and the correct manner in which newcomers should be admitted. There are also instructions for electing the Grand Master, and notes on the relative position of the Templars to other Orders and to the Pope.

How far is it possible to speculate upon the existence of a secret rule? Travelling adventurers, especially those coming into contact with Eastern civilizations, were more likely to encounter esoteric teachings than those who stayed quietly at home, tending their orchards. Byzantium was a rich, ancient and flourishing culture at the time of the Templars; secrets as old as Rome itself could well have been preserved there. As the tides of war flow over ancient cities, they wash away the covers of formerly safe hiding places. A hidden chamber, once deep within a castle wall, will yield its secret to the first soldier who scrambles over the broken stone after the siege engines have done their work.

Many of the early Templars were reformed soldiers of fortune. Might some of them have acquired treasures during their plundering careers, treasures whose real significance and value they realized only dimly? Now that they had been admitted to the loyal brotherhood, was it not probable that their earlier plunder should be given to their Order? Travelling adventurers tend to talk to fellow spirits about their travels and their adventures. A tale from Damascus ties up with a story from Acre. A legend from Cyprus can be linked with a fable heard in Eschcol.

The Templars had contact with Egypt, and Egypt was the traditional origin of the Hermetic texts. There are repeated references to Hermeticism and Hermetic secrets in the stories surrounding the treasure of Rennes. Abbé Saunière was said to have consulted leading experts on Hermeticism during his work on the manuscripts and gravestone inscriptions. Hermeticism is sufficiently deep, complex and ancient to warrant a full volume on its own, but in essence it is concerned with magic, alchemy and hidden secrets. Mercury or Hermes, winged messenger of the classical gods, is shown with the serpent-entwined staff, or caduceus, symbolizing wisdom. In the second century, this classical Hermes gives way to Hermes Mercurius Trismegistus, or Hermes the Thrice-Great; his Egyptian equivalent is Thoth. Hermeticism falls into two main sections: popular, which deals with magic; and higher, which deals with theology, philosophy and the development of the soul.

It is well within the bounds of possibility that a secret, inner, theological and philosophical rule existed, known only to the highest officers of the Templars. This rule may have had a surprising amount in common with the Manichee faith, a Babylonian version of Gnostic dualism. Gnostic dualism is said to be expressed in one of two equal and opposite ways.

The aescetic, purist dualist — for example, a Cathar — expresses his contempt for all things earthly by avoiding them and regarding matter as evil. The excessive dualist, contemptuous of the physical universe because he believes it to be the work of an evil — or ignorant — demiurge, and of no consequence when compared to the world of spirit, indulges in whatever lifestyle he wishes. To him, if matter is unreal or unimportant, his treatment of it can have no moral consequences. The resultant free sexual behaviour, the refusal to fast or abstain from alcohol and the procuring of bodily satisfactions by any means available made the excessive Gnostics vulnerable to charges of immorality.

Furthermore, if a Gnostic Christian believed that Christ was a being of pure spirit, whose illusory human body was attacked by Satan, *Rex Mundi,* or the demiurge via the cross, then such a Gnostic Christian would regard the cross not as a sacred symbol of salvation, but as a sign of the enemy's attempt to destroy the divine, spiritual redeemer. In consequence, a Gnostic Christian would be more likely to despise the cross than to venerate it. One of the most serious charges levelled against the Templars was that they spat on, or near, the cross. Did they really do so? And, if they did, was it because their secret rule had this Gnostic or Manichaean flavour?

Bernard of Clairvaux died in 1153, but well before his death the Templars were successfully established in almost all the Christian kingdoms. Louis VII (born 1120, reigned 1137-80) granted them land near Paris which became their European headquarters. Henry I (born 1068, reigned 1100-35) gave the Templars more lands in Normandy. Stephen (born 1094, reigned 1135-54), who was Henry's nephew, gave them Cressing and Witham in Essex. His wife, Matilda, granted them the manor of Cowley in Oxfordshire. Eugene III (Pope 1145-53) granted them the right to have their own hallowed graveyards. Adrian IV (Pope 1154-59) added the right to have their own churches. They paid no tithes; they were exempt from general censures and Vatican decrees unless named in them specifically. This privilege and independence led to continual friction between Templars and the local church authorities, but as long as they were needed to keep open the routes to the Holy Land, the Templars were safe. Their decline and fall was directly linked to the decline and fall of the Latin Kingdom of Jerusalem.

The end of the Latin Kingdom of Jerusalem has the sombre majesty of a Greek tragedy. Gérard de Riderfort, a French adventurer, entered the service of Raymond, Count of Tripoli, was disappointed, left Raymond and joined the Templars where he patiently plotted Raymond's overthrow. Gérard became Grand Master of the Templars in 1184.

On the death of Baldwin IV, King of Jerusalem, his young nephew, Baldwin V, became king, with Raymond as guardian. The lad died in 1186. Gérard and his Templars moved in and crowned Sibylla (the dead boy's mother) and her husband, Guy de Lusignan, who was Raymond's rival. The frustrated Raymond now made an unholy alliance with the Sultan. Gérard and the Templars, accompanied by the Hospitallers, rode north. There was a hopeless battle against 7,000 Saracens, but Gérard and three knights cut their way through and got to Nazareth. Guy and Raymond then patched up their quarrel.

The rash courage of the Templars provoked the battle of Hittin (a military disaster for Christendom), and both Gérard and King Guy were captured by Saladin and held for a year. Most of the Templars and Hospitallers were executed immediately after the battle, but Raymond escaped.

One by one the Christian fortresses fell to Saladin, and on October 3rd 1187, Jerusalem itself surrendered. The Templars used some of their enormous wealth to buy safe conduct for the poorer Christians. More of their money was given to Conrad of Montferrat to pay for the defence of Tyre.

Yet again, the Christian princes quarrelled. Conrad would not accept King Guy, so the Hospitallers and Templars went with him to the siege of Acre. In the desperate battle of October 4th, 1189, their Grand Master, not wishing to survive his brothers in the Order, rode to his death with them.

When Acre fell, the Templars bought Cyprus from Richard of England for 1,000,000 besants, could not raise it all, and transferred the island to King Guy. When Acre was recovered, the Templars returned there. Later they built the great defence works of Castle Pilgrim, close by on a craggy spur of sea-wet rock, approachable only from the east; and it was from here that the Fifth Crusade set out against the Egyptians in May,1218. The Templars again lived up to their motto "First to attack and last to retreat". They were the heroes of Damietta.

Unfortunately the Templars were opposed to Frederick II because he was excommunicated. There was further trouble with Richard of Cornwall. The Hospitallers and Teutonic Knights disagreed with the Templars, but the Templars defeated both rival orders. Then came the Christian disaster of 1244, when the Sultan of Babylon called in the Kharizmians – a barbarian horde displaced by the Mongols. On October 18th the Christian army was virtually wiped out: 300 Templars rode into battle – eighteen survived; sixteen Hospitallers were left alive out of 200. The sad downhill trail continued: only three Templars lived through the battle of Mansura in 1250; the Egyptians, under the Mameluke Bibars, ground their way relentlessly northwards, capturing one Christian fortress after another. By 1272, the Templars were seriously weakened, but they still had enough strength left for bitter internecine warfare. Tripoli fell in 1290, and Acre the year after. A handful of Templars sailed for Cyprus and set up a new headquarters there.

The power of the Templars in Palestine and the Middle East was scarcely the tip of their iceberg. Their estates ranged from Ireland to the Mediterranean, from Denmark to Spain, but their true wealth lay in their banking activities. In its heyday, their Temple in Paris was the financial centre of the world. They were not only financiers on the grand scale, but also politicians and theologians: they acted as guardians of disputed castles; they were godparents to royal children; they attended the Lateran Council in 1215.

The suppression of the Order began with the insolvency and jealousy of the treacherous King Philip IV of France (born 1268, reigned 1285-1314). Having used Jewish and Lombard wealth, Philip exiled the Jews and Lombards. He then began to look greedily towards the Templars' wealth. He needed an excuse to attack them, and, if he once dared to attack, he was wise enough to know that he must destroy the Order completely or it would destroy him.

Their enemies told strange stories in whispers about the secret rites of the Templars. It was said that they possessed a magical head of bronze named Baphomet, and that it uttered oracles and prophecies. Some said this was the bronze-coated head of John the Baptist. Others claimed Baphomet to be an Arabian god with the head and hooves of a goat, a black candle between its horns, human hands, female breasts, the scales of a fish and the wings of an eagle. The Templars were said at their initiation to trample on the cross and to spit on it. They were accused of sodomy. In support of the suggestion that the Templars were black magicians, it was claimed that Jacques de Molay, their last Grand Master, cursed the French royal family even as he died in the flames, and reputedly it was this curse which brought Louis XVI from imprisonment to the guillotine 500 years later. (It must be disappointing for any self-respecting black magician to place an order and have to wait 500 years for delivery!)

In 1305, Esquiu de Floyran, who lived at Béziers not far from Rennes-le-Château, claimed to know the secrets of the Templars and betrayed them to King Jaime II of Aragon and Cataluna (1291-1327). Jaime had every reason to be grateful to the Templars and did not receive Esquiu with wild enthusiasm, but the thought of Templar treasure may have overcome the king's principles later. Esquiu was promised a share of the plunder if he could substantiate his charges. He then approached Philip IV of France, who was keen to exploit the opportunity Esquiu presented. At Philip's orders twelve spies were insinuated into the Templars to collect information while Philip made overtures to Pope Clement V. The divided loyalties of Clement are a significant factor in the Rennes mystery. He was related to the Blancheforts, and there had once been a Blanchefort Grand Master of the Templars. But Clement was also Philip's man; what was he to do? Clement stalled. He set up an inquiry into the Templars. He played for time. Did he secretly warn the Blancheforts? If so, it seems to have made little difference to the Templars' readiness to defend themselves, but the Templars of Bézu, near Rennes-le-Château, were said to have concealed their major treasures so effectively that Philip's men never located them.

Tired of Clement's delaying tactics, Philip turned instead to his henchman, William, Grand Inquisitor of Paris, because the Inquisition could act without the Pope. Philip's spies denounced the Templars to the Inquisition and the Inquisition demanded their arrest − turning, naturally, to Philip to put the demands into effect. On the night of Friday, October 13th, 1307, the arrests were made. Jacques de Molay, the Grand Master, was himself arrested in Paris.

Torture produced the required "confessions", some of them ludicrous in the extreme. Trials and councils, debates and discussions dragged on for nearly seven years. Much of the Templars' wealth and property was transferred to the Knights of St. John in 1312. On March 14th, 1314, Jacques de Molay withdrew his confession, testified to the innocence of his order and died in the flames.

Philip IV was also dead before the year ended!

The Priory of Sion

One of the main factors discernible in Templarism was the possible existence of a secret inner group, or hidden order, among the hierarchy. It is possible that this secret society existed even earlier than the Templars and that its members later infiltrated the Knights and became their inner core. The contents of the church at Rennes and the strange codes on documents and stones there all carry some evidence for the existence of a secret society calling itself The Priory of Sion. Knowledge of the Priory is very sketchy and speculative, but without some attempt to peer through the mist which enshrouds it, it will remain difficult to get close to the secret of Saunière's treasure.

The Priory of Sion could be one of the most ancient, powerful and remarkable secret societies in the world; it could be the last vestigial trace of an inner group of Knights Templars; or it could merely be the imaginings of one or two twentieth century crypto-politicians linked to the mysterious M. Plantard. It may be connected with Rosicrucianism, with Hermeticism, Cabalism, Mysticism and various other forms of magic. Is it possible to combine all these ideas about the Priory into one general theory? Its title is hardly copyright, and more than one individual or group may have used it at more than one time for more than one purpose.

The first theory of the Priory is that it could have originated as a group of very early Roman Christians, drawing some support from Jewish-Christian communities scattered throughout the Roman Empire, but strongest in the East. With or without much historical foundation, the Priory may have believed that the traditional lost treasures of the Temple of Jerusalem were still in existence and recoverable. Their quest for these treasures had both physical and spiritual aspects. In some ways their search resembled the later ideals of the Arthurian cycle and the knights' quest for the Holy Grail.

The physical aim of the search was the recovery of the gold and silver vessels and religious treasures which had once adorned the altars of Solomon's Temple and Herod's Temple. The spiritual objective was the recovery of faith and religious purpose, "purification of the soul" and a platonic "reunification of the world of ideals with the material world". The rediscovery and restitution of the physical treasure would be the sacramental indication that the spiritual objectives were also accomplished – "the outward and visible signs of the inward and spiritual truths".

Following this theory of the origins of the Priory leads to the Gnostics and Manichaeans who flourished in the early centuries of Christianity and whose "heretical" views may well have appealed to the members of the Priory in their quest for "truth" and "purity". Heretical sects that proclaimed their custodianship of hidden secrets could well have attracted the attention of members of the Priory, determined to leave no stone unturned in their quest for lost treasures – both spiritual and physical.

From the followers of Mani to the followers of Bogomil, the trail – though faint – can be traced, and from Bogomil to the Cathars of Razès is a shorter step than from Mani to Bogomil. Was the Priory there, too, following the Gnostic, Manichaean, Cathar trail from its earliest beginnings? Were some members of the Priory also Cathars? Might those select Cathars who escaped the flames of Montségur with their treasure also have belonged to the ancient Priory of Sion?

The second theory of the Priory of Sion, while not necessarily directly contradicting the first, suggests a rather later point of origin. According to this second hypothesis, the Priory was the secret inner hierarchy of the Templars — those who knew the Hidden Order as distinct from the Open Order. It was this inner élite of Templars who supposedly knew the so-called magical and alchemical secrets on which Templar wealth was allegedly founded, who knew the locations of their secret mines and laboratories (for example, the mine of Blanchefort and the Tower of Alchemy at Rennes) and who knew the truth about Baphomet. This Baphomet allusion (already referred to in an earlier passage) is itself worth further investigation. Some experts in the history of the occult — the late Dennis Wheatley among them — believe that Baphomet is intended to represent a composite eastern philosophical symbol of the Absolute. The head is the head of a goat, and a black candle is placed upright between the horns. There is a five-pointed star in the middle of the forehead. The prominent female breasts are bright blue, and the wings which spring from the shoulder blades are golden-brown like the wings of eagles. The abdomen is green and scaly like a reptile and the organs of both sexes are present — Baphomet is hermaphroditic. The legs are hairy and goat-like and end in cloven hooves. Each hand points with two contiguous fingers at a crescent moon. The left hand points down at a black crescent; the right points up at a white one. Baphomet sits on a cube whose faces may represent the six directions of time and space; north, south, east, west, past and future. The twelve right angles of the cube are possibly the twelve "houses" of the zodiac. Beneath Baphomet's hooves lies a globe, probably the symbol of the world — like *Rex Mundi,* Baphomet is said to be ruler of the earth.

Another theory suggests that the word "Baphomet" is formed from *Baphos* and refers to water. The Baphomet of the Templars, according to this theory, was a magical severed head, covered in gold leaf or bronze, and able to utter accurate oracles when questioned in conjunction with the performance of appropriate rites and incantations. This head, once John the Baptist's (hence *Baphos*), had been taken from Herod's palace after being struck off to gratify Salome. It has been suggested that, recognizing the latent oracular power of so potent a relic, a member of the Priory of Sion rescued the head and preserved it in gold leaf in a casket packed with magical herbs and spices. This, of course, takes the Priory back to the first half of the first century, and gives some credence to the idea that it may have been connected with the Essenes or other secret pre-Christian religious societies.

The Templars were certainly accused in the wilder rumours spread by their opponents of taking profane orders from a supernatural brazen head that spoke miraculously.

Another Baphomet theory suggests that, etymologically, the name comes from Mahommed via the Spanish *Mafomat* and the Provençal *Bafomet.* It is much more likely, however, that the word simply transliterates into Wisdom using the Atbash Cipher, and that the Templars revered personified Divine Wisdom which they encoded as Baphomet.

If the inner core Templars were also members of the Priory of Sion, what became of them after 1314 when Jacques de Molay died in the flames? Many Templars and sympathisers survived the persecution. Generally, the main result of persecution is to drive the persecuted into hiding and to make them more secretive than before. With an organization such as the Templars and its supposed inner group, the Priory, who were already famous for their secrecy, what further precautions might have been taken to elude their enemies? Did the Priory go so deeply underground in the fourteenth, fifteenth and sixteenth centuries that, for all practical purposes, it might as well have ceased to exist? These were the years when itinerant alchemists including Flamel and Paracelsus travelled all over Christendom – and beyond.

After these underground centuries of the wandering alchemists, which was a period when an accusation of wizardry, witchcraft or heresy could send the accused to the noose or the stake via the torture chamber, there is some evidence that the Priory began to pursue its affairs again more vigorously in the late sixteenth century.

If the Priory actually existed at all, it seems likely that its members recognized one another by using the code words *Et in Arcadia ego*. The physical Arcadia is a mountainous region of the Peloponnese. It is traditionally associated with the nature god, Pan, who closely resembles the odd statue inside Saunière's church, the one which is often referred to as Asmodeus or *Rex Mundi*. Pan is also linked by ancient legends to shepherds and a state of Eden-like rustic innocence as we have already noted. Guercino painted a picture showing shepherds examining a skull, and the phrase *Et in Arcadia ego* is associated with it. The generally accepted interpretation is "Even here, in the perfect land of Arcadia, I, death, am present". Other suggestions are, "Though I am now dead, I, too, was once in Arcadia, the land of perfect happiness", or, "Even though my body is dead my soul lives happily in Arcadia now". To a member of the Priory, it may have meant ubiquity as well as immortality. "Even in Arcadia (in the perfect land, the land of youth, the ideal country, the furthest imaginable place) the Priory is present"; as the psalmist speaks of the Spirit of God, from whom there is no escape in heaven or in Sheol, in the east or across the sea to the west, or in the darkness (Psalm 139: 7-12); or the more sinister words in *Nineteen Eighty-Four* by George Orwell: "The Thought Police are everywhere." Is this what the Latin motto really means? It is also the main theme of the famous Poussin painting, "Shepherds of Arcadia," which may have helped Saunière to find the treasure. It crops up again on the parchments and tombstones at Rennes.[2]

The late sixteenth and early seventeenth centuries were the period when the great English Elizabethans travelled extensively on the Continent. This was the heyday of the creative writers, artists, poets, actors and adventurers. This was the age during which Sir Philip Sidney wrote his famous and mysterious *Arcadia* with its coded watermarks, which were dealt with in the chapter on codes and ciphers. This was the epoch during which Francis and Anthony Bacon were possibly involved with a strange continental

---

[2]The phrase has recently been taken up as the name of a concert agency. Fritz Spiegl writes in "Classic CD" (August 1990 issue, page 11) about Et In Arcadia Ego Ltd. - "a name that starts off poetically but tails off in the prosaically fiscal disclaimer of the limited company. The address is not in Arcady but in London, NW6." PVST

secret society which could have been the Priory of Sion, or the Rosicrucians, or the former encapsulated within the latter. This was the period during which the wealthy lawyer Anson bought Shugborough Hall in Staffordshire, the same Shugborough in whose grounds now stands the Shepherd Monument bearing the inscription *Et in Arcadia ego* as well as its mysterious cipher. This was the time during which the Fouquet brothers were influential in France, and Poussin in Rome was apparently in the process of communicating vital secrets to them. The Priory could just possibly have been the link connecting this brotherhood of powerful and secretive men. If the Priory existed, and if the Rosicrucians existed as a genuine society, had the former infiltrated the latter?

Paracelsus

If there ever was a character who fitted the profile of a Hermeticist, a Rosicrucian, a master alchemist and a member (or Master?) of the Priory of Sion perfectly, that man was Paracelsus. His full name was Auroelus Philippus Theophrastus Paracelsus Bombast von Hohenheim, and he was born in Einsideln near Zurich in 1493. Paracelsus travelled extremely widely: he visited almost every part of the known world. He had an audience with the Cham of Tartary; he studied magic in Egypt and Arabia; he visited India; and finally settled in Basle in 1524 as Professor of Medicine at the University. His brilliant unorthodoxy led to a bitter quarrel with the Galenic school of medicine and there is strong evidence that someone of the Galenic persuasion poisoned him in 1541 — at least the circumstances of his death provided serious grounds for suspicion.

His teachings and writings exceeded the strangeness and excitement of his life: he foreshadowed Mesmer and Descartes and believed absolutely in the power of the mind and the will. "Resolute imagination," he wrote, "is the beginning of the magical operations . . . Because men do not perfectly believe and imagine, the result is that arts are uncertain when they might be wholly certain."

This is not a million miles away from Christ's own teaching about the vital importance of faith. Paracelsus believed — and, at least to his own satisfaction, proved — that humanity is infused with (or in constant close contact with) a universal spirit which directs and governs the physical body. Did he foreshadow the Gaia Hypothesis here? Was he getting at something like "The Force" in the *Star Wars* films?

Paracelsus was a truly amazing character — what he did and what he wrote deserve complete volumes on their own. If there was any significant manifestation of the Rennes mystery in this old proto-Rosicrucian's day, he is almost certain to have been aware of it and to have had a hand in it. Why did Saunière leave those rose emblems among the cryptic decorations in his church? All known Rosicrucian societies have included the rose and the cross among their symbols, but the Rosicrucian cross may be much older than Christianity. The Jewish Cabala gives symbolic meaning to both signs. Some alchemists regarded the cross, like the square, as the symbol of the four elements. Hindus regarded it as the emblem of creation.

The curious old Fountain of the Tritons outside the house in Montazels where Saunière was born.

Chasubles worn by Bérenger Saunière while he was Priest at Rennes-le-Château.

M. Fa;in, the sculptor, owner of Château Hautpoul, with a scale model of his home.

Exterior view of Château Hautpoul

The broken tombstone in the cemetery at Rennes-le-Château.

Statue of St. Mary Magdalen between Stations of the Cross XII and XIII in the Church at Rennes-le-Château.

Marcel Captier demonstrating the secret compartment in the ancient pulpit support, allegedly found by his great grandfather in Saunière's time.

Christ being baptised by John: statue in the church at Rennes-le-Château.

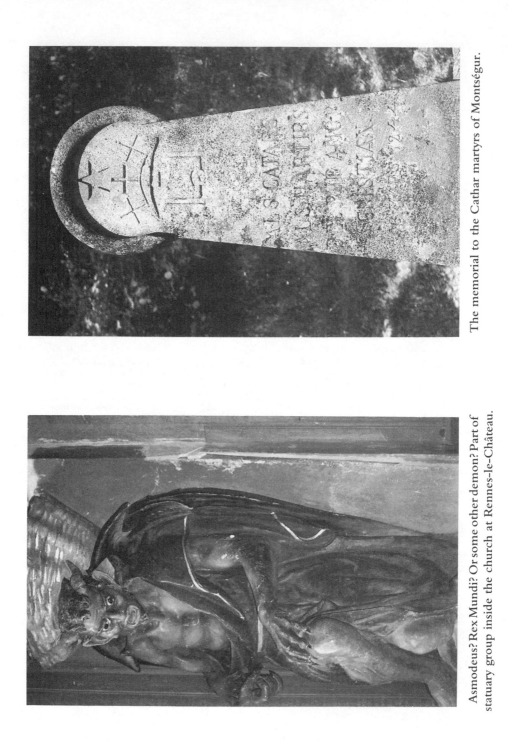

The memorial to the Cathar martyrs of Montségur.

Asmodeus? Rex Mundi? Or some other demon? Part of statuary group inside the church at Rennes-le-Château.

Lionel Fanthorpe discussing the role of Abbé Boudet with Pierre Bren, co-author of *L'occultisme dévoilé* and an expert on Boudet.

Twelfth Station of the Cross in the church at Rennes-les-Bains. Note the skull.

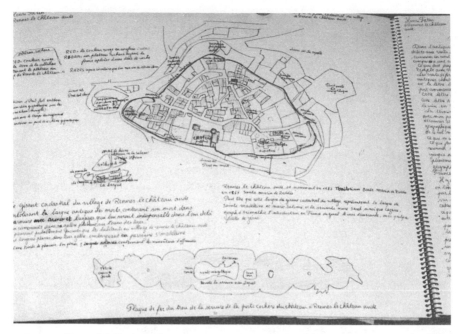

A page from M. Fatin's fascinating manuscript history of Rennes-le-Château, showing the outline of Rennes as the corpse of a giant warrior in a "ship of the dead".

Station X: the dice are cast for Christ's robe. Note the 3, 4, 5 faces. Perhaps a clue to a right-angled triangle? But just as 3^2 plus 4^2 equals 5^2, so 3^3 plus 4^3 plus 5^3 equals 6^3 (6x6x6)! All very curious!!

First Station of the Cross in the church at Rennes. Note that the lad attending
Pontius Pilate is black.

Are these curious ancient arches in Château Hautpoul the same ones that are
depicted on the knight's gravestone in the Museum?

Painting of Christ and Mary in the church at Rennes-les-Bains.

The Cathar fortress of Quéribus.

Lionel Fanthorpe, co-author, in the stronghold of Montségur.

The almost inaccessible Cathar stronghold of Montségur.

Poussin's "The Shepherds of Arcadia."

The Tomb of Arques as it was in 1975.

The site where the Tomb of Arques once stood.

The mysterious "bag of gold" below the feet of Christ: mural in the church at Rennes-le-Château.

M. Rousset, the doyen of Coustaussa, who showed us how to find Abbé Gélis's grave.

Interior of St. Sulpice, Paris.

Ancient Visigothic Cross in the cemetery at Cassaignes.

Part of the curious inscription on Abbé Boudet's grave at Axat.

Patricia Fanthorpe on the shore of Oak Island, Mahone Bay, Nova Scotia, with the mysterious Frog Island in the background.

Lionel Fanthorpe discussing the Oak Island mystery with Dan Blankenship of Triton Alliance, near Dan's home on Oak Island.

Entrance to the Triton Alliance shaft on Oak Island.

Rosicrucians Revisited - Links with the Priory?

In the thirteenth century poem, *Roman de la Rosa*, which was partly translated into English by Chaucer (et al.) as the *Romaunt of the Rose*, the rose may be the symbol of illumination, of the acquisition of knowledge and enlightenment. It may also be the symbol of love. The first 4,000 lines were written by Guillame de Lorris in 1240; the remaining 18,000 lines were added about forty years later by Jean de Meung. The *Roman* is set in a beautiful walled garden, which represents the dream world of courtesy, chivalry and medieval ideals. The harsh realities of life, such as treachery, betrayal, theft, sickness, old age, poverty and death, are painted on the outside walls. In the second part of the work, Jean de Meung gives a cynical, natural and realistic account of human relationships. Reason is one of the allegorical characters of the poem. There is a very close parallel indeed between the hypostatization of Reason and of Wisdom (Baphomet?). They are, in fact, almost synonymous. She plays only a minor part in the first 4,000 lines, but Jean de Meung makes much of her attempt to dissuade man from the extravagant nonsense of courtly love in the second, rational section of the poem. Chaucer's version is a powerful satire on the abuses of thirteenth century religion. In each version, however, whatever the correct understanding of the complex symbolism and allegory, it is the rose which is the object of the quest. If this was early Rosicrucianism and if it was another camouflaged vehicle for the Priory of Sion, could Guillame de Lorris, Jean de Meung and even Chaucer himself have been involved in it?

The rose is also identified with the sun, the heart of Zoroastrian worship. In ancient Egypt it was the symbol of rebirth and even, perhaps, of reincarnation. Lakshmi, the Hindu goddess of love and creation, features a rose among her emblems. The rose was also a symbol of secrecy, particularly a symbol of secret love affairs. One of the ancient Dionysian festivals was known as the Rosalia, and Dionysus was connected with the mysteries of Eleusis. If Rosicrucianism goes back that far and carries the Priory of Sion back with it, its roots are very deep indeed.

Some modern Rosicrucians regard the rose as the symbol of man, stretching out his arm to the sun. Yet another alternative is that the derivation of the word Rosicrucian is from *ros* meaning "dew" rather than from *rosa*. Ancient alchemists regarded dew as a vital solvent possessing magical properties.[3]

In the early seventeenth century, Rosicrucianism played no small part in the failure of Frederick V's attempt to secure the throne of Bohemia.

---

[3]My friend Paul Townsend has suggested two further possibilities for the derivation of the name.

The first is that the element "ros" is the Celtic word for "heath" (modern Welsh "rhos"). From "heath" = "countryside" comes the English word "heathen". The name "Rosicrucian" would therefore convey the idea of bringing the "cross" to the "heathen" – in other words, an evangelical movement.

The other possibility is that "ros" is related to various words for "red", e.g. French "rouge", German "roth", Italian "rosso", etc. "Rosicrucian" would therefore simply imply "red cross" – invoking the most familiar Templar symbol. Is the anonymous Red Cross Knight in Book I of Spenser's "Faerie Queene", vaguely identified with St George, a Templar? (Note that the modern Red Cross medical organisation has no connection here - their symbol is a simple "negative" of the Swiss flag.)

Frederick, Elector of the Palatinate, married the English Princess Elizabeth, daughter of James I, and, bravely but unwisely, accepted the throne of Bohemia. This was regarded as a direct challenge by the Habsburgs, and after one short winter in Prague, Frederick and Elizabeth fled to spend the rest of their lives in impoverished exile. Their son, Prince Rupert, was later to distinguish himself as a dashing and valiant cavalry commander with the ill-starred cavaliers of Charles I. During the Bohemian misadventure, James I might well have supported his daughter despite his paralytic fear of the Habsburgs, had it not been for the Rosicrucian support for Elizabeth and Frederick. James I's fear of the Habsburgs was second only to his abject dread of witchcraft, magic and anything unorthodox – including Rosicrucianism. Consequently, he refused to send an English force to help his son-in-law, thus incurring the deep hostility of Parliament, who were unanimous in their support of the English princess. These were the seeds of that parliamentary discontent which led eventually to Cromwell and the decapitation of Charles I, seeds watered by the Rosicrucian dew. It is interesting to speculate how far Francis Bacon, then at the height of his power, was involved in the Bohemian adventure, and how far its failure dragged him down as well as ruining the fortunes of Frederick and Elizabeth. If any of the great English statesmen of the time were Rosicrucians, or members of the Priory, Francis Bacon is a leading candidate; and it is even more likely that his quiet, loyal brother Anthony, who spent so much time on the Continent, was even more involved in deep and secret political and religious intrigues.

As we have already noted the most famous document of Rosicrucianism is the *Fama Fraternatis* which appeared in 1614. Most of it is devoted to the life of Christian Rosencreutz (C.R.C.?). According to *Fama Fraternatis* Rosencreutz died in 1484 at the age of 106 and was buried in a hidden tomb on the door of which was carved: "I shall open after 120 years". In 1604, the authors of *Fama Fraternatis* claimed that they had discovered and entered this tomb. It was a seven-sided vault, inexplicably illuminated. Rosencreutz's body, perfectly preserved, lay beneath an altar in the centre; nearby were magic mirrors and a mysterious manuscript called *The Book T*.

Secret tombs provide links with Poussin's "Shepherds of Arcadia", the monument at Shugborough, the tomb of Arques, and the strange Rennes legend of Ignace Parris, a young shepherd who found a cave, gold, skeletons – and his own swift death. Then there is Victor Hugo's story of the entombed treasure of the Marquis de Fabrice and the inhuman cruelty and greed of Ratbert.

What of the R.C. seal? What of the rose? A watermark of 1440-60 on a manuscript of the Spenser copy of the Apocalypse shows a letter P with a rose growing from it. Is this a link between the Priory of Sion and the Rosicrucians? An early copy of Ben Jonson's *Cynthia's Revels* bears the watermark I R C. Could it mean Jonson Rosy Cross? Double candlesticks, surmounted by grapes and carrying the letters C R or R C, are used as watermarks in Clark's *Examples*, dated 1656. In the 1638 edition of *History of Life and Death*, the watermarks include a lidded vase surmounted by a crescent and bearing the letters R C.

The Rennes parchments end with a cryptic P S, which is possibly the sign of the Priory of Sion. If it was indeed Abbé Bigou who left those

123

parchments in or near the altar, he was possibly a member of the Priory.[4]

Coming more closely up to date, The *Secret Dossiers* of Henri Lobineau record Charles Nodier (1801-44), Victor Hugo (1844-85), Claude Debussy (1885-1918) and Jean Cocteau (1918-63) as being among the most recent Grand Masters of the Priory. There was even a rumour current in Wales at the time of Barnes Wallis's death that he, too, had been a Grand Master – and the same was said of Isaac Newton!

There is also some evidence of a French friendly society, presumably similar to such perfectly legitimate and respectable organizations as the Oddfellows or Foresters in England, which was registered in 1956 as "The Priory of Sion" and recorded at the Sous-Préfecture of Saint-Julien-en-Génévois (Savoie) – but it is curiously hard to trace.

Real or imaginary? Ancient as Eleusis or modern as the welfare state, the bouncing bomb and the swing-wing aircraft? What and where is the Priory of Sion, and what keys does it hold to the mystery of Rennes-le-Château? The enigmatic M. Plantard may well be the only living man who could answer those intriguing questions.

Another man of mystery who cannot be ignored is the Bavarian Knight, Wolfram von Eschenbach, to whom we are indebted for the story of Parzival, the Grail Knight. Wolfram, who wrote sometime between 1190 and 1220, says that he got the basic facts from Kyot de Provence who in turn got his information from an eastern astrologer, Flegetanis, and from the writings of Mazadan which he discovered in Anjou.

In Wolfram's version, Parzival goes to seek the mysterious Grail Castle. His uncle, a hermit, tells Parzival that many brave Templars live there as guardians of the Grail, which he describes as a kind of magical stone which bestows healing and longevity. The stone is described as *lapsit exillis* which might mean "stone *ex caelis*" – fallen from the heavens. This produces an interesting nexus with the ancient stone sacred to the Earth Mother, or Venus-Aphrodite, and believed to be of meteoric origin. Alternatively, the Latin might be a corruption of *lapis elixir*, the stone from which the Elixir of Life is made.

In addition to its healing and life sustaining powers, Wolfram's Grail is a cornucopia: it provides ample quantities of all types of food and drink.

The Troubadours

The Grail bearer is a beautiful, queenly woman, Repanse de Schoye; a name which might be a corruption of the French phrase *réponse de choix* – the chosen response – or *réponse de la joie* – the joyful response. The visitor to the Grail castle has to make the right response: to ask the appropriate and acceptable questions. The enigmatic Kyot from whom Wolfram obtained his information may have been a mysterious troubadour named Guiot, whom Wolfram could have met at the Chivalric Festival in Mayence in 1184. This was the occasion when Frederick Barbarossa, the Holy Roman Emperor, conferred knighthood on his sons, and it is almost certain that a Bavarian knight like Wolfram would have

---

[4]There is also, in view of the RC/PS connection, the intriguing possibility of the letter pairs P/R, C/S being simple transliterations between the Roman and old Greek alphabets. The ancient form of the upper-case sigma is "C", a form which was incorporated into the Cyrillic (Russian, Bulgarian, Serbian) alphabet and survives there to this day. PVST

attended such an important occasion. Guiot (or Kyot) provides a link with the French *troubadours*, the German *Minnesingers* and their possible role in the mysteries surrounding Rennes-le-Château.

The very name *troubadour* has interesting derivations. These poets and musicians from southern France, northern Spain and northern Italy wrote in the *langue d'oc* and flourished from roughly the end of the eleventh century to the closing years of the thirteenth. The modern French *troubadour* derives from the Occitanian *trobador* which is the accusative singular form of *trobaire*, "poet", which in turn comes from *trobar* meaning "to create, find or invent". The modern French *trouver* is similar.

To be a *troubadour* then was to be an inventive writer, a creator of new songs and poems, an innovator of elaborate lyrics. Some troubadours were kings and princes — Richard the Lion Heart, for example. Others were itinerant adventurers who literally sang for their suppers.

There was something of an apprenticeship system among troubadours; many of them were accompanied by *joglars* who provided their music and sometimes sang the songs the troubadours had written. There were probably no more than 400 troubadours all told during their two centuries of flourishing activity.

It would be difficult to overestimate their influence. They spoke freely on almost every topic, were involved in politics, and created a special romantic atmosphere around the ladies of the many courts they visited.

The fall of the Cathars and the ravaging of the Languedoc by the Albigensian Crusaders also brought about the decline and fall of the troubadours. When the quarrel between Rome and the Cathars flared up into open warfare in 1209 the barons of northern France were all too eager to descend upon the rich lands of the Count of Toulouse. Tragically for the troubadours, nearly all their patrons and protectors were either Cathars or Cathar sympathisers. When the Albigensians went down their supporters were inevitably dragged down with them into the general disaster and desolation of the Languedoc.

Guiraut Riquier, the last of the real troubadours, lived from 1230 to 1294. He was born in Narbonne and his patron was Alphonso the Wise of Castile. "The gathering darkness," wrote Guiraut, "makes it useless to be a troubadour . . . Songs are for joy, not sadness . . . I have come into the world too late . . . "

These talented, intelligent and widely travelled, singing adventurers knew every court and castle of the Languedoc. What strange secrets did they learn and share and record, perhaps, in their complex and elaborate *chansonniers* (song books)? What better, or safer, cover for a member of a mysterious secret society (such as the Priory of Sion was believed to be) than the guise of a wandering minstrel?[5] Believing himself to be the last of his kind in the tragic twilight of the Languedoc, did Guiraut Riquier in particular commit what he knew to musical codes and metrical ciphers hidden among the *leys d'amors* (love songs) and *sirventes* (political satires) in his chansonniers?

---

[5]Compare with Gilbert and Sullivan's "The Mikado", where "A wand'ring minstrel I/A thing of shreds and patches,/Of ballads, songs and snatches/And dreamy lullaby" turns out to be none other than the son of the Mikado himself. PVST

The Man in the Iron Mask

From the mysteries which the troubadours and Minnesingers may have known, we pass to a very different riddle — yet one which is not so far from them when we recall the famous episode in which Blondin the Minstrel found the castle where Richard the Lion Heart was imprisoned. The Man in the Iron Mask — who was he and what was the real reason behind his bizarre and prolonged incarceration?

What connection — if any — could the masked prisoner possibly have with the mystery of Rennes-le-Château? The conditions of his lengthy imprisonment were strange. No one except St. Mars, King Louis XIV's trusted agent and prison governor, was to speak to the masked prisoner, or to listen to anything he might try to say. If anyone did, he was to be executed immediately. The prisoner was treated with great respect and courtesy as if he were of royal blood, or at least of very high rank.

The whole mysterious affair has all the hallmarks of a classic "stand-off" situation. The masked prisoner is so potentially dangerous that he must never be allowed to escape and must never be allowed to communicate with anybody. Yet — for some unexplained reason — he is so valuable that he must be kept alive. Simple political pragmatism in the seventeenth century dictated that when a potentially dangerous opponent or rival fell into your hands you simply killed him . . . unless, of course, he was the sole possessor of a secret of such importance that you, yourself, wanted badly enough to run all the risks entailed in keeping him alive.

Fouquet junior met Nicolas Poussin in Rome and wrote the famous letter to Fouquet senior. Suppose that Poussin subsequently disclosed his amazing secret — whatever it was — to the brothers. Assume that Louis XIV discovered — or at least strongly suspected — that the elder Fouquet had access to something which he, Louis, desperately wanted: ultimate weapons like the ones which Napier described; the secret of transmutation; the Elixir of Life?

Fouquet and Louis are both sophisticated pragmatists and realists; both are politically astute. Fouquet knows that as soon as Louis has the information, he, Fouquet is expendable. Louis knows that if Fouquet can escape, or get word to his family, friends or supporters, the power of the great secret can all too easily be turned on the man responsible for the long imprisonment . . . Power like that can all too easily reverse the roles of captor and captive.

There are other contenders, of course, but Fouquet is as likely a candidate as any for the dubious honour of being the Man in the Iron Mask, and, if he was, then the secret he withheld from Louis for all those years was in all probability linked to the secret of Rennes-le-Château.

It has also been suggested by some researchers that the secrets of the Cathars, the troubadours, the Templars, the Alchemists and the Rosicrucians eventually found their way into the safe keeping of the Freemasons. Mrs. Henry Pott makes an interesting comment about this in her book about Sir Francis Bacon's secret society: "With Freemasonry the occult fraternity has only this much to do, i.e., that some of the Rosicrucians were also Freemasons . . . "

That seems to be the sum and essence of it: modern Freemasonry is in no sense the inheritor of the Rosicrucian or any other "mystic" or "magical" mantle from remote antiquity or even from the medieval world. Co-author Lionel Fanthorpe's father and elder brother Hugh were both long-serving Freemasons and Lionel Fanthorpe himself was a Master Mason and a member of Bishop Bowers Lodge while the authors were living in Norwich in the 1970's. None of them ever encountered anything unpleasant, objectionable, strange, eerie, bizarre or mysterious in the sense that Rosicrucianism, Hermeticism and Alchemy purport to be the repositories of arcane and esoteric supernatural knowledge. There may well have been Freemasons who were also members of the Priory, the Order of the Rose Cross, the New Templars or any other mystic fraternity – but English Freemasonry is simply and unconnectedly contemporary with those organisations. It is not derived from – nor in any sense dependent upon – them.

The Inklings (Tolkien, Lewis, Charles Williams) and George MacDonald

We have already mentioned the serious possibility that Professor J. R. R. Tolkien was one of those who may have known more than most about the mystery of Rennes-le-Château. When Gandalf and his companions reach Moria, a vast and sinister labyrinth below a mountain, they are involved with the treasure chamber and the burial place of a dead king. Over and above everything else, however, hovers the malevolent presence of The One Ring, made by Sauron, the Lord of Evil, long ages ago. Its power is dark and mysterious. Beside the value of the One Ring, any mere treasure of silver, gold and jewels shrinks into insignificance. The whole story is the story of a great quest, and the reinstatement of a "lost" king – almost parallel to the reinstatement of Dagobert II. Is it possible that Tolkien's *Lord of the Rings* contains hints and clues in the same way that Victor Hugo's poetry is supposed to do?

Tolkien was a close friend of Professor C. S. Lewis, and Lewis's brilliantly imaginative writings might also contain hints about the Rennes-le-Château enigma. At least one knowledgeable Rennes researcher (see Conclusions) describes Rennes as "a gateway to the Invisible", and she could well be right. C. S. Lewis's writings are full of mysterious gateways to enchanted worlds: there are the magic rings which lead to the mysterious Wood-between-the-Worlds in *The Magician's Nephew*, there is the wardrobe in *The Lion, the Witch and the Wardrobe* which leads to the other world of Narnia; there is the door in the wall at the back of the gym in Experiment House which takes Jill and Eustace to Aslan's Mountain.

In *Till We have Faces*, which is based on the myth of Cupid and Psyche, Lewis refers to that curious ancient statuette of the goddess which was believed to have fallen from the sky. In *That Hideous Strength*, a mysterious ancient magician (Merlin) sleeps in a curious underground chamber near an ancient university – which from its description sounds uncannily like Durham, but is never positively identified.

Most mysterious of all is the sixty-four page fragment called *The Dark Tower* which was providentially rescued from a bonfire by the happy intervention of Fred Paxford (the gardener) and Father Walter Hooper, immediately after Lewis's death. In *The Dark Tower* Lewis begins the story of a strange parallel universe, a different probability track, to which human beings can occasionally gain access – yet another example of doors into unknown worlds.

Charles Williams was also a member of that very exclusive group "The Inklings" of which Tolkien and Lewis were the most prominent members. Williams shared their interests to a very great extent but was himself something of an expert on the Tarot. His mystical and mysterious novel, *The Greater Trumps,* is centred around the Tarot pack as integrally as *Alice through the Looking Glass* is centred around the chess board.

Three brilliantly intelligent, sensitive and imaginative men all equally interested in other worlds, in the arcane, the romantic and the mysterious: each in his own subtle way referring to curious things that could link up with the Rennes-le-Château mystery . . . It might be only a coincidence, of course, or it could be that they knew something . . .

Brilliant thinker and superb stylist that he was in his own right, Lewis was also a very generous man. He always gave massive credit to George MacDonald: "I have never concealed the fact that I regarded MacDonald as my master," wrote Lewis, "indeed I fancy I have never written a book in which I did not quote from him." Lewis always regarded the old Scots divine as his mentor, and praised him accordingly. Two of MacDonald's great fantasy stories were *Phantastes* and *Lilith*. In the latter, there is a mysterious old mansion, or castle, which has a library where, by a peculiar arrangement of mirrors, it is possible to move from our world into a very strange realm.

In real life the young George MacDonald spent some time working in the library of a great house, or castle, in Scotland, and that experience flavoured many of his subsequent books. The precise location and identity of that great house, or castle, has never been discovered: what if it was none other than Merchiston Castle near Edinburgh, home of the mysterious John Napier, mathematician and inventor? What if the young George MacDonald found something in that library, and later incorporated at least part of it in coded or symbolic form into some of his mysterious books about fascinating unknown worlds? What if MacDonald's clues eventually set Lewis, Tolkien and Charles Williams thinking along the same track? Pure speculation, of course, but by no means impossible.

MacDonald was a contemporary of Bérenger Saunière, and both were clergymen though of very different denominations.

Nikola Tesla

Another contemporary of theirs was one of the strangest and most brilliant men of the late nineteenth and early twentieth centuries: Nikola Tesla, born on July 10, 1856 at Smiljan in Croatia. As a child, Tesla had an amazing facility for mental arithmetic: mathematical calculations just seemed to happen in his head faster than he could write them down.

One day in 1882, Tesla was walking through Budapest with his friend Szigeti when he saw a sudden strange vision: it gave him the idea for his revolutionary invention — the alternating current motor.

Tesla went to the USA in 1884 and worked with Edison for a while before establishing his own Tesla Laboratory in New York, where he died on January 7th, 1943.

Kit Pedler, writing in Colin Wilson's superb collection *Men of Mystery* (W.H.Allen, London, 1977) describes an alternative framework of science: one in which the individual "scientist" is an integral part of a system in which he, or she, also has a vital creative and formative role. This is coming very close to what Paracelsus says about "magic" and to what Michell and Rickard say about phenomenalism. Outstanding but unorthodox geniuses like da Vinci, Napier and Tesla all seem to have been in contact with Pedler's "alternative framework".

A colleague was once told by Tesla that he had not only invented and built, but was actually in the process of carrying out test runs on several electrical machines. Tesla was telling the simple truth as he saw it, but those machines existed only in his framework of reality.

O'Neill says in his biography of Tesla that Nature seemed to be constantly staging spectacular demonstrations for him, revealing the secrets of some of her mightiest forces.

What if the heart of the enigma with which all our Men of Mystery seem to have been involved was some form of superior communication? But communication with what? Or with whom?

CHAPTER EIGHT

THE HABSBURG CONNECTION

Austriae est imperare orbi universo
(Motto of the Habsburg Emperor Frederick III)

The problem of Rennes-le-Château is to try to find a way through the tangled threads which seem to connect the village and its mysterious treasure with the Jews of the Old Testament, Romans, Visigoths, Albigensians, Templars, Alchemists, Rosicrucians and those who came after. The clues, however, never seem to lead to answers – only to other clues. The light at the end of the tunnel is not an exit; it shines on the entrances to a hundred more tunnels, each longer and more tortuous than that from which the explorers have just emerged.

Victor Hugo's strange story of Ratbert and the tragedy of Fabrice, Isora and the hidden treasure points vaguely in the direction of the ancient House of Habsburg. Here is a noble old European family, powerful and ancient enough to have been involved in some of the earliest treasure episodes, but tired, fragile and moving into its twilight by the time Bérenger Saunière came on the scene.

There are particular aspects of the Habsburg connection which may be significant in unravelling the mystery of Rennes: their early connection with the Visigoths, the death of Crown Prince Rudolf at Mayerling and the mysterious end of Johann Salvator.

The very earliest Habsburgs are difficult to trace accurately – not because there is a paucity of genealogical evidence, but because there is a flood of legend. Court historians and reward-motivated royal genealogists had tried on and off for six centuries to connect the Habsburgs with Julius Caesar and back, beyond him, to the Trojan Prince Aeneas. Others attempted to link the Habsburgs with the Carolingians, or the more legitimate Merovingians, and so, following the old Frankish legends, back to the Trojans again, albeit by an alternative route.

It may well be, Frankish and Roman legends apart, that the first historically reliable Habsburg was a certain Guntram who flourished in the middle of the tenth century. This Guntram had a grandson who died round about 1040. His name, like others of the period, has been subjected to the vagaries of non-formalized spelling and has suffered again in translation. One acceptable spelling is Radbot and this is close to the name Ratbert which Victor Hugo uses to identify the villain who destroyed Fabrice and his granddaughter.

If the treasure of Rennes-le-Château does involve Carolingians and Merovingians, together with Victor Hugo's legend of Fabrice's hidden treasure, then Radbot/Ratbert may be one of the links connecting Rennes with the Habsburgs, or, at least, opening up a Habsburg dimension to the curious events centred upon Rennes.

There is some local hearsay evidence to suggest that Bérenger Saunière found a treasure which had immense symbolic value. This is not incompatible with its having passed from Palestine to Rome and having been known to pious Albigensians and crusading Templars. A religious relic of extreme age and unquestioned authenticity would be priceless − provided the finder could reach a market. Two obvious potential buyers spring to mind: the Vatican and the Holy Roman Empire. For Saunière, the former was ruled out because he worked for it. A serving priest could hardly ask the Pope to pay for a holy relic found in or near a Catholic church. It would be like a jeweller's assistant finding a diamond ring which had been hidden under the floorboards of his employer's shop and then asking the proprietor to pay for it!

So if what Saunière had found included a relic he was left with one customer only − the Archducal Dynasty who had been Holy Roman Emperors for more than five centuries. The punctilious Franz Josef would be unlikely to wish to be seen entertaining a mercenary priest who had obtained a sacred relic by dubious means. Yet, on more than one occasion, the Emperor does not seem to have been completely averse to putting political or dynastic expediency before the letter of that moral law to which he was ostensibly a dedicated subscriber. It would have been in keeping with Franz Josef's attitude to get what he wanted by using a junior member of the dynasty as his confidential agent. His nephew, Johann Salvator, could have been involved in this way.

Younger members of the dynasty were certainly not afraid of involvement in risky adventures if it seemed that the light at the end of the tunnel justified taking a chance with the intervening shadows. Maximilian's tragic flirtation with Mexico serves as an example. Egged on by the wily and unreliable Napoleon III (with him as a friend, who needed enemies?), the hapless Maximilian enjoyed a brief titular rule as Emperor of Mexico and finished up facing a firing squad on a hill just outside Queretaro.

Before his death, Maximilian wrote a last letter to Franz Josef asking the Emperor to "remember kindly" the Belgian and Austrian soldiers who had served faithfully during the Mexican fiasco. One by one they struggled across the world and presented themselves at the Hofburg. Among these returning veterans three very strange characters presented themselves. They gave their names as the Archpriest Roccatani, Don José Maroto and Antonio de la Rosa (could there be any possible connection with the Rosicrucians?) and asked for an audience with the Emperor himself. They claimed to have a priceless secret for his ears alone: transmutation. They also claimed to be devoted servants of the Habsburgs, whom they said they regarded as the last bastion of legitimacy and the ultimate stronghold of true religion. The audience probably went well because this was more or less the way Franz Josef thought of the Habsburgs! Their offer was to transmute silver into gold, and the three itinerant philosophers asked for an initial stake of five million gulden in pure silver from the imperial mint. Despite the keen surveillance of a professor of chemistry appointed by the Emperor to keep an eye on things, over 90,000 gulden were unaccounted for when the experiment was terminated. Is it just another odd coincidence which links the Habsburgs with alchemy and Rennes-le-Château? Maximilian had not been afraid of adventure — neither had Johann Salvator.

Johann was a descendant of that cadet branch of the Habsburg family who became Grand Dukes of Tuscany. These Tuscan rulers were almost autonomous under the wider Habsburg aegis. Some perceptive historians have described them as Latinized Habsburgs. They were informal, imaginative and happy — everything that Franz Josef was not. Leopold II, who was Johann's father, was forced to leave Tuscany in 1859 after the Emperor's defeat at Solferino. His eldest son, Ferdinand, reluctantly renounced his claim to Tuscany, but was allowed to retain his title for life. Ferdinand's younger brother Karl was an expert locksmith. The next brother Ludwig was an intelligent eccentric: a brilliant linguist who dressed like the peasants and kept (so rumour suggested) a crew of beautiful girls on his boat by disguising them as boys. Johann, the youngest brother, was in fact seventeen years younger than Ferdinand. His mother was Maria Antonia, daughter of Francis I, King of the Two Sicilies. She was a strong-willed woman and a devout Catholic who seems to have written off Ferdinand and Karl as nonentities; her disapproval of Ludwig was monolithic. All her hopes for the future were, therefore, centred on Johann, and this must have affected his psychological development significantly. He was undoubtedly a very able man, but impatient and eager for opportunities to exercise real power. They never came.

Johann's Christianity wavered until he was on the verge of becoming a freethinker. Maria Antonia was desperately anxious about this, but he wrote to reassure her, "I can say that I am not a bad Christian".

He had architectural talent, and his work on the improvements and restoration of Schloss Orth was impressive.

He passed military and naval examinations like an Olympic athlete, taking hurdles en route to a gold medal. It was part of his determination to show the older generation of Habsburgs that he was a man to be reckoned with. Franz Josef and Archduke Albrecht grudgingly recognised Johann's ability, but steadfastly refused to give him power or to listen seriously to his ideas.

Unharnessed talent runs wild if frustrated. Dillinger and Capone might have been great leaders if society had had a niche for them. Johann wrote indiscreetly, and his work was traced — his promotion was blocked indefinitely. Conservative circles next to the Emperor regarded him as "unreliable".

Shortly after the death of Crown Prince Rudolf at the Mayerling hunting lodge, Johann renounced his title and studied for a master's certificate in the merchant navy. He acquired his certificate and sailed for South America in the Saint Margaret on March 26th, 1890. His faithful mistress, Milli Stubel, joined him at Buenos Aires, and they set off together on July 12th to round Cape Horn in the Saint Margaret. It was a dangerous route, the weather was appalling and Johann had little experience of the sea. There is no reliable evidence that they were ever seen again but rumours circulated for years that he was in India, Japan or South America. He was not officially presumed dead until 1911.

The possibility of Johann Salvator's involvement in the Rennes affair hinges on a question of dates. When, exactly, did Bérenger Saunière find his treasure? Or did he find it in instalments? Suppose that the relic, if it existed, turned up earlier than the other valuables. Suppose Saunière makes discreet enquiries in the Hofburg some time between 1886 and 1888, and is told that Johann will see him. The relic, treasure, secret or whatever it is, passes to Johann in return for the promise of regular cash payments to Saunière. There is some evidence that bank accounts for Saunière and for Salvator were opened in the same Austrian bank on the same day and that money was transferred periodically from Johann's account to Bérenger's.

Johann was an ambitious and frustrated young man, as was his cousin, Rudolf the Crown Prince. Such men are likely to get together. Suppose that they did, and suppose also that whatever it was that Saunière had brought to Johann might have had some political value. If it was the same thing that Poussin wrote of to Fouquet, kings would have given much to possess it. Kings were notoriously fond of power. It is possible that what was found at Rennes was a power source: an artefact, a relic, a focus, a psychological or sociological rallying point. Its precise nature is unimportant at this stage of the argument. Armed with this power source, the two frustrated young Habsburg princes might have been tempted to try to stage a coup. They could have been so desperate and so deluded that they were eager to grasp at any straw: transmutation, divination, the elixir of life, or the support of some ubiquitous secret society – real or imagined. Each man was a tragic mixture of Hamlet and Macbeth.

Rudolf, born in 1858, was six years younger than Johann. His mother Elisabeth, was beautiful, independent, sensitive and intelligent. She had been at war with her mother-in-law for years and was not in love with Franz Josef. She sorted out her problems by taking long tours away from the Hofburg. She was, perhaps, the one person who could have helped and understood Rudolf, but the long trips abroad which she needed for her own psychological defence meant that she was not often there when he needed a confidant. Because her mother-in-law had wrecked Elisabeth's relationship with Franz Josef, she kept well away from Rudolf after his disastrous marriage.

Rudolf was a delicate, nervous boy and needed perceptive, sympathetic handling. His first tutor was the old-fashioned Count Gondrecourt who gave him military drill in the snow to "toughen" him; he once locked him in the zoo, shouting that a wild boar was loose, to "strengthen his nerves". The best thing Elisabeth ever did for Rudolf was to tell Franz Josef that either Gondrecourt went or she did.

Rudolf's next tutor was Count Joseph Latour von Thurnberg. Latour was ideal for Rudolf, and in later life they became firm friends, but even Latour was not really close to the unhappy, frustrated, idealistic, young, liberal heir to the old, traditional, conservative, Catholic monarchy.

Like Johann, Rudolf wrote indiscreetly, and made friends who were *persona non grata* to the Austrian hierarchy. One of the most notable of those was Moritz Szeps, the gifted editor of the liberal *Neues Wiener Tagblatt*, who came to the prince's apartment by a backstairs route to avoid the guards posted by Rudolf's suspicious uncle Albrecht.

Rudolf was quick-tempered and careless, unless the apparent carelessness was a cloak for a deeper and more sinister deliberation. In the late

1880's, Rudolf almost shot Franz Josef "accidentally" during a hunting expedition. The prince was ordered off the field for the rest of the day, but apart from that the Emperor took no action.

There were persistent rumours that Rudolf and Johann were planning a coup, and that on its successful completion they would divide the Austro-Hungarian Empire between them.

It was at the end of 1888 that Maria Vetsera came into Rudolf's orbit. She was an attractive eighteen-year-old minor countess whose mother Hélène, was a social climber. Countess Marie Larisch was instrumental in arranging the prince's assignations with Maria. Larisch was as discontented and frustrated as Rudolf himself. They were the same age, and it seemed at one time that they might marry, but Larisch, although physically attractive and energetic, was strangely devious and sinister. Her motives in "helping" Rudolf and Maria to get together may have been far from benign.

Maria herself was rather an odd girl with wildly extravagant romantic ideas and strange illusions about the juxtaposition of love and death. Her imagination ran down deep, dark tunnels where romantic ecstasy and morbidity formed the stalagmites and stalactites waiting to trip or impale it. If there was a sound political reason for killing Rudolf, Maria Vetsera unwittingly provided the ideal cover story. There can be little doubt that Count Taafe's secret police and Archduke Albrecht's guards were well aware of Rudolf's involvement with Vetsera and of her character.

Amid a chaos of conflicting reports, the elements of the Mayerling tragedy emerge like the outline of a gaunt ship disguised by swirling mists. Rudolf and Maria were at Mayerling together. In the early hours of Wednesday, January 30th, 1889, they died together in the bedroom of the prince's hunting lodge. The official attempts to mask the story of the lovers' suicide pact were so grotesquely clumsy that it is almost possible to believe that they were never intended to mask it. Modern politicians often use a supposed "leak" to ensure that information intended for publication is not only made known but attracts attention. Let a government spend millions on free road-safety pamphlets and subsidized highway codes: few people will read them or act on their advice. Let it be whispered that a controversial new speed limit or parking restriction may be introduced during the next parliamentary session, and every motorist will lobby his MP in fury. Human curiosity is such that we are most interested in things which we believe others may not want us to know.

The Austrian government of 1889 could have been sufficiently subtle and astute to use that psychological approach. Perhaps the "cover-up" of the prince's "suicide with Maria" was intended to be blown so that attention would focus on his liaison with the young countess. Was Rudolf really killed because he and Johann had been plotting against the establishment with the aid of something which Saunière had made available to them?

The sinister and unreliable Countess Larisch enters the story once more. She claimed in her memoirs that Rudolf had entrusted her with the custody of a locked steel box which was to be given to no one unless he used the password R.I.O.U. On the day of his funeral, she was given a message which included that password. Later in the evening, as arranged in the message, she met a heavily cloaked Johann Salvator who took the box, telling her that it contained evidence so damning to Rudolf and himself that if Franz Josef had seen it both young men would have been court martialled and shot.

Years later, the sister of Milli Stubel (Johann's mistress), sold her memoirs to a Viennese paper and confirmed the story of the steel box, adding that it contained a number of documents in code. She maintained that Johann had given it to Milli for safe custody. The question is: did it go down with the Saint Margaret off Cape Horn in 1890? The coded documents in that box may have held clues to the mystery of Rennes-le-Château as well as to the intrigues of the young Habsburg princes. Do those clues now lie somewhere on the bed of the South Atlantic?

How, then, can we summarize the Habsburg connection in the affair of Rennes-le-Château? Firstly, some Habsburg genealogists have claimed links with the Merovingian and Carolingian kings. Secondly, Radbot, an early Habsburg, may have been the same person as Victor Hugo's Ratbert, despite the date problem. Thirdly, if Saunière wanted to sell a religious relic, the Habsburgs were still Holy Roman Emperors in all but name. Fourthly, if it were not merely a religious relic but a supposed power source, or even a combination of the two, Saunière might still have considered that the Habsburgs were the best prospective customers. After all, they had entertained Roccatani, Maroto and de la Rosa after the Mexican tragedy. Fifthly, if there is any truth in the suggestion that Saunière dealt with Johann, it seems very odd that both he and Rudolf should die shortly afterwards and in suspicious circumstances. The Saint Margaret could have gone down in a storm; she could just as well have been sabotaged. Rudolf might have shot Maria, then himself; they could also have been shot by the Austrian secret police and their bodies suitably arranged.

Saunière's watchtower has a strategic view of the mountains and a sturdy steel door. It would be as good a stronghold as any for a man who suspected that Franz Josef's agents might come looking for him.

CHAPTER NINE

PRIESTS AND PRELATES

Corruptio optimi pessima.

The Rennes-le-Château enigma not only involves men of mystery, like the alchemists and Rosicrucians, and ancient noble families like the Habsburgs: it embroils a surprising number of priests as well. Some of them were almost as mysterious in their own ways as Flamel, Paracelsus and Tesla.

Bérenger Saunière

Bérenger Saunière, the best known of them, was born in the tiny hilltop village of Montazels close to Couiza in the high valley of the Aude on April 11th, 1852. His father worked for the Marquis of Cazemayou, and the family were loyal monarchists. Bérenger was the oldest of seven children, and his brother, Alfred, also became a priest. Their attractive terraced house overlooked an eighteenth century fountain decorated with three enigmatic stone Tritons.

In 1874 Bérenger passed the entrance examination for the Grand Diocesan Seminary where he studied for five years. He was ordained in June 1879, and on July 16th was appointed as Assistant Priest in the Parish of Alet. Three years later he became Curé of Clat, where he stayed for a further three years. On June 1st, 1885, he was appointed as Parish Priest of Rennes-le-Château. As an enthusiastic and traditional Royalist and a strong anti-Republican, Bérenger proceeded to preach two powerful anti-Republican sermons on Sunday October 4th and Sunday October 18th that year. As a result he fell foul of the victorious anti-clerical Republican politicians in Aude after the election. In January of 1886 he was nominated as a lecturer in the Seminary at Narbonne, but in July of the same year he was re-appointed as Curé of Rennes-le-Château.

In 1887 some extensive work was carried out in his little church of St. Mary Magdalen, principally in connection with replacing the altar. The old altar was said to have stood on two stone Visigothic pillars, one of which was allegedly hollow and was believed to have contained the mysterious coded parchments with their odd message about Poussin, Teniers and the blue apples.

It was in 1888 that Saunière and the Abbé Boudet of Rennes-les-Bains got to know each other. Henri Boudet was fifteen years older than Saunière and possessed a deep, complex and scholarly mind. There is no doubt that he exerted a powerful influence over the younger priest.

On July 1st, 1889, Monseigneur Félix Arsène Billard, the Bishop of

Carcassonne, made a special visit to Rennes-le-Château.

During the period between May 4th and June 12th, 1890, Saunière was also placed in charge of the Parish of Antugnac, about seven kilometres from Rennes-le-Château.

In 1891 he erected the statue of Our Lady of Lourdes, with the inscription *Pénitence! Pénitence!* below it. It was during this same year that he uncovered the famous *dalle du chevalier* which is currently on display in the museum at Rennes. It is a very ancient carved stone – old enough to be Visigothic or Merovingian. Its primitive carving might represent a knight carrying a child on horseback, although some authorities have suggested that it is meant to depict the Holy Family's flight into Egypt to avoid Herod's barbaric cruelty.

In 1897 Saunière created the "Terrain Fleury" wall decoration at the south of the church, near the confessional; and, at the same time, the very peculiar *bénitier* (holy water stoup) was built. According to Émile Saunière the grimacing demon at the base of this curious arrangement is meant to represent, or personify, Republicanism, which Bérenger greatly disliked: it's certainly one possible explanation! The inscription reads: "By this sign (i.e., the sign of the cross) you will conquer him." The letters B.S. on this strange statuary are either the initials of Bérenger Saunière or a combination of Boudet-Saunière to show that both priests had a hand in designing the work.

In 1899 Saunière purchased various parcels of land around the church and presbytery – all in the name of Marie Dénarnaud his young housekeeper. Massive building projects went on for the next few years: the Villa Bethania, the Magdalen Tower, the orangeries and promenades. Money was obviously coming in from somewhere to pay for all these expensive projects . . . but from where?

Unfortunately, on January 28th, 1908, Saunière fell foul of the new bishop, the unpleasantly inquisitive, bureaucratic and persistent de Beauséjour. Monseigneur Billard had been an ideal bishop: a good and tolerant man – prepared to live and let live as far as Saunière was concerned. Although Bérenger fought off de Beauséjour successfully most of the time with the nonchalant contempt that such a bishop richly deserved, there can be little doubt that de Beauséjour and his bureaucratic henchmen in the diocesan hierarchy eventually wore Saunière down, and were largely responsible for the deterioration of his once robust health.

By 1915 de Beauséjour's spite had deprived Saunière of his parish title. In 1916 he made a pilgrimage to Lourdes in the hope of recovering his health and spirits. He came home full of plans for a new tower fifty metres high, for a rampart all around the village, for a piped water supply to each home . . . but these grand designs were never realised.

According to Émile Saunière's account of his famous relative's life, Bérenger had a heart attack on January 20th, 1917, sent for his friend, the Abbé Rivière, Priest of Espéraza, to hear his final confession, and died on January 22nd.

Rumours and dimming local memories supply most of the other sinister and curious information which has accumulated around Saunière's death: it is said that mysterious visitors called shortly before Saunière had his "heart attack"; that his coffin was ordered and paid for in advance; that

Father Rivière was so shocked by Saunière's last confession that he himself became ill and was unable to work for several months afterwards; that Saunière's parishioners filed past his body as he sat in state covered by a red cloth from which each mourner plucked a pompom as a souvenir . . .

Marie lived on until 1953 having promised that she would reveal her old master's secret when she knew herself to be dying. She had a stroke two weeks before her death which left her speechless and paralysed, and, although she tried very hard to whisper the secret to Noël Corbu, who had befriended her during her declining years, nothing intelligible came out . . .

She and Saunière lie buried side by side at the west end of the little cemetery alongside the church of St. Mary Magdalen.

Abbé Boudet

Was Henri Jean-Jacques Boudet the power behind Bérenger Saunière? Those who have studied his role in the mystery closely, declare that Saunière was only the highly visible puppet who attracted all the limelight while Boudet the puppet master remained concealed in the shadows behind the stage.

Boudet was born on November 16th, 1837, at Quillan, into a poor family. Fortunately a neighbouring clergyman detected the boy's intelligence and generously paid for his education. On Christmas Day 1861, the twenty-four year old Boudet was ordained; in 1872 Bishop Billard appointed him as Parish Priest of Rennes-les-Bains. Like Saunière a few years later, Boudet was a tireless walker. In view of Saunière's strange interests in stones, one of Boudet's comments to Gassaud (another neighbouring priest) may be significant: "I enjoy the greenery on fine days," he wrote, "but I like the winter when the greenery no longer hides the stones . . ."

Boudet's tantalising and enigmatic book *La Vraie Langue Celtique et le Cromleck de Rennes-les-Bains* was more or less completed in 1880, but it took another six years of re-setting and typographical modification before it finally came off the press in 1886, at Boudet's own expense.

From 1886 to 1914 only ninety-eight copies were sold; 100 were given away to libraries, V.I.P's and charities; 200 more were given to interested visitors who had come to Rennes-les-Bains for the "water cure" — it was in its heyday a fashionable thermal health spa. This left 102 copies which were destroyed in 1914. The original run of 500 copies cost 5382 gold francs to produce . . . all very strange. Some sources indicate that the unpleasant Bishop de Beauséjour ordered the last of Boudet's books to be destroyed in 1914 when he allegedly also deprived the sick old priest of his living. Other sources indicate that Boudet himself had them destroyed. De Beauséjour seems a prime suspect, but there is said to be evidence from Boudet's own correspondence to indicate that the destruction was in accordance with his wishes.

Boudet's death and burial were almost as strange as his book. His mother and sister had died in 1895 and 1896 and been buried in the cemetery at Rennes-les-Bains. When de Beauséjour removed Boudet from his Parish in 1914, he was 77 years old and reported to be gravely ill with intestinal cancer. He retired to Axat where his brother Edmond, a lawyer, had lived until his death on May 5th, 1907. It was strongly rumoured — although such stories are difficult to substantiate — that Boudet, despite his grave illness, did not die of natural causes. He is alleged to have been visited by some sinister strangers and died in agony a few hours later. Similar rumours circulated in connection with the death of Napoleon I. The official line was that the former Emperor had died of stomach cancer: the rumour was that he had been poisoned. It was also rumoured that despite Saunière's deteriorating health in 1917 he had rallied considerably and was showing signs of a full recovery before the same sinister visitors called on him just before his "heart attack" of January 20th.

Poisoned or not, Boudet was interred beside his brother Edmond and on the stone which covers them both is the carved "book" with its cryptic inscription. It may be simply the Greek word for fish (the early Christian acrostic); it could be a clue to pages 310 and 311 of Boudet's book; or it might mean something entirely different but of equally mysterious significance.

Maurice Guinguand is reported to have given an account of a local lawyer's, or notary's, visit to Saunière in 1884, or 1885. This man asked for the priest's help in translating certain Latin documents connected with the ownership of land once belonging to Paul Urbain de Fleury, who had died in the 1850's. By a very odd coincidence, a few months later, this notary died as the result of a shooting accident which took place while he was in Saunière's company.

There have been several other sinister events — in and around Rennes-le-Château — before, during and after Saunière's time.

Monge and Montroux
On May 27th, 1732, Abbé Bernard Monge, the incumbent at Niort-de-Saux, was found by the gate of his presbytery garden with a fractured skull. The man responsible was François de Montroux, the legal guardian of young Marie de Nègre d'Ables, who was later to marry François d'Hautpoul, Lord of Blanchefort, and eventually, as his widow, to lie beneath one of the strangest tombstones ever carved.

Montroux was banished, but during his absence he lent François d'Hautpoul the money to buy the late Abbé Monge's former presbytery. The whole discreditable episode is vaguely reminiscent of Ahab, Jezebel and Naboth's vineyard.

The Murder of Gélis - Saunière again?
Jean-Antoine-Maurice Gélis was born on April 1st, 1827 at Villesequelande in the Aude, and was appointed as the Priest of Coustaussa near Rennes-le-Château in 1857. By 1897, when he was in his seventieth year, he had become a timid, suspicious old recluse. He would open the sturdy door of his presbytery only to his niece when she brought his meals and clean laundry. He took the food and clothes indoors while she waited on the step until he had re-secured the door. Despite these elaborate precautions, the old man was brutally murdered during the Eve of All Saints' Day, 1897. Whoever he had admitted — for there were no signs of a forced entry — had struck him first with the heavy old nineteenth century fire tongs and then — as the old man had struggled towards the window to attract attention and shout for help — with an axe.

The local paper, *Courrier de l'Aude* reported fourteen grisly wounds to the head and multiple skull fractures. The floor, walls and ceiling were splashed with blood. Three great pools of it lay on the floor – but the murderer had left neither hand nor foot print anywhere. Despite the wild savagery of the attack, Gélis's body had been laid out reverently with the hands across the chest. There was a considerable quantity of cash lying quite conspicuously about the house – none of that had been taken, but the presbytery had been ransacked.

Whoever had murdered the old priest had been desperate to find something. Had he found it? According to the account in the *Courrier de l'Aude* masked men had broken in and searched the presbytery a few years previously. Perhaps that was why old Gélis had been so cautious?

One grim theory even points the finger of suspicion towards Saunière. Suppose that Boudet and Saunière in the process of working out their decodings of the cryptic parchments had passed a document or two to Gélis to decipher. Suppose further that it had contained just enough information to arouse his curiosity and suspicion and that he had stubbornly refused to return it until the other two told him more. It would never have crossed the old man's mind that a brother priest would raise a hand against him – but Saunière was no ordinary priest. Perhaps, as we have already hinted, he had never felt any genuine vocation, that he had endured the long years of boredom and deprivation in the seminary simply to become the Priest of Rennes-le-Château in order to be in the most advantageous place to look for the legendary treasure?

What emerges from a long, close study of Bérenger Saunière is a picture of a man with great determination and stamina; a man of remarkable physical and mental strength; a great individualist, verging on the eccentric; a proud, impulsive and energetic man, who will not take no for an answer and who, in his prime, is capable of successfully defying both civil and ecclesiastical authorities; a libidinous and passionate man whose emotional needs encompass the devoted Marie Dénarnaud, the flamboyantly exciting Emma Calvé . . . and several others. Saunière is not a man to tangle with unless your own muscle, stamina and ruthless aggression are at least the equal of his. Querulous old Gélis came nowhere near playing in the same league as Saunière. To butcher a man in a moment of wild anger and then solemnly and reverently lay out his corpse is not characteristic of any ordinary murderer.

Now tie in the rumours of Saunière's deathbed confession and the traumatic effect it had on Rivière. Did Saunière murmur something like this?

"Father . . . I have sinned . . . I shot and killed a notary . . . I also struck down helpless old Father Gélis . . ." Did Rivière turn pale with shocked revulsion to think that hands which had committed at least two murders had celebrated Mass for years afterwards as though nothing untoward had ever happened? And was that *all* that Saunière confessed to? Was there any mention of obscene black magic? Of the Convocation of Venus? Of dark ceremonies involving sexual rituals with Marie or Emma Calvé? If Rivière's mind was strong enough and resilient enough to absorb all that, did Saunière say even more? " . . . I found and systematically robbed the ancient tombs of Merovingian Kings and nobles . . . I passed through a secret doorway into a forbidden realm . . . Rivière, my friend, what you think of as reality is not reality at all . . ." The dying Saunière draws his last weak breath and subsides into silence.

Gérard de Sède

Gérard de Sède, author of *Le Trésor Maudit de Rennes-le-Château*, tells of his 1963 meeting with a scholarly old priest called Joseph Courtauly, who was in charge of the Parish of Villarzel-du-Razès. Like the unfortunate Abbé Gélis of Coustaussa, the aged Courtauly had become very suspicious in his old age. He even refused to admit his Vicar-General on one occasion. Gérard de Sède was told by Courtauly that in 1908, when he was eighteen, he had spent two months as Saunière's guest in Rennes-le-Château. He had even been allowed to assist with some of the painting in the church, but Saunière had been insistent about the finest details of the work. Courtauly had also met Boudet whom he regarded as an amazing character. He recalled that Boudet had had trouble with the Bishop in 1914 and that – according to Courtauly's account – Boudet's books had been burnt in front of him. These comprised not only the residual copies of *La Vraie Langue Celtique* but also a work entitled *Lazarus*. (The Biblical Lazarus was the brother of Martha and Mary of Bethany, who might have been the same woman as Mary Magdalen. It was this same Biblical Lazarus whom Jesus raised from the tomb.) Courtauly recalled that Abbé Rescanière, the diocesan missionary, had been appointed to Rennes-les-Bains in May of 1914. Not surprisingly, he too had become very interested in the Boudet-Saunière mystery; but in the early hours of the morning of February 1st, 1915, two mysterious visitors arrived . . . Father Rescanière was found dead . . . his visitors were never traced.

According to Gérard de Sède, the old priest then showed him a superb collection of Merovingian and Visigothic gold coins which he said Saunière had given to him. Courtauly died in 1964; whatever else he might have been able to disclose about the Rennes mystery died with him.

The 1956 Corpses

In March or April of 1956, M. Descadeillas, Dr. Malacan, M. Brunon (an optician), and M. Despeyronat were excavating part of Saunière's garden when they exhumed three decaying corpses, all male and aged between thirty and forty. Strips of flesh, hair and even the recognisable remains of a moustache still clung to the skeletons. All three had been shot. The police were called. An inquest was opened. No conclusions were ever reached.

Were they from World War II? World War I? Or did those three corpses pay secret, silent tribute to Saunière's strength, speed and prowess with a gun? Had they been members of whatever strange, underground organisation had sent "visitors" to silence Gélis, Rescanière, Boudet and eventually – when he was no longer at his peak – the redoubtable Saunière himself?

Could they even have been three members of Count Taafe's Austro-Hungarian Habsburg secret police intent on dealing with Saunière and Marie as they had already dealt with Rudolf and Maria Vetsera? If so they had fatally underestimated their intended victims: from all that we can hypothesize about the reckless and colourful Warrior Priest of Rennes-le-Château, Saunière might almost have been the last of the Templars; first to attack and last to retreat.

Noël Corbu and Abbé Boyer

Marie Dénarnaud made over the estate to M. Noël Corbu who treated the old lady with great courtesy, consideration and kindness in her declining years. If anyone heard anything at all of her incoherent dying whispers on January 29th, 1953, it was Noël Corbu. On May 20th, 1968, M. Corbu himself was killed in a horrendous car crash on the road between Castelnaudary and Carcassonne. Less than a month later, Abbé Boyer, Vicar General in the Carcassonne Diocese, another investigator who was keenly interested in the Rennes affair, narrowly escaped the same fate when his car crashed near the Devil's Bridge on the Carcassonne road. Although severely injured, he recovered.

Abbé Mazières

Abbé Maurice-René Mazières was the Parish Priest of Villesequelande near Carcassonne when Gérard de Sède was carrying out his research. Father Mazières, who had been a lawyer before taking Holy Orders, was a very sensible and level headed man. He told de Sède: "This Rennes affair is very gripping, but I must warn you . . . it is also dangerous . . ."

Abbé Duvilla and the Couiza War Memorial

Another very interesting priest was Abbé Duvilla of Couiza, who went to that parish in 1917 – the same year that Bérenger Saunière died. Duvilla had once been a lecturer at the Grand Seminary and was a man of formidable scholarship. He had also been the Curé of Axat where he had often been visited by Boudet and by Johann of Habsburg. Johann had apparently been in the habit of lodging with Boudet's sister-in-law whenever he came to the village.

Duvilla commissioned a sculptor named Giscard to create a war memorial for him to go in his church at Couiza. Incidentally, this Giscard was the same artist who had made the fourteen Stations of the Cross for Saunière for his Church of St. Mary Magdalen at Rennes. This very strange war memorial shows a dead or dying soldier with his right knee uncovered, his left hand over his heart, and his right hand still holding his rifle. The right index finger points towards – and is almost touching – a strange round stone. The figure of Christ on the cross carved in the centre of this memorial is exchanging a long, meaningful look with the dying soldier. An angel on the right of the tableau holds out a crown to the fallen warrior. According to Gérard de Sède, the symbolism in this unusual memorial would be exactly right for a Scottish Freemason who had achieved the rank of Chevalier in the Order of the Rose-Croix. If de Sède is right, then the memorial does not only honour the heroes of Couiza who died in World War I: it commemorates one hero in particular – Bérenger Saunière, Warrior Priest of Rennes-le-Château and Chevalier of the Rose-Croix – who fell in 1917.

CHAPTER TEN

THE OVERSEAS ENIGMA

Qua ducitis adsum.

A number of earlier researchers have claimed to find links between the Sinclair family of Scotland and the ancient Norman Saint-Clairs, who were alleged to be connected with a Priory of Sion event which supposedly took place at Gisors. At one time the Knights Templars had their Scottish headquarters close to the Sinclair estates at Rosslyn. The chapel at Rosslyn dating from the middle of the fifteenth century has traditional associations both with Rosicrucianism and Scottish Freemasonry. Thory's early nineteenth century history of Freemasonry and Gould's later work on the same theme both indicate that from a very early date in the seventeenth century the Sinclairs were regarded as the hereditary Grand Masters of Freemasonry in Scotland. How many of the Templar secrets actually found their way to Rosslyn is anybody's guess — but it is a very interesting area of speculation.

Slane is one of the most attractive and interesting villages in Ireland. It stands where the road from Derry to Dublin cuts the road which links Drogheda with Navan. The village layout is quaintly octagonal, and one folktale says that the four fine Georgian houses which are such a prominent feature were originally designed to house the Priest, the Doctor, the Magistrate and the Constable. Not far away are the enigmatic ruins of Castle Dexter, believed by some historians to be of Flemish origin, or, at least, to have belonged to the Fleming family — an interesting possible continental connection.

There are two very curious stone coffin lids set on either side of the church door, on one of which the inscription appears to have been cut as a mirror image reminiscent of the Shepherd Monument at Shugborough and the chess boards on which the final knights' tours have to be executed to decipher the "blue apples" code.

The Hill of Slane, a mile from the village centre, has strong associations with St. Patrick himself. Erc, the first Bishop of Slane, was a good and courageous man who defied the local druids in order to give due honour to St. Patrick. Erc's tomb still stands in the ancient graveyard at the top of the hill, close to the monastery which he founded there, on the site of which a small Franciscan friary was later built. It was to the original monastery founded by Erc, however, that the infant King Dagobert II was sent when Grimoald, the Mayor of the Palace, attempted to usurp the throne of Austrasia for his own son Childebert in 653. The other Austrasian lords arrested Grimoald and sent him to Paris where King Clovis promptly

143

executed him. According to evidence provided by Archdall and Mezeray, Dagobert II was recalled from Slane in 674 and reigned for almost three years before being assassinated.

The enigma of Rennes now moves to England. Our chapter on codes and ciphers has already touched briefly on the Shepherd Monument at Shugborough Hall in Staffordshire, and its puzzling inscription, but there is still more to be said about the significance of this strange marble bas-relief which so curiously reverses Poussin's original composition, Admiral George Anson died in 1762 and such was his fame that a poem to honour his memory was read in Parliament. This is recorded in Erdeswick's Survey of Staffordshire published in 1844:

> Upon that storied marble cast thine eye.
> The scene commands a moralising sigh.
> E'en in Arcadia's bless'd Elysian plains,
> Amidst the laughing nymphs and sportive swains,
> See festal joy subside, with melting grace,
> And pity visit the half-smiling face;
> Where now the dance, the lute, the nuptial feast,
> The passion throbbing in the lover's breast,
> Life's emblem here, in youth and vernal bloom,
> But reason's finger pointing at the tomb!

That stanza seems to relate quite unequivocally to the Shepherd Monument at Shugborough.

The vast fortune which Admiral Anson acquired came, ostensibly, from overseas gold. His richly exciting and adventurous life took him all the way around the world. Did he ever go to Nova Scotia or, more particularly, to Oak Island in Mahone Bay, near the fishing village of Chester? If he never went there in person did he arrange for an expedition to go there under the command of one of his trusted subordinates?

Michael Bradley's fascinating book, *The Holy Grail Across the Atlantic,* provides a number of important clues linking the mysteries of Rennes-le-Château with the mysteries of the Oak Island Money Pit.

Bradley discovered that there are two Oak Islands, not one, and that their relationship to each other is very curious. The better known of the two, the one in Mahone Bay, was the scene of our own research visit in 1988 to gather data for our unsolved mystery lectures and a forthcoming book. This Oak Island is close to the mouth of the Gold River, which flows south across Nova Scotia and empties into the Atlantic.

The lesser known of the two is an island no longer, although it was until the 1930's when the dyke building programme to counteract the worst effects of the great depression turned it into the tip of a peninsula. Thousands of acres of fertile land were reclaimed from the waters of the Bay of Fundy. When this northern Oak Island was an island, it lay at the mouth of the Gaspareau River. Michael Bradley goes on to tell of his discovery of what sounds very much like the ruin of an ancient castle – almost exactly midway between these two Oak Islands. It is on the central Nova Scotian water table from which the Gaspareau and the Gold River flow north and south respectively. By a curious coincidence, if you stand on either of the Oak Islands and look towards the mainland you will see the mouth of the river to your right. Follow the river and you will reach the enigmatic site of what may have been the ancient castle.

As knowledgeable old Abbé Boudet might well have written in *La Vraie Langue Celtique*, the old Celtic word for "oak" is *duir*, "right side" is *de*, *duir* meant "door" as well as "oak". In Welsh, which is very closely related to old Celtic, *derw* is "oak", *drws* is "door" and *dwr* is "water". Bradley's etymology makes a great deal of sense: the two Oak Islands are probably clues to water-doors via the rivers on their right hand sides.

His ideas about the origin of the oak trees on the two islands are also convincing. Oaks are unlikely to be self-seeded: Bradley says acorns don't float. Supposing that you wanted to provide a clue, a marker, or a signpost, which would be obvious to those in the know but of no significance to the uninitiated. There were plenty of oak trees on the shore. They would not look out of place or odd on an offshore island — but they would not have got there without human intervention, according to Bradley. There's another Celtic-Welsh word that's worth examining en route: the word is *dwyrain* — it means "east". Is that the direction from which the oak-planters came? Bradley is making out a respectable case for the existence of an important and interesting site midway between the two Oak Islands. Who built it? Why? And when?

While we were making a detailed site study of the Mahone Bay Oak Island in 1988,we had the pleasure of meeting one of the most knowledgeable writers and researchers in the area: George Young, a recently retired professional surveyor. His extensive firsthand experience of the locality leads him to a similar conclusion to Michael Bradley's about the geological origins of the Money Pit: it is a natural limestone blow hole, about seventy metres deep. At its base lies a large and mysterious cavern connected to the surrounding Atlantic and, possibly, to part of the course of a subterranean river as well. Its natural origin by no means negates the theories about something of great historical interest (and, perhaps, of great financial value) being buried there.

The recent history of the Oak Island Money Pit begins in 1795 when young Daniel McGinnis and his two teenaged friends, John Smith and Anthony Vaughan, dug into a circular, saucer-shaped depression about thirteen feet across, which Daniel had found in a clearing in the south east corner of the island. A sturdy solitary oak stood above this depression and — in some accounts — from one of its lopped branches hung a decaying block and tackle of the type used on early sailing ships.

Two feet down the boys discovered a layer of flat stones, like paving stones: they were not of local origin as far as the young explorers could judge. As the boys continued their work they unearthed platforms of oak logs at ten foot intervals down to a depth of about thirty feet. At this juncture, as not a single brass farthing had yet appeared to reward them for all their heavy digging, the boys abandoned the project for the time being.

Attempts to enlist further assistance were not very successful for two reasons: first, life as a Nova Scotian farmer or fisherman in 1795 was hard and time consuming; second, Oak Island was regarded — and still is today by some of the local residents — as a place of ill-omen.

Some years before the McGinnis gang found the clearing and the top of the shaft, strange lights had been seen on the island. It was rumoured that two or three fishermen who had rowed out to investigate had never returned. Pirates, perhaps, had murdered them?

John Smith, one of the three original discoverers grew up, built a house on Oak Island and began to farm the eastern end of it. David McGinnis joined him and began farming an area in the south west.

In the spring of 1803, the three original excavators — now part of the Onslow Company led by Simeon Lynds — got down to the ninety foot level. Every ten feet, or so, they discovered yet another horizontal platform of oak logs. They also encountered coconut fibre, putty and charcoal strata: and Oak Island was a long way — 2000 kilometres — from the nearest coconut trees. At the ninety foot level they found a curiously inscribed stone. Its "message" is ambiguous.

Oak Island stone

Symbols	Word		Key			
▽ ⛨ ⋮ ⌀ △ ✓	FꟼORTY		A = .		N = ✕	
▽ ⋮ ⋮ △	FEET		B = †		O = ⋮	
† ⋮ ⊏ ⋱ ☐	BELOW		C =		P = ⊖	
△ ☐ ⋱	TWO		D = ◫		Q =	
‡ ∴ ⊏⊏ ∴ ⋱ ✕	MILLION		E = ⋮		R = ⌀	
⊖ ⋱ + ✕ ◫ ⊙	POUNDS		F =		S = ⊙	
· ⌀ ⋮	ARE		G =		T = △	
† + ⌀ ∴ ⋮ ◫	BURIED		H = .		U = +	
			I = ∴		V =	
			J =		W = ☐	
			K =		X =	
			L = ⊏		Y = ✓	
			M = ‡		Z =	

There is reliable evidence that this stone actually existed: it is mentioned in the early records left by the Onslow Company. John Smith cemented it into the fireplace of his home on Oak Island; then it was taken to Halifax by a bookbinder named Creighton, who was treasurer to another Oak Island syndicate. He displayed it in his shop window to attract investments. In 1865, a language professor from Dalhousie University in Halifax deciphered it along the lines shown in the above diagram. A friend of the authors, computer engineer Paul Townsend, reached exactly the same conclusion in a matter of minutes when he checked it for us a few months ago.[1]

---

[1]To reach this decipherment a minor emendment to the text of the message is necessary. The first character is a point-down triangle, and the second looks like a badly carved six-pointed star. None of the other characters, however, appears "badly carved" in any way. Eventually, I reached the conclusion that this "six-pointed star" was in fact a second point-down triangle, carved in error and promptly crossed through with two diagonal lines. When this character is ignored, the remainder of the message decodes into "FORTY FEET BELOW TWO MILLION POUNDS ARE BURIED" by a simple substitution cipher, very much along the lines of the "Dancing Men" in the Sherlock Holmes story by Sir Arthur Conan Doyle. PVST

The problem is that the stone itself vanished in 1919 when the Creighton bookbindery was closed and has not been seen since. Harry Marshall, however, the son of a former Creighton partner, swore an affidavit regarding the stone on March 27th, 1935. He said basically that the stone was two feet long, fifteen inches wide and ten inches thick. It was as dark and hard as Swedish granite and very finely grained. When Harry Marshall had seen it there had been no trace of any inscription on it — either carved or painted — but he also testified that it had been used as a base block for beating leather in the bookbindery for over thirty years. That would have effectively obliterated any message it might once have carried.

The second theory of the inscription's meaning was brought to our attention by George Young who has made detailed studies of the local coast line and tidal levels over a number of years and has concluded that within historical times the water was at least thirty feet lower in the Oak Island area than it is today. His researches have led him to conclude that the earliest visitors from the old world may well have been Phoenician or Egyptian merchants. He is of the opinion that these early visitors would have established friendly relationships with the local Amerindian tribes, and that far more Micmac words than coincidence can account for are very similar indeed to Arabic and Egyptian words. If, as is certainly possible, these earliest Mediterranean seafarers reached Nova Scotia centuries before the Christian Era, there is no reason at all why later parties should not have repeated their epic voyage.

Suppose, for the sake of argument, that a party of religious refugees — spiritual fore-runners of the "Mayflower" men — left Egypt or North Africa in the fourth or fifth century to escape the ravages of the Vandals. It is well known that Gaiseric the Vandal was responsible for prolonged and vicious persecution of the Christians in the second half of the fifth century. Early in the sixth century the Vandal Empire covered much of the north coast of Africa immediately south of Sardinia, including the city of Hippo, where Bishop Augustine, the Christian philosopher, had flourished from 396 to 430.

George Young's investigations into the Oak Island mystery have led him to hypothesize a small group of Coptic Christian refugees settling there almost 1500 years ago under the leadership of an Arif, or sub-Priest. When this holy man eventually died, he was buried at the bottom of the Money Pit, with log platforms arranged at regular intervals to prevent the weight of the re-filled clay from crushing his sarcophagus. Young's fascinating ideas are powerfully reinforced by the work of Professor Barry Fell of Harvard University who says that far from being written in a simple English language alphabet code, the inscription on the mysterious stone was carved out in a Libyan script, and the words form part of a Libyan-Arabic dialect. Professor Fell translates the inscription as a religious exhortation to the group of refugees:

> "The people will perish in misery if they forget the Lord, alas. The Arif, he is to pray for an end or mitigation to escape contagion of plague and winter hardships."

George Young compounds an already strange mystery by referring to what several historians accept as the authentic remains of a mid-fourteenth century Norse church at Newport, Rhode Island. Others believe the building to have been a medieval lighthouse.

The Italian adventurer Giovanni de Verrazano visited the site in 1524 during his coastal explorations from Florida to Labrador. He recorded that the people he met on Rhode Island were very light-skinned and highly civilised: but they had no knowledge of who had built the ancient stone tower.

According to Young's research, a party of considerable size reached the Oak Island area round about 1384. Were these the same men who had built the Church (or lighthouse?) on Rhode Island? Had they, or their descendants on Rhode Island, inter-married with the indigenous Amerindians in that neighbourhood to produce the friendly and civilised people who welcomed Giovanni in 1524?

In 1946, Magnus Bjorndal and Peer Loofald translated some Norse runes found in the Rhode Island tower. These runes claimed that the tower had been "built as the Bishop's seat," i.e., the "Cathedral" of his "diocese". Suppose that instead of − or in addition to − a Coptic Christian Arif, a fourteenth century Norse bishop lies buried in the Oak Island Money Pit?

To resume the narrative of the Pit itself: at the ninety foot level the Onslow Company found and removed the mysterious dark stone.

The problem with the transliteration of the coded stone's message into English is that it's too simple. It seems much more likely that that message was concocted in the 1860's and then either cut or painted on to the stone to tempt potential investors. Suppose, however, that the original 1803 stone contained something like the strange Libyan-Arabic script which Professor Fell deciphered, or, at least, a far more complex code than the rather facile and superficial "FORTY FEET BELOW . . ." message. What if that stone was treated rather like a lithic version of a palimpsest in the 1860's: some trivial message having been superimposed for commercial reasons over an original and ancient one which really was of interest and significance?

Having located and removed the stone the Onslow team kept on digging. At ninety-three feet they were excavating two tubs of water for every tub of soil. As darkness fell they probed the floor of the pit. A few feet down their crowbar struck something hard: wood, iron, treasure chests, the roof of a burial chamber? They decided to cease operations for the night.

When they returned at first light there were twenty metres of water in the pit. Bailing had no effect on it. For the time being they gave up. Returning the following year they sank a second shaft four and a half metres to the south east of the original Money Pit. This, too, flooded when the earth between the two pits collapsed. The Onslow Company gave up altogether; John Smith went on farming; the pits were filled in for safety.

In 1849 a new group, the Truro Company, had a go at the Money Pit. Daniel McGinnis had died, but Smith and Vaughan (now in their seventies) were still around, and so was Simeon Lynds of the old Onslow Company. Jotham B. McCully was appointed as drilling engineer. On June 2nd, 1862, Jotham wrote to a friend telling him what they had found. His exploratory drillings and core samples had revealed a spruce platform five inches thick at exactly ninety-eight feet (which was where the Onslow men had said it was). The auger had fallen twelve inches then gone through four inches of oak. Beneath that there were "loose objects" of some kind (treasure or the bones of a dead holy man still wrapped in his robes?) and the auger brought up three links of an ancient chain — possibly, but not definitely gold. Then came eight inches of oak (the bottom of the upper chest — or sarcophagus — and the lid of the lower chest — or sarcophagus?). This was followed by more loose metal, a further four inches of oak (the bottom of the lower chest, or sarcophagus?), and another spruce platform. These upper and lower platforms were about six feet apart. Below the deeper platform the auger encountered more loose clay, suggesting that the pit went deeper than the tomb, or treasure chamber, situated between the two spruce platforms at ninety-eight feet and one hundred and four feet respectively.

The Truro Company sank a few more holes and some of this work was done under the direction of a foreman named John Pitbladdo. He was seen to pocket something that the auger brought up and subsequently left Oak Island rather suddenly. John Gammell, a major Truro shareholder, actually saw the incident, and, when he asked what had been found, Pitbladdo said he would show it to all the directors together at their next meeting: he didn't!

Shortly afterwards, Pitbladdo and Charles Archibald, manager of the Acadia Iron Works in Londonderry, Nova Scotia, made an all out effort to buy John Smith's land: they failed, but the most probable conclusion is that the wily Pitbladdo had found something of such value in the core samples that he was prepared to stake everything — including his reputation — to gain control of the important part of Oak Island.

The Truro team were very determined. They tried again the following summer: what they discovered was a series of fan-shaped, man-made drains under layers of coconut fibre and eel grass running nearly one hundred and fifty feet along the shore of Smith's cove. These drains fed at least one flood tunnel which connected with the Money Pit about one hundred feet down.

Whoever had built the original Money Pit, or modified an existing natural sinkhole, had created a flooding system which the best of nineteenth and twentieth century mining technology has so far been unable to neutralize.

To describe in detail every shaft and tunnel sunk by syndicate after syndicate and company after company from then to the present day would require a large and profusely illustrated volume all to itself. There is no better book on the subject than George Young's *Ancient Peoples and Modern Ghosts* available from the author at "Queensland", Hubbards, Nova Scotia, Canada; other excellent accounts are given by D'Arcy O'Connor in *The Big Dig* published by Ballantine Books of New York, and by Rupert Furneaux in *Money Pit: The Mystery of Oak Island* published by Fontana.

When we were carrying out our own research on Oak Island in the Mahone Bay area in 1988, the island was a hive of industry set in a bewildering mass of old collapsed shafts, flooded diggings, abandoned workings, labyrinthine underground tunnels and enigmatic ruins. The work there is presently in the hands of the Triton Alliance Limited headed by David Tobias, and their man in charge of the island is Dan Blankenship to whom we spoke at length during our visit in 1988. It's an interesting coincidence yet again that the mystery of Oak Island is now being investigated by a team with same name as the strange characters from ancient Greek mythology who adorn the old fountain in Montazels, immediately outside the house where Saunière was born. Arcadian Shepherds in Shugborough and Tritons on Oak Island near what was once Acadia in Nova Scotia?

Another intriguing aspect of the Oak Island mystery is that several of the most active investigators and their closest associates during the 1930's — Hedden, Blair and Harris, for example — were believed to be Freemasons of high rank. D'Arcy O'Connor records that Blair once referred to Hedden as a brother Mason in a letter to Harris, in which he expressed his deep disappointment that Hedden was postponing his explorations indefinitely. (Like many of his predecessors Hedden was running out of funds.) Is it just possible that not only some of the highest ranking trans-Atlantic Freemasons, but whatever European secret society the Bacon brothers were involved in had some special knowledge of the Oak Island mystery?

One of the most amazing Oak Island theories concerns the four hundred year old controversy about whether Sir Francis Bacon was the real author of the plays which bear Shakespeare's name. Eminent supporters of the Bacon claim have included Coleridge, the poet, and Disraeli, the Prime Minister. The argument begins with the suggestion that William Shakespeare, who probably left Stratford's free grammar school when he was only thirteen to become an apprentice to a local tradesman because the fortunes of his father, John Shakespeare, were dramatically declining, had nowhere near the necessary educational background to have written the plays that bear his name. He married Anne (or Agnes) Hathaway (who was eight years older than he was) in 1582 when he was eighteen. In 1584 he annoyed Sir Thomas Lucy by poaching on his estate and had to leave Stratford rather hurriedly. There is then a long gap in what is known with any certainty of Shakespeare's life history until 1592, when he surfaces again as an actor with some plays credited to him.

Genius, of course, is independent of formal education: leaving school at thirteen to enter the University of Life may well have sharpened Shakespeare's latent talent rather than hindered it. But the stubborn fact remains: if we are looking for an alternative author — a man of equal genius with a germane educational and cultural background in addition — Sir Francis Bacon is a very prominent candidate.

Bacon was undoubtedly highly intelligent as well as being a very secretive and mysterious character. He was a talented all-rounder: a writer, linguist, lawyer, scientist, philosopher and statesman.

The Elizabethan court tended to look down on actors, poets and play-wrights, so it was by no means rare for a courtier with literary or dramatic talent to use a pseudonym, or even to give some other real person the credit for his work. The Baconians argue that this is what happened with the plays attributed to Shakespeare: Sir Francis wrote them but attributed them to Master William. Some of the more extreme Baconians even go so far as to hint that Shakespeare was not Bacon's only pen name. They wonder if he also wrote some, at least, of the works attributed to Edmund Spenser and Christopher Marlowe. It is, undeniably, a possibility.

One major plank in the Baconian argument is that very, very few — if any — genuine, original manuscripts in Shakespeare's own hand, (or Spenser's or Marlowe's for that matter!) are known to exist. Is it not just slightly curious that they have all — or almost all — disappeared? Enthusiastic Baconians would argue that the real reason for the scarcity is that those precious manuscripts are so clearly in Bacon's elegant and distinctive hand, that they were all carefully hidden away in some very secure place at his instigation.

Dr. Burrell F. Ruth told a group of students at Iowa State College as long ago as December 3rd, 1948, that Sir Francis must have prized those original documents very highly and had, therefore, arranged for them to be hidden securely until the world had become a better place — the home of a highly civilized humanity to whom he would like the truth about his authorship to be revealed.

Bacon, as we have noted, was a scientist as well as a statesman and author. His book, *Sylva Sylvarum,* describes a technique for preserving documents in mercury, and a method of creating artificial water sources not unlike the ingenious drainage systems found in Smith's cove to the east of Oak Island.

Even more curious was the expedition of Dr. Orville Ward Owen who followed what he believed to be Baconian ciphers which led him to a mysterious underground chamber beneath the riverbed at the mouth of the River Wye in the west of England. The chamber was empty when Dr. Owen examined it, but he was convinced that certain symbols cut into the walls were Baconian. He concluded that Bacon had intended to hide his manuscripts there, then changed his mind and decided on somewhere more secure and much further away. Oak Island? There are one or two other pointers in this direction: in 1610 Bacon was one of a number of men to whom James I granted lands in Newfoundland — so he had some connection with that area; furthermore, among the many oddities said to have been found on Oak Island were a number of stone jars of old-fashioned design — and traces of mercury were alleged to have been detected in them.

Another famous name connected with Oak Island is that of William Kidd, who was hanged for piracy in 1701. He is not the strongest of contenders: the Oak Island structures seem far older and more complicated than anything a crew of privateers could have managed. However, Kidd's adventures were not so much earlier than Shugborough's Admiral Anson's. Young George was still only a child when Kidd was hanged, but Anson's epic voyage was inspired by the earlier adventures of Woodes Rogers, a daring privateer, who was a contemporary of Kidd.

There is also a strange tale told by Andrew Spedon in *Rambles Among the Blue Noses* which appeared in 1863. Spedon said that Kidd had a lieutenant named Lawrence who jumped overboard and swam for it to escape being arrested with Kidd when their ship reached Boston harbour. Lawrence is said to have been befriended and hidden by Dutch settlers, to whom, before his death, he gave the information that Kidd had left a vast treasure buried on, or near, the coast of Nova Scotia. Could there have been any remote connection between this Lieutenant Lawrence (if he was ever anything more than a figment of Spedon's imagination) and the enigmatic Lawrence family — also of American origin — who were connected with the mysterious Tomb of Arques near Rennes-le-Château?

By far the widest spread of the convoluted net of the Rennes-le-Château mystery, however, is daringly hypothesized in the stylish and elegant prose of Jean Robin, the skilled, sensitive and imaginative author of *Opération Orth*. In this far reaching study, Robin focuses first on Archduke Johann — or Jean — Salvator, the young Habsburg Prince who was contemporary with the tragic Rudolf of Mayerling, and who was also acquainted with both Saunière and Boudet. After the lovers' death in the hunting lodge, Johann — having assumed the name of Orth — set sail for South America and was never seen again.

Robin goes on to explain how an incredibly powerful "artefact" or "talisman" of some description was transported in great secrecy from the cemetery of Millau (a little town in the Languedoc) to Bear Island, part of the remote Spitzberg Archipelago. From there, Robin's amazing story leads to subterranean labyrinths in South America, and awesome eschatological predictions . . .

The mystery of Rennes-le-Château is no more confined to that small mountaintop village than a bullet is confined to the gun in whose magazine it rests while waiting for a finger to pull the trigger.

CHAPTER ELEVEN

GLIMPSES AND GLANCES:
IMPRESSIONS OF SOME CONTEMPORARY RENNES
INVESTIGATORS

Qui docet, discit.

If the number of objects it attracts is a measure of a body's gravity, Rennes-le-Château is a veritable black hole among the earth's strange and mysterious places. Writers and artists, historians and archaeologists, journalists and broadcasters, mystics and priests, scientists and prospectors . . . Rennes draws them all inexorably into her mysterious web.

Perhaps there is also a sense in which Rennes affects all her adherents like a metaphysical mirror. While grudgingly yielding only a grain or two of fact about herself, Rennes holds up a revealing glass which reflects her investigators harshly and starkly.

In his article entitled *Fernseed and Elephants*, C. S. Lewis illustrated the mortal danger inherent in all attempts at comment and criticism: the commentator or critic never really knows all the facts. He, or she, can never get inside the heart and mind of the subject, can never fully appreciate the circumstances under which the other person worked. Of all Christ's teachings, "Judge not, that ye be not judged" is among the greatest – and is sadly the most neglected! The authors approach this section of the work with some reluctance and hesitation, aware that with the best of intentions they may be doing scant justice to colleagues in the field who have laboured hard and long, and whose only offence is to have arrived at a different conclusion from ours! Where we have made that kind of error, we ask forgiveness in advance.

What follows is only a series of glimpses and glances; where an important contemporary work has not been studied and commented on, we hope to make amends in later editions and revisions.

Perhaps the best place to start the survey is with our old friend, Henri Buthion.

Henri Buthion

When we made our second research visit to Rennes in the 1970's we stayed at what was then M. Henri Buthion's small hotel: the very place where Saunière had lived almost a century before. Henri cooked superbly (the authors still remember the fish!) and looked after us, our expedition photographer, Peter Rice, and our artist friend, Patrick Kirby, very well indeed – in the highest traditions of French hospitality.

On an unforgettable August evening after a strenuous day on the mountains, the four of us sat enthralled as Henri gave us his version of the Rennes mystery. The gist of what he said was that as a child Bérenger Saunière used to say, "Let's go up to Rennes-le-Château to look for the treasure." Henri himself had heard this from an actual witness, and he went on to say what a bad state of repair the little church was in when Saunière arrived: woodwork was worm-eaten and rotten; plaster statues were crumbling and collapsing; there was no stained glass left in the windows; everything was a wreck and the wind and rain were getting in. Henri asserts strongly – in the face of counter-arguments from some other Rennes experts – that as the result of a visit from a local benefactress, Saunière was able to carry out some preliminary restoration work on the altar, and that during this refurbishment the famous coded parchment scrolls were discovered in or near one of the altar pillars. According to Henri, Saunière examined the documents for about two hours and then ordered his builders to stop work. About two weeks later, Saunière went to visit Abbé Grasseau at St. Paul de Fenouillère because Grasseau was in contact with the hermetic centres in Paris. It was in this way, said Henri, that Saunière made contact with "the Parisian set".

On his return to Rennes, according to Henri Buthion's version, Saunière pointed to a spot on the church floor and said, "We'll dig here!" At a depth of about half a metre they encountered the Knight's Tombstone (the one that's now on display in the little museum at Rennes). It was lying face down, and they raised it carefully. One of the builders thought he saw something glinting underneath. Saunière said, "It's Sunday tomorrow. We can't have a hole in the middle of the church floor. Stop work now and come back on Monday morning."

On their return on the Monday morning, the builders lifted the stone at once. "Hey! There's nothing underneath it now," they exclaimed. They could tell that it had been moved and replaced. "Well, yes, I did it," Saunière explained. "It was from that time onwards," went on Henri, "that Saunière began making his journeys abroad taking heavy suitcases with him." Henri went on to say that the grandsons of the men who had carried the priest's cases for him commented on how heavy they were. Saunière made two or three of these mysterious overseas trips, explained Henri, and then began restoring and rebuilding his church in the Carolingian style. He believes that Saunière chose to make Carolingian style (his words) restorations because it was the ancient Carolingian documents (his words again) that led him to the treasure. Henri also said that there was an ancient genealogy among the parchments, one which said that Sigebert IV, the five year old son of Dagobert II, had escaped from the ambush in which his father was killed. Their descendants became the Counts of Razès. Henri was absolutely certain that the ancient stone dated from the eighth century and that it was meant to depict a horseman leading a child. It was also Henri's view that the stone was once part of the tomb of Sigebert IV and that it was originally immured in the wall where the statue of St. Anthony of Padua stands today. He is a keen and knowledgeable student of church architecture and argues that the external pattern of the church goes back at least to Visigothic or Lombardic times. He comments particularly on the two Carolingian bays and the tower.

Henri believes that certain additions were made by the Blancheforts in the Templar style of architecture, and that there were at one time two tombs built into the walls: one of these was ultimately used to make the stairs which lead up to the present pulpit, but the one on the opposite side was hidden – not by Saunière, but by Bigou. According to Henri, it was also Bigou who moved the contents of that tomb and hid them somewhere in the church before concealing the hole in the wall. He says that this hole was re-discovered in the 1960's when some official excavations were made in the church: but it was then completely empty.

Henri says that there is little doubt that Saunière found at least one very special and valuable prize in a tomb in the centre of the church: a thirteenth century chalice and some gold crowns from the reign of St. Louis (King Louis IX). According to Henri, Saunière gave four such crowns to a family from Carcassonne. "They are extremely rare," he said. "Only eight are known to exist in the whole world."

Henri is also convinced that Saunière found treasure of a sacred nature: something infinitely more valuable than gold or jewels, and that in order to capitalise on its unique religious worth he did a deal – or deals – with either the Vatican or the Habsburgs. Henri thinks that this explains what he describes as the frequent visits of Johann (Jean) of Habsburg to Rennes-le-Château.

Henri also tells how Saunière financed missions to Africa and paid for the building of convents and monasteries – as well as the huge sums he spent in Rennes itself. Commenting on Saunière's apparent financial difficulties towards the end of his life, he believes that these were due to the political problems then existing between the French and Austrian Governments, and spying charges levelled against Saunière which would made it very imprudent for him to have been seen receiving money from Austria.

Turning to the subject of Marie Dénarnaud, in whose name Saunière had bought all the land, Henri described her as an ordinary peasant girl, very shrewd and intelligent, almost sly according to some of those who knew her. Sadly, after Saunière's death, Henri explained, she failed to keep things in good repair. She kept rabbits and chickens on the estate. She grew flowers in the huge greenhouses where he had cultivated oranges and lemon trees. "The garden turned into a wilderness," Henri said sadly. "She let everything go." Even the once exquisitely elegant Villa Bethania fell open to the elements and became uninhabitable. (Authors' note: As previously mentioned, this is where we stayed for a few days during one of our trips to Rennes in the 1970's. Even though M. Corbu – and later Henri himself – had worked wonders of restoration on it by then, there was still something in its atmosphere reminiscent of lines from Edgar Allan Poe's *The Fall of the House of Usher*: "I felt that I breathed an atmosphere of sorrow. An air of stern, deep, and irredeemable gloom hung over and pervaded all.")

Henri told us that he had taken over the presbytery in 1966. At that time the floorboards were rotten and the staircases were falling down: Marie had abandoned everything, and this neglect had persisted for thirty-five years. Henri tells of how his predecessor, M. Corbu, had taken over from Marie, given her a life annuity, looked after her and treated her kindly. But by the time M. Corbu acquired the estate the library door of the tower was missing — it had been stolen — and the interior had been exposed to the weather. The furniture, however, was very strong and solid and all Saunière's books were still there, including a seventeenth century Bible in twenty-four volumes.

Henri then related how Marie had promised M. Corbu that she would tell him something which would make him rich before she died, but she died following a stroke which left her unable to communicate. He then referred to the episode of the ancient rings which Marie owned. On being asked where the ones she was wearing had come from, she took them off and never wore them again. Henri also says that Gérard de Sède, a pioneer researcher of the Rennes mystery, claimed that in a letter written in the year of her death Marie asked for one of those ancient rings to be sold. Henri uses this data to support the theory that part, at least, of the Rennes treasure was of the traditional kind — gold and jewels of some sort. He then argues very astutely that if the treasure had been only gold, silver and jewels there would have been little difficulty in selling it locally. Certainly Toulouse, Carcassonne or Narbonne would have contained possible buyers. Even Marseilles would have been nearer, safer and more convenient than Austria.

To use Henri Buthion's words: "It must have been something absolutely beyond price." That very significant comment re-awakens echoes of the old Cathar statement about whatever it was that was smuggled away from the siege of Montségur: *pecuniam infinitam* — unlimited wealth.

At the end of 1990, Lionel had an opportunity to visit Dr. Arthur Guirdham, the renowned authority on Catharism, to ask what he thought the four heroic mountaineers from Montségur had carried down its precipitous sides under cover of darkness. "Books," said the doctor, "esoteric manuscripts of some kind. I think that's the most probable answer."

Could it have been those same books, or the secret knowledge within them, which Saunière discovered six centuries later and possibly sold to Johann (Jean) Salvator, the Habsburg prince? Could such books have contained information which Henri Buthion described as "something absolutely beyond price" or what the Inquisition records called *pecuniam infinitam*? Or could they have contained information about the whereabouts of something and secret instructions about how to operate it?

Henri Buthion also has interesting ideas about alchemy, transmutation and the mysterious Nicholas Flamel. He believes that transmutation might have been possible, even that Flamel might have known how to do it, but that it was not the source of his wealth. Henri thinks that the important aspect of transmutation is spiritual rather than physical, and that no one has the right to use it to acquire material wealth. In his opinion, Flamel's wealth came because he helped a Jewish community (who had been exiled from Lyons) to recover treasure that was rightfully theirs. Flamel dealt faithfully and honourably with his Jewish friends and was rewarded accordingly. Henri also said that Flamel, although not immortal, did have the secret of some sort of rejuvenating medicine, or elixir of youth, and that he had used it to help the French King — who had shown his gratitude as generously as Flamel's Jewish friends had done.

From the possibility of alchemy, Henri turned next to the mysterious and contentious subject of the so-called Priory of Sion. He thinks that

Saunière did contact a secret society to help him decipher the coded manuscripts, but that the priest's association with whatever secret society it was ended at that. Henri also wonders whether Rennes was one of the Priory of Sion's headquarters during the seventeenth century.

He spoke next of the mysterious tombstone codes which he has studied in great depth and on which he is undoubtedly an important authority. *Redis*, he said, stood for the ancient Visigothic capital, and was carved on the tombs of ancient warriors and nobles whose treasures had been buried with them. The words *regis, cellis, arcis*, he explained, were understood to mean, in addition: "There is treasure at Rennes in the hiding place of the king in the citadel."

Henri moved on from these enigmatic local tombstones to the "Arcadian" tomb which Poussin had painted, and its connection with the neighbouring village of Arques. The *redis, regis, cellis, arcis* inscription could also mean: "Go to Rennes to the tomb of the King at Arques". Henri maintains strongly that there are two versions of Poussin's "Shepherds of Arcadia" in the Louvre, but that the Louvre authorities don't talk about them — which he finds very strange. Only one is on show there. (At this point in our conversation Henri produced a colour reproduction of the version said not to be on show!)

He told us that in Saunière's time only the foundations of the ancient tomb of Arques could be seen. According to Henri, this earlier tomb had been pulled down by Colbert — Minister of Finance to Louis XIV — who had also undertaken extensive excavations at Chateau Blanchefort. This can be proved, he says by its inclusion in the report of the Intendent of Languedoc. Henri maintains that the "modern" tomb — the one which we examined closely in the 1970's, but which was recently demolished — was erected by Lawrence over the foundations of the ancient tomb in 1904/1905.

Henri then produced a copy of another Poussin painting showing King Midas bathing in the River Pactol with the water god watching him. In the Languedoc the name for the river which flows by the site of the tomb of Arques is: The River of the King's Gold.

Henri tells his fascinating story quietly, simply, impressively and with great conviction. It is soundly argued and very well worth hearing. Although it appears to answer several of the Rennes questions very satisfactorily, it raises almost as many.

The matter of the Louvre paintings to which Henri refers is a curious one: certainly the letters reproduced in our Correspondence Appendix support his view of the affair. When we wrote to the Louvre asking for information about the second or "hidden" version of "The Shepherds of Arcadia" we received a polite denial of its existence. When Peter Rice, our photographer on one of the early expeditions, called in person one Saturday and asked to see it, he was told that it did exist but that it could not be seen at week-ends: all very curious.

Henri Fatin

Less than a stone's throw from Henri Buthion's home in what was once Saunière's grand estate stands the ancient and mysterious Château Hautpoul — the home of M. Henri Fatin.

Henri (son of the late M. Marius Fatin who bought Château Hautpoul in 1946 and lived there until his death in 1967) has spent the whole of his life in this strange, deeply historic place. Henri is a very talented sculptor and an avid collector. When he and his sister showed us around their unusual and atmospheric home it was an unforgettable experience. As you move from room to stairway, from courtyard to oubliette, from deep Romano-Visigothic foundations to lofty but decaying seventeenth century walls, it is like walking under the lintels of history, moving through twenty centuries in a single afternoon. A serious and knowledgeable student of astronomy, astrology, geology, archaeology and prehistory, Henri showed us a wide range of samples from his amazing collection of pottery, fossils and ancient artefacts found in and around Rennes — and very generously gave us some interesting items to keep. He also showed us a few beautifully illustrated and carefully annotated pages from the hand-produced book about Rennes and Château Hautpoul which he and his father began compiling together, and on which Henri is still working. It was from M. Fatin that the idea of Rennes itself resembling a "Ship of the Dead" bearing a great dead warrior came. This unusual theory of his is significantly reinforced by an extract from the twelfth century Anglo-Latin author, Gervase of Tilbury, given in full in the appendix entitled "Shipping the Dead".

Gervase, a relative of Patrick, Earl of Salisbury, lived the life of a scholarly adventurer. Despite being a Clerk in Holy Orders he rose to become Marshall of Arles under Emperor Otto IV and married a rich and beautiful young heiress. His contemporary account of mysterious, silent and unmanned "ships of the dead" bearing their cargoes of corpses and treasure down the River Rhône to the cemetery at Arles makes strange and compelling reading. Does it have any connection at all with the enigmatic coded text of the supposed Rennes parchments? "This treasure belongs to King Dagobert II . . . and he is there dead."

Not far from M. Fatin's château and adjacent to the ancient church is the small but excellent museum run by Antoine Captier and his wife, Claire Corbu, daughter of the late M. Noël Corbu who befriended and cared for Marie Dénarnaud in her declining years. First class conducted tours are available for museum visitors and the brightly vivacious, effervescent, ever helpful and fluently bilingual Celia Brooke is on hand to help the many English-speaking visitors. It is also possible to meet Antoine's brother, the official Village Guardian, Marcel Captier, who is a gifted artist and illustrator, and is also a very well-informed source of information about the Rennes mystery. The Captier brothers' great grandfather was Saunière's bellringer, and it was he who discovered the mysterious little glass vial hidden in the secret compartment in the old pulpit balustrade which can now be seen in the museum. But, as always with Rennes-le-Château, not only is there some evidence that this balustrade is solid and could not possibly have contained anything at all, but also that it could well be a reproduction installed in Saunière's time!

Baigent, Leigh and Lincoln

The Baigent, Leigh and Lincoln team have also bored pretty deeply into the Rennes mystery, but, unlike Paul Smith, they give the impression that they had a particular objective or conclusion in mind before they began their explorations. That seems to us a great pity. Their love of historical mystery and the intriguing way they build up the suspense in their books makes exciting and entertaining reading – which is why the anticlimax of what we believe to be their very badly mistaken conclusion is so much more of a disappointment. We cannot help thinking that if once they could disentangle themselves from the mare's nest of the Jesus-married-Mary-Magdalen/Merovingian/Priory-of-Sion theories and start looking for an alternative explanation of their extensive research and fascinating clues they could well produce something really startling and significant.

Robert Heinlein, the talented SF author, once wrote a novel called *The Unpleasant Profession of Jonathan Hoag*. It began brilliantly. The suspense and mystery were genuinely gripping . . . but it petered out into a mundane ending which did not live up to the promise of the earlier parts of the story. Sadly, there is a *Jonathan Hoag* quality about the Rennes work of Baigent, Leigh and Lincoln. The reader is left wishing that it had ended as well as it began.

Henry Lincoln's new book *The Holy Place* which is currently being released by Jonathan Cape, concentrates on his latest theory, the result of some twenty years' research and reflection on the data, that there exists in the Rennes area an astounding pentacle of mountain peaks and an even more astounding artificial structure which surrounds it! If he is right – and he could well be – his discoveries generate a whole new series of very challenging and fascinating questions. Who built it, and when? How did they do it, and why? What began as a local mystery centred on Bérenger Saunière's inexplicable wealth, grew to include the Jesus-and-Mary-Magdalen theories and the Priory of Sion, codes in paintings, clues in cartography, traces on tombstones and ciphers in parchments, mysterious genealogies and hints of alchemy and black magic. Henry Lincoln's latest researches look as if they may be taking the bounds of the Rennes mystery further still.

Paul Smith

No bloodhound with a nose for truth could ever hope to be in the same league as Paul Smith. If he were an income tax inspector, a Scotland Yard fraud squad superintendent or a district auditor, the careless and the dishonest would cringe and tremble at the sound of his name. Undoubtedly, Paul could also have made a high reputation for himself as an analytical chemist – if chemistry had interested him as much as Rennes does. His appetite for facts is voracious. He devours all the relevant data, cross references it thoroughly, re-checks everything three times and still keeps a question mark handy in case he's overlooked something. Paul goes to war with two battle cries emblazoned across his banner: "Who said so?", and "Where did he get it from?" His appendix to the present volume, for which the authors and publishers are most grateful, is a mine of tightly compressed, granite hard information.

Stanley James

Stanley James is a weaver of webs; and he does it with immense skill and delicacy. As though by magic, he produces one convoluted thread after another, working them into intricate patterns and complicated designs. He is no stubborn fact-sifter as Paul Smith is; neither does he decide on an answer and deliberately build a subsequent framework of questions in order to reach it. His writing gives the impression that he has the heart of a connoisseur, or a truly sophisticated collector. Yet somewhere in that curator's heart of his, there is a reluctance to discard any piece which might, eventually, be shown to have value or importance. If he were a prophet's disciple he would not only wish to preserve the holy man's left sandal but the grass on which it trod, the soil below that grass and the bird now flying overhead whose fleeting shadow once passed over the sacred turf! He approaches the codes, the ciphers, the symbols and the real and supposed clues in and around Rennes like a wise old Victorian gardener bent on propagation. He grafts an idea here, cross-pollinates a theory or two there, takes a slender cutting of fact, dusts it with his own patent brand of hormone hypothesis powder and watches it lovingly while it takes root. If he has a fault at all, it is that he is too good and subtle a weaver, too skilful and successful a gardener. The reader cannot help but admire his emulation of Adam's ability and Arachne's skill, but is left wondering whether the webs of derivation which he has woven are somehow becoming too heavy and elaborate to be sustained by the slender threads of fact attaching them to the cavern walls.

Stanley James has the kind of ingenuity which can find the letter A cut into the wall of a cave and deduce: that its apex is pointing in a significant direction; that its cross bar forms an isosceles triangle the bisector of which (if drawn) would mark an important point on the map; that its three sides represent Boudet, Saunière and Bigou in chronological order; that their names lead to their parishes and that we must take measurements from there; that the letter A if laid on the floor of the church at Rennes with its apex towards the altar would indicate two important paintings or statues with its "feet"; that one of these would be a saint with an A in his name and − as A is pronounced like "Aix" in "Aix-les-Bains" − that it is, therefore, probable that the treasure hunter should pay a visit to Aix-les-Bains in Savoie, 15 kilometres north of Chambery, and search the museum there which occupies the site of the old Roman temple . . . and so on . . and so on . . .

One acceptable definition of intelligence is that it is the ability to see connections − whether Stanley James's theories are right or not, there can be no doubt about the very considerable intelligence that lies behind them. All his ideas are contained in his previously quoted book *The Treasure Maps of Rennes-le-Château,* which is still available and deserves to be read.

Elizabeth van Buren

Just as it is easy to admire Stanley James's wonderfully woven webs of interconnected derivations − even if they might sometimes seem to cross gulfs which are a shade too wide for them − so it is equally easy to admire Elizabeth van Buren's towering heights of mysticism and imagination. St. Paul once wrote of a man (he may, modestly, have chosen to refer to himself in the third person in this passage) who was "caught up to the third heaven" where he heard "inexpressible things which man is not permitted to tell" (II Corinthians, chapter 12 : 2 et seq.).

Like all gifted and intuitive writers, M. van Buren makes sudden psychic bounds and mystic leaps which are not always easy for the reader to follow, and she also sees connections which, while they are perfectly clear and obvious to her, are sometimes less discernible to the reader who is not used to her style and way of thinking. The extent of her research is vast: the towering edifices of her esoteric thought rest on very broad foundations of knowledge. She is a daring, poetic writer – as most mystics are – and, in consequence, her faith and philosophy are a million kilometres away from the traditional orthodoxy which we defend. Her work combines speculative cosmology, astrology, alternative pre-history, and, almost inevitably, an awesome and ominous eschatology. Through the ever-thinning veil of the observed material universe, M. van Buren sees brief but vivid glimpses of the eternal, invisible world and – as far as the limit-ations of language will allow – she seeks to share those glimpses with her readers. She writes with the passionate conviction of the pure in heart and those with the gift of spiritual simplicity and directness. She talks freely of cosmic wonders and mysterious multi-dimensional realities with a delightful and disarming frankness and ordinariness: the kind which most people use to discuss such things as dinner menus, the price of petrol, or the best route from Paris to Toulouse.

M. van Buren's finely tuned instincts and exquisitely sensitive intuitions tell her that something of immense importance may be happening at Rennes: she could be wrong, of course, but time will tell . . .

Émile Saunière

The country families in and around Rennes-le-Château have been there for generations. Bérenger Saunière himself was born in the house behind the Fountain of the Tritons in Montazels. The Saunières belong in the district. Émile, who is related to Bérenger, lives nearby, and has written two very useful and authoritative volumes entitled *Moi, Bérenger Saunière* which throw a fascinating light on his famous kinsman. M. Émile Saunière is also closely involved with the "Association Terre de Rhedae" set up in 1989 with the main aim of protecting the domaine and preserving the cultural history of Rennes-le-Château.

Robin, Herrera and Markale

Jean Robin, a master of stylishly elegant French prose, and a thoughtful metaphysical and philosophical writer, has produced two distinguished volumes on the Rennes mystery, in which he refers with particular admirat-ion to the work and thought of René Guénon. Robin writes from an eschatological perspective, and states that we are living in a pre-Apocalyptic age. He believes that France holds the key to this mysterious eschatology – but he does not say this from any spirit of excessive nationalism; rather, he regards France in a very deep and esoteric sense as "the Kingdom of the Grail". He also accepts and understands that a privileged function of this sort inevitably has its dark side – like The Force in *Star Wars* – and that this negative aspect has been revealed throughout the centuries in such tragedies as the massacre of the Cathars during the Albigensian Crusade, the destruction of the Templars by the odious Philippe le Bel, the Revolution with its accompanying Terror at the end of the eighteenth century and the Napoleonic Wars. Robin sees both sides of the coin and says very perceptively: *corruptio optimi pessima* — the corruption of the best produces the worst; the fallen saint is the worst kind of sinner. (Was Saunière, in that sense, a "fallen" priest? If so what exactly did he tell Abbé Rivière during that last dramatic confession?)

Jean Robin argues very convincingly that Rennes-le-Château has always constituted one of the two poles of these French mysteries for reasons that relate to what he describes as its "sacred geography". Rennes summarises and encapsulates these two components — the light and the dark side of the mission of France. Robin believes that it is the dark, dangerous and sinister side which currently prevails, but that a final Redemption — the Ultimate Triumph of Goodness and Light — is surely coming. He very strongly recommends Guénon's book, *The Reign of Quality and Signs of the Times.* The thoughts of this remarkably talented man have taken research into the Rennes mystery an astronomical distance from the simple legend of a poor country priest who found a buried treasure.

In his richly metaphorical prose Herrera describes Rennes-le-Château as the "Doorway into the Dragon", the "Centre of the World". In his work on Rennes entitled *A Multidimensional Doorway into the Dragon*, Herrera refers in depth to Mount Bugarach, which he describes as an extinct volcano, and speculates on the possibility that Saunière and Jules Verne knew one another. He then considers the possibility that Verne's *Journey to the Centre of the Earth* actually refers to Mount Bugarach; certainly, he says, Verne has a character called Captain Bugarach in his novel *Clovis Dardentor*, and there is a farm called "Les Capitaines" at the foot of Mount Bugarach.

Herrera adds his quota to the sinister whispers that circulate in and around the Rennes mystery. He tells of a close friend of his — a regular visitor to the Razès — a man named Daniel Bettex, who was once a senior Swiss security officer. "Don't ask too many questions about the Vatican and its Secular Orders," Bettex warned Herrera. "They have top secret matters to attend to in this region." Herrera never saw Bettex alive again. He seems to have died of the same inexplicable cardiovascular lesions which might have killed old Abbé Boudet and his successor at Rennes-les-Bains, Abbé Rescanière.

Herrera never hesitates to invoke the macrocosmic, the metaphysical and the eschatological in his conclusions about the nature of the mystery pervading Rennes-le-Château.

Jean Markale's researches are rather more localised than Herrera's, and the results appear in his book *Rennes-le-Château et l'énigme de l'or maudit.*

When travelling in the Razès, Markale was fascinated by Montségur, but reported feeling strangely uneasy in Rennes-le-Château itself. He experienced equally curious sensations in the tiny village of Monthoumet near Bugarach, where he said it was "as if the local people were living in another world". For him it seemed that Rennes-le-Château was almost outside space and time.

His most interesting hypothesis is that Bérenger Saunière was being blackmailed by the local schoolmaster, a man named Jamet, who also worked as secretary at the Mairie. Markale's work indicates that Saunière gave both money and jewels to Jamet, and that the blackmail did not begin until after the murder of Gélis.

Markale also refers to an ancient tradition which relates that the treasure of the Visigoths is buried "between the mountains of Alaric and Alaricou," which is possibly between Carcassonne and Narbonne.

He argues a firm case for a Templar-Cathar connection and suggests that the former protected the latter and helped them to salvage some of their valuables from the ever encroaching persecution.

Markale also emphasizes some possible links between the ancient and noble family Aniort who befriended the Cathars in 1209 (and were consequently excommunicated and lost their castles), Trencavel le Jeune and the King of France. King Louis IX restored the Aniort castles to them and the excommunication was annulled. For Markale this raises a fascinating question: what price did they pay, or what major secrets did they reveal, in order to gain Louis IX's pardon with such alacrity?

Markale also goes deeply into the connections between Rennes-le-Château and St. Sulpice in Paris; the "Confrèrie du Saint-Sacrement," Nicholas Fouquet and the then Bishop of Alet, Nicolas Pavillon.

Markale argues that it must have been Marie de Nègre d'Ables who had custody of the ancient Aniort documents in 1732 when she married François d'Hautpoul, and that those documents might well have contained evidence for the persistence of the Merovingian line, evidence attested to by no less a witness than Blanche de Castille herself.

Did Bigou, chaplain to Marie de Nègre, conceal those documents – along with some Aniort gold and jewellery – in the church at Rennes before leaving for Spain where he died in exile in 1794?

Markale is also very interested in the role played by the Countess de Chambord (a Habsburg according to some knowledgeable sources) and her gift of 3000 gold francs to Saunière for the renovation of the church at Rennes.

Summary

As we said at the outset, this has been only a series of very brief glimpses at a great many pieces of fascinating contemporary work. It is simply not possible to include more in this present volume – however interesting, and however deserving – but we greatly hope to do so in future revisions.

The bibliography contains a list of the key books by researchers into the mystery. Not all are now readily available, but the serious student is directed to these along with the source documents listed in *Rennes-le-Château: A Bibliography* by John M. Saul and Janice A. Glaholm.

For a very detailed and extensive survey of the whole subject, there is nothing better than *Les Archives du Trésor de Rennes-le-Château* by Pierre Jarnac. Apart from the authors mentioned earlier in this chapter, the major writers are René Descadeillas, Gérard de Sède, Franck Marie, Jean-Luc Chaumeil, Jean-Michel Thibaux, Claire Corbu with Antoine and Marcel Captier, Pierre Jarnac, Jean Alain Sipra and the team of Claude Boumendil and Gilbert Tappa.

CHAPTER TWELVE

CONCLUSIONS

Saepe stilum vertas, iterum quae digna legi sint scripturus.

Edward de Bono, the lateral thinking pioneer and great problem solving expert, once said something to the effect that you can reach a solution in an hour, a better one in a day, a better one still in a week: but the best one — never! What he meant, of course, was that you can go on revising, improving, adjusting, modifying and polishing indefinitely: what has to be decided is a purely practical issue — at what point do you call a halt to the refining process and say, "OK. This is it; it may not be the end of the line, but this is where I'm stopping the train"?

What are the possible solutions to the Rennes-le-Château mystery?

It could, of course, be a colossal hoax. We do not for one moment think that it is, but the possibility has to be examined. There have been numerous elaborate and highly successful hoaxes over the years. "Piltdown Man" (1912) was the apparently fossilized fragments of a cranium and jawbone found in a gravel formation at Barkham Manor on Piltdown Common, near Lewes. It happened during the Saunière period. It was not until 1926 that any objections were raised: the gravels were found to be far less ancient than had been previously thought. By 1954 "Piltdown Man" was revealed as a comparatively recent human cranium deposited in the proximity of the jaw of an orangutan; both had been skilfully disguised. Charles Dawson, a lawyer and antiquarian who died in 1916, was given the blame for perpetrating the hoax.

One could add the tragic death of Dr. Paul Kammerer, author of *The Inheritance of Acquired Characteristics* (1924). Someone injected India ink into the "thumb" of a midwife toad which became the basis of his theories. When Dr. Noble of the American Museum of Natural History in New York published the results of his close examinations of the toad in 1926 — the ink had washed out in the water in the dissecting dish — Kammerer committed suicide.

Almost as sad was the decline and accelerated death of Johann Beringer (note the near-coincidence of names with Bérenger Saunière! Another example of such a near-coincidence will be found in the Appendices), a Professor at the University of Wurzburg. Beringer's students planted some "fossils" and ridiculously inscribed clay tablets for Beringer to find. One of these even bore what purported to be God's signature, but Beringer was completely taken in. Even when his sheepishly penitent students told him it was all a hoax, he refused to believe them.

The bitter truth finally dawned on him, however: he spent the last of his money buying back all the copies of his book which he could locate. He died heart-broken and practically destitute.

There is also the much more recent controversy over the Archaeopteryx ("ancient wing") "fossils" of what may, or may not, have been some sort of bird prototype. Von Schlotheim reported finding some in the Upper Jurassic beds near Solnhofen in Bavaria in 1820, but they are now lost. All that currently "survives" of the Archaeopteryx from the Upper Jurassic period is one feather, one fragmentary skeleton and two more or less complete skeletons — scarcely enough for Sunday lunch!

Some recent work by a scientific photographer at Cardiff, however, has led to very grave suspicious that the so-called Archaeopteryx remains were doctored with the same loving care as "Piltdown Man". Scientific camera work seems to have revealed that every feather impression is identical: did some skilful hoaxer simply use one feather over and over again to produce the appearance of fossilized, feathery wings?

Archaeopteryx macroura — if genuine — is about the size of a small crow with a disproportionately long tail consisting of some twenty vertebrae of a reptilian type. The supposedly fossilised remains had feathery impressions all along this tail. Is it unreasonable to suspect that another Charles Dawson had added these feather impressions to the genuine fossil of some small Upper Jurassic snake?

If the Rennes-le-Château mystery is explicable in terms of a hoax, then the hoaxer must be a twisted genius and his degree of eccentricity must be matched by prodigious wealth. His skills as an artificer, fabricator, historian, archaeologist, linguist and cryptographer must be — or have been — well above average. When did he operate and whom did he set out to deceive? Are we looking for one hoax, or a series? One hoaxer in the distant past, or a whole succession of whimsical, capricious eccentrics with enough time, energy and money — and sufficient talent — to create hoaxes and forgeries of sufficient calibre to deceive serious researchers over a long period?

Saunière's income can scarcely have been a hoax. It isn't possible to spend on that scale for over twenty years without paying the craftsmen, builders and suppliers more or less regularly. Whatever else was bogus, however many red herrings swam up and down the Aude, one stubborn contradiction of the hoax theory remains obdurate and immovable: Saunière had real and substantial assets of some sort — and he didn't have them before he came to Rennes.

So what of the secret blood-line theories and the Priory of Sion — beside which a will-o'-the-wisp has the density of lead Christmas pudding?

Apart from the fact that there isn't one shred of real evidence for the "Jesus married Mary Magdalen and their descendants became the Merovingians" theory (while there is a mountain of evidence against it — cemented by the blood of martyrs and reinforced by the testimony of saints) — its greatest and most obvious weakness is that it doesn't explain Saunière's wealth. Purely and simply: it's not an income generator.

Let's examine the angles objectively. The first idea might be that some wealthy vested interest (the Vatican, the Habsburgs as the vestigial traces of the Holy Roman Empire, even the Bishop of Carcassonne?) paid Saunière very handsomely to keep it quiet. It won't hold water. Can you seriously imagine any Pope, Bishop or ethereal remnant of a Holy Roman Emperor quietly and cynically absorbing some so-called "proof" that everything he had believed in was based on an error? Would such a man pay an insignificant country priest a small fortune to keep silent about his "discoveries"? If the hypothetical powerful vested interests who wanted things kept quiet had been as immoral, as cynical and as pragmatic as that, they would have silenced Saunière far more cheaply, efficiently and permanently!

Men who achieve positions of that magnitude are politically shrewd, and wise in the ways of the world. They know from experience that absolute secrecy can rarely be bought, and that only the dead can be trusted not to speak. The whole idea of paying Saunière not to reveal the so-called "secret" about Jesus and Mary Magdalen would strike such a man as unsound and impractical. There was another problem: if Saunière had "discovered a secret" someone must have put it there in the first place. Saunière would not be the only man who knew it. There is no point in putting a golden plug in an unreliable kitchen sink when the bath and washbasin taps are full on.

To a man with the intelligence of Franz Josef Habsburg, or the Pope, another thought would instantly occur: there can be no such "proof" as Saunière claims to have found. The Church has always had many vicious and unscrupulous opponents — pernicious liars as well as savage persecutors. They were around at the time of Christ's resurrection.

"Tell everyone that the disciples came and stole his body while you were asleep," said the influential priests to the Roman tomb guards. "If you get into trouble for sleeping on duty, we'll square it with the Governor."

What could anyone find, or claim to have found, which would provide "incontrovertible proof"? A mummified body in a sarcophagus could be anyone at all, no matter how many false labels describe it as being the body of Jesus. Fanatical anti-Christian plotters who were prepared to bribe Roman guards to lie, would not have been above arranging for the embalmed body of some hapless, unidentified vagrant — or, better still, the body of a crucified felon — to be placed in a suitably labelled sarcophagus and referred to as the body of Jesus.

What other "evidence" could there have been? An ancient parchment purporting to be an eyewitness account of Jesus's death and burial — without any resurrection? Forged by some rabid, anti-Christian propagandist, what does that prove?

The Lincoln team were not the first to suggest that Jesus was married. One of the familiar arguments is that he was often addressed as "Rabbi" and that it was normal practice for a Rabbi to be both a husband and a father. There is little or no evidence, however, to suggest that the term was used other than as a general mark of courtesy and respect when directed towards Jesus. The constant attacks made on his work by the Pharisees and Sadducees indicate that he was not an officially recognized Rabbi. Much New Testament evidence suggests that he was entirely independent. Whereas the scribes made it a point of their scholarship always to quote a scriptural authority or precedent, St. Matthew writes of Jesus: "He taught as one having authority (i.e., within himself) and not as their scribes." (Matthew 7:29.)

His only recorded public legitimisation by any other religious leader or group was his encounter with John the Baptist, and John was the first to declare that any such process of recognition should have been the other way round. The Baptist regarded himself as unworthy even to unfasten Christ's sandals (John 1:27). On at least one occasion Jesus was directly interrogated about the source of the authority he assumed (Matthew 21:23).

If then, he was not an "official" Rabbi, some of the pro-marriage arguments break down. If a salesman calls you "sir" because he wants to sell you something, you don't immediately become a recognized and invested knight. Neither do you acquire a suit of armour. Arguing a wife for Christ merely because he was addressed as "Rabbi" is broadly parallel reasoning. As we have already noted, some sort of case can be made for identifying Mary Magdalen with Mary of Bethany, and with the unnamed woman taken in adultery, who was saved from stoning by Christ's intervention. She may also have been the unnamed woman who poured the ointment over his feet. But it is not a strong case, and it is certainly not conclusive.

According to Lincoln's team, the tradition was merely an attempt by the early church leaders to blacken her reputation. They had apparently decided that the secret of her marriage to Jesus had to be suppressed at all costs. However, taken in conjunction with Christ's teaching that those who are forgiven most will tend to express most gratitude (Luke 7:47), the prostitution tradition centred on Mary Magdalen can be defended to some extent.

There is, however, a further pro-marriage argument which the Lincoln team have omitted. Christ was a master of Old Testament scholarship. He would have been sensitively aware of the anguished message of the prophet Hosea, who wrote of the parallel between Israel's spiritual infidelity to Yahweh and the sexual infidelity of his wife, Gomer. Her series of extramarital encounters terminated in the slave market where Hosea eventually found, rescued and forgave her, before reinstating her at home. The compassion and understanding shown by Christ to the unnamed woman taken in adultery becomes infinitely deeper and more significant if it is suggested that it was his own wife whom the hypocritical mob were planning to stone. It would also explain the love and devotion she demonstrated later when anointing his feet (John 12:3); her long, heartbreaking vigil by the cross, and her visit to the tomb even before it was light.

His implacable opponents among the Scribes and Pharisees directed some of their most pointed questions towards marriage and sexual ethics. Could they have been trying to exploit what they mistakenly believed to be a weak spot in Christ's defences — a wife who had not always observed the sanctity of their marriage? For example, Christ's teaching that sexual thoughts are morally equivalent to sexual acts (Matthew 5:28) seems a perfect counter to the hypocrisy underlying the ostentatious puritanism and respectability of his opponents. However, it is not Christ's conjectural marriage to Mary Magdalen, nor even the possibility that they might have had children, which lies at the heart of our disagreement with the Lincoln team.

Christ's divinity and humanity are, if anything, enhanced and endorsed by the thought that he might have been a husband and father. His transcendent spirituality is increased rather than diminished by this possibility of his total involvement in the human experience. The inevitable redemptive suffering of the Son of God, who was also the Son of Man, could only have been made more poignant by his knowledge that those on earth who loved him best were being hurt most by his pain and approaching death — and by their inability to help him. If Christ had decided to remain unmarried it would have been to spare his hypothetical family's feelings at his crucifixion rather than because he felt that marriage and fatherhood were inimical to his unique role.

The clearest indication of his attitude to marriage is probably to be found in Matthew 19:3 - 12, where he pronounces unequivocally against divorce. He goes on to answer the disciples' subsequent surprised comment by indicating that for particular people in specific circumstances marriage may not be appropriate. (The medical missionary working in malarial swamps? Among lepers? In a society where persecution and martyrdom are everyday occurrences? A single man may gladly undertake risks to which he would not expose a wife and family. A dedicated old religious scholar cannot pore single-mindedly over his Aramaic scrolls and Syriac codices when as a parent he urgently needs to discuss his son's money problems.)

Whether Christ considered that his own mission precluded marriage was a matter between Him and his Father, and neither Lincoln's researches nor ours could attempt to reveal that decision conclusively. Lincoln thinks Jesus was married; on balance we think he wasn't. The essence of the debate seems to be that either celibate or married priests can do excellent work in the locations to which God has called them. Christ's marital status is not a major issue, but the Lincoln team's insinuations that someone else died in his place, or that he recovered and retreated, are fundamental, and must be refuted absolutely.

In any philosophical consideration of the nature of human autonomy, certain limits to freedom are axiomatic. We cannot perform two mutually exclusive activities, such as standing and sitting, simultaneously. We are not free to act in ways for which we lack the necessary strength, stamina, skills or physical equipment; we cannot lift buildings on the palms of our hands, run non-stop around the earth, count the visible stars in five minutes using only eyes and brains, nor flap feathered pinions and fly to the sun. Neither can we perform actions which are at variance with our psychological and sociological patterns of behaviour. A seventeenth century Puritan girl would not have been able to participate in the sexual freedom of Polynesian islanders. A vegetarian does not relish rare steak — with or without the added risk of BSE! A loving parent can no more harm her child, nor by inaction allow the child to be harmed, than an Asimovian robot can harm a human being. We cannot retain our identity and integrity — we literally cease to be ourselves — if we begin to act in ways which would contradict our fundamental character patterns.

A once loyal hero who runs and leaves his friends to die thereby automatically ceases to be a loyal hero. His actions re-define him as a coward and a traitor. The hero remains a hero because he does not run. The former coward who suddenly finds the courage to stay and fight to the death ceases at that moment of decision to be a coward and becomes a new and different character. Some of us can, of course, change and perhaps even re-change, throughout our lives. Scrooge moves from meanness to generosity as *Christmas Carol* progresses. Sydney Carton's character changes from recklessness and superficiality to altruistic heroism in *A Tale of Two Cities*. But there are some indelible characters whose central and most recognizable characteristic is their innate immutability.

Such men and women become the granite landmarks by which their friends and acquaintances navigate. Socrates, Confucius and − above all − Jesus, were neither fluid nor plastic men. No matter how gravely Lincoln's team may suspect some of the New Testament records, the picture of Christ emerges clearly as that of a strong, fearless, resolute and charismatic leader.

From the twelve year old boy who debated with priests and rabbis in the Temple to the lonely spiritual wrestler facing temptation in the wilderness, Jesus personifies courage, strength and stability. He is the healer who pours out his energy unstintingly for the sick. He is also the inspired and practically inexhaustible teacher whose unique blend of parables, patience and persistence enables him to communicate effectively with curious crowds on the one hand and his occasionally dull disciples on the other. He touches lepers. He mixes with social outcasts. He goes on fearlessly with his work despite Herod's murder of John the Baptist. Christ confronts Priests, Levites, Scribes, Pharisees, Sadducees, Romans, Zealots and Samaritans − every dangerous and potentially hostile faction in the boiling cauldron of political and religious vitriol which comprised first century Palestine. He antagonises the money changers in the Temple precincts. He dares to proclaim his Messiahship openly by riding into Jerusalem at the head of an excited crowd. With calm resolution he faces the lonely anguish of Gethsemane, the irony of Judas's betrayal, the sorrow of Peter's denial and the humiliating agony of scourging and crucifixion. Even on the brink of death he begins reciting the twenty-second psalm, a psalm in which we proceed from lonely agony and derision through prophetic optimism to final triumphant glory. Surely no words could be more appropriate for a man undergoing that kind of torture?

One fundamental and irrefutable argument for the historicity of the crucifixion and the genuine physical death of Christ is his character. He would not have run away from his enemies. He could not have allowed another man to die in his place. In the highly unlikely event that he had somehow managed to survive the scourging, the nails, and the spear thrust in his side, he would have been back preaching, teaching and healing as soon as he could stand. He could not, he would not, have retreated to a hermitage and a life of quiet meditation in Egypt or India. It is just conceivable that he might have sent his hypothetical family to safety across the Mediterranean, but he himself would have continued to work for the coming of his Father's Kingdom just as energetically and relentlessly as he had done before in the face of all danger and all opposition.

But what about Mary Magdalen herself? Suppose all the wildest hypotheses were true and Mary was the wife whom Jesus saved from the mob, the wife who later poured the precious ointment together with her absolute love and gratitude at her husband's feet − could she have left Palestine if he had survived the crucifixion and gone on with his ministry? Could such a truly strong and loving woman have left such a man in those – or in any – circumstances? Never!

The evidence for the resurrection is infinitely stronger than any "evidence" which can be concocted against it. Those who had known, loved and followed Jesus during his earthly ministry testified fearlessly that He had risen from the dead in a genuine, substantial form – that he could walk to Emmaus with them, break bread, eat fish and honeycomb, talk to them and be touched by them. If you know that your faith is a sham because you have seen your dead hero's body lying unresurrected in its tomb, you do not go out of your way to proclaim that he is alive – especially when to do so is to risk incurring a similar agonising death yourself.

Subjective experiences can provide much better evidence than some opponents of Christianity will admit. Every effect has a cause. The countless men and women who turn dramatically from drug addiction, crime, vice, abject cowardice, alcoholism, savage aggression, boasting or compulsive lying to lead a gentle, caring, loving and stable Christian life will say that this behavioural miracle has happened – and continues to happen for them on a renewable daily basis – because of a genuine relationship which they now enjoy with the living Christ. It is not their imagination. It is not wishful thinking. It is not some curious trick of the mind – Christ is real, and his reality is continually demonstrated in the reconstructed lives of those who love and trust him.

So it is reasonable to argue that whatever Saunière found, it was not some weird anti-Christian fabrication or forgery with which to blackmail the ecclesiastical authorities. They would not have paid. Nothing could have provided "proof" of what was so palpably untrue. There was nothing, therefore, with which Saunière could have enforced his demands for money.

Some researchers have accused Saunière of abusing the seal of the confessional. We can't prove that he didn't: but it seems highly unlikely. As with Max Redlich, the gangster hero of the prize-winning *Schindler's Ark*, there are some things which certain characters just will not do. During the Nazi occupation, Max Redlich, a notorious gangster, was rounded up with other Jews and told to trample over and spit upon the sacred scrolls of the *Torah* (Law). Refusal meant death. Redlich said, "I've done many dirty things in my time – but I'm not doing that." The Nazis killed him. There can be no doubt that men of Max's calibre enjoy God's hospitality at a far higher table than we shall aspire to at the Everlasting Feast.

Saunière may have done many things which subsequently he bitterly regretted – but he doesn't have the characteristic stamp of a despicable little blackmailer. The homely temptations of Marie Dénarnaud's passionate young body, and the occasional exotic headiness of Emma Calvé's sophisticated, cosmopolitan womanhood might well have appealed to him. Blackmail would not. To have lost that fiery temper of his and battered obstinate and querulous old Gélis to a bloody pulp if the elderly priest had obstructed and irritated him over some failure to return hypothetical coded documents – that might have been a strong possibility for a Saunière-type personality. It would also have fitted the evidence of immediate remorse – the careful and dignified laying out of the man he had just butchered. Saunière's sins seem to have been very human sins: ostentation; flamboyance; colourful extravagance; cavalier independence of spirit; extroverted prodigality; passionate fury and passionate love. Whatever else he was, he was never deliberately and premeditatively cruel, mean, jealous, petty or spiteful. The nibbling rodent sins of minute and restrictive formalistic bureaucrats could never be laid at the door of his presbytery. He might have been King Herod. He could never have been a Pharisee.

He didn't find anything to embarrass the church, or the ghost of the Holy Roman Empire, because there was nothing to find. He didn't entangle wealthy penitents in the slow but terrible coils of a blackmailer's net because he was too big, too passionate, too fiery and too liberal a personality ever to have been a blackmailer. He might have eloped with a parishioner's wife, or fractured a Republican politician's jaw after a heated argument — but he simply wasn't the type to be an extortioner. Blackmail wasn't his mental habitat, any more than giraffes live in underground dens or foxes stretch up to chew leaves on high branches.

Was he just a sordid grave robber? He might have been. Saunière's bellringer and verger, whose descendants still live in Rennes, maintained that there was a small secret compartment hidden within an old pulpit balustrade — the evidence is on display in the village museum. Within this compartment — so the old bellringer averred — was a small glass bottle containing a tiny parchment. The verger gave it to the priest . . . Shortly afterwards, so this version of the story goes, Saunière located the entrance to an old Visigothic or Merovingian catacomb which lay deep below the floor of the church. Again, according to this variation, Saunière and Marie systematically took the valuables from the royal coffins they found there.

It was also suggested that the tiny parchment had held clues which led to an old burial register and plans showing the hidden tombs of other wealthy nobles interred in and around Rennes in bygone centuries. Saunière's long trips into the countryside "to gather stones for his grotto" were, according to this version, simply a cover for his rural tomb raiding activities.

Was this the disclosure which so shocked Rivière when he took Saunière's final confession — that this man of God whose duty was to bless the dead, lay them to rest and pray for their souls, was instead disturbing ancient graves and robbing those who rested there?

It's not entirely out of character. Saunière was a pragmatist, as far as can be judged from the evidence available in this day and age. It might have seemed reasonable to him that as the dead Visigothic and Merovingian nobles had no further use for their earthly wealth, there was no moral or logical reason why he shouldn't enjoy it.

The invincible Doctor Occam — one of the sharpest minds of the fourteenth century — put forward the intellectual principle still known and valued today as "Occam's Razor": entities must not be unnecessarily multiplied. Or, if a simple solution fits the facts, don't invent complications.

Was there ever anything more at Rennes than a simple case of grave robbery? Were all the other apparently amazing facts no more than an accretion of rumours, legends, coincidences and exaggerations? We are, of course, still left with scope for historical conjecture about the precise nature of the treasure: was it gold bullion, silver ingots, ancient coins, plate or precious stones? Did it contain one or more priceless special pieces from Sion or Rome?

"Mere" treasure seems to be something of an anticlimax after all the tantalising question marks which have been raised in other areas. Like Dorothy in the Land of Oz, the researcher feels as if he, or she, had looked behind a forbidden screen only to find something disappointingly mundane and simple.

It does seem probable that Saunière discovered an ancient treasure of some sort and cashed in at least part of it, but that by no means ends, or solves, the rest of the mystery. There have been several good comedy thrillers in which the villain — to avoid capture — empties a satchel or two of stolen notes among his pursuers and escapes in the ensuing confusion while everyone scrambles to pick them up.

There is more than one dark rumour circulating among contemporary Rennes researchers to the effect that the physical, or monetary, treasure was itself something of a distraction or decoy. Perhaps it had the same effect on Saunière as the satchel of high denomination notes has on the posse in the typical comedy thriller: it occupied his attention so that something of infinitely greater value could be kept safely concealed from him.

Aladdin's wicked uncle, Shalmanazar, in the story of the genie in the lamp, told the boy that he could help himself to as many jewels and as much gold as he wanted . . . as long as he brought the lamp — the infinitely greater treasure — to Shalmanazar. In the tale of the magic tinder box which had powers only marginally inferior to those of Aladdin's lamp, the witch sent the itinerant soldier of fortune into the sinister cave guarded by the gigantic dogs (an echo of Cerberus). Here he was able to fill his pockets first with copper, then silver and finally gold. One form of money was, in a sense, acting as a shield, or as camouflage, for something very much more valuable. Finally, the magic tinderbox itself — the true treasure — was "protected" by the distraction afforded by the gold.

Suppose that the coded parchments which Saunière allegedly found in, or near, the altar (and was said to have taken to the expert palaeographers at St. Sulpice to be decoded) actually existed and really referred to some great lost secret — the Philosopher's Stone; the Elixir of Life; the Emerald Tablets of Hermes Trismegistus; the Key to a Fourth Dimensional Doorway; the secret of operating the Urim and Thummim; the Ark of the Covenant; even the Holy Grail itself . . .

What better way to safeguard this one priceless treasure than by diverting and distracting the searchers with gold, silver and jewels? The discovery of a precious "lid" may mean that what it covers is infinitely more precious; or the discoverer — especially if he's greedy and impatient — may mistake that rich and ornate "cover" for the treasure itself and go away clutching baubles while leaving the real treasure safely concealed.

Politico-religious pressure? No. Blackmail? No. Grave robbery? Possibly. Ancient treasure from Jerusalem, Rome, the Cathars, or the Hospitallers of St. John? Probably . . . but with a lot more lying behind the mystery than "mere" treasure.

One possibility often discussed is that Saunière found something of great importance in terms of an ancient imperial treasure that also served as a dynastic emblem, something that would be of inestimable value to the Habsburgs. Clutching his priceless symbol of ancient rights and powers − whatever it was − Saunière visited the powerful Austro-Hungarian ruling house and was referred to Prince Rudolf and Prince Johann (or Jean) − but their every move was closely and suspiciously monitored by Count Taafe's Secret Police.

Saunière, much stronger than the unhappy Rudolf and much wilier and better able to defend himself than Johann, takes numerous wise precautions. Sheets of vital confidential information are given to several trusted friends and accomplices: Marie Dénarnaud; Emma Calvé; Abbé Gélis (was it, perhaps, Taafe's secret police who murdered him?); Abbé Boudet; Monseigneur Billard of Carcassonne . . . and others. "If anything happens to me inform the press, the French Government, the Vatican . . . that those responsible are Count Taafe's men . . ." Documents in safe places were not enough: a watchtower with a steel door is built. It has commanding views. It is so designed that if the attack is from above, the steel door shuts off access to the ground floor. If the attack comes at ground level, the steel door can be slammed in the enemies' faces as the occupant of the tower vaults over the parapet and escapes.

Saunière and Boudet were known to be close collaborators. The link between Johann Salvator and the Boudet family in Axat was also close. Were those frequent Habsburg visits connected with a vast payment being made to Saunière and Boudet in instalments? Was Johann a financial courier? Accounts vary, but there is evidence that Saunière's fortune might have faltered during the period before his death. During World War I it must have been very difficult to transfer funds from Austria to France. The major question concerning the identity of the priceless object which may have been transferred to the Habsburgs remains unanswered and tantalising.

One fascinating legend tells how the Centurion, Gaius Longinus, pierced Christ's side with a lance. The historical fact of the piercing is recorded in St. John: 33 - 37, but the soldier is not named in the gospel account. Supposedly retrieved by Joseph of Arimathea along with the Grail and other sacred relics, the Lance of Longinus underwent a long and chequered history, passing through good hands and bad, but always exerting massive supernatural power. Like all legends it is fragmentary and confused − the Lance accompanies the Grail during the ceremonies in the mysterious castle of Anfortas, the wounded Fisher King. One Holy Lance came to Paris with St. Louis after he returned from the Crusades; another was kept in the Vatican; a third was in Cracow in Poland; the fourth − probably the oldest and the one with the strongest claim to authenticity − was in the hands of the Habsburgs until Hitler annexed Austria and took the Lance to Nuremberg. A consistent feature of the legend is that the Lance confers power on its holder, but death follows swiftly if he loses it. Charlemagne carried it through more than forty victories, but died soon after dropping it accidentally. Frederick Barbarossa survived sixty-seven years of successful medieval warfare, with its accompanying savagery and carnage; but died shortly after letting go of the Lance while fording a Sicilian river.

Dr. Walter Johannes Stein, who knew Hitler before the First World War, said that Hitler was fascinated by the Lance legends and was determined to gain possession of it. Eventually he did — only to lose it again. On April 30th, 1945, U.S. Army Lieutenant William Horn broke through the steel doors of the Nuremberg vault where the Lance lay and formally took possession of it on behalf of the United States Government. That night Hitler shot himself. Mere superstition? Only coincidence? Perhaps it was, but it suggests the kind of power which a politico-dynastic talisman may be able to exert over the minds of those who credit it with supernatural powers.

Tolkien said very much the same thing about the One Great Ring in his Middle Earth saga. It gave vast power to the man or woman who could wield it, but it also exacted a high price: death usually followed its loss.[1]

Baring Gould tells how he excavated a Gallo-Roman palace at Pont d'Oli (Pons Aulae) near Pau in southwestern France, and discovered an amazing mosaic pavement there. "The most northerly chamber," he wrote, "measured twenty-six feet by twenty-two feet . . . the pavement was . . . most elaborate and beautiful. It was bordered by an exquisite running pattern of vines and grape bunches . . . The pattern within this border was of circles, containing . . . roses alternately folded and expanded. This design was . . . interrupted by a . . . cross measuring nineteen feet eight inches by thirteen feet, with its head towards the south . . . " Baring Gould goes on to describe a figure within this cross carrying a trident — very probably Neptune, but just possibly Longinus carrying his lance. The devout Catholic labourers who uncovered the mosaic under Baring Gould's direction thought that the figure represented Christ himself.

---

[1]Interestingly in this context, at the Council of Elrond in Book II of "The Fellowship of the Ring", the dwarf Glóin reports how the dwarf-king Dáin was visited by an emissary from Mordor who promised the return of the surviving Rings from the Seven Rings of the Dwarves, if the One Ring were returned. The request was phrased thus: "As a small token only of your friendship Sauron asks this: that you should find this thief [Bilbo], and get from him, willing or no, a little ring, the least of rings, that once he stole. It is but a trifle that Sauron fancies. . ." This ties in with the "misdirection" idea — the Ruling Ring is described as the "least of rings" — a "trifle". PVST

Another theory which some researchers have considered is that the treasure of Rennes included the famous emerald tablets of Hermes Trismegistus. It is a fascinating idea, but it begs the question of whether Hermes Trismegistus himself existed − let alone whether his famous emerald tablets did! Often identified with Thoth, the Egyptian scribe of the gods, Hermes may or may not have been a real person. Like Merlin in the Arthurian legends, Hermes seems to fade into and out of history. In that special sense in which Michell and Rickard use the word, Thoth (or Hermes) is a typical phenomenon.

If for the sake of progressing the argument a little further we assume that he might have had some basis in historical reality, where did he come from and where did his supernormal power and knowledge come from? Was he an extra-terrestrial? Did he have the same time-defying powers as the Flamels and the Comte de St. Germain were alleged to have had? (That is, of course, if they ever existed!) Following the faint and elusive scent of Hermes Trismegistus absorbs the full concentration of that eager quartet of bloodhounds: Conjecture, Speculation, Hypothesis and Assumption!

Whatever other secrets might have been engraved on the mythical emeralds, it has been thought that they were ingeniously cut or carved into the form of a tesseract, which is a three-dimensional "shadow" of a four-dimensional hypercube − a figure having yet another dimension at right-angles to the three with which we are familiar. *(See Appendix I for a discussion of the mathematics of the tesseract, together with illustrations)*. Members of some ancient mystic cults have been said to meditate for hours upon the tesseract until they experienced a shift of perception − a sort of gateway to the fourth dimension perhaps? In an altered state of consciousness following their lengthy meditation on the tesseract were they able to establish contact with someone − or something − else? The great question arises: is the so-called "hallucination" which occurs in an altered state of consciousness simply a malfunction of the observer, or is the observer in that state able to experience an alternative reality? Did the amazing mind of Nikola Tesla just imagine his electrical machines in an exceptionally vivid way? Did he "make" them in some strange manner from a sort of "phenomenalist material" (what Victorian spiritualists might have called ectoplasm) which most people cannot manipulate? Or did he have access to another dimension, an alternative reality, where he didn't so much have to imagine or create new machines as to observe and analyse machines which already existed there?

More than one serious and well-informed Rennes researcher has suggested that the real secret is "a doorway to the Invisible" − if that nerve-tingling hypothesis comes anywhere near the truth, then the key which opens that doorway could just be the emerald tesseract of Hermes Trismegistus.

If the mysterious Rennes treasure had some precious Jewish object as its centre piece, something which had been brought from Sion in Jerusalem, it might have been the Urim and Thummim. When the Jewish exiles returned from their Babylonian captivity and came up against a question which they found difficult to answer, a question for which they could find no relevant data, they agreed to postpone the problem "until there should rise up a Priest with Urim and Thummim." (Nehemiah

7 : 65) There is wide disagreement and wild conjecture about what the true and original Urim and Thummim really were. The Hebrew root of Urim means lights or fires. The root of Thummim means "perfection" or "completeness". It is not clear whether the two words should be taken together to mean "perfect or complete illumination" or whether each stands for a number of separate things. The word Urim occurs by itself once or twice (Numbers 27 : 21; 1 Samuel 28 : 6) but Thummim never occurs by itself.

The words appear for the first time as part of the description of the High Priest's robes and equipment. Over the ephod he is to wear a "breastplate of judgement" made of fine linen folded square and doubled, a "span" wide and a "span" long. Its colours are to be gold, scarlet and purple. In this "breastplate" are to be set twelve jewels, in four rows of three, and each jewel is to be inscribed with the name of one of the twelve tribes of Israel. The Urim and Thummim are to be placed inside this sacred "breastplate" in much the same way that the Tables of the Covenant are placed inside the Ark. The Urim and Thummim might have been given to Moses at the same time as the great tablets containing the Law. There is no account of Urim and Thummim being made by Moses or Aaron. There are no special sacred instructions for their manufacture. Ben Nachman and Hottinger have suggested that they were of supernatural origin and unlike anything else on earth.

Other scholars and historians have suggested that Urim and Thummim gave their answers as light fell on certain letters carved on them and so spelled out the answers. Josephus thinks that they were identical with the sardonyxes on the shoulders of the ephod, that they gleamed brightly before a victory or an acceptable sacrifice, but were dark before a disaster. Epiphanius thought of them as a single diamond: bright in times of peace; red during a war; dull as a sign of imminent death.

Another theory identifies them as a golden plate, or a large precious stone, on which was engraved the sacred and mystical name of Yahweh, the *Shem-hammephorash* of the Jewish cabbalists. According to this theory, the Priest would fix his gaze on the Sacred Name and stand by the Holy of Holies listening for the voice of God. Levi ben Gershon believed that the main function of Urim and Thummim was to enable the Priest to reach an altered state of consciousness, an ecstasy, in which he could clearly receive messages from God. The old cabbalistic book *Zohar* goes so far as to say that there were forty-two letters engraved on the Urim.

It's an odd coincidence that Douglas Adams' famous science fiction comedy *The Hitchhiker's Guide to the Galaxy* contains the statement that the answer to the riddle of the universe is forty-two, but, unfortunately no-one knows the question!

Spencer argued etymologically that the Urim were the same things as the Teraphim − miniature anthropomorphic idols, rather like dolls[2] − which is both reasonable and possible. He went on to speculate, however, that there was some strange supernatural means by which these images were made to speak to the Priest, which seems infinitely less likely!

---

[2]Some at least must have been life-sized, for Michal (David's first wife − and the daughter of King Saul) to use one for the "dummy in bed" trick to conceal David's escape from Saul (1 Samuel 19 : 11-17). PVST

Zullig and Winer both thought that the Urim were bright, cut and polished precious stones — possibly diamonds — while Thummim were round, uncut and thus still "complete". Both kinds were engraved with words or letters. Zullig and Winer suggested that the Priest (who alone knew the meanings of the resulting configurations) threw the stones on a sacred table, or even on the Ark, and gave his answers according to the pattern in which they fell.

Yet another idea is that they originated in Egypt, where the priestly judges (with whose appearance, robes, accessories and function Moses would certainly have been familiar) wore an image of Alatheia ("Perfect Truth") hanging around their necks. These Egyptian images were usually carved from sapphire. Egyptian Priests also wore over their hearts the sacred scarab emblem signifying light and life, the sun and the universe, creation and resurrection. Depending upon the wealth and rank of the wearer, these pectoral symbols could be made from blue porcelain, jasper, cornelian, lapis lazuli or amethyst.

Did the Jewish priesthood modify and extract all that was highest and best in Egyptian thought — the principles of Complete Truth and Perfect Light — and encapsulate them in the symbolism of their own Urim and Thummim?

Dean Trench adds another interesting idea about the nature of the Urim and Thummim: he refers to the "white stone" of Revelation 2 : 17 as indicative of the nature of the Old Testament oracular stones. A stone representing light must by its nature be as pure, clear and white as possible — a diamond? A crystal? When the redeemed soul is given his, or her, white stone in Heaven, Dean Trench sees it as a symbol of the priesthood of all believers: that which was once the special privilege and prerogative of the High Priest alone is now given to all.

If the Urim and Thummim were precious stones derived from the Egyptian prototypes, how were they used? The consensus seems to be that they acted in some way as a focus for the priest's mind — inducing an almost trance-like state in which he was able to prophesy.

How closely do they tie in with older Egyptian ideas? From the time of Joseph the Dreamer until the Exodus led by Moses the Law Bringer, the Jews were exposed to Egyptian culture at first hand. When Moses led his people out of Egypt they took a great many Egyptian valuables with them. Pharaoh, who appears to have been a very stubborn and determined man — but not previously a stupid one — sent the flower of the Egyptian army with the best of its chariots and horses over an extremely dangerous sea bed in order to recapture the Israelites. Fully aware of the fatal risk they were running the Egyptian charioteers went unquestioningly to their doom . . . Had Pharaoh discovered that some sacred and priceless Egyptian treasure had disappeared with the Israelites? Were the forerunners of Urim and Thummim missing from their jewelled caskets in the inner sanctum of an Egyptian temple? Were the emerald tablets, the mystic tesseract of Hermes Trismegistus, missing as well? Or were those two sacred and mysterious treasures one and the same thing? Were Urim and Thummim simply the later Hebrew names for the emerald tablets?

There is an even older legend which might link the two artefacts, and provide a further nexus between Israel and Egypt. According to this account while Abraham and Sarah (his wife and step-sister) were travelling from Ur of the Chaldees, they came to a strange cave in the wilderness. Sarah, full of curiosity, went in. According to the legend she discovered the recumbent form of Hermes Trismegistus in some form of suspended animation: his emerald tablets lay beside him. Greatly daring, she touched one of the magical stones and immediately Hermes started to wake up. Sarah fled from the cave. What if some shred of truth lies within the legend? Suppose Sarah told Abraham — a man of immense wisdom, faith and courage. Suppose that Abraham went back to the cave and actually recovered the emerald tablets? Were they then passed down from father to son until they went back to Egypt with Jacob the aged patriarch at the time of Joseph's ascendancy? During the later years of persecution and forced labour in Goshen, did the Egyptians take them from Joseph's descendants — only to lose them again when Moses led the Israelites out of Egypt and over the Red Sea to safety?

Another school of thought has suggested that the priceless heart of the Rennes treasure is the Ark of the Covenant. Did it make its way to Babylon at the time of the captivity? Or is the account in 2 Maccabees 2:4, the correct one? According to this Maccabean record, which is normally historically reliable, the prophet Jeremiah received a divine command to conceal the Ark in a cave high on the slopes of Mount Pisgah and then to seal and cover the entrance. Certain priests followed the prophet to try to ascertain the location of the hiding place but were unable to find it. Jeremiah told the inquisitive priests in no uncertain terms that it was no concern of theirs — God Himself would arrange for it to be revealed in his own good time in accordance with the divine plan.

It requires no very great stretch of the imagination to envisage a group of adventurous Templars or Knights of St. John finding the Ark and bringing it in secret to a safe hiding place in Château Blanchefort, or Bézu . . . to be transferred at some later date to the labyrinth of Merovingian tombs below the Church at Rennes, or even to the deepest and safest dungeon of the ancient Château Hautpoul. Was that the secret of secrets which the Cathars would rather die than reveal? Did the Albigensians know where the Ark was hidden?

Going off on a completely different tack, we sail towards the reefs and shoals guarding the treacherous marshes and quagmires that mark the boundaries of "von Däniken Land". The problem with von Däniken's theories, as set out in *Chariots of the Gods* and his other sensational volumes, is that a perfectly sound and feasible basic idea — the possibility that at some remote period in prehistory Planet Earth was visited by aliens from another planet — is excitably and unreliably embroidered, then buried under a mass of unsupported conjectures and very dubious data.

Because an over-enthusiastic pioneer gets carried away by his own zeal and impatience now and again, we ought not to dismiss all his ideas as fabrications, errors and exaggerations. Von Däniken wrote carelessly about vast and amazing subterranean tunnels in South America: Jean Robin's elegant and stylish *Opération Orth* makes mysterious tunnels under South America sound much more plausible. So let's suppose just for one wild, irresponsible moment that underneath von Däniken's ramshackle mountain of loosely cobbled myths, legends, pseudo-facts and misunderstandings there is some real evidence for an extra-terrestrial visit in the remote past. If only ten percent of his data can be proved correct, it presents a serious case for his basic theory.

Now let's take that supposition further: if an extra-terrestrial did reach Earth millennia ago, and left some sort of amazing artefact behind when he either died or left, might not some élite group have found it and tried to use it? Anything ancient, alien and only imperfectly understood is unlikely to function reliably. If it works at all it will work spasmodically and unpredictably. Let's tack on another hypothesis: suppose our dying alien is befriended by some reasonably pleasant and caring human beings to whom he entrusts as best he can (in view of their limited intelligence and almost non-existent technological background) the secrets of operating the marvellous machine he is bequeathing to them. If the first group of "guardians" who had the benefit of their alien "master's" direct personal tuition can't operate it perfectly, how will the next generation manage? And the next? And the thirty-fifth? The *modus operandi* may well have evolved into something like a religious liturgy, or ritual, by that time: something like the alleged Secret Rule of the Templars? The codes of the Alchemists? The mystic writings of the Rosicrucians? The hidden ciphers of the Freemasons?

An unreliable old miracle machine holding out the tantalising promise of wealth and fame, power and longevity, time travel, access to the fourth dimension — and who knows what else — is all too likely to let the user down at a crucial moment. That much fits in with what can be conjectured about some of the people who might have used it with sporadic success in the past. The Cathars led a charmed life for centuries in a world full of dangerous enemies — then their protection crumbled and failed. The Templars enjoyed military and economic success for many years — they were defeated by the odious Philip IV. Fouquet was in contact with Poussin, and Fouquet lived in more regal state than the King for a time. Had Poussin passed Fouquet the secret of the alien X-machine? Did Fouquet overreach himself and end his days in the Bastille as the Man in the Iron Mask? Did the two tragic young Habsburg Princes try to use it against Franz Josef and his "minder", Count Taafe? Was it the failure of the machine which brought them down? Saunière himself flourished mightily for a while — but the end of his life seems to have been sadly clouded. Was there a mysterious "artefact-from-beyond-the-stars" and did it inevitably fail all its owners sooner or later?

There are those who say that the secret of Rennes-le-Château is the secret of alchemy, of real transmutation of base metals into gold. Modern chemists and physicists say that it can be done only at such enormous cost in a nuclear laboratory that it's much cheaper to dig your gold out with a pick and shovel.

But one tower of the ancient Château Hautpoul was known as The Tower of Alchemy, and the strange group of statues inside the door of Saunière's church could symbolise the alchemical elements: earth, air, fire and water.

It seems highly improbable that anything available to medieval alchemists could have effected a transmutation which modern science can perform only by recourse to prohibitively expensive nuclear forces, but there was the inexplicable case of Price and old Dr. Irish . . . not to mention the strange wanderer who brought the Philosopher's Stone to Irish in the first place.

The alchemical transmutation of metal seems a very improbable solution, but it's not totally impossible. The same might well be said of the other alchemical dream — the elixir of life: highly unlikely but not totally out of the question.

There are apparent discrepancies and wide variations in human life spans: external physical circumstances such as chronic malnutrition and exhaustion can shorten life dramatically as it did for the workers in the Industrial Revolution. The right food, clean air and water, peace of mind and the right amount of exercise can extend life significantly. Many Hunzas live for well over a century enjoying their apricot rich diet in a pollution-free environment. If such simple, common sense factors can double or treble a "normal" human life span, might there not be some secret, rejuvenating elixir which would be even more effective in promoting longevity?

Semi-miraculous drugs and new prophylactic techniques seem to appear quite suddenly and regularly in medical history: penicillin from mould; smallpox vaccinations from cowpox; interferon; vitamin C to prevent scurvy on board ship; pasteurisation; antiseptic and aseptic surgery; the identification of blood groups and the ensuing transfusion techniques; insulin to control diabetes; organ transplants . . . each in its own way an elixir of life to many who would otherwise have died.

Did some ancient Chaldean magician, an Egyptian healer-priest, or even a wise Macedonian physician like St. Luke discover a blend of rare herbs and spices which could significantly prolong human life? Did the Comte de St. Germain have that formula? Did the Flamels have it? Is there even the remotest chance that those three very enigmatic characters are still with us?

Some serious attention must be paid to Bremna Agostini's theory of the Convocation of Venus being performed at Rennes-le-Château. Her knowledge of esoteric matters is considerable and she has friends and acquaintances who know even more. In outline the Convocation of Venus theory states that Saunière with the regular cooperation of Marie — and probably the occasional cooperation of Emma as well — performed the ritual continually and obtain from it enough more or less accurate predictions to sell to wealthy enquirers. (The proprietors of the Delphic Oracle grew prosperous in much the same way!)

The arguments in favour of the Convocation of Venus theory include the so-called "natural pentagons" on the ground near Rennes, which allegedly augment the Venusian planetary pentagon, and the supposed shock which Rivière is alleged to have received when Saunière made his final confession. "Father . . . I confess that my wealth came from regular black magic rituals of a sexual nature, which I used to predict the future for the rich and credulous . . ."

The theory is of academic interest but scarcely more than that. Admittedly, the Delphic confidence trick produced enormous wealth in its day, but the nineteenth century was a more rational period. To go for the Convocation of Venus theory means taking on board all sorts of highly volatile theological and philosophical explosives. If the future can be predicted accurately it must already exist. If it already exists we can do nothing about it. If we can do nothing about it we have no free will. If we have no free will we cannot choose good or evil. . . .The implications are massive.

We cannot prove that we have free will, of course. What we confidently believe to be our own autonomous decisions may be induced from elsewhere. In the last resort we are thrown back on good old gut reaction: all our instincts tell us that when we think we are making a decision we really are making a decision. It's one of those situations where you survive by throwing the elaborate sophistications and refinements of logic and philosophy overboard and keeping afloat with the pumps of instinct and the bailer of old-fashioned common sense!

Another idea which cannot be ignored is M. Fatin's theory about the layout of Rennes itself, the giant outline of a sleeping warrior and the idea of a ship of the dead. Several other serious researchers, both in the Rennes area and in other mysterious sites like Glastonbury, have claimed to see the resemblance of zodiac type configurations in the topography of the land as well as in the distant stellar constellations.

If M. Fatin is right, the question arises as to who this dead − or sleeping − warrior might be? Some have suggested King Arthur; others have argued a case for Hermes Trismegistus; he could be a Roman general; he might be a Celtic Warlord, a Visigothic Prince or even a Merovingian King. A Rosicrucian? An alchemist? A significant saint? Whoever he is, it is quite probable that his treasure went into his tomb with him, and it is equally probable that Saunière ferreted some of it out again!

In our earlier volume we looked carefully at the theory of a mysterious artefact accompanied by wealth in some form − or the means of creating wealth − and tended by an ancient and mysterious group of "Guardians". We considered that such an object might have passed through the hands of the Cathars and the Templars (or, as later research may now be indicating, the Knights of St.John) before being hidden away securely in Château Blanchefort, or below the church of St. Mary Magdalen at Rennes. We looked at the serious possibility that Saunière could then have transferred it to the Habsburgs and that it might well have ended up at the bottom of the Atlantic locked in the hold of the ill-starred Lady Margaret. It also seemed possible that Count Taafe acquired it before Johann (or Jean) Salvator left Europe: in which case it may now be in the hands of one of his descendants, or back in the custody of the Habsburgs.

This still seems to us to be a strong possibility, but our current research has led us to another hypothesis which we believe to be even more likely. It goes like this.

Earlier on we laid particular emphasis on the persistent and recurring symbolism of the mother/virgin/harlot goddess theme surrounding Rennes: since the beginning there have been strange paradoxes in these seemingly contradictory "goddess" legends. This has led us to wonder whether Something − or Someone − of immense size and power was making "contact" with those who were sensitive enough to be aware of "her".

Poets and singers have their "muses"; artists and sculptors their "inspirations"; contemplative saints and sages their "insights" and "illuminations". Sensitive, creative minds often seem to feel that the best of what they do is coming to them from outside. Are they right? If so what might that mysterious source — or those mysterious sources — really be?

The *Star Wars* film trilogy, as well as being highly entertaining, posed an interesting metaphysical question: what was the strange Force which the Jedi Knights were able to use, and which had a dark aspect as well as a benign one? Is there any truth behind James Lovelock's Gaia hypothesis, and, if so, is it the same truth that underlies both the mystery of Rennes and the idea of the Force in *Star Wars*?

Lovelock's work began with his studies of the possibility that life might exist on Mars, and this led him to question the nature of life on earth. The Gaia hypothesis suggests that all life on earth ought to be viewed as one vast living being — perhaps a huge single organism, perhaps a massive Gestalt life form. This being, according to the Gaia hypothesis, has the power to alter the planetary environment in order to survive. Very important aspects of this immense unified organism are the feedback systems which "maintain" and "control" the environmental conditions essential for life. One clear example of what Lovelock means can be seen in the atmospheric balance. The composition of the earth's atmosphere — approximately 79% nitrogen, 20% oxygen, with argon, carbon dioxide and minute traces of other gases making up the rest — seems to have been stable and constant throughout the planet's history. That stability in turn has made life possible. The Gaia hypothesis seems to be suggesting reciprocality: life creates and maintains the biosphere in which it exists by the use of its own biological feedback systems.

From this fundamental idea which originated with Lovelock, it is by no means a quantum leap to hypothesize that Gaia has a mind as well as a colossal "body".

It is difficult enough for two human minds from the same period and the same culture to communicate with each other effectively. It is harder to understand men and women of other times and other cultures. To try to communicate with another species — a cetacean or an anthropoid ape — is even more challenging. How hard might it be to try to make contact with the much larger and very different mind of Gaia — if "she" exists, and if "she" has awareness and intelligence?

What might the preconditions for such hypothetical "contact" be? Firstly, the human mind may need to be of a particular type: receptive, finely tuned, sensitive — what some people might describe as "psychic". Secondly, that human mind may also need to be in a particular state of consciousness: the famous "trance" of the medium or the mystic; a light hypnosis; a dreamy reverie; an open, empty, quiet, tranquil and receptive state. Roy Norvill, writing in *Hermes Unveiled* (Ashgrove Press, Bath, 1986) says that the secret of acquiring knowledge is to concentrate the mind absolutely in a single direction. He quotes the examples of Sir Isaac Newton who said that he discovered the principle of gravitation "by thinking on it continually", and of Paracelsus who said, " . . . the activity of the Universal Mind can only come to the consciousness of those whose spheres of mind are capable of receiving its impressions . . . "

Are these ideas so very far removed from Jung's semi-mystical theories about the collective unconscious? What was it that Tesla was in touch with? Where did Napier's ideas for his mysterious weapons come from?

In order to make contact with another human being we either have to be close enough to hear what she's saying, or to see what he's writing or signalling, or we have to use long distance technical methods of some sort: telephone, radio or television. What if the secret of Rennes-le-Château — in addition to its ancient treasure cache — is that the centre of one of its mysterious pentagons is the ideal place to be in order to communicate with Gaia?

Part of what we see and hear when we communicate with another human being is governed — at least in part — by what we want to see and hear and what we expect to see and hear. May it not also be so with Gaia? If the lonely and the lost are subconsciously seeking a mother figure to sustain them, it is the protective and maternal aspect of her that they locate: the bird bringing food to her fledglings; the ewe caring for her lamb. If the saintly, contemplative and spiritual seeker longs subconsciously for holiness, beauty and purity it is the virgin aspect of Gaia which he finds: the opening bud, the first falling snowflake, crystal clear water springing from clean rocks. It is the prodigal who finds the harlot Gaia: in seeking to exploit and dominate her, he is himself ultimately exploited and defeated. In tearing away her foliage veil and brutally ravaging her tropical forests, he eventually destroys himself as well. The pleasure is tawdry; the rewards are ephemeral; the damage to both harlot and patron can be massive and enduring.

Is the secret of Rennes an artefact which enables human beings to contact Gaia? Is it simply the place, the Rennes area, the "doorway to the invisible"?

What is of the very greatest importance is that Gaia should not be confused with, nor mistaken for, her Creator. Huge as "she" is — if she really exists as a conscious personality — she is only another of God's creatures, a being like ourselves, but of a different order and on a larger scale. Her wisdom, experience and knowledge compared to ours may well be as those of a mature woman compared to a young child's. Gaia may frequently have been mistaken for a goddess in the past, but — if she exists — she is only on a slightly higher rung on that same ladder of God's creation on which we all stand. We may learn much from her. We may benefit enormously from loving and respecting her and cooperating with her, but she is as dependent upon God the Father, Christ and the Holy Spirit as the rest of us are.

APPENDIX A

CHRONOLOGY OF RENNES-LE-CHÂTEAU

The authors and publishers are very grateful to Paul Smith, one of the most accurate and painstaking of all the Rennes-le-Château researchers, for permission to include his Chronology.

c410   Possible *Rhedae*, major Visigothic strategic outpost in Septimania. (Rennes-le-Château, Châteaux de Blanchefort and Bézu/"Albedun" are all constructed on Visigothic foundations forming an isosceles triangle with angles 36^0, 72^0, 72^0.

1210   Destruction of the Château de Blanchefort, during the Crusade against the Cathars.

1633   Guillaume de Catel's account, stating that workers were imported all the way from Germany to excavate the mines by Rennes-les-Bains (*Mémoires de l'Histoire du Languedoc, Tome I*, p. 51).

1645   Legend of the shepherd "Jean" (*Folklore (Aude)*, Nr. 8, p. 137, 1938).
         Legend of the shepherd Ignace Paris (Noël Corbu, *Essai Historique sur Rennes-le-Château*, 1962).

1709   *Antiquités des Bains de Monferran communement appelés les Bains de Rennes* by Abbé Antoine Delmas, vicar at Rennes-les-Bains.

1732   Marriage of Marie de Nègre d'Ables to François d'Hautpoul, first Marquis de Blanchefort.

1780   Jean-Baptiste Siau, notary at Espéraza, refused to give the Hautpoul family will to Pierre Françoise d'Hautpoul, under the pretext: "It would be unwise of me to let a will of such great consequence out of my hands". (*Rennes et ses derniers seigneurs* by René Descadeillas, pp. 7-8)

c1780   Legend of the "Devil's Treasure" (*Voyages à Rennes-les-Bains* by Auguste de Labouisse-Rochefort, pp. 469-471, 1832).

1781   Death of Marie de Nègre d'Ables, Countess Hautpoul-Blanchefort: the mysterious epitaph on her tombstone containing errors which point out the words *MORT épée* (*Excursion de 25 Juin 1905 à Rennes-le-Château* by Elie Tisseyre, *Bulletin de la Société d'Études Scientifiques de l'Aude, Tome XVII*, pp. 98–106, 1906).

"1872" "Death" of Abbé Jean Vié, vicar at Rennes-les-Bains, whose epitaph reveals that he was named priest when 32, and "died" 32 years later (the chessboard motif: 32 "white years" before becoming priest, then 32 "black years" as a priest).

1880 "In the Middle Ages it was believed that the precious metals extracted from the Blanchefort mine came, not from a vein in the rock, but from a store of gold and silver ingots buried in the dungeons of the fortress by its first masters, the Visigothic kings." (*Histoire du comté de Razès et du diocèse d'Alet*, by Louis Fédié).

1885 François-Bérenger Saunière (1852-1917) appointed Parish Priest of Rennes-le-Château, at the Church of St. Mary Magdalen.

1886 Saunière temporarily transferred to the Seminary at Narbonne for delivering anti-Republican, right-wing sermons during the elections.

1887 Saunière reinstated at Rennes-le-Château: began renovating his church — moved the "Knight's Stone" which lay face-down before the main Altar (which was probably the entrance to the Hautpoul family burial vault beneath the church), and made his fateful discovery . . .
Church renovation details (1887-1900) are introduced by the character as below.
■ New Altar (700Frs; F. D. Monna, Toulouse)
■ Stained-Glass Windows (1350Frs; Henri Feur, Bordeaux)

1890-91 Saunière in charge by interim at Antugnac, near Rennes-le-Château.

1891 Visigothic Pillar/Statue of the Lourdes Virgin: ceremony June 21st.
"Lettre de Granès. Découverte d'un tombeau, le soir pluie." (Saunière's diary, September 21st).
"Vu curé de Névian — Chez Gélis — Chez Carrière — Vu Cros en secret." (Saunière's diary, September 29th).
■ Statue of St. Mary Magdalen above church entrance (150Frs; Giscard, Toulouse)
■ Pulpit (750Frs; Giscard, Toulouse)

1892 Treasurer of the *Conseil de Fabrique* resigned stating he found the duties of the post contrary to his beliefs; replaced by Guillaume Dénarnaud. (The Church's income rose from

239.60Frs 1886 to 1914.80Frs in 1888, returning to its original level in 1893).

1893   Confessional (700Frs; M. Mestre, Limoux).

1895   Letters of complaint sent against Saunière to the *Préfet de l'Aude*, regarding his clandestine activities in the cemetery.

1897   ■ Statues of the Saints (720Frs; Giscard, Toulouse)
        ■ Stations of the Cross (600Frs; Giscard, Toulouse)
        ■ Jesus/Baptist Font, etc. (404Frs; Giscard, Toulouse)
        ■ Devil/Angels Holy Water Stoup (300Frs; Giscard, Toulouse)
        ■ *Bas-Relief* of Jesus Christ on the Mount (800Frs; Giscard, Toulouse)
        ■ The Calvary; church consecrated by Mgr. Billard (June 6th).

1898   Collecting-trunk made from oak (400Frs; M. Mestre, Limoux).

c1900   *Bas-Relief* of St. Mary Magdalen at the foot of the Altar (reverse image of a stained-glass window from Puichéric church).

1902   Mgr. Paul-Félix Beuvain de Beauséjour replaces Mgr. Félix-Arsène Billard as Bishop of Carcassonne.

1901-05 Villa Béthanie; Tour Magdala; gardens and terraces, etc.

Owner:	Mlle. Marie Dénarnaud
Promoter:	Abbé Bérenger Saunière
Architect:	Tiburce Caminade (Limoux)
Master-Builder:	Elie Bot (Luc-sur-Aude)
Plasterer:	Tisseyre
Carpenters:	Oscar Vila (Couiza)
	Jean Idrac (Toulouse)
Painters:	Georges Castex (Limoux)
	V. Laffon
Ironmonger:	Charles Dénarnaud (Alet)
Papers/Paints:	Duchesne (Paris)
Tile-Flooring:	Taillefer (Trèbes)
Materials:	Sté des Chaux et Ciments d'Albi
	Ciments Bethelot de Grenoble

"1903"(?) Galibert family erect the "Poussin-Tomb" at Les Pontils in Peyrolles (dismantled April 9th 1988).

1905-06 Separation of the Church from State in France. Saunière's superiors demand he show his accounts and give an explanation of his source of wealth.

1909   Saunière transferred to Coustouge: replaced by Abbé Marty at Rennes-le-Château; but he refused his nomination and built a private altar in the Villa Béthanie.

1910–11   Saunière's trial before the Carcassonne Bishopric, to account for his source of wealth.

1911   Bishop of Carcassonne issues a strong warning against Saunière, accusing him of simony and forbidding him to administer the Sacraments: Carcassonne February 1st (*Semaine Religieuse de Carcassonne*, February 3rd). Following three sentences against him (dated July 23rd 1910, November 5th 1910 and December 5th 1911), Saunière sought assistance from Rome, unsuccessfully. He never regained his position as Parish Priest of Rennes-le-Château.

1915   Reminder to the local population of Saunière's interdiction in *Semaine Religieuse de Carcassonne*, July 3rd.

1917   Death of Saunière, his interdiction being lifted only *in articulo mortis* ("at the moment of death"). He is not described as a priest in the obituary column of *Semaine Religieuse de Carcassonne* of January 27th.

1931   Pamphlet version of Elie Tisseyre's 1906 article deposited in the Municipal Library of Carcassonne, by "Marty".

1946   Noël Corbu purchases Saunière's old estate held in Marie Dénarnaud's name.

1953   Marie Dénarnaud dies aged 85; Noël Corbu inherits her archives relating to Bérenger Saunière.

1956   First popular account of the Saunière mystery: *La Fabuleuse Découverte du Curé aux Milliards de Rennes-le-Château* by Albert Salamon (appearing in *La Dépêche du Midi*, January 12th, 13th and 14th).

1962   *Essai Historique sur Rennes-le-Château* by Noël Corbu (5-page MS deposited in the *Archives de l'Aude*, Carcassonne); possible transcript of a 1955/56 tape-recording made for the tourists to Rennes-le-Château.

1964   Henri Buthion acquires Saunière's old estate.

1968   Noël Corbu tragically killed in a car crash.

1974   *Mythologie du Trésor de Rennes: Histoire véritable de l'Abbé Saunière, Curé de Rennes-le-Château* by René Descadeillas (*Mémoires de la Société des Arts et des Sciences de Carcassonne, Années 1971-72, 4me série, Tome VII, 2me partie*).

1983   *Le Fabuleux Trésor de Rennes-le-Château! Le Secret de l'Abbé Saunière* by Jacques Rivière (Éditions Bélisane).

| 1985 | *Histoire du Trésor de Rennes-le-Château* by Pierre Jarnac (Éditions Bélisane). |
| | *L'Héritage de l'Abbé Saunière* by Claire Corbu and Antoine Captier (Éditions Bélisane). |

1985   *Histoire du Trésor de Rennes-le-Château* by Pierre Jarnac (Éditions Bélisane).
L'Héritage de l'Abbé Saunière by Claire Corbu and Antoine Captier (Éditions Bélisane).

1987   *Les Archives de Rennes-le-Château, Tome 1* by Pierre Jarnac (Éditions Bélisane).

1988   *Les Archives de Rennes-le-Château, Tome 2* by Pierre Jarnac (Éditions Bélisane).

1989   Formation of Association Terre de Rhedae (May), devoted to historical research of the mystery. Its President, Antoine Captier, is curator of the Saunière Museum at Rennes.

APPENDIX B

GERVASE OF TILBURY'S ACCOUNT OF "SHIPPING THE DEAD" TO ARLES (CIRCA 1210)

The Anglo-Latin writer, priest, scholar and adventurer, Gervase of Tilbury, was related to Patrick, Earl of Salisbury. Before 1177 Gervase taught Law in Bologna. Later he worked for Henry fitz Henry in England, for William of Champagne (the Cardinal Archbishop of Rheims) and William II of Sicily. Shortly before 1200 he was employed by Emperor Otto IV, who promoted him to be Marshall of the Kingdom of Arles, where, despite being in holy orders, he married a rich and beautiful young heiress.

His *Otia Imperialia* trilogy was written for the Emperor in 1211. It is a fascinating mixture of political theory, geography, history and folklore.

Cathars, Templars and the Knights of St. John were all flourishing in the vicinity of Arles at the time. The famous Venus of Arles was discovered in the remains of the Roman Theatre there in 1651 — during the period when Poussin was painting. Marie de Nègre's tombstone records her as "Dame d'Arles".

What Gervase says about floating corpses and treasure *could* be linked to M. Fatin's ideas about Rennes-le-Château being laid out to resemble a "ship of the dead" bearing a giant warrior.

Gervase's text (*Otia Imperialia*, Decisio iii, c.90) follows, in both the original Latin and in an English translation. The authors wish to thank Father Martin I. Williams, Vicar of the parish of St. German, Roath, for advice on the mediaeval Latin.

Insigne mirum ac ex divina virtute miraculum audi, Princeps Sacratissime. Caput regni Burgundionum, quod Arelatense dicitur, civitas est Arelas, antiquissimis dotata privilegiis. Hanc ordinatus ab Apostolis Petro et Paulo, Trophimus, qui . . . deliberavit coemeterium solemne ad meridianam urbis partem constituere, in quo omnium orthodoxorum corpora sepulturae traderentur, ut, sicut ab Arelatensi ecclesia tota Gallia fidei sumsit exordium, ita et mortui in Christo undecunque advecti sepulturae communis haberent beneficium. Facta itaque consecratione solemni per manus sanctissimorum antistitum ad Orientalem Portam, ubi nunc est

Most Sacred Prince, let me tell you of a remarkable wonder and miracle of divine power. The capital of the kingdom of Burgundy (known as the Arlesian kingdom) is the city of Arles, the recipient of ancient privilege. It was Trophimus, who had been ordained by the Apostles Peter and Paul, who . . . determined to set aside a proper cemetery in the central part of the city, in which the bodies of all the faithful could be brought for burial, that as the whole of Gaul received the faith initially from the church of Arles, so also the dead in Christ by being brought there from all over the country might have the benefit of a common burial ground. The solemn consecration was ecclesia ab ipsis in honorem B. Virginis consecrata, illis Christus, pridem in carne familiariter agnitus, apparuit, opus eorum sua benedictione profundens, dato coemeterio ac illis sepeliendis munere, ut quicunque inibi sepelirentur, nullas in cadaveribus suis paterentur diabolicas illusiones. Ex hujusmodi ergo Dominicae benedictionis munere, apud omnes majoris auctoritatis Galliarum principes ac clericos inolevit, quod maxima patentum pars illuc sepulturam habent, et quidam in plaustris, alii in curribus, nonnulli in equis, plurimi per dependulum fluentis Rhodani ad coemeterium Campi Elisii deferebantur. Est ergo omni admiratione dignissimum, quod nullus in thecis positus mortuus ultimos civitatis Arelatensis terminos, quod Rochestam nominant, quantalibet vi ventorum aut tempestate compulsus praeterit, sed infra semper subsistens in aqua rotatur donec applicet, aut ad ripam fluminis ductus coemeterio sacro inferatur. Mirandis magis miranda succedunt, quae oculis conspeximus sub innumera utriusque sexus hominum multitudine. Solent, ergo praemisimus, mortui in doliis bituminatis ac in thecis corpora mortuorum a longinquis regionibus fluminis Rhodani dimitti cum pecunia sigillata, quae coemeterio tam sacro, nomine eleemosynae, confertur. Uno aliquo die, nondum decennio delapso, dolium cum mortuo suo descendit inter illud angustum, quod ex alternis ripis castrum Tarasconense et castrum Belliquadri prospectant. Exilientes adolescentes Belliquadri dolium ad terram trahunt, et relicto mortuo pecuniam reconditam rapiunt. Depulsum dolium inter impetuosi amnis fluctus subsistit, et nec vi fluminis praecipitis nec juvenum impulsibus potuit descendere, verum rotans et in se revolvens, eosdem circinabat fluminis fluctus ... Tandem, restituto censu, confestim mortuus sine omni impellentis adjutorio viam aggreditur, et infra modicam horam

therefore performed at the hands of the most holy bishops at the East Gate, where the church consecrated by them in honour of the Blessed Virgin now stands. To them Christ himself appeared, as of old he was intimately recognisable in human flesh; he lavished his blessing on their work, granting to the cemetery and to its occupants that whoever might be buried there should suffer in their corpse no mockery of the devil. As a result, therefore, of this gift of the Lord's benediction, it was borne in upon all the principal rulers and clergy of Gaul that the great majority of those to whom they had access had right of burial there. And so some in wagons, others in chariots, a number on horse back, but the majority borne downstream on the River Rhône, were brought to the cemetery of the Elysian Field. It is quite astonishing that no dead person placed in a coffin ever overshot the outer boundary of the City of Arles (which they call Rocheta), driven by whatever force of wind or tempest, but remaining close to the shore, the coffin circles in the water until it lands, or else is borne into the sacred cemetery by the direct current of the river. Marvels succeed to marvels which we have seen with our own eyes in the case of innumerable multitudes of people of either sex. As we have said, the dead are usually sent in vessels of bitumen and in coffins from distant reaches of the river Rhône, with figured coinage, which is offered as alms to so sacred a cemetery. On one occasion, less than ten years ago, a vessel with its corpse came downstream into that strait which is overlooked on one side by the camp of the Tasconians and on the other by that of the Belliquadri. Some youths of Belliquadri jumped out and dragged the vessel to shore, and, leaving the dead body, seized the money laid within it. The vessel having been pushed out again into the river stood still amidst its fierce currents, and neither the force of the headlong flood nor the thrusts of the apud civitatem Arelatensem applicans, sepulturae honorifice traditur.

young men could make it go downstream. Turning and turning about on itself, it circled those same waves of the stream . . . At last, when the whole sum of money was restored, the body forthwith pursued its way without the help of anyone impelling it, and within a short space of time, landing at Arles, was given an honourable burial.

APPENDIX C

THE KOGI OF COLOMBIA

Before the Spanish Conquest, the ancient, indigenous Chibcha peoples were the dominant race in what is now Colombia. Their population of close to 500,000 seems to have been concentrated in the high valleys around the modern cities of Bogotá and Tunja. They were intensive agriculturalists, craftsmen and traders: fruit, vegetables, pottery and cotton cloth changed hands at the weekly markets in their larger villages. Trade with their neighbours brought in large quantities of gold which they used for religious ceremonies, personal adornment and ornaments.

Descent was matrilineal: chiefs and religious leaders were succeeded by sons of their sisters. Land, however, was inherited patrilineally.

The present-day Kogi of northern Colombia were recently visited for the first time by Alan Ereira (whom they call "Mr. BBC"). The brilliant and thought-provoking documentary which he produced as a result of that visit was shown on BBC 1 on Tuesday, December 4th, 1990.

In essence, Ereira's programme revealed that the Kogi are descended in an undisturbed line from an ancient South American civilisation who had learned to live *with* nature, to co-operate (as some might rephrase it) with Gaia herself. Their simplistically wise priest-rulers believe that the Kogi, high on their secret mountain, are the *Elder Brothers*: they refer to the rest of humanity as the *Younger Brothers*. The Kogi asked Alan Ereira to broadcast a solemn warning to the world — a request which his superb documentary fulfilled with great clarity and dignity. Fundamentally, Kogi priest-rulers believe that mining and other world-wide industrial exploitation are mortally wounding the Great Earth Mother (Gaia?) on whom we all depend — *Elder Brothers* and *Younger Brothers* alike.

If the strange "natural pentagon" at Rennes-le-Château is one of Gaia's "sensory organs" or "communication channels", is the secret mountain of the Kogi another?

Is it only by the strangest of coincidences that the *River Magdalena* runs close by the Kogi's mountain citadel, and that the city of *Santa Marta* (surely the Hispanic rendering of St. Martha, sister of Mary of Bethany, who might also have been Mary Magdalen) is only a few miles away?

Is there the remotest possibility that the hypothetical refugees who might have established themselves on Oak Island were a group of the Kogi's ancestors escaping with their gold and their strange nature secrets from the sixteenth century Spanish invaders?

Could the mysterious Colombian Kogi, and their belief in the Great Earth Mother, have any connection — however remote — with Jean Robin and von Däniken's ideas about tunnels under South America?

Map of Colombia showing Bogota, Tunja and the Magdalena River.

APPENDIX D

THE VIGENÈRE SQUARE CIPHER

In Chapter 6 (Codes, Ciphers and Cryptograms), an entirely new approach to the decipherment of the long coded inscription was made using the purely numerical "position value" method. This obviated the old Tableau Vigenère technique. However, since the Vigenère system has become almost traditional as an aid to decoding the tombstone and parchment ciphers, its use is explained briefly in this Appendix.

To produce a French Vigenère table, write out the 25-letter French alphabet (the same as our own alphabet with the letter W removed) twenty-five times in the form of a square. The first horizontal line is written normally from A to Z; the line below it begins with B and ends with A, Z in this line being the penultimate letter; the twenty-fifth and last line begins with Z followed by A, and ends with Y.

```
A B C D E F G H I J K L M N O P Q R S T U V X Y Z
B C D E F G H I J K L M N O P Q R S T U V X Y Z A
C D E F G H I J K L M N O P Q R S T U V X Y Z A B
D E F G H I J K L M N O P Q R S T U V X Y Z A B C
E F G H I J K L M N O P Q R S T U V X Y Z A B C D
F G H I J K L M N O P Q R S T U V X Y Z A B C D E
G H I J K L M N O P Q R S T U V X Y Z A B C D E F
H I J K L M N O P Q R S T U V X Y Z A B C D E F G
I J K L M N O P Q R S T U V X Y Z A B C D E F G H
J K L M N O P Q R S T U V X Y Z A B C D E F G H I
K L M N O P Q R S T U V X Y Z A B C D E F G H I J
L M N O P Q R S T U V X Y Z A B C D E F G H I J K
M N O P Q R S T U V X Y Z A B C D E F G H I J K L
N O P Q R S T U V X Y Z A B C D E F G H I J K L M
O P Q R S T U V X Y Z A B C D E F G H I J K L M N
P Q R S T U V X Y Z A B C D E F G H I J K L M N O
Q R S T U V X Y Z A B C D E F G H I J K L M N O P
R S T U V X Y Z A B C D E F G H I J K L M N O P Q
S T U V X Y Z A B C D E F G H I J K L M N O P Q R
T U V X Y Z A B C D E F G H I J K L M N O P Q R S
U V X Y Z A B C D E F G H I J K L M N O P Q R S T
V X Y Z A B C D E F G H I J K L M N O P Q R S T U
X Y Z A B C D E F G H I J K L M N O P Q R S T U V
Y Z A B C D E F G H I J K L M N O P Q R S T U V X
Z A B C D E F G H I J K L M N O P Q R S T U V X Y
```

It will be seen that the uppermost horizontal line and the first (far left) vertical line are normal alphabets. To use the square to decode a message write out the key words (*MORT épée* in the case of the tombstone) over and over again below the ciphered version. The key word indicates which of the horizontal alphabets is to be used to find the letter.

For example, suppose that the key word is SAUNIERE and that the cipher reads:

BRJFGNMOBAXQFJMO

Copy the key word as often as necessary until every letter of the cipher is covered by a letter of the repeated key word.

Cipher: B R J F GNMOB A X Q F J MO . . .
Key Word: S A U N I E R E S A U N I E R E . . .

Locate the letter B (the letter from the encoded message) along the top row of the square, then follow that column vertically until you reach the row with S (the first letter from the keyword) leftmost. The letter found at the intersection of that column and row is T, which becomes the first letter of the plaintext. The second letter is R, found in column R, row A — which row is just the unshifted alphabet at the top of the square. Similarly, column J, row U gives E, the third letter of the message. Continuing to the end gives the decoded message *Trésor est à Rennes . . .*

Cipher: B R J F GNMOB A X Q F J MO . . .
Key Word: S A U N I E R E S A U N I E R E . . .
Clear: T R E S O R E S T A R E N N E S . . .

It is important to note that letter changes via a Tableau Vigenère can be effected in two ways: either by the method demonstrated above, i.e. by finding the alphabet indicated by the keyword, looking for the cipher letter along the top line and then finding its partner by descending vertically into the keyword alphabet, or the other way round.

Note that the Tableau Vigenère system is *not* equivalent to the position value addition system described in Chapter 6. The *Trésor est à Rennes* message emerged from the position value system from a different original:

AQIEFMLNAZVPEILN

Let us see what happens when we attempt to decipher this by the Vigenère method, using the same keyword SAUNIERE:

Cipher: A Q I E FMLNA Z V P E I L N . . .
Key Word: S A U N I E R E S A U N I E R E . . .
"Clear":   S Q D R N Q D R S Z Q D M M D R . . .

It doesn't work! Complete decipherment requires that one slight refinement be performed on the text — one of the "alphabetic shifts" that feature so prominently in the Vigenère analysis of the long coded inscription given below. We replace each letter with the next letter in the alphabet, i.e., S becomes T, Q becomes R, etc. Only when this is done is the plain message *Trésor est à Rennes* revealed.

Let us consider again the long coded inscription. In their original form, the 128 letters of the coded inscription run as follows:

VCPSJQROVYMYYDLTPEFRBOXTODJLBKNJFQUEP
AJYNPPBFEIELRGHIIRYBTTCVTGDLUCCVMTEJHP
NPGSVQJHGMLFTSVJLZQMTOXANPEMUPHKORPK
HVJCMCATLVQXGGNDT

The key word is *MORTépée*, which has to be written sixteen times below the letters like this:

Cipher: V C P S J Q R O V Y M Y Y D L T P E F R B O X T . . .
Key word: M O R T E P E E M O R T E P E E M O R T E P E E . . .

The key letter M directs us to the M alphabet line of the Tableau Vigenère which changes V into I; the key letter O directs us to the O alphabet line of the Tableau Vigenère which changes C into Q; the key letter R directs us to the R alphabet line of the Tableau Vigenère which changes P into H . . . and so on. The letter transformation, using the Vigenère method, begins like this:

Cipher: V C P S J Q R O V Y M Y Y D L T P E F R B O X T . . .
Key word: M O R T E P E E M O R T E P E E M O R T E P E E . . .
Stage 1:   I Q H M N G V S I M E R C S P Y C S X L F E B Y . . .

The full text at this stage is:

IQHMNGVSIMERCSPYCSXLFEBYBRBFFARNRFMYT
PNCAEHUJTMIYGYBMYVCNILVAJKHYJTVACYIVV
HHTVXADYZAQBJYFKBFDGQYBLRHTTQZCVCIVF
OLIYTGGPYPIFOAKDHY

The next complication is an alphabetic shift as described above. Following this alphabet shift we have the Stage 2 text − a whole new string of 128 letters:

JRINOHXTJNFSDTQZDTYMGFCZCSCGGBSOSGNZ
UQODBFIVKUNJZHZCNZXDOJMXBKLIZKUXBDZJ
XXIIUXYBEZABRCKZGLCGEHRZCMSIUURADXDJX
GPMJZUHHQZQJGPBLEIZ

Now we have to use a different keyword: the whole of the inscription from the gravestone of Marie de Nègre, including the "(P. S.)" and "prae cum". To complicate matters still further, this new keyword has to be used backwards. We start in the bottom right-hand corner and work from right to left and from the lowest line upwards:-

Cipher:	J R I N O H X T J N F S D T Q Z . . . Z Q J G P B L E I Z
Key word:	M U C E A R P S P E C A P N I T . . . E L B O N T I G T C
Stage 3:	V M K R O Z M M Z R H S S H Z S . . . D C K U D U T K C B

The full text at this stage is:

VMKROZMMZRHSSHZSDVQQOASDTBZDDMHQVSF
DDMCDKNQRHZZNDKDERCPQODCBTOFVZHDLT
HCNBDICMLDFLBNBDDOCRGQVZHZCGZSLNZDR
DAHBDKDQMDDZHDDCKUDUTKCB

Next comes yet another alphabet shift, giving the Stage 4 text:

XNLSPANNASITTIATEXRRPBTEUCAEENIRXTGEE
NDELORSIAAOELEFSDQRPEDCUPGXAIEMUIDOCE
JDNMEGMCOCEEPDSHRXAIADHATMOAESEBICEL
ERNEEAIEEDLVEVULDC

This brings us to precisely the same point as the more efficient position value method given in Chapter 6. There a single decipherment stage was used, in place of the four stages given above. By either method, the text is now ready for the knight's tour transformation.

APPENDIX E

THE TOWNSEND CIPHER

So much has been written about the complexity of the hypothetical codes on the parchments which Saunière is said to have found in or near the Visigothic altar pillar, that an antidote to their complexity makes a refreshing change — not to mention a challenge to a lot of conventional thinking about the secret of Rennes-le-Château.

It is no exaggeration to say that Paul Townsend, the compiler of this appendix, is a computer genius with few equals, but his alternative hypothesis, and the spoof "tombstone code" which he has concocted, bring esoteric cryptographers down to earth with something of a bump.

We present his hypothesis without comment — other than to reiterate that he is an extremely able man, and his ideas are well worth careful consideration.

An Enquiry into the Affairs of Joe Bloggs (Deceased)

The story begins with the tombstone of the proverbial Joe Bloggs, a reproduction of which is shown below. He was well-known as the brother of the equally proverbial Fred, but his recently discovered tombstone gives some further details of his family and — most importantly — reveals that he was probably Supreme Grand Master of the Priory of Sion.

Spoof tombstone

HERE LIETH
SIR JOSEpH BLOGGS
BELoVED HUSBAND
OF EMMELINE
BROTHER OF F
REDERICK FATHER OF
ANDREW SARAH AND
PETER DIED ИINTH
AUGUST NINETEEN
SIXTY FOUR AGeD
SEVENTY TWO YEAЯS
REQUIESCAT IN
PACE

P.S.

As with the Rennes tombstone, there are several "funnies" in the inscription:

    (a) Three letters — the P of "JOSEPH", the O of "BELOVED" and the E of "AGED" — are in lower case.

    (b) The H of "LIETH" and the A of "ANDREW" are missing their crossbars.

    (c) The F of "FREDERICK" is detached from the rest of the name, isolated on the previous line.

    (d) The T of "NINETEEN" has a spurious crossbar approximately halfway up.

    (e) The first N of "NINTH" and the R of "YEARS" have been carved in mirror-image form.

The above imperfections in the inscription highlight the letters A,E,F,H,N,O,P,R,T. There has been much speculation regarding what these letters represent, but the most likely rendering is FANTHORPE, the surname of a priest from Wales and one of the co-authors of at least one book about the Rennes mystery.

The Long Coded Inscription

We have heard of the following inscription, corresponding to the long coded manuscript alleged to have been found behind the altar at Rennes:

AS I FWALKED THKROUGH THE WFILDERNESS POF THIS WOKRLD TI LIGHTEZD ON A ICERTIAIN PLACEN WHERE WASB A DEN AVND I LAID MEH DOWN NIN THAT PLACWE TO SLEEP SAND AS IZ SLEPT ID DREAMED AL DREAM I QDREAMED ANCD BEHOLD NI SAW AA MAN CPLOTHEVD WITH RAGIS STANDIFNGP IN AR CERTAIN PKLACE WITAH HIS FAGCE FROM HIVS OWN HOUWSE A XBOOK INN HIS HHAND ANDN AW GREAT BRURDEN UPAON HIS BACK TI LOOKIED AND SAEW HIM OPEN MTHE BOOGK AND READV THEREIN ANTD AS HE READL HE WEWPT AND KTREMBLERD AND NOT FBEINGZ ABLEP LONGER TOJ CONTAIN HQE BRAKE OUYT WITH A LAFMENTABKLE CRY SUAYING WHXAT SHDALL I DOL IN THISL PLIGHKT THERPEFORE CHE WENT OHOME AND RRESTRAVINEDL HIMTSELF BAS LONG ASH HE COULZD THATZ HIS WIFE RAND CHILIDREN SHOULED NOT PHERCEVIVE HIZS DISTRESS UBUT HE COULRD NOT BJE SILENTT LONG BECIAUSE THAPT HIS TROUBYLE IYNCREASED WHEDREFORE ABT LENGTH XHE BRAKER HIS MIND TOL HIS WIZFE ANVD CHGILDRENW AND TPHUS HE BWEGANH TO TGALK TOJ THEM O TMYF DEAR WIIFE SAAID HE ATND YOU TTHE CHILFDREN OF MUY BOWELS I XYOUR DEIAR FRYIEND AMB INU MYSELF UNDOONE BYP REASON SOF A HBURDEN THAT QLIETH HARD JUPON MEW MOREOVER HI AM FORZ

CERTAINR INFORMED NTHAT THIS OAUR CITHY
WIXLL BE BNURNED LWITH FIKRE FROM HQEAVEN
INX WHICRH FEARFULW OVERTHROZW BOTH
MYLSELF WITH STHEE MY WFIFE AND YOUS MY
SWVEET BABESP SHALL MTISERABLY COFME TO
RSUIN AEXCEPT XTHE WHICH YEST I LSEE NOT
SHOME WAYR OFM ESCAPNE CAN HBE FOUEND
WVHEREBYS WE JMAY BE DELIVERED

One recognises the opening paragraphs of John Bunyan's *Pilgrim's Progress*, into which some one hundred and sixty-two additional letters have been inserted. The number 162 is significant — it is the same number of letters as on our concocted tombstone inscription.

There are three main steps to decoding the message. Firstly, the letters of the message have to be extracted. Here they are shown in upper case, with all the remaining letters rendered into lower case for clarity:

as i Fwalked thKrough the wFilderness Pof this woKrld Ti
lighteZd on a IcertIain placeN where wasB a den aVnd i laid
meH down Nin that placWe to sleep Sand as iZ slept iD
dreamed aL dream i Qdreamed anCd behold Ni saw aA man
cPlotheVd with ragIs standiFngP in aR certain pKlace witAh
his faGce from hiVs own houWse a Xbook inN his Hhand
andN aW great bRurden upAon his back Ti lookIed and saEw
him open Mthe booGk and readV therein anTd as he readL
he weWpt and KtrembleRd and not FbeingZ ableP longer
toJ contain hQe brake ouYt with a laFmentabKle cry sUaying
whXat shDall i doL in thisL plighKt therPefore Che went
Ohome and rRestraVinedL himTself Bas long asH he coulZd
thatZ his wife Rand chilIdren shoulEd not pHerceVive hiZs
distress Ubut he coulRd not bJe silenTt long becIause thaPt
his troubYle iYncreased wheDrefore aBt length Xhe brakeR
his mind toL his wiZfe anVd chGildrenW and tPhus he
bWeganH to tGalk toJ them o TmyF dear wiIfe sAaid he
aTnd you Tthe chilFdren of mUy bowels i Xyour deIar
frYiend amB inU myself undOone byP reason Sof a Hburden
that Qlieth hard Jupon meW moreover Hi am forZ certainR
informed Nthat this oAur citHy wiXll be bNurned Lwith
fiKre from hQeaven inX whicRh fearfulW overthroZw both
myLself with Sthee my wFife and youS my swVeet babesP
shall mTiserably coFme to rSuin Aexcept Xthe which yeSt i
Lsee not sHome wayR ofM escapNe can Hbe fouEnd
wVherebyS we Jmay be delivered

The number of additional letters, 162, is twice the square of 9. We write the letters, taking them in the order in which they appear in the inscription, into a double 9 x 9 grid, filling up the left grid and then the right:

F	K	F	P	K	T	Z	I	I
N	B	V	H	N	W	S	Z	D
L	Q	C	N	A	P	V	I	F
P	R	K	A	G	V	W	X	N
H	N	W	R	A	T	I	E	M
G	V	T	L	W	K	R	F	Z
P	J	Q	Y	F	K	U	X	D
L	L	K	P	C	O	R	V	L
T	B	H	Z	Z	R	I	E	H

V	Z	U	R	J	T	I	P	Y
Y	D	B	X	R	L	Z	V	G
W	P	W	H	G	J	T	F	I
A	T	T	F	U	X	I	Y	B
U	O	P	S	H	Q	J	W	H
Z	R	N	A	H	X	N	L	K
Q	X	R	W	Z	L	S	F	S
V	P	T	F	S	A	X	S	L
H	R	M	N	H	E	V	S	J

A suitable transposition is now required. We remain with the double 9 x 9 grid, and this time generate a 9 x 9 magic square in the left grid using a standard technique, as described in *A Number for Your Thoughts* by Malcolm E. Lines (Adam Hilger Ltd., Bristol, 1986), section 13. The right grid contains a mirror-image duplicate of the same magic square:

47	58	69	80	1	12	23	34	45
57	68	79	9	11	22	33	44	46
67	78	8	10	21	32	43	54	56
77	7	18	20	31	42	53	55	66
6	17	.19	30	41	52	63	65	76
16	27	29	40	51	62	64	75	5
26	28	39	50	61	72	74	4	15
36	38	49	60	71	73	3	14	25
37	48	59	70	81	2	13	24	35

45	34	23	12	1	80	69	58	47
46	44	33	22	11	9	79	68	57
56	54	43	32	21	10	8	78	67
66	55	53	42	31	20	18	7	77
76	65	63	52	41	30	19	17	6
5	75	64	62	51	40	29	27	16
15	4	74	72	61	50	39	28	26
25	14	3	73	71	60	49	38	36
35	24	13	2	81	70	59	48	37

We now read the letters off in the order specified by the numbering of the squares in the above magic squares, the left grid then the right. This gives:

KRRXZHRCHNNTIVDGNKWAAWZELPVJTRGPSIHL
TLQLAVVZIDFBKYWTWIXFNKHPFKIRENLBFZCKO
UFMPQVPZJNTXZHYTLJRRMPQKWIJXGXURVSLFN
QUHBZHLJSSXHFWDVYYSXLHSTPTWGPVAZAPNO
AIVIESWFRRUBFZTH

When this sequence of letters is decoded using the Vigenère Square technique (using the English alphabet, and the keyword FANTHORPE), the following highly suggestive message is revealed:

FREE STANDING POPPY GRAND SQUARE TENIERS
HOLDS THE KEY FOR RICHES FAR ABOVE
MEASURING JUSTICE AVENGES THE HERETIC THE
EXTENDED HAND BANISHES FEAR FORTY FEET
BELOW TWO MILLION POUNDS ARE BURIED

Yes — very suggestive, particularly in the reference to Teniers and including a copy of a familiar inscription — that alleged to be the meaning of the mysterious carvings on the Money Pit tablet. This final message is (as the reader may wish to check) a perfect anagram of the tombstone inscription.

Explanation

Well, of course, it is all concocted. Unfortunately, it was not possible to get anything better than a series of disjointed phrases as above out of the tombstone letters, but that does not matter. The original BERGERE PAS DE TENTATION message is no better in this respect.

The first germ of my hypothesis is a curious "flaw" in the original Rennes tombstone message — reproduced in my concoction. This is that the anagram uses *all* the letters on the tombstone, even those of *MORT épée* [FANTHORPE] itself. It seems rather odd to decode a message and find within it the keyword to use for the decoding! One does not expect a locked safe to contain its own key.

Secondly, the Rennes encipherment was so complex, involving two Vigenère transformations with different keywords, plus transpositions and further alphabetic shifts, that I do not believe that Saunière — or anybody else in his time — would have been able to decipher the message had it been genuine. In our own century, the wartime codebreakers did manage to "crack" the ciphers produced by the German "Enigma" machine (a mechanical implementation of a multi-stage Vigenère square), but they required their own machinery in the form of Colossus (a purpose-built electro-mechanical computer) with various sundry pieces of additional equipment, knowledge of the Enigma machine itself, *and* a fair idea of what the contents of the messages would be (e.g. weather reports, or particular lightships being destroyed).[1]

I therefore began with the idea that Saunière had gone the other way, and *enciphered* the message. I therefore set out to determine how difficult (or, as it turned out, how easy) it would be to construct something similar, beginning with a concocted tombstone inscription containing some "funny" letters which gave the keyword when taken together. Finding the anagram only required an hour or so with modern technological aid (an anagram-exploring program running on an IBM-compatible Personal Computer) to turn up the "FREE STANDING POPPY" nonsense. In

---

[1] An excellent account of Allied codebreaking activities during WWII is contained in Chapter 6 of *The Secret War* by Brian Johnson (Arrow Books, London, 1979). This book accompanied a series of BBC documentary programmes transmitted in 1978.

Saunière's time, the easiest way to play with the letters would have been to write them on small pieces of paper and attempt to arrange them all into a series of sensible words. (Was this the inspiration for the game of Scrabble?!)

My hypothesis is, therefore, that the BERGERE PAS DE TENTATION anagram is a red herring, devised, probably by Saunière himself, to supply an ostensible "use" for the letters *MORT épée* of the tombstone inscription once he had become aware of its survival despite his obliteration of it from the tombstone itself; and thereby detract attention from further research on the *real* meaning of *MORT épée*. Saunière (or whoever) should have excluded the key letters *MORT épée* from the anagram and attempted to concoct some meaningful-looking nonsense from the 120 remaining letters.

APPENDIX F

THE ASIMOV-ECO CONNECTION

Isaac Asimov

The authors gratefully acknowledge a fascinating idea which was sent to them by Chris Kirk of New Oscott, Birmingham, shortly after their first volume on the Rennes mystery was published in 1982.

Chris made a detailed study of Isaac Asimov's *Foundation* trilogy after reading our 1982 comments about the similarity of names in the Rennes mystery and those used by Tolkien in *Lord of the Rings*. If Tolkien, he wondered, why not Asimov?

Chris's first point is that Asimov's books refer to an open Foundation of physical scientists, and a *secret or hidden Foundation* (the Second Foundation) whose aim is the preservation of the "Seldon Plan" to form a new galactic empire. Is this a parallel of the Open and Closed Orders of the Knights Templar, he asks.

Kirk's second point is that the background to Asimov's *Foundation* trilogy is a crumbling galactic empire and a lineage of emperors. On page 140 of Volume Two in the Panther edition, entitled *Foundation and Empire*, the Emperor Dagobert IX is mentioned. His son, Dagobert X, is later killed by a character called The Mule. A heroine in Volume Three (page 71 in the Panther edition) is called Arcadia. The instigator of the whole plot is a character called Hari Seldon. The name is an anagram of "Sion Herald"!

As an afterthought, Chris adds that the transmutation of base metals into gold features prominently in Part IV of Volume I, *Foundation*, especially on page 122 of the Panther edition.

So, is it possible to add Isaac Asimov to the list of writers (so far including Victor Hugo, Jules Verne, George MacDonald, J. R. R. Tolkien, Charles Williams and C. S. Lewis) who might have known about Rennes and dropped a few hints to that effect into their work?

Umberto Eco

If anything, even more probable than an Asimov connection, is the possibility that Umberto Eco is dropping extremely erudite and subtle hints first in *The Name of the Rose* and later in *Foucault's Pendulum*?

The very word "Rose" in the first title may be significant. The mystery is set in an ancient monastery and centres on a curious lost work of philosophy. Strangely, one of the monks is called *Berengar* — the second case we have come across (after Prof. Beringer in Chapter 12) of somebody who bears a name similar to that of Bérenger Saunière. Even more strangely, there is almost an element of anticlimax in the *dénouement*. Jorge, the grim, blind librarian, has kept secret the second book of the *Poetics* of Aristotle because it dealt with *laughter*. The explanation isn't really adequate. The secret was guarded so carefully. Men died to keep it safe. The reader is left asking *why*.

Is Eco doing what Lewis Carroll and Boudet perhaps did? Is the "secret" not really hidden in Aristotle's treatise on humour? Is there some subtle camouflage within the camouflage? Eco's towering intellect is more than capable of that sort of double concealment.

What then of *Foucault's Pendulum*?

Jean Bernard Leon Foucault was born in Paris on September 18th, 1819. His father was a publisher. Jean Bernard studied medicine and then turned his attention to experimental physics. With Armand Fizeau, who was also born in September 1819, Foucault carried out a series of important experiments concerned with the behaviour of heat and light: forms of *energy*.

Perhaps Foucault's most memorable achievement was the demonstration of the diurnal motion of the earth using a long, heavy, freely suspended pendulum, which was subsequently named after him. He also invented the gyroscope (which still seems to possess some only partially explained power to defy gravity!). Foucault died of paralysis in 1868 in Paris, but his friend and collaborator, Armand Fizeau, lived on until 1896 — well into Saunière's time.

Eco's second book, like his first, has the underlying and persistent theme of a secret that is no secret: the paradox of a mystery which *in one sense does not exist*. His text swings like Foucault's Pendulum itself, seemingly independent of the earth and those who crawl about their mundane business across its surface. Yet scattered throughout the whole work are intriguing *hints* and *innuendoes*, suggestions of dark secret societies and their relentless pursuit of arcane knowledge. There are whispers of alchemists . . . of transmutation . . . and of much, much *more* . . .

APPENDIX G

ON THE TRAIL OF THE PAINTINGS

Among the many subsidiary mysteries that surround Rennes-le-Château is that of who is misinformed about the various so-called "significant" paintings, who is responsible for such misinformation as appears to be circulating, and whether there is some secret, sinister *reason* for it, or whether it's just one more good old-fashioned human error laced up with a bit of honest, understandable and forgivable record bungling?

Prior to the great ninth day picture sale of August 10th, 1842, there were in Shugborough Hall, Staffordshire, one or two paintings by Teniers, Guercino and Poussin — at least, they were there according to the auctioneer's catalogue.

When we wrote to the Louvre as long ago as November 1976, we were told that the second version of "The Shepherds of Arcadia", which Henri Buthion had told us about, did *not* exist — although he had shown us what certainly looked like a reproduction of a slightly modified Poussin canvas. When our expedition photographer of the time, Peter Rice of Ipswich, called in person one Saturday and asked to see it, he was told that it *did exist* but that it couldn't be seen at weekends!

The Shugborough sale catalogue and the subsequent "hunt-the-Poussin" correspondence make interesting reading.

Ninth Day's Sale,

AT SHUGBOROUGH HALL, NEAR STAFFORD,

On WEDNESDAY, the 10th Day of AUGUST, 1842,

Commencing at Twelve o'Clock precisely.

THE AUCTION DUTY IS TO BE PAID BY THE PURCHASERS.

No. 19.—The valuable Collection of Pictures.

IN THE HOUSEKEEPER'S ROOM.

	LOT	
RUSSELL	1	A pair of Portraits of Ladies, in crayons
—DANCE	2	The Holy Family
MARTIRELLI	3	Landscape with Figures
DITTO	4	Ditto, the companion —
	5	A Monk Reading
VIVIANI	6	Architectural Ruins with Figures
GUERCINO	7	A Sybil.
ELMER	8	Dead Game
ITALIAN	9	Emblematical Figures
ITALIAN	10	Ditto, the companion

IN THE CHINA ROOM.

P. PANINI	11	Architectural Ruins with Figures
MIGNON	12	A group of Flowers
	13	Landscape with Figures
	14	Drawing of Venus, framed and glazed

o

210

IN THE STEWARD'S ROOM.

AMICONI - -	15	Joseph and Potiphar's Wife *Webb — ...*
BOGDANE -	16	A Peacock and other Birds in a Landscape *Grant.*
DITTO - - -	17	Dogs, &c., the companion - *ditto*
GUISEPPE CHIARI -	18	The discovery of Calista, *formerly in the collection of Mr. Edwin* *... for Lord ...*
	19	A Landscape with Figures *... Bought ...*
RUSSELL - -	20	A pair of Portraits of Ladies, in crayons *...*
DITTO - - -	21	Ditto *... near Market ...*
SOLIMENA -	22	Venus and Cupids *... for Lord Lichfield.*
	23	A large Historical Picture *... Bought ...*
PADUANINO - -	24	Danae in the Golden Shower *... for Soul*

IN LOWER BED CHAMBER.

MODERN - -	25	View of Mount Vesuvius from Naples *Hodges*
DITTO - - -	26	View near Naples, the companion — *ditto*

IN THE BILLIARD ROOM.

OCHIALLI - -	27	View in Rome, with Buildings and Figures *...*
ITALIAN - -	28	Cupid holding an Urn *Long. ...*
ZUCCARELLI -	29	A View in Italy, with Buildings, Water a Figures, one of his most elegant and cl pictures (engraved) *Walsh ...*
DITTO - -	30	Ditto, with Female and Child on Horseb: attended by a Dog, the companion picture, equal in quality *... for Lord ...*
WOUVERMANS -	31	A Landscape, with Horse and Figures *...*
VAN TOLL - -	32	The Pedlar — *ditto* -
SIR JOSHUA REYNOLDS	33	Portrait of Sir Charles Sanders *ditto*
	34	Girl seated with a Horn Book *...*
	35	Vessels at Sea, curious *... 53 ...*
POUSSIN - -	36	Small Landscape with Figures *Wyatt ...*
	37	Upright ditto *...*
GAINSBOROUGH	38	Landscape with a Windmill *...*
H. SWANEVELDT -	39	Ruins of the Temple of Peace *...*

255.17/— —

ANTI DRAWING ROOM.

	WM. VANDEVELDE	55	A STORM AT SEA, with Vessels in Distress, upright *King 6 Woodstock Bell*
	LUCA PENNI -	56	HOLY FAMILY *Samax - sea address*
	PLACIDO - -	57	Head of the Magdalen, after the celebrated picture by Guido, in the Barberini Palace, *from Mr. Fouquier's collection Hodges*
	N. BERGHEM - -	58	Exterior of a Cottage, with Figures and Cattle, full of subject, and sweetly painted; *a choice gem of the master*
	F. LAURI -	59	Venus, Satyr and Cupid in a Landscape, *formerly in Mr. Fouquier's collection*
	D. TENIERS -	60	An upright Landscape, with the Chateau of Teniers and Two Flemish Peasants in conversation on the left, *a pleasing specimen*
	B. CASTIGLIONE -	61	Landscape, Cattle and Figures, circular
	DITTO - -	62	Ditto, the companion -
	P. BRILL -	63	Rocky Landscape, with St. Anthony
	DITTO - -	64	Ditto, with St. Jerome, the companion -
	ARTOIS - -	65	View in Flanders, with Figures -
	YELLOWLES - -	66	Small Portrait of a Lady
	C. POELEMBERG -	67	A Landscape, with romantic scenery and Nymphs Bathing, circular; *a pleasing specimen of the master*
	K. DU JARDIN, 1651	68	Three Sheep and a Cow in a Landscape, *a little bijou of high quality by this rare and much esteemed master, formerly in the collection of Mr. Fouquier*
	GONZALES -	69	Small Portrait of a Man in a Ruff
	BREUGHEL - -	70	Landscape with Figures coming down a Road, circular
	ANGELLUS -	71	Dutch Exterior with a Woman selling Vegetables, *highly finished*
	DOMENICHINO -	72	UPRIGHT LANDSCAPE, with Tobit and the Angel
	DITTO -	73	DITTO, with Moses and the Burning Bush, the companion
	B. PETERS - -	74	Sea Piece, with Dutch Boats, &c.
	WM. VANDEVELDE	75	A BRISK GALE, with a Man of War riding in front, and a Dutch Boat with other Vessels in the offing, *a charming composition of his finest time, and in high preservation*
	DITTO - -	76	DITTO, its companion, *equal in quality and beauty of composition with the preceding*

5 1 12   P. PANINI - - 90   *An upright View of the* INTERIOR OF THE PAN-
THEON AT ROME, with numerous Figures, and
an effect of Sunshine from the Cupulo, truly
magical; *from Mr. Fouquier's collection* *Davis two*

2 11 3   J. BASSANO - 91   THE ANGEL APPEARING TO THE SHEPHERDS,
a brilliant specimen of the master *Cockburne. etc.*

2 1   LE BRUN - - 92   THE DEPARTURE OF RINALDO FROM ARMIDA,
formerly in the collection of Sir Luke Schaub *Wood*

6 9   P. PANINI - 93   View of the COLOSSEUM AT ROME, with various
Buildings and Figures

DITTO - - 94   View of the PIAZZA DEL POPOLO, the companion,
of equal merit; *from Mr. Fouquier's collection*

HORIZONTI - - 95   AN ITALIAN LANDSCAPE, with Buildings and
Figures, *an elegant composition*

25 11   DITTO - - 96   DITTO, with Figures in the foreground on the
borders of a Lake; *the companion to the preceding*

6 11 1   G. POUSSIN - - 97   A MOUNTAINOUS LANDSCAPE, with
Classical Buildings, on the left a group of
Figures reposing under the shadow of some
Trees; *a fine specimen of this much esteemed
master*

43 1   DITTO - - 98   A WOODY SCENE with Figures, its companion, painted with great freedom of pencil, *and
formerly in the collection of Sir Luke Schaub*

1188 12   WM. VANDEVELDE   99   A CALM, WITH MEN OF WAR AT
ANCHOR, and an infinity of Vessels, Boats
and Figures, beautifully composed, painted in
his finest time, and embracing every quality for
which this highly esteemed master was so
eminently distinguished. *This splendid picture
may be pronounced, without fear of contradiction,
one of his most capital productions in existence,
truly a chef d'œuvre*

341   A. CUYP - 100   A VIEW NEAR DORT, WITH A WOMAN
MILKING A COW on the banks of a River, and
Three Cows standing behind her, a distant View
of a Village, with Dutch Boats sailing along,
forming one of the most charming compositions
that can be conceived, with an effect of light
that illumines the whole, which produces a scene
completely true to nature. *This very desirable
picture is in a state of pristine purity*

1624 15 —

9th November 1976

Au Conservateur du Departement de Peinture,
Le Louvre,
75 Paris.

Monsieur,

Je suis en train d'achever le premier jet d'un livre sur les tresors de Rennes-le-Chateau et je m'interesse surtout aux peintures de Nicolas Poussin "Bergeres d'Arcadie" et "L'Automne".

Lors d'une recente visite au Louvre j'ai pu acheter une reproduction en diapositive et en carte postale des "Bergeres d'Arcadie", mais depuis lors en m'a dit qu'il existe au Louvre une seconde version de cette peinture que l'en n'expose pas. Serait-il possible, Monsieur, de m'envoyer une reproduction de cette seconde version et d'autres versions qui puissent exister dans les archives du Louvre?

Je m'interesse aussi a une peinture de Teniere representant St. Antoine. Je ne connais pas le titre de cet oeuvre mais il montre le saint qui n'est pas en train d'etre tente, au contraire de la plupart des peintures de Teniere de St. Antoine ou le sujet de la Tentation est en evidence.

Je serais tres heureux de payer en avance tous les reproductions, photographies ou livrets dont vous puissiez me fournir, pour m'aider a repondre aux questions que j'ai posees ci-dessus. Voudriez-vous me faire savoir les frais d'affranchissement et d'emballage, etc.?

Veuilles trouver ci-encles un coupon-repense international.

Veuillez agreer, monsieur, l'expression de mes sentiments les plus distinguees.

(R. L. Fanthorpe, B.A., A.C.P., A.M.B.I.M.)

PALAIS DU LOUVRE (PAVILLON DES ARTS)

TÉLÉPHONE : 260.39.26

PARIS, LE 15 Décembre 1976

75041 PARIS CEDEX 01

JF/yb/ 1611

Monsieur ,

En réponse à votre récente lettre du 9 novembre,
je puis vous assurer qu'il n'existe au Louvre aucune
version des Bergers d'Arcadie de Poussin : on vous a
mal renseigné. Certes, il existe beaucoup de copies de
tableaux célèbres. Je suppose que les détails ne vous
intéressent pas.

Je vous signale également qu'il vous est facile
de consulter en Angleterre l'oeuvre magistrale sur
Poussin rédigé par votre compatriote Sir Anthony Blunt.

Quant à Teniers, ici encore vous êtes mal renseigné
car nous avons deux tableaux représentant Saint Antoine
mais chaque fois le saint est bien représenté en train
d'être tenté, ainsi votre spéculation ne s'avère pas juste.

Agréez, je vous prie, Monsieur, l'expression de
mes sentiments distingués .

Jacques Foucart
Conservateur au Département des Peintures
Chef du Service d'Etude et Documentation

Monsieur E.L. FANTHORPE

215

26th **Sept**.1977

**CHATSWORTH
BAKEWELL**
DERBYSHIRE
DE4. 1PN.

Dear Sir,

In reply to your letter of the 7th I am now able to send you the enclosed photograph of the Poussin Shepherds in Arcady in the collection here, together with a commercial colour slide.

This painting, which is No.501 in the Chatsworth catalogue, is on canvas and measures 40 x 32 inches. It was at Devonshire House, London, in the mid-18th century, and was probably acquired by the 2nd or 3rd Duke of Devonshire. It was previously in the collections of Mme du Housset and Comte Loménce de Brienne. For information on Poussin you should refer to the books and articles by Friedlander, Panofsky, Blunt and others, and especially to the Mellon Lectures on the artist given by Sir Anthony Blunt at the National Gallery, Washington, in 1958 which were published in 2 volumes by Pantheon Books as Bollinger Series XXXV.7. The Chatsworth painting is discussed in detail and illustrated.

Also in the collection here is another Poussin - Holy Family with Putti in a Classical Landscape (No.502), which was purchased by the 3rd Duke of Devonshire at the Hay Sale in 1737. There are also several drawings by the artist, including The Rape of the Sabines and Apollo and Daphne.

Yours faithfully,

R. L. Fanthorpe, Esq.,

216

20 AUBREY WALK · LONDON · W · 8

727 4468 : 727 4469

R. Lionel Fanthorpe Esq., B.A.,

29th July, 1977

Dear Mr Fanthorpe,

Thank you very much for your letter concerning the connection between Shugborough and Rennes.

I think the easiest way to obtain the best information would be to write to either the National Trust representative for Shugborough who is Merlin Waterson, The National Trust, Attingham Park, Shrewsbury, or the County Archivist, who is Mr F. B. Stitt, Staffordshire Record Office, County Buildings, Eastgate Street, Stafford ST16 2LZ, who also has considerable knowledge of the house and the pictures in general.

As you may know Shugborough was handed over to the National Trust in the Fifties and all the documents were handed over to the County Archivist at that time.

Yours sincerely,

The Earl of Lichfield

Staffordshire County Council

The Museum of Staffordshire Life
Shugborough
Great Haywood Stafford

Curator: Mrs Pamela Murray, B.A., A.M.A.
telephone/Little Haywood 388

L. Fanthorpe, Esq.,

our ref PM/NR 9780(b)/5/En.T.

your ref

date 6th September, 1977

Dear Mr. Fanthorpe,

   Your letter to Mr. Stitt has been forwarded to me, although I'm afraid I cannot be of much help to you. The collections at Shugborough do not include versions of the paintings you refer to. In addition to the existing collections, checks have been made in Mr. Stitt's Office, the National Trust Office at Attingham and also our own inventories made some years ago.

   I am sorry I cannot be of any assistance to you in this matter.

                         Yours sincerely,

                         Pamela M Murray

                         Curator.

❧ The National Trust for Places of Historic Interest or Natural Beauty

Attingham Park, Shrewsbury, SY4 4TP Telephone: Upton Magna (074 377) 659

Historic Buildings Representative
for the West Midlands & North Wales: J. M. Waterson

R. Lionel Fanthorpe Esq., B.A.,

My ref: CR/AB

Your ref:

13th December 1977

Dear Mr. Fanthorpe,

    Thank you for your letter of the 17th August. I am very sorry to have been so long in replying.

    We seem to have no record of versions of Poussin's Bergers D'Arcadie or Teniers St. Anthony in the Shugborough collection. If it transpires that these pictures have at any time been in the Shugborough collection, I shall of course let you know.

                    Yours sincerely,

C. Howell

APPENDIX H

THE MYSTERY OF SAUNIÈRE'S BEDROOM CEILING

One of the most intriguing things about Rennes-le-Château is that information about the mystery comes in small instalments from many unsuspected sources. The tale of Saunière's bedroom ceiling comes via a very roundabout route.

The Russian Revolution led to the murder of the Tsar's family on July 17th,1918. At that time a loyal old Cossack named Basile Kikof fled from Russia. He married a girl named Anastasia. The two exiles arrived in France in 1928 and worked wherever they could until 1950, when they reached Rennes-le-Château. Here, Anastasia Kikof befriended the eighty-year-old Marie Dénarnaud, and the two women became friends and confidantes.

According to what Anastasia said to a reporter, whose article appeared in Littoral on June 10th,1983, what was left of the treasure was concealed in the false ceiling of Saunière's bedroom. With the collaboration of other local residents at the time, the Kikof family searched the ceiling: there was nothing there. Had it once been there? The question cannot now be answered satisfactorily . . . but it does provide one more microscopic clue to the Rennes mystery.

APPENDIX I

THE MANDELBROT ENIGMA AND THE
RIDDLE OF THE TESSERACT

In this Appendix, written mostly by our friend Paul Townsend, M.Sc, we discuss two mathematical constructions — the Mandelbrot set (with some variations upon it) and the Tesseract, both of which refer back to points raised in the main text of this book, and both of which involve extensions to the mathematics of the 'real world'. The authors and publishers wish to express their grateful thanks to Paul Townsend for writing graphic programs showing the "Bearskin Rug" pattern and an animated tesseract on screen, and for his kind permission to reproduce photographs and line illustrations generated by these programs.

Complex Numbers — The Mandelbrot Set and Others

Through the ages, mathematicians have bestowed derogatory tags upon concepts which, at first, seemed to be blemishes upon the ideally spotless face of the Queen of Sciences. We speak, for example, of a division of two whole numbers which does not produce a whole number answer as being a "vulgar" fraction. Gradually, of course, the new concept is integrated into mathematics and gains general acceptance — the vulgar fraction is now usually known by the more polite expression *ratio*. When it was found that the division of the diagonal of a square by its side could not be expressed even as a ratio, this and similar quantities were termed *irrational* — a word which originally meant simply "without ratio", but has entered general currency with the meaning "odd", "eccentric" or "illogical".

The name "complex numbers" is a similar misnomer, and is particularly unfortunate since, far from complicating mathematics, the use of complex numbers simplifies and unifies a large number of concepts. For example, every quadratic equation has exactly two solutions (no dependence on b^2-4ac or other such parameters), and such diverse concepts as the sine and cosine functions of trigonometry, and the raising of one number to the power of another, join into a single larger whole — the de Moivre function.

The mathematics of complex numbers seems to have begun in the 16th century with the Italian mathematician Cardan. Cardan's original problem was to find two numbers which gave the sum 10 when added, and the product 40 when multiplied together.

Two numbers which add to 10 may be represented by the expressions $(5+P)$ and $(5-P)$, where P is some number. For example, setting $P=2$ gives the numbers 7 and 3. When these two expressions are added, the +P and

-P cancel each other out, leaving only the two 5's which add to 10.

The two expressions are recognised as a case of the "difference of two squares" theorem: their product is given by:

$$(5+P)(5-P) = 5^2\text{-}P^2$$

Since 5^2 is the unalterable constant 25, our hope of finding a solution to Cardan's problem rests in the P^2 term. Unfortunately, for $5^2\text{-}P^2$ to have the value 40 requires that P^2 equals -15. Since all numbers, whether positive or negative, have positive squares, Cardan's problem seems impossible to solve.

But mathematicians don't like a problem being branded "impossible" so quickly. It was soon determined that a whole new class of numbers, namely those with negative squares, could be introduced into mathematics without at the same time introducing any contradictions. Since such numbers did not appear to fit into the "real world", they were branded "imaginary" − another instance of the derogatory tags referred to above. The imaginary numbers could be combined with the ordinary "real" numbers to produce the compound numbers referred to as "complex". Mathematicians now give the solution to Cardan's problem as the pair of complex numbers:

$$5 + \sqrt{\ } - 15 \text{ and } 5 - \sqrt{\ } - 15$$

Just as the real numbers can be plotted on a line, representing the magnitude of the number by the length of the line from a given origin, so complex numbers can be plotted on a *plane*, usually referred to as the *Argand diagram*, where the real component is plotted horizontally and the imaginary component plotted vertically. The complex number $5 + \sqrt{\ } -$ 15 is represented by a point 5 units east, and $\sqrt{15}$ (nearly 4) units north, of the origin. By Pythagoras' theorem, the distance of this point from the origin (known as the *modulus* of the number) along a straight line is $\sqrt{40}$ (approximately 6.3), the appearance of "40" reflecting the conditions of Cardan's problem.

Quadratic equations can be solved directly, simply by inserting the a, b and c parameters into a formula and pulling out the two answers. However, such cases are rare − there is no formula, for example, for solving more typical equations such as:

$$2z - 2 - z \, Ln(z) = 0$$

This one appeared in the doctoral thesis of the authors' daughter Stephanie. Its solution ($z = 4.921554$ to six decimal places) had to be found by numerical techniques. In such circumstances, mathematicians resort to an *iteration* scheme, constructed as follows:

(1) Express the equation in the form:

$$x = [\text{some expression involving x}]$$

which is more elegantly written ("f" is read "function of"):

$$x = f(x)$$

(2) Estimate (or guess) an approximate solution.
(3) Evaluate f(x) for the approximate solution.
(4) Use the result from step 3 as the new approximate solution.
(5) Return to step 3.

It is hoped that, eventually, the value of f(x) computed from step 3 will be equal to the value of x that went into the expression. The iteration scheme is then said to *converge* to this final value, which may be computed as accurately as desired by running the iteration scheme enough times. Unfortunately, a badly constructed iteration scheme, or an initial estimate too far from the true solution, will result in x moving further and further from the solution, eventually heading to infinity. Such a scheme is said to *diverge*.

Consider the equation:

$$x^2 - x + c = 0$$

where c is some constant. Although this is a simple quadratic, solvable using the formula, we use it here as an illustration of the iteration scheme. Step 1 requires that the equation be transformed into the form $x = f(x)$. The following is the simplest of many such transformations:

$$x = x^2 + c$$

We shall examine below two cases of this equation, using two different values of c: -0.5 and +0.5. In each case, our initial guess at the solution will be zero.

Iteration Loops	$x = x^2 - 0.5$	$x = x^2 + 0.5$
0 (start)	0	0
1	−0.5	+0.5
2	−0.25	+0.75
3	−0.4375	+1.0625
4	−0.308594	+1.628906
5	−0.404770	+3.153336
6	−0.336161	+10.44353
7	−0.386996	+109.5672
8	−0.350234	+12005.48
9	−0.377336	
10	−0.357618	(diverges)
11	−0.372110	
12	−0.361534	
13	−0.369293	
etc. to		
97	−0.366025	
98	−0.366025	
99	−0.366025	
100	−0.366025	

We find that, whereas $x^2 - 0.5$ converged to a single value, $x^2 + 0.5$ diverged. The next term of the latter sequence (not shown in the table) exceeded 140,000,000 and in subsequent terms the number of *digits* in the number doubled each time.

Further experimentation shows that convergence to a single value is found for values of c in the range -0.75 to +0.25 inclusive. Divergence is found for c more negative than -2, or more positive than +0.25. Between the limits of -2 and -0.75 comes a more complicated regime: the values of x do not converge to a single value, but to a series of two or more different values which appear in turn. However, such behaviour can still be classed as "finite" since the x values do not diverge to infinity.

To sum up the above discussion, we find that only real values of c falling between the limits of -2 and +0.25 remain finite, while all other numbers diverge.

We now introduce Mandelbrot and his set. The "Mandelbrot Set" emerged as a solution to a problem in "fractal geometry", a branch of mathematics too complicated to outline in any great detail. Basically, it is concerned with the mathematics of infinite complexity. To give the stock example, how long is the coastline of Britain? Even if no allowance is made for tides, erosion and other dynamical factors, the answer still depends on your scale of measurement. If you measure the coastline as shown on a road map with a scale of, say, five miles to the inch, features less than 100 yards across would be below the resolution of the printing process, and could not be shown with any great accuracy. It would not, therefore, be surprising if the answer were significantly less than that obtained if you were to tour the entire coast of Britain armed with (a) a metre rule, (b) a suitably long piece of string, (c) a gauge capable of tracking the contours of the smallest pebble with $1/100''$ accuracy, (d) an apparatus perhaps based on an electron microscope which could plot the surfaces of the tiniest grain of sand down to the atomic scale.

The Mandelbrot Set is the set of constants c which remain finite under the iteration scheme $x=x^2+c$ which we have discussed above, with the twist that *complex* values are admitted for c. When the entire Argand diagram is checked for divergence under this iteration scheme, with points that remain finite coloured in while points which diverge are left blank, the pattern that emerges is one of infinite complexity. Nowhere is the boundary between finite and divergent behaviour absolutely smooth, but smaller and smaller "nodules" are visible, upon infinitely finer and finer scales. No matter how much the diagram is magnified, there is always detail below the resolution of the picture. The set even contains miniatures of itself! We have the paradoxical situation of a figure of finite area (since the entire set must lie within a circle of radius 2 drawn about the origin) but with an infinitely long surface. A beautiful series of successively magnified views of the Mandelbrot Set is shown in the colour plates in James Gleick's excellent book *Chaos: Making a New Science* (Heinemann, London, 1988).

What has all this to do with our subject? We take up the reference in Chapter 5 to Bayley and Campbell's exposition of the curious properties of the number five. It is found that, when the power in the iteration scheme $x=x^2+c$ is raised above 2, totally different patterns emerge. The pattern of interest here is that which results from plotting those values of c which remain finite under the iteration scheme $x=x^6+c$. The resulting pattern has fivefold rotational symmetry (i.e. it can be rotated by one-fifth of a turn and look the same as before). Each of the major branches of the pattern terminates in what looks very much like a "foot" with five "toes".

When this pattern appeared for the first time on our friend Paul Townsend's computer display, he immediately dubbed it the "bearskin rug". Is this the "Quinotaur" of Chapter 2, the name arising from the pentagonal symmetry and its resemblance to the flattened-out skin of some kind of animal?

When magnified, the pattern shows similar fivefold divisions down to infinitely finer scales. Is the approximate fivefold symmetry of higher lifeforms, mentioned by Campbell, simply a variation on this pattern? Does the $x=x^6+c$ iteration scheme have this physical significance, just as the classic Mandelbrot set emerges unexpectedly as the shape of the physical boundary between magnetised and nonmagnetised regions in metals as discovered by Peitgen and Richter (*Chaos* p.236)?

Four-Dimensional Space — The Tesseract

In classical Euclidean geometry: a point has no magnitude; an infinite number of points make a line, which has length but no breadth; an infinite number of lines make a plane, which has length and breadth but no thickness; and an infinite number of planes make a three dimensional or "solid" figure. In the "real world", that is as far as we go.

To specify a position on a flat, two dimensional shape (e.g. a map), we need two sets of imaginary lines running at right-angles to one another (e.g. parallels of latitude and lines of longitude). To specify positions in a "solid" we have to introduce a third set of lines running at right angles to both the other dimensions — the pilot of an aircraft will want to know not only his position (latitude and longitude) but also his height.

If there were four dimensions of space — not merely the three with which we are familiar from our everyday life experiences — the fourth dimension would have to go off at right-angles to each of the other three.

Because our minds are understandably circumscribed by the three-dimensional world in which we have always lived, most of us find it impossible to imagine such a shape as a four-dimensional hypercube. Pure mathematics is, however, equal to the task and can readily elucidate the properties of spaces of four, five, six or more dimensions.[2]

Although a true four-dimensional figure cannot be constructed, it is perfectly possible to build a three-dimensional *model* of a four-dimensional hypercube.

Suppose we constructed a cube from twelve equal lengths of wire representing its edges. Looking at this cube from above one of its faces, we would see a large square (i.e., the top face) containing a smaller square (i.e., the bottom face) within it, and the outer corners of the inner square would be joined to the corresponding inner corners of the outer square by lines (i.e., the four vertical edges).

The three-dimensional model of the hypercube — the *tesseract* — usually takes the analogous form of a cube inside a cube, where the external corners of the smaller internal cube are connected to the internal corners of the larger, enveloping cube. In this way four spatial dimensions can be

---

[2]For further discussion of the geometry of hyperspaces, the reader is referred to Martin Gardner's excellent recreational mathematics books, published in the Pelican series: *Mathematical Carnival*, Chapter 4, "Cubes and Hypercubes," and *Mathematical Circus*, Chapter 3, "Spheres and Hyperspheres." PVST

represented in three, much as a two-dimensional shadow can be cast on a flat surface by a three-dimensional human being standing in a patch of sunlight. Although some of the edges and faces of the hypercube as represented appear to be larger than others, this effect must be regarded as a perspective distortion — all edges and faces are "really" equal in four-dimensional space. The four-dimensional hypercube has 16 vertices, 32 edges, 24 faces and 8 bounding cubes.

The arrangement of the edges of the hypercube — four edges meeting at each corner — permit a re-entrant tour of all the edges, reminiscent of the knight's tours of the chessboard which featured so largely in the chapter on codes and ciphers. In such a tour, all 32 edges are traversed once each, and each corner is visited twice before we return to the starting point. No such complete tour of the edges is possible on an ordinary cube — at best only nine of the twelve edges may be traversed.

There is some interesting evidence that a thirteenth century Catalonian mystic and numerologist drew a two dimensional sketch of a tesseract — or, perhaps, built a three dimensional model of one — and achieved an altered state of mind by contemplating it. Some modern investigations into psi-powers at universities with research departments interested in extra-sensory perception have seemed to suggest that prolonged gazing at a

tesseract (or a sketch of one) may induce a state of mind in which psychic abilities in certain "sensitive" individuals are enhanced.

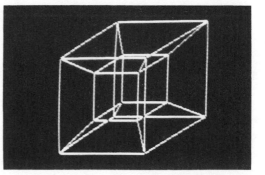

The tesseract, supercube or hypercube may be no more than an interesting and un-usual mathematical diversion: it could just be part of the key to something extremely in-teresting and mysterious.

BIBLIOGRAPHY

TITLES ON RENNES-LE-CHÂTEAU

Baigent M., Leigh, R. and Lincoln H, *The Holy Blood and the Holy Grail.* Jonathan Cape, London, 1982.

Boudet, H., *La Vraie Langue Celtique et le Cromleck de Rennes-les-Bains.* Bélisane, Nice, 1984. (Facsimile of 1886 original.)

Bradley, M., *Holy Grail Across The Atlantic.* Hounslow Press, Canada, 1988.

Captier, A. et al., *Rennes-le-Château.* Bélisane, Nice, 1985.

Corbu, C. and Captier, A., *L'Héritage de l'Abbé Saunière.* Bélisane, Nice, 1985.

Descadeillas, R., *Mythologie du Trésor de Rennes-le-Château.* Carcassonne, 1974.

De Larouanne, U., *La Voie de Dieu et du Cromlech de Rennes-les Bains, Tinena.* Quillan, 1981.

De Larouanne, U., *Géographie Sacrée du Haut-Razès, Tinena.* Quillan, 1982.

De Monts, B., *Bérenger Saunière Curé à Rennes-le-Château.* Bélisane, Nice, 1989.

De Sède, G., *Rennes-le-Château, le dossier, les impostures, les phantasmes, les hypothèses.* Editions Robert Laffont, Paris, 1988.

Elie, H., *A la Gloire de Jésus Christ.* Vogels, Couiza, 1983.

Fanthorpe, P. and Fanthorpe, L., *The Holy Grail Revealed: The Mysterious Treasure of Rennes-le-Château.* Newcastle Press, California, USA, 1982.

Fédié, L., *Le Comté de Razès et le Diocèse d'Alet.* Carcassonne,1880.(Reprinted Brussels, 1979).

James, S., *The Treasure Maps of Rennes-le-Château.* Seven Lights Publishing, Bow, UK, 1984.

Jarnac, P., *Histoire du Trésor de Rennes-le-Château.* Cabestany, 1984.

Jarnac, P., *Les Archives du Trésor de Rennes-le-Château.* Bélisane, Nice, 1987.

Kletzky-Pradère, T., *Rennes-le-Château: Guide du Visiteur.* Maquette Jean-Luc Ganz, 1990.

Lincoln, H., *The Holy Place.* Jonathan Cape, London, 1991.

Marie, F., *Rennes-le-Château: Étude Critique, S.R.E.S.* Bagneux, 1978.

Marie, F., *La Résurrection du Grand Cocu, S.R.E.S.* Bagneux, 1981.

Marie, F., *Le Surprenant Message de Jules Verne, Vérités Anciennes.* Malakoff, 1981.

Markale, J., *Rennes-le-Château.* Pygmalion, Paris, 1989.

Monteils, J., *Nouveaux Trésors à Rennes-le-Château.* Les Éditions de l'Ocotogone, France, 1974.

Riviére, J., *Le Fabuleux Trésor de Rennes-le-Château.* Bélisane, Nice,1983.

Robin, J., *Operation Orth.* Guy Trédaniel, Paris, 1989.

Robin, J., *La Colline Envoutée.* Guy Trédaniel, Paris, 1982.

Saunière, B., *Mon Enseignement à Antugnac.* Bélisane, Nice, 1984.

Saunière, E., *Moi, Bérenger Saunière (Two Volumes)*. Émile Saunière, Espéraza, France, 1989.
Serrus, G., *Pays Cathares*, Loubatières, Portet-sur-Garonne, 1990.
Van Buren, E., *Refuge of the Apocalypse*. C.W.Daniel, Saffron Walden, UK, 1986.
Wood, D., *GenIsis*. Baton Press, Kent, UK, 1985.

GENERAL REFERENCES

Alexander, W.L., *The Ancient British Church*. The Religious Tract Society, London, 1889.
Armstrong, R. (Ed.), *Treasure and Treasure Hunters*. Hamish Hamilton Ltd., London, 1969.
Baigent M. and Leigh, R., *The Temple and the Lodge*. Jonathan Cape, London, 1989.
Baigent, M., Leigh R. and Lincoln H., *The Messianic Legacy*. Jonathan Cape, London, 1986.
Bammel, E.M. and Moule, C.F.D. (Ed.), *Jesus and the Politics of His Day*. Cambridge University Press, 1984.
Barber, R., *King Arthur in Legend and History*. Sphere, London, 1973.
Baring-Gould, S., *Curious Myths of the Middle Ages*. Rivingtons, London, 1884.
Barker, M., *The Lost Prophet*. SPCK, 1989.
Birks, W. and Gilbert, R.A., *The Treasure of Montségur*. Crucible (The Aquarian Press), Wellingborough, UK, 1987.
Bord, J. and Bord, C., *Mysterious Britain*. Paladin, Herts., 1976.
Branigan, K. (Ed.), *The Atlas of Archaeology*. MacDonald, London, 1982.
Brooke, D. (Anthologist), *Private Letters Pagan and Christian*. Ernest Benn Ltd., London, 1929.
Brown, F., *Nostradamus*. Tower, NY, 1970.
Bullock, A. *et al.* (Ed.), *The Fontana Dictionary of Modern Thought*. Fontana Paperbacks, London, 1988.
Butler, W.V., *The Greatest Magicians on Earth*. Pan Books Ltd., London, 1977.
Carr, D.E., *Energy and the Earth Machine*. Sphere, London, 1978.
Castries, Duc de., *Lives of the Kings and Queens of France*. Weidenfeld and Nicolson, London, 1979.
Chadwick, N., *The Celts*. Pelican Books (Penguin), UK, 1971.
Delaney, F., *The Celts*. Grafton Books, London, 1989.
Downs, N., *Basic Documents in Medieval History*. Van Nostrand, Toronto, 1959.
Duriez, C., *The C. S. Lewis Handbook*. Monarch Publishers, Essex, 1990.
Eco, U., *Foucault's Pendulum*. Picador, London, 1990.
Eco, U., *The Name of the Rose*. Picador, London, 1984.
Farmer, D.H., *The Oxford Dictionary of Saints*. Oxford University Press, 1982.

Fisher, H.A.L., *A History of Europe, Volume I, From Earliest Times to 1713*. Fontana/Collins, Glasgow, 1935.

Frazer, J. G., *Magic and Religion*. Watts and Co., London, 1944.

Frazer, J. G., *The Golden Bough*. The Macmillan Co., 1923.

Furneaux, R., *Money Pit — The Mystery of Oak Island*. Fontana/Collins, 1976.

Gardner, M., *Mathematical Carnival*. Pelican Books (Penguin), UK, 1978.

Gardner, M., *Mathematical Circus*. Pelican Books (Penguin), UK, 1979.

Garnier, P., *Montségur, le Trace du Château*. Association pour la Promotion de l'Archéologie en Midi-Pyrénées. France, 1989.

Gettings, F., *Secret Symbolism in Occult Art*. Harmony Books, NY, 1987.

Giardini, C., *The Life and Times of Victor Hugo*. Hamlyn Publishing Group, UK, 1969.

Gleick, J., *Chaos: Making a New Science*. Heinemann Ltd., London, 1988.

Glover, T.R., *The Jesus of History*. SCM, London, 1920.

Green, R.L., *King Arthur*. Puffin, 1972.

Gribble, L., *Famous Historical Mysteries*. Target, London, 1974.

Guirdham, A., *The Cathars and Reincarnation*. Neville Spearman, UK, 1976.

Hannay, O.J., *The Wisdom of the Desert*. Methuen, 1904.

Hassrick, R.B., *North American Indians*. Derbibooks, NJ, 1974.

Hawking, S.W., *A Brief History of Time*. Bantam Press, 1988.

Higenbottam, F., *Codes and Ciphers*. English Universities Press Ltd., London, 1973.

Hughes, J., *The World Atlas of Archaeology*. Mitchell Beazley, 1985.

Hugo, V., *La Légende des Siècles*. Librarie Gallimard, France, 1950.

Huzinga, J., *The Waning of the Middle Ages*. Pelican, 1953.

James, E., *The Franks*. Basil Blackwell, 1988.

James, S., *Missing Pharaohs: Missing Tombs*. Maxbow Publishing, UK, 1986.

Johnson, B., *The Secret War*. Arrow Books, London, 1979.

Joinville and Villehardouin, (Tr. by M.R.B. Shaw), *Chronicles of the Crusades*. Penguin, London, 1983.

Kent, J.P.C. and Painter, K.S., *Wealth of the Roman World*. British Museum Publications Ltd., London, 1977.

Kitto, J., *The Bible History of the Holy Land*. George Routledge and Co, London and NY, 19th century.

Knight, G., *The Secret Tradition in Arthurian Legend*. Aquarian Press, 1983.

Kopal, Z., *The Realm of the Terrestrial Planets*. The Institute of Physics, Bristol and London, 1979.

Lines, M.E., *A Number for Your Thoughts*. Adam Hilger Ltd., Bristol, 1986.

McKitterick, R., *The Frankish Kingdoms under the Carolingians*. Longman, 1983.

Melegari, Vezio., *Hidden Treasures*. Collins International, Franklin Watts, Inc., 1972.

Michell, J. and Rickard, R., *Phenomena: A Book of Wonders.* Thames and Hudson, 1977.
Munro, R.W., *Highland Clans and Tartans.* Peerage Books, London, 1987.
Myers, A.R., *England in the Middle Ages.* Penguin Books, 1985.
Norvill, R., *Hermes Unveiled.* Ashgrove Press, Bath, UK, 1986.
Nova Scotia Travel Guide., Dept. of Tourism and Culture, Halifax, Nova Scotia, Current edition.
O'Connor, D'A., *The Big Dig.* Ballantyne, NY, 1988.
Orden, W., *The Outline of Art.* George Newnes, London, undated.
Palmer, D.G., *Sliced Bread.* Ceridwen Press, Cardiff, 1988.
Pott, H., *Francis Bacon and his Secret Society.* Sampson Low, Marston and Co. Ltd., London, 1891.
Pounds, N.J.G., *An Historical Geography of Europe, 450 BC − 1330 AD.* Cambridge University Press, 1973.
Ridley, B.K., *Time, Space and Things.* Penguin, 1976.
Schonfield, H.J., *Those Incredible Christians.* Bernard Geiss Associates, 1968.
Serrus, G., *Pays Cathares.* Éditions Loubatières, Toulouse, 1990.
Sitchin, Z., *The Wars of Gods and Men.* Avon Books, NY, 1985.
Smith, C.T., *An Historical Geography of Western Europe before 1800.* Longman, 1967.
Smith, W. (Ed.), *Dictionary of the Bible (Three Volumes).* John Murray, London, 1863.
Spence, L., *The Encyclopedia of the Occult.* Bracken Books, London, 1988.
The Tartan Map., John Bartholomew and Son Ltd., Edinburgh.
Todd, M., *Everyday Life of the Barbarians.* Dorset Press, NY, 1972.
Van Buren, E., *The Sign of the Dove.* Neville Spearman, UK, 1983.
Vaughan, C.J., *Characteristics of Christ's Teaching.* Alexander Strahan, 1866.
Vaughn, A., *Incredible Coincidences.* Corgi Books, London, 1981.
Verne, J., *Journey to the Centre of the Earth.* Original, Paris, 1864. Penguin Edition, London, 1965.
Von Däniken, E., *Chariot of the Gods.* Souvenir Press, London, 1970.
Von Däniken, E., *Return to the Stars.* Souvenir Press, London, 1970.
Wallace-Hadrill, J.M., *Early Medieval History.* Basil Blackwell, Oxford, 1975.
Webb, A.E., *Glastonbury.* Avalon Press, Glastonbury, 1929.
Wheatley, D. *The Devil and All His Works.* Arrow Books, London, 1973.
Whiston, W. (Tr.), *The Works of Flavius Josephus.* Milner and Co. Ltd., London. Undated.
Wise, L.F., *World Rulers from Ancient Times to the Present.* Ward Lock Educational, London, 1967.
Wistar Comfort, W. (Ed.), *Arthurian Romances by Chrétien de Troyes.* J.M.Dent and Sons, 1913.
Young, G., *Ancient Peoples and Modern Ghosts.* George Young, Nova Scotia, 1980.

INDEX

Adam and Eve, 37

Adams, Douglas, 176

Adonis, 84, 85

Adoptionists, 41

Agostini, Bremna, 79, 180

Alaric, 23, 67

Albigensians (see Cathars)

Alchemy, 2, 17, 68, 82, 86, 95, 112

Ansegesil, 31

Anson Family, 96-98, 102-103, 121, 144, 151

Aphrodite (see Venus)

Archeopteryx, 165

Ark of the Covenant, 178

Arnulf, 30

Arques, Tomb of, 11, 17, 23, 62, 63, 65, 68,

Asmodeus, 21, 69, 120

Atargatis, 25

Ataulphe, 67

Atbash Cipher, 88-91, 96, 119

Atomic Number, 56

Atomic Weight, 56

Austrasia, 28

L'Automne (Poussin), 98

Aven, 15, 16, 38

Bacon, Anthony, 93, 96, 100, 120

Bacon, Dr. Benjamin Wisner, 91

Bacon, Sir Francis, 7, 92, 93, 98, 100-102, 106, 126, 150

Bacon, Sir Nicholas, 96, 100, 101

Baigent, Leigh and Lincoln, 8, 24, 46, 49-51, 159, 167

Baphomet, 88, 91, 117, 119, 122

Baring-Gould S., 39, 174

Bayley, Barry, 55

de Beauséjour, Bishop Beuvain, 36

Begga, 31

Beringer, Johann, 164

Bigou, Abbé, 33, 67, 68, 76, 123

Billard, Monseigneur, 33, 36

Blanchefort, 2, 11, 14, 16, 33, 44, 83, 87, 113, 117, 119

Blankenship, Dan, 10, 149

Boat (Ship) of the Dead, 12, 13, 18, 19, 62, 95

Bode, Johann Elert, 56

Bogomils, 42, 68, 118

deBono, Edward, 109, 164

Boudet, Henri, 4, 5, 8, 11, 14, 15, 19, 20, 84, 98, 99, 138-139, 145

de Bouillon (St. Omer) Godfroi, 113

Boyer, Abbé, 142

Boyle, Robert, 7

Bradley, Michael, 6, 144

Bren, Pierre, 8

Bres, Nimian, 110

Brooke, Celia, 7

Buddhism, 49

Bugarach, 68

van Buren, Elizabeth, 8, 18, 68, 69, 161

Buthion, Henri, 7, 61, 154-157

Cabala, 121
Cagliostro, 108
Cajuns, 6
Calvé Emma, 62, 170
Camelot, 18
Campbell, J.C., 55, 56
Captier, Antoine, 7
Captier, Marcel, 7
Carolingians, 29, 31, 32
Carroll, Lewis, 1, 68
Cathars, 2, 7, 12, 16, 32, 33, 41,
    42-44, 83, 84, 94, 102, 113, 114,
    118, 125
Charlemagne, 32
Celts, 1, 22, 23
Charles Martel, 30, 31, 32
Chateaubriand, François-René de,
    61
Chatsworth House, 60, 62, 63, 96
Chess, 76
Chiasmus, 53
Childebert, 27, 28, 143
Childeric I, 25, 26, 27, 62
Chilperic, 27
Christianity, 36, 39, 40, 41, 42, 49,
    50-53, 84-118, 121
Clairvaux, Bernard of, 115
Clodion, 10, 24, 27, 38
Clotaire I, 26, 27
Clotaire II, 26, 27, 30
Clovis I, 26, 27, 28, 143
Clovis II, 27
Cocteau, Jean, 124
Colbert, Jean Baptiste, 65, 66
Le Comte de St. Germain, 7, 108-
    109, 110, 111, 175
Conques, 66
Constantine, 66

Convocation of Venus, 3, 7, 180
Corbu, Claire, 8
Corbu, Noël, 8, 142
Cortés, Hernán, 46
Coustaussa, 12, 13, 17, 67
Crusades, 2, 95, 98, 115
Crystallography, 56

Dagobert I, 27, 28
Dagobert II, 1, 26, 28, 29, 30, 87,
    143
Dagon, 25
Dalle du chevalier (see Knight's
    Gravestone)
von Däniken, Erich, 14, 78
Debussy, Claude, 6
Dee, Dr. John, 100
Delacroix, Eugène, 66
Delaney, Frank, 40
Demeter (Ceres), 38
Dénarnaud Marie, 3, 5, 33, 63, 84,
    108, 142, 170
Dirac, Paul, 47
Dossiers Secrets, 28
Druids, 22
Duvilla, Abbé, 142

Ea, 25
Earth, 57
Easter Island, 93
Ebionites, 41
Egypt, 44, 47
Einstein, Albert, 48, 63
Eleusinian Mysteries, 39, 122
Elixir of Life, 2, 3, 112, 126
Emerald Tablets, 3

Eryx, 38
Eschcol, 98
von Eschenbach, Wolfram, 124
Essenes, 119
Et in Arcadia Ego, 6, 11, 59, 63, 82, 120
Eugenius, Emperor, 38

Fatin, Henri, 9, 12, 14, 18, 19, 22, 38, 62, 158, 181
Fibonacci, Leonardo, 57
Flamel, Nicolas, 7, 109-110, 175
Fleury Family, 67, 69, 85
de Floyran, Esquiu, 117
Fludd, Robert, 112
Foix, 16
Fountain of the Tritons, 18, 19
de la Fontaine, Jean, 65, 66
Fouquet, Nicolas, 2, 3, 63, 65, 66, 80, 106, 111, 126
Frankland, Edward, 4
Freemasons, 15, 126
Furneaux, Rupert, 149

Gaia Hypothesis, 45, 121, 182-183
Galibert, Jean, 63
Gardner, Martin, 57
Gavelle, Robert, 63
Gélis, Abbé, 12, 14, 20, 139-141, 170
Gervase of Tilbury, 158
Glanvill, Joseph, 110
Glastonbury, 18, 40
Gnosticism, 12, 22, 40, 41, 42, 45, 114, 115, 118
Golden Age, 63

Golden Mean, 56-59, 70
Gregorian Calendar, 67
Grimoald, 28, 31, 32, 143
Gringonneur, Jacques, 86
Guercino (Giovanni Francesco Barbieri), 6, 63
Guinguand, Maurice, 20
Guirdham, Dr. Arthur, 42

Habsburgs, 2, 4, 11, 16, 64, 104, 123, 124, 130-135, 152, 166
Hautpoul Family, 2, 9, 12, 14, 18, 19, 21, 22, 33, 67, 179
Hawking, Stephen, 48
Heisenberg, Werner, 47, 48, 49, 63
Herbert, George, 98
Hermes Trismegistus (Thoth), 3, 44, 71, 94, 114, 175, 181
Hermeticism, 17, 40, 45, 67, 86, 118, 121
Herrera, Manuel, 162
Hilderson, Arthur, 95
Hitler, Adolf, 173
Hokhmah, 91
Holy Grail, 4, 18, 124
Holy Roman Empire, 15
Horselberg, 39
Horselloch, 39, 40
Horus, 3, 38
Hospitallers, 115, 116, 117
Hugo, Victor, 7, 103-106, 123
Huguenots, 102
Huygens, Christiaan, 65

Inklings, 127-128
Irish, Dr., 110-111

Isiac Mysteries, 39
Islam, 49
Isis, 3, 38

James, Stanley, 8, 14, 16, 18, 38, 69, 160
Jarnac, Pierre, 8, 11, 62, 63
Jesus Christ, 166-173, passim
Jonson, Ben, 96, 123
Joseph of Arimathea, 18, 40, 51
Jung, Carl, 49, 182
Jupiter, 48

Kammerer, Paul, 164
Kidd, William, 151
King Arthur, 4, 18
King Charles VI, 86
King Francois II, 4
King Louis XIV, 2, 3, 64, 66, 67, 126
King Louis XV, 109
King Philip IV, 91, 106, 116, 117
Knight's Gravestone (Dalle du Chevalier), 5, 19, 29, 106
Knights of the Round Table, 4, 18
Knights of St. John (see Hospitallers)
Knights Templar (see Templars)
Knight's Tour, 75, 76, 77, 78, 79, 96

Labarum, 66
Lanigan, J., 28
de Laplace, Marquis, 48
Law of Planetary Distances, 56, 58

Lawrence, Louis Bertram, 16, 62
Leigh, Richard (see under Baigent, Leigh and Lincoln)
Lewis, C.S., 94, 127, 153
Lincoln, Henry (see also under Baigent, Leigh and Lincoln), 67, 159, 208
Lobineau, Henri, 28, 124
Longinus, Gaius, 173
Louvre, 61, 62, 66, 96
Lovelock, James E., 45, 182-183
Lucie-Smith, Edward, 61

Macaulay, Lord, 101
MacDonald, George, 128
Mahomet (Mohammed), 50, 119
Major Arcana (see Tarot)
Manichaeanism, 40, 41, 94, 114, 118
Man in the Iron Mask, 3, 7, 126-127
Markale, Jean, 162
Marlowe, Christopher, 95
Mars, 45
Mary Magdalen, 3, 5, 27, 39, 40, 51, 52, 61, 71, 72, 85, 166
Mary Magdalen, Church of St., 18, 21, 69-72
Mayors of the Palace, 29-30, 32
Mazières, Abbé, 142
Melchior, Friedrich, 108
Mercury, 37
Mérovée, 10, 24, 25, 27, 32, 38, 65
Merovingians, 3, 10, 24, 26, 27, 29, 30, 38, 113
Merovingian Genealogy, 27
de Meung, Jean, 122

Mezeray, 27
Michell, John, 49
Minnesinger, 39
Minor Arcana (see Tarot)
de Molay, Jacques, 117
Monarchus, Georgios, 41
Money Pit, 6, 10, 144-152
Monge, Abbé Bernard, 139
Montazels, 9, 10, 15, 17, 20, 33, 36
de Montfort, Simon, 33
Montségur, 2, 16, 44, 118
Moses, 95

Napier, John, 106-108
Nazca Lines, 14
de Nègre, Marie, 5, 18, 19, 33, 59,
   67, 74-76, 91
Neustria, 31
Newton, Sir Isaac, 7, 50, 65
Nicetas, Bishop, 42
Nodier, Charles, 123
Norvill, Roy, 182
Nova Scotia, 6, 10, 96, 144

Oak Island, 6, 10, 96, 144-152
Occam's Razor, 171
O'Connor, Darcy, 149
Orwell, George, 120
Osiris, 3, 38
Ovid, 60
Owen, Dr. Orville Ward, 151

Pan, 120
Palmer, David, 52, 53, 54
Paris Meridian, 6, 64-68

Paracelsus, 112, 121, 182
Parzifal, 124
Paulicians, 41, 42, 44
Paul of Samosata, 41
de Payns, Hugues, 113
Pedler, Kit, 128
Pentacle, 16, 21, 56
Pentagon, 56-58
Pentagram, 56-58
Pépin of Herstal, 31
Pépin the Old, 31
Pépin the Short, 31, 32
Perrault, Charles, 65
Perrault, Claude, 65
Peyrepertuse, 16, 32
Pharisees, 84
Philosopher's Stone, 2, 111, 112, 180
Photius, 41
Pilate, Pontius, 18, 19, 20, 71, 72
Planck, Max, 48
Pleiades, 87
Poe, Edgar Allan, 155
Pott, Mrs. Henry, 98, 126
Poussin, Nicolas, 3, 5, 6, 10, 11, 14,
   16, 23, 24, 59, 60-64, 70, 71, 80,
   86, 87, 93, 96, 98, 100, 103, 106,
   120, 121, 123, 126, 144
Poseidonius, 22
Price, James, 110-111
Priory of Sion, 3, 7, 64, 93, 100, 102,
   103, 104, 112, 117-121, 122-124
Puilaurens, 2, 16
Puivert, 2, 16
Pythagoras, 56, 88

Quéribus, 2, 16, 32
Quinotaur, 25

Ratbert, 104
Règne, Arlette, 8
Rescanière, Abbé, 20
Rex Mundi, 84, 86, 87, 95, 114, 115, 119, 120
Rhode Island, 148
Rickard, R.J.M., 49
Rivière, Abbé, 171
Robin, Jean, 8, 152, 162, 178
Rosicrucians, 2, 59, 93, 111-112, 118, 121, 122-123, 126
Rosslyn, 143

Salvator, Johann (Jean Orth, see under Habsburgs)
Santiago de la Compostela, 66
Saturn, 48
Saunière, Bérenger, 136-138, passim
Saunière, Émile, 8, 137, 160
Schidlof, Leo, 28
Schonfield, Dr. Hugh, 88
Schrödinger, Erwin, 47, 63
Sède, Gérard de, 15, 20, 61, 141, 142
Semiramis, 25
Septimania, 30
Seth, 38
Shakespeare, William, 150
Shepherd Monument, 6, 10, 93, 96-98, 102, 103, 121, 144
Shepherds of Arcadia, 6, 10, 14, 59, 60-62, 71, 86, 96, 120, 123
Ship of the Dead (see Boat)
Shugborough Hall, 5, 10, 64, 93, 96-98, 102, 121, 123, 144
Sicambria, 32
Sidney, Sir Philip, 98, 120
Sigebert III, 26, 27, 28, 29, 106

Simon, Pierre, 48
Sirjean Gaston, Dr., 26
Slane, Ireland, 28, 143
Smith, Paul, 8, 163
Solar System, 58, 87
Solomon's Temple, 2, 23
St. Andrew, 93
St. Anthony of Padua, 21, 69
St. Anthony the Hermit, 21, 64, 70, 71
St. Foy, 66
St. Germaine, 21, 70
St. James, 50
St. John, 21, 41, 61, 70, 72, 119, 166
St. Mark, 51
St. Mary Magdalen, Church of, 1, 18, 20, 21, 65, 69-72
St. Patrick, 143
St. Paul, 50, 53
St. Peter, 51, 61
St. Roch, 21, 65, 71
St. Roseline, 68
St. Sulpice (Sulpicius), 65, 66
St. Wilfrid, 28
Stations of the Cross, 19, 20, 69-72, 86
Stonehenge, 22
Synchronicity, 49

Taafe, Count, 134, 141, 173
Tannhäuser, 3, 39, 40
Tarot, 85-87, 95
Tectosages, 1, 9, 30, 40
Templars, 1, 2, 8, 16, 33, 41, 44, 86, 87, 91, 98, 102, 106, 112-119, 124, 143

Teniers, David (Father & Son), 7, 63-64, 71, 93, 100, 103
Tesla, Nikola, 128-129, 175
Thoth (see Hermes Trismegistus)
Titias, Daniel, 56
Titus, 2, 23
Tolkien, J.R.R., 94, 95, 127, 174
Trastamarre, Count of, 33
Trencavels, 32
Tritons, 9, 10, 24, 25, 32
Triton Alliance, 149
Troubadours, 1, 39, 124-125
Truro Company, 149

Urim and Thummim, 172, 175, 176-177
Urquhart, Sir Thomas, 107
Usson, 2

Valhalla, 68
Vaughan, Alan, 49

Venus (Goddess), 3, 37, 38, 39
Venus (Planet), 3, 37, 57, 58
Verne, Jules, 65
Vetsera, Maria, 134-135, 141
Vikings, 68
da Vinci, Leonardo, 7
Visigoths, 1, 2, 11, 16, 23, 24, 30
Voisin Family, 33, 67

Wagner, Richard, 39
Walpole, Horace, 108
Watermarks, 92-94, 102, 123
Williams, Charles, 94, 128
Wilson, Colin, 8, 128
Wood, David, 67
Wren, P.C., 113

Young, George, 147, 148

Zodiac, 17, 18
Zoroaster, 40, 122

Lionel and Patricia Fanthorpe have a mutual fascination for real-life, unsolved mysteries. *Secrets of Rennes-le-Château* is their second endeavor together, shedding light on the many unexplained mysteries at Rennes.

A member of Mensa since 1964, Lionel is an ordained Anglican priest of the Church of Wales, a renowned lecturer, a writer of theological and educational works, as well as over 200 novels and collections of stories, including children's stories, fiction, and science fiction fantasy. Patricia, whose interest in the mysterious was sparked by her husband, is not only his co-investigator of Rennes but also the administrator of their management consultancy practice and is Lionel's agent and publicity executive.